Editors

Ian Davis, BA; LLB; Dip Lg Pr. Director of Legal Services, Registers of Scotland

Alistair Rennie, LLB. Deputy Keeper, Registers of Scotland.

DEDICATED TO THE MEMORY OF DAVID WILLIAMSON, KEEPER OF THE
REGISTERS OF SCOTLAND 1973 - 1982, WHO DID SO MUCH TO INTRODUCE A
SYSTEM OF LAND REGISTRATION IN SCOTLAND.

A guide to land registration in Scotland

Registration of Title Practice Book

The policy and practice of land registration in Scotland

First published 1981
Second edition 2000. (including amendments 08/01)

Registers of Scotland *Executive Agency*
Meadowbank House, 153 London Road, Edinburgh EH8 7AU

email: keeper@ros.gov.uk

www.ros.gov.uk

ISBN 0953 418 014

PREFACE TO SECOND EDITION

The first edition of the Practice Book was published in 1981 as a result of a collaborative venture under the auspices of the Joint Consultative Committee of the Law Society of Scotland and the Keeper of the Registers of Scotland (the 'JCC'). Amendments were incorporated in 1981 and 1983. The principal objective of the Practice Book was to provide conveyancing practitioners in Scotland with a detailed instruction on how the new system of land registration, as introduced by the Land Registration (Scotland) Act 1979, would alter the way in which they carried out a conveyancing transaction in an operational area. The Practice Book was well received and over the years has proved valuable for both practitioners and Agency staff. An indication of both its usefulness and standing is the fact it has been referred to as a source of Agency policy in numerous court cases.

Since its original publication the continued expansion and development of the system of land registration has necessitated changes in practices and policy. In addition, the courts, in a number of landmark judgements, have commented on various aspects of the 1979 Act. These judgements have had important implications for land registration. Moreover, experience in operating land registration has led to the development and promulgation of policies for dealing with an ever-increasing range of conveyancing issues. Accordingly, two years ago the JCC agreed that a review of the Practice Book was overdue. The JCC realised that any updated Practice Book would have to act not only as a guide to practitioners on the current practice in the land register but also explain the reasons why certain registration policies had been adopted.

The second edition, like the first edition, is the product of close collaboration between the Law Society and the Agency. It includes a large number of new sections covering those issues on which, over the years, practitioners have sought the keeper's advice. Thus for the first time readers will find useful guidance on such diverse topics as salmon fishings, liferents, crofting and servitudes to name but a few. The second edition contains guidance on many of the routine issues which arise in the course of registration. There are also explanations on how difficult areas of substantive law are dealt with in the context of land registration. I hope that the second edition, which builds on the experience of nearly 20 years, will be particularly valuable to practitioners.

In the preparation of this edition I would acknowledge the hard work of a number of people in the Agency and in the Law Society. In particular I would like to thank Alistair Rennie, the Deputy Keeper, and Ian Davis, the Agency's Director of Legal Services, who jointly edited the book and made contributions to much of the text. I would also thank John King who "managed the project" and updated much of the text and others in the Agency who contributed in a variety of ways.

My thanks also go to those members of the Law Society of Scotland who have been involved in this project, and in particular Paul Carnan, Lynsey Lewin, John McNeill, Ramsay Milne and Sandy Weatherhead, for their work in compiling the chapter on missives and also for their contributions and comments on the rest of the text.

Alan Ramage
Keeper of the Registers of Scotland
Chairman, Joint Consultative Committee

CONTENTS

CHAPTER 1

History and development of land registration

CHAPTER 2

Implications of land registration

CHAPTER 3

Reports, searches and enquiries

CHAPTER 4

Maps and plans in registration of title

CHAPTER 5

Application for registration

CHAPTER 6

1979 Act - Interaction with Substantive Conveyancing Law

CHAPTER 7

Rectification of The Register and Indemnity

CHAPTER 8

Missives and Conveyancing Procedures

Table of Cases

Table of Statutes

Table of Statutory Instruments

Note:- *details of the Land Registration (Scotland) Act 1979 Commencement Orders are given at para 1.8*

Glossary

Absorption
The merging of two fees as in a consolidation of property with superiority or on the termination of a lease otherwise than by expiry of its natural term (sections 2(1)(a)(iv), 2(4)(a) and 8(2)(b)).

Certificate of Title
Includes a land certificate and a charge certificate (Rule 2)

Certificate Plan
Facsimile of the title plan included in a land certificate

Charge Certificate
A duly authenticated certificate issued to an applicant on the registration of a heritable security (section 5(3)).

Commencement Date
The appointed day on which an area becomes operational (section 30(2)). See para 1.8.

Dealing
Any transaction which on registration causes an amendment to be made to the title sheet of a registered interest in land (section 5(1)).

Dealing with the whole
A dealing with the whole of a registered interest. Paradoxically, this expression includes a dealing with a part of a registered interest in respect of which the Keeper does not require to make up a separate title sheet (section 5(1)).

Deed inducing Registration
The deed which is the immediate cause of a first registration in the Land Register.

First Registration
The registration in the Land Register of a previously unregistered interest in land (section 6(1)).

Indemnity
Provision is made in the Act for a person who suffers loss in certain circumstances to be indemnified by the Keeper to the extent of that loss (section 12).

Index Map
Consists of a series of ordnance maps held by the Keeper and on which are delineated by him properties in respect of which interests are registered (rule 23)(a)).

Interest in land
Any estate, interest, servitude or other heritable right in or over land including a heritable security but excluding a lease which is not a long lease (section 28).

Land
Includes buildings and other structures and land covered with water (section 28).

Land Certificate
A duly authenticated copy of the title sheet issued to an applicant on the registration of any interest which is not a heritable security (section 5(2)).

Long Lease
A probative lease -

(a) exceeding 20 years; or

(b) which is subject to any provision whereby any person holding the interest of the grantor is under a future obligation, if so requested by the grantee to renew the Lease so that the total duration could (in terms of the Lease as renewed, and without any subsequent agreement, express or implied, between the persons holding the interests of the grantor and the grantee) extend for more than 20 years (section 28).

Noting
Information which is not registrable may be noted on a title sheet on application being made to the Keeper (sections 6(4) and 12(3)(h) and Rule 13)

Office Copy
A duly authenticated copy of a title sheet, part thereof or of any document referred to in a title sheet issued to any person applying for same (section 11(3)).

Operational Area
An area in respect of which the provisions of the Act relating to registration have come into operation (section 11(3)).

Overriding Interest
A convenient label for those "real" rights or restrictions which did not, before

commencement of the Act, require to be recorded in the Register of Sasines and do not in terms of the Act require registration to make them real. Overriding interests included servitudes, rights of crofters, public rights of way &c. (section 28(1)).

Recorded / Registered
These words are both used (especially in leasehold property) in connection with the Register of Sasines.

In this publication and in papers issued by the Keeper, recorded is restricted in use to the Register of Sasines and registered to the Land Register.

Rectification
An inaccuracy in the Land Register may be corrected by the Keeper, by the insertion, cancellation or amendment of anything therein. Such correction may normally not be made to the prejudice of a proprietor in possession (section 9 and rule 20).

Report
Reports are issued for interests in land about to be registered and those which have been registered. For the former, they contain information from both the Register of Sasines and the Land Register and for the latter from the Land Register. Both also provide for Reports from the Register of Inhibitions and Adjudications (section 27(b) and Rule 24).

Search
The word search continues to be used in respect of the Register of Sasines from which there are issued Searches and Interim Reports for interests in land which are unregistered and not about to be registered.

Title Plan
The plan, based on the ordnance map, prepared by the Keeper and forming part of the title sheet (section 6(1)(a) and Rule 4(2)).

Title Sheet
A title sheet is the record of an individual property in the Land Register. It is made up and maintained by the Keeper in respect of each interest in land which is not a heritable security, liferent or incorporeal heritable right. It consists of a property section (including a plan of the land to which the interest relates, a proprietorship section, a charges section and a burdens section (section 6(1) and Rules 3,4,5,6,and 7).

Transfer of Part
A dealing with only a part of a registered interest which creates a new interest in land in respect of which the Keeper is required to make up a new title sheet. Again, paradoxically, this includes a grant of a feu or a long lease of the whole of a registered interest (section 5(1)).

Unregistered
Used to signify an interest in land which has not been registered in the Land Register whether or not the interest or the land affected by the interest is held on a sasine title.

Voluntary Registration
A registration, the application for which has been accepted although outwith the terms of section 2(1)(a) (sections 2(1)(b) and 11(1)).

Chapter 1 - History and Development of Land Registration

1.1 In Scotland, registers relating to a wide range of subject matter have been kept for centuries. In Volume 1 of the Acts of Parliament of Scotland there is a copy of an Inventory of 1282 of the registers and records then in Edinburgh Castle. The continued existence of the Scottish registers was safeguarded by article 24 of the Treaty of Union in 1707 which stipulated that all records, rolls and registers both public and private 'should continue to be keeped as they are'.

The need for registration

1.2 Although the idea of registration of property interests had begun to take root in the late 16th century, there remained significant doubt as to benefits. A number of Acts of Parliament provided for arrangements that were intended to make land transactions secure by providing for Notaries appointed by the King to be formally examined before admittance to office and for records to be kept. Notwithstanding this it would seem that chaos ensued with inadequate notarial records being kept and inappropriate behaviour being frequent. Moreover there was evidence of secret conveyancing in the Royal Burghs from the terms of an Act of 1567[1] which reads

> *ITEM, Forasmeikle as the great hurt, done of befoir within Burgh, be giving of saisings privatlie, without ane Baillie, and ane common Clerke of Burgh, quhairthrow our Soveraine Lordis lieges, may be defrauded greatlie, Theirfore it is statute, and ordained be our Soveraine lord, with advise and consent of his Regent, and the three Estaites of this present Parliament, that na saising be given within Burgh of ony maner of land, or tenement within the samin, in any time cumming bot by ane of the Baillies of the Burgh, and common Clerke theirof. And gif ony saising beis utherwaies given heirafter to be null and of nane avail force nor effect.*

Despite legislative action the problem still persisted. An act of 1579 [2] required that amongst others *'all writings importing heritable title'* required to be subscribed and sealed by the principal parties if they were literate or otherwise by two *'famous'* notaries before four *'famous'* witnesses who were to be present at the execution and designed by their address or some other means by which they might be clearly identified.

[1] c.27
[2] c.80

One early register, the Register of the Secretary, was suppressed by an Act of the Convention of the Estates dated 27 Jan 1609 on the grounds that it was *'serving for little or no use than to acquire gain and commodity to the clerks keepers thereof, and to draw his Majesty's good subjects to needless, extraordinary and most unnecessary trouble, turmoil, fasherie and expense'*. However, in 1617 the statute 'Anent the registration of Reversions, Seasings and others Writs[3]' was passed. This statute is known as The Registration Act 1617 and has formed the basis for the General Register of Sasines, a register that formed the chief security in Scotland of the rights in land and other heritable property. The Register is regulated by the Land Registers (Scotland) Act 1868[4].

The Registration Act 1617

1.3 The Act is forthright in its description of the mischief which it was intended to remedy and the solution which was prescribed, beginning:

> *OUR Sovereigne Lord, considering the great hurt suffered sustained by his Majesties Lieges, by the fraudulent dealing of parties, who having annalied their lands, and received great summes of money therefore, Yet by their injust concealing of some private Right formerly made by them, render the subsequent alienation done for great summes of money, altogether unprofitable: which can not be avoided unless the saids private rights be made publick and patent to his Highnes Lieges: for remedy thereof, and of the many inconveniences which may ensue thereupon: His Majesty with advice and consent of the Estates of Parliament, statutes and ordeins, That there shall be ane publick Register, in which all Reversions, Regresses, assignations of the same, Renunciations of Wadsets, and grants of Redemption, and siklike all instruments of Seasing shall be registrat …And if it shall happen any of the saids Writs, which are appointed to be Registrated as said is not to be duly registrated within the space of threescore dayes: then, in that case, his Majesty, with advice and consent foresaid, decernes the same to make no faith in Judgement by way of action or exception in prejudice of a third party, who hath acquired a perfect and lawful Right to the saids Lands and Heritages.*

The register was to be *'patent to all Our Sovereign Lords Lieges, and extracts thereof to be given … to all who have adoe with the same, which shall make as great faith as the originals'*. The Register was to be kept under the authority of the Lord Clerk Register but *'for the greater ease of the lieges'* the registers would be compiled by Deputes resident in sixteen Burghs to serve surrounding sheriffdoms. The

[3]c.16
[4]c.64

'evidents' of the transaction were to be presented to the registrar who was required to record the same within 48 hours of receipt. Registration was achieved by *'ingrossing'* the whole text of the document in the register. The *'evidents'* were then returned to the presenter marked with the day, month and year of registration together with the number of the pages of the register on which the text was to be found.

Thus from the first quarter of the 17th century the conveyance of title to land in Scotland, in addition to a signed and witnessed writing and a notarial instrument narrating that sasine had been given, came also to include registration in a public register. Whether it was intended that registration should become an essential element of the process of completing title or whether title was complete once the notarial Instrument of Sasine was obtained remained an open question. The matter was settled with the decision of the majority of the Court of Session in *Young v Leith*[5] who held that title was not complete until registration was completed. Registration was not simply to give notice or publicity of the transaction or simply to provide information as to the true owner of an interest in land. Registration was an essential part of the transaction without which the grantee would not have a real right in the property. The creation of the register was a deliberate, considered act of public policy for the protection of the lieges. The Scottish registers have been public since their inception, in contrast to the Land Register in England and Wales which, until 3 December 1990, was open only to proprietors or their solicitors.

The Register of Sasines underwent several organisational changes until the local registers were finally closed and the whole registration process centralised in Edinburgh, although records continued to be kept according to the 33 county divisions of Scotland. Separate registers kept for the Royal Burghs were also closed and properties in the burghs gradually came to be registered in the Register of Sasines. By the turn of the 20th century the Register comprised the Record Volume (a verbatim transcript of all deeds recorded) and the Minute Book (a sequential series of minutes or abstracts of the recorded deeds in the order of registration) indexed by name and place. In addition, from 1876 onwards there has been kept a search sheet which is in essence a ledger for each property in Scotland on which are entered in sequence all deeds affecting that property. The number of search sheets now runs to over 1.6 million.

[5] 1844 6 D 370

The move to a system of registration of title

1.4 The Register of Sasines is a register of deeds in which documents are lodged from which the quality and state of title requires to be deduced by the solicitor acting for a purchaser. The deeds themselves may have a plan attached, but it is sufficient to incorporate a verbal description of the property to which the deed relates, or a reference to an earlier deed containing such a description. In practice the deed referred to may be of some considerable antiquity and the description therein may be either so vague as to be of little use or may indeed be inaccurate as a result of natural processes or other changes in circumstance. In addition, the fact that a deed appears in the register does not guarantee its validity, merely that it is *ex facie* competent to be recorded. By contrast a system of registration of title is designed to be definitive as to the nature and extent of title, the land being identified by reference to a map. In this system an official examines the progress of deeds relating to a property and makes up a formal certificate of title beyond which no further examination need, in principle, be made. The extent of the property is plotted onto a map, and the property is allocated a unique identifying number. Except for any 'over-riding interests' as defined in statute, the formal title sheet is determinative of title. In most cases, title, once issued, is indefeasible. Should someone with a better claim to the land emerge and establish their claim they do not recover 'their' property but rather have a remedy against the State in indemnity.

Pressure to introduce registration of title in Scotland began shortly after it was introduced in England, and as in England a series of Enquiries took place into the introduction of registration of title into Scotland. A Royal Commission under Lord Dunedin reported in 1910, with the final authoritative report on the principle of land registration emerging from a committee under the chairmanship of Lord Reid in July 1963[6]. The majority of the Reid Committee recommended that it was *'practicable to introduce a system of registration of title to land in Scotland'* which complied with four conditions which they established as requiring to be fulfilled by any replacement for the existing system of registration of deeds. These were as follows:

1. *It must retain the merits of the existing system as regards security, flexibility and publicity.*

2. *It must in the long run result in a substantial saving in time occupied in legal work and in cost to the public.*

3. *Its character must be such as to prevent dislocation or substantial practical difficulties during the transitional period while it is being introduced: it must therefore be in the nature of an evolution or development of the present system.*

[6] *Registration of Title to Land in Scotland, HMSO, 1963, Cmnd 2032*

4. *The first registration of title of any subjects must not be unduly expensive. In particular we would not favour any system which required intimation to neighbouring proprietors as a preliminary to such registration because that would inevitably stir up disputes and involve expense in many cases in settling or litigating questions which are at present dormant. So the existing rights of neighbouring proprietors must be adequately safeguarded without their having to intervene.*

The practicalities of the scheme were considered in detail by a further committee under the chairmanship of Professor Henry which reported in 1969 following the operation of a pilot scheme. The Henry Report[7] differed in a number of respects from the recommendations of the Reid Report and both differed in some respects from the eventual scheme of land registration that emerged for Scotland.

Changes in land law

1.5 In recommending the introduction to Scotland of a system of registration of title, the Reid Committee considered that any such system should build on the long-established system of registration of writs. Changes to the existing substantive law relating to land rights could, consequently, be kept to a minimum. The Henry Committee, established later to prepare a detailed scheme for the introduction of registration of title, endorsed that recommendation. The Act, in implementing most of the recommendations of the Henry Committee, adhered to this principle. The Act has, however, had a major impact on the legal profession as regards conveyancing practice, particularly with missives where there is a strong emphasis on the purchaser obtaining a land certificate with full indemnity thereby obtaining the benefits of the state guarantee of title.

Although the Act did not alter the underlying principles of substantive conveyancing law, it did however introduce a number of necessary changes. The main legal changes which the registration provisions of the Act introduced in operational areas are summarised as follows:

- In general terms registration in the Land Register supersedes recording in the Register of Sasines as a means of completing a real right. Recording in the Sasine Register will, however, remain appropriate in certain instances in terms of section 2(2) of the Act.

---

[7] *Scheme for the Introduction of Registration of Title to Land in Scotland, HMSO, 1969, Cmnd 4137*

- Registration is necessary in an operational area to perfect a real right in long leases, land held under udal tenure and kindly tenancies as per section 3(3). Previously such real rights could be perfected by possession without the need for recording in the Sasine Register.

- Once an interest in land has been registered in the Land Register, title flows not from a progress of title deeds, but from the register itself.

- A registered interest is subject only to matters set out in the title sheet of that interest and to overriding interests (per section 28(1), the Interpretation section which defines overriding interests, and section 6(4) dealing with the noting on a title sheet of overriding interests). It is not necessary to look further than the title sheet to ascertain the extent of the registered interest, the proprietor(s), the charges against the property and the rights and burdens relating to it.

- The Act introduced the concept of a guaranteed title to interests in land backed by a statutory indemnity scheme. The accuracy of the Land Register and official reports issued by the Keeper are covered by the indemnity provisions at section 12. The consequence is that, unless indemnity has been excluded in respect of any part of the registered interest, the title sheet can be relied on absolutely. Moreover, information given in writing by the Keeper, or *via* direct link to the register, also attracts the statutory protection against loss suffered. Registration may, as a result of inadequate or incorrect information supplied by an applicant or through an error by the Keeper, or through subsequent judicial pronouncement, occasion an inaccuracy in the register that will invoke the section 9 (rectification) provisions (see *Short's Trustee v Keeper of the Registers of Scotland*[8], and *Kaur v Singh*[9]). A person suffering loss in terms of section 12 may be able to claim indemnity (see chapter 7).

- The circumstances in which the Register can be rectified are severely circumscribed by the provisions in section 9(3)(a)(i)-(iv) and (b).

- Deeds presented for recording in the Sasine Register and applications for registration in the Land Register received by the Keeper on the same day will be deemed to have been received and recorded and registered contemporaneously (see section 7 which was applied to the whole of Scotland by the first commencement order).

---

[8]1994 SLT 65, 1996 SLT 166
[9]1997 SCLR 1075

- Discrepancies as to common boundaries may in some cases be resolved by a formal agreement without the need for excambion or conveyance. Such agreement, when registered in the Land Register or recorded in the Register of Sasines will bind singular successors (see section 19). Where the interests involved are registered, the submission of a docqueted plan alone may be sufficient to enable the Keeper to give effect to the parties' intentions.

- The 1979 Act introduced a number of new terms and concepts into conveyancing parlance, e.g. 'proprietor in possession', 'overriding interest', 'land/charge certificate' etc. Many of the terms in the Act were drawn from equivalent English provisions and it is true to say that problems in interpreting what is meant by these within the context of the Act has attracted both academic and judicial criticism of the drafting of the Act itself (see for instance Lord Jauncey in *Short's Trustee v. Keeper of the Registers of Scotland*).

Appeals

1.6 It is a feature of almost all State systems of registration of title that a form of appeal be provided for those who wish to challenge anything done or omitted to be done by the official in charge of the Land Register or his staff. In this respect the 1979 Act is no different and the matter is dealt with under section 25(1) which permits an appeal on either a question of fact or law to the Lands Tribunal for Scotland. At the time the Act was drafted it was considered that an appeal to the Lands Tribunal would be cheaper and possibly receive more expeditious consideration than simply leaving the complaining party with a right of appeal to the Court. The right of appeal to the Lands Tribunal is, however, not exclusive of other avenues of recourse. Section 25(2) preserves a right of recourse to the Court should someone wish to bypass the Lands Tribunal.

Under the law relating to *res judicata* once an appeal has been dismissed in a court of first instance, the appellant cannot seek to appeal in another court of first instance (section 25(3)). So an unsuccessful action brought before the Lands Tribunal cannot be brought in the Court of Session as a court of first instance. Likewise the unsuccessful appellant to the Court of Session cannot try his luck at the Lands Tribunal. The unsuccessful appellant may in each case appeal to a higher court.

Section 25(4) provides that no appeal is permissible against the Keeper's refusal to accept a voluntary registration whether within or outwith an operational area. This section was introduced in light of evidence which showed that unrestricted voluntary registration caused serious disruption in Her Majesty's Land Registry and could, therefore, have the same effect in Scotland.

Commencement provisions and operational areas

1.7 The system of land registration in Scotland was introduced by the Land Registration (Scotland) Act 1979. The Act was supplemented by the Land Registration (Scotland) Rules 1980[10], which provided the tools to operate the new system. The original Rules have been enhanced by four sets of Land Registration (Scotland) (Amendment) Rules promulgated under section 27[11].

The Land Register came into being on 4 April 1979, the date on which section 1 came into force. Certain miscellaneous provisions of the Act (sections 16 to 23) which do not relate exclusively to registration of title also came into force on that date. In terms of section 30, however, the main provisions relating to land registration only come into force on such day or days as the First Minister may appoint by statutory instrument. The Act envisaged the progressive introduction of the land register over Scotland on an area by area basis, each area corresponding to an existing registration Division of the General Register of Sasines. In some cases more than one such area is designated as an operational area at the same time.

1.8 The first commencement order (Land Registration (Scotland) Act 1979 (Commencement No. 1) Order 1980[12]) brought the registration provisions into force for the county of Renfrew on 6 April 1981. It was envisaged that land registration would extend to the rest of the counties under a nine year rolling programme. Although this original projection proved over-optimistic, progress is being made and so far 22 counties have become Land Register operational areas. The remaining 11 counties are scheduled to become operational areas by April 2003.

The operational areas and the commencement dates on which they became so are as follows:

AREA	DATE OF COMMENCEMENT	ORDER
County of Renfrew	6 April 1981	S.I. 1980 No. 1412
County of Dumbarton	4 October 1982	S.I. 1982 No. 520
County of Lanark	3 January 1984	S.I. 1983 No. 745
County of the Barony and Regality of Glasgow	30 September 1985	S.I. 1985 No. 501
County of Clackmannan	1 October 1992	S.I. 1992 No. 815
County of Stirling	1 April 1993	S.I. 1992 No. 2060
County of West Lothian	1 October 1993	S.I. 1993 No. 922.
County of Fife	1 April 1995	S.I. 1994 No. 2588

[10] 1980 No.1413
[11] 1982 No.974, 1988 No.1143, 1995 No. 248 and 1998 No.3100
[12] 1980 No.1412

County of Aberdeen	1 April 1996	S.I. 1995 No. 2547
County of Kincardine	1 April 1996	S.I. 1995 No. 2547
County of Ayr	1 April 1997	S.I. 1996 No. 2490
County of Dumfries	1 April 1997	S.I. 1996 No. 2490
County of Kirkcudbright	1 April 1997	S.I. 1996 No. 2490
County of Wigtown	1 April 1997	S.I. 1996 No. 2490
County of Angus	1 April 1999	S.I. 1998 No. 1810
County of Kinross	1 April 1999	S.I. 1998 No. 1810
County of Perth	1 April 1999	S.I. 1998 No. 1810
County of Berwick	1 October 1999	S.I. 1998 No. 2980
County of East Lothian	1 October 1999	S.I. 1998 No. 2980
County of Peebles	1 October 1999	S.I. 1998 No. 2980
County of Roxburgh	1 October 1999	S.I. 1998 No. 2980
County of Selkirk	1 October 1999	S.I. 1998 No. 2980

The timetable for the introduction of registration of title to the remaining areas is as follows:

AREA	PROPOSED DATE OF COMMENCEMENT
County of Argyll County of Bute	1 April 2000
County of Midlothian	1 April 2001
County of Inverness County of Nairn	1 April 2002
County of Banff County of Caithness County of Moray County of Orkney and Zetland County of Ross and Cromarty County of Sutherland	1 April 2003

1.9 The first commencement order made the county of Renfrew the first operational area and brought all the registration provisions of the Act into force for the whole country except for sub-sections (1) and (2) of section 2 (registrable transactions) and section 3(3) (long leases etc.). It was decided to apply the registration provisions (other than those three sub-sections which relate to first registrations) to the whole of Scotland as soon as the county of Renfrew became operational. This was to ensure the following:

• that no problems would arise in cases where the Keeper exercised his discretion under section 11(1) to accept for registration in the Land Register interests in land which lie in an area not yet operational; and

- that the ranking provisions contained in section 7 would apply throughout the whole country.

By virtue of the exclusion of the operation of sections 2(1) (and (2) and 3(3)) in the initial commencement order, section 8 applies. Consequently, all writs relating to property in other parts of Scotland fall to be recorded in the Sasine Register until such time as those excluded subsections are brought into force for a particular county or counties. Voluntary registrations may, of course, be accepted under section 11(1). By excluding section 3(3) from those areas yet to be subject to a commencement order, a real right in a long lease, or in respect of udal tenure or a kindly tenancy, can continue to be obtained by possession or recording in the Sasine Register. When registration of title is extended to a further county, sections 2(1) and (2) and 3(3) are brought into force by the commencement order for that county.

Chapter 2 - Implications of Land Registration

Changes in conveyancing procedures

2.1 From the date on which an area becomes an operational area in the Land Register, section 8(4) prohibits the Keeper from accepting for recording in the Sasine Register any deed relating to an interest which is registrable in terms of section 2.

2.2 The main practical effects of transacting with property located in an operational area may be summarised as follows:

- Registration of title is a map based system and descriptions of registered interests are based on the ordnance map. The extent of the registered interest is shown on the title plan. Written descriptions on the title sheet will, in practically every application for registration, be used only to supplement information given on such plans.

- When a county becomes operational for land registration the provisions of section 2 determine when unregistered land can enter the Land Register. It follows that deeds which induce first registration in the Land Register are not acceptable for recording in the Sasine Register. The minute book (*i.e.* the record of deeds recorded in the Sasine Register) does not reveal the transfer of either the whole or a part of property to the Land Register. It should be noted however that examination of the search sheet does contain details of the transfer of property to the land register.

- When a transaction will induce first registration in the Land Register or affect a registered interest, the clauses in the missives relating to the exhibition or delivery of writs and searches will differ from those appropriate to a transaction involving a recording in the Sasine Register.

- Writs in respect of which an application for registration is being made do not require to bear a warrant of registration but must be accompanied by the appropriate application form duly signed and completed by the applicant or the applicant's solicitor (see rule 9).

- The examination of title required in connection with a transaction which will induce a first registration is similar to that carried out in connection with a transaction involving recording in the Register of Sasines. Upon completion of registration, the resultant land certificate sets out in readily accessible form the position relating to all matters relevant to the title as at the date of that certificate, except for any overriding interests not noted. There is, however, one case where, despite the interest being registered, an examination of prior titles may still be appropriate. That is where an interest has been registered with an exclusion of indemnity.

- It is not necessary to deduce the title of an uninfeft granter in a deed relating to a registered interest, nor to expede a notice of title to a registered interest, provided in either case that the necessary links in title are produced to the Keeper (see section 15(3)).

- Occasionally there are technical defects in applications for registration, most commonly in the deeds and documents submitted. Such defects may, at the Keeper's discretion, be ignored when giving effect to the application. In cases where, prior to land registration, a defective title would have required to be backed by defective title insurance, the Keeper may exercise his discretion and register the title without excluding indemnity. (Enquiries as to whether the Keeper will overlook a particular title defect should be directed to the Pre-Registration Enquiries Section - see para 3.21).

- A document forming part of, or submitted in support, of an application may, at the Keeper's discretion, be returned for amendment or correction without the entire application being withdrawn or rejected. In such a case and in terms of Rule 11 of the Land Registration (Scotland) Rules 1980[1], the application will retain its original date of registration provided that the document is corrected or amended and timeously returned to the Keeper.

- A deed relating to a registered interest in land, executed after registration of the interest, must bear the title number as per the terms of section 4(2)(d).

- Deeds relating to a registered interest need only describe the subjects by reference to the title number. Such a deed will import all rights, burdens, conditions and other matters referred to in the title sheet without the need for any specific reference to them (see section 15(1) and (2)). However, where new burdens are being created or rights granted, these must be set out at length in the dispositive clause or in a separate deed of conditions.

[1] 1980 No. 1413

Registrable transactions: first registration

2.3 Transactions which induce first registration are set out in section 2(1)(a). Generally, only a transfer for valuable consideration will induce first registration. However, section 2(1)(a) also lists a limited number of circumstances in which a gratuitous transaction will induce first registration.

In terms of section 2(1)(a), the following transactions fall to be registered in the Land Register:

- conveyance on sale;

- the grant of a feu, even if there is no valuable consideration or if the feu grant implements remedial conveyancing, such as a charter of novodamus;

- the grant of a long lease (as defined in section 28(1)), (*i.e.* a lease for more than 20 years), whether for valuable consideration or not. A lease for less than 20 years but which contains provisions which could oblige the landlord to extend it to exceed 20 years will also induce first registration;

- a contract of ground annual (so far as effective in terms of section 2(2) of the Land Tenure Reform (Scotland) Act 1974[2]), whether for valuable consideration or not;

- a conveyance in consideration of marriage;

- any disposition *ad perpetuam remanentiam* or minute of consolidation, if the superiority is already registered;

- a renunciation of a long lease, if the landlord's interest is already registered;

- any transfer of a long lease, subjects held under udal tenure, or a kindly tenancy, whether for valuable consideration or not. A transfer of the tenant's interest in a long lease is registrable even if the lease has less than 20 years still to run, or is already recorded in the Register of Sasines;

- a conveyance on sale, feu or long lease of salmon fishings.

[2] c.38

Transaction not inducing registration

2.4 The following transactions do not induce first registration:

- a gratuitous transfer, other than in those instances mentioned above. For example, both a disposition for love, favour and affection, certified under exempt instrument category L (see the Stamp Duty (Exempt Instruments) Regulations 1987[3]), and a conveyance to a beneficiary under a will or on intestate succession would normally be treated as gifts and thus would not induce first registration;

- a disposition *ad perpetuam remanentiam*, even if for valuable consideration, if the superiority is not registered;

- a renunciation of a long lease, if the landlords' interest is not registered;

- a heritable security or discharge of a security over an unregistered interest. Similarly, a reconveyance (or a discharge under section 40 of the Conveyancing and Feudal Reform (Scotland) Act 1970[4]) of an *ex facie* absolute disposition does not induce first registration;

- the grant of a liferent, even if for valuable consideration;

- a grant or transfer of an incorporeal heritable right (other than salmon fishings) even if for valuable consideration, *e.g.*, a deed of servitude for valuable consideration, where neither the dominant tenement nor the servient tenement is registered in the Land Register, would not induce first registration;

- any deed relating to heritable property not already mentioned in the preceding paragraph.

Valuable consideration

2.5 The Act does not define the term 'valuable consideration'. While clearly this must include monetary payment of the full market value, the Keeper believes that the term affords a broader interpretation and in practice this has been interpreted by the Keeper to include the following:

[3]1987 No. 516
[4]c. 35

- monetary payment of less than full market value, *e.g.* a disposition where the consideration is a nominal amount;

- the purchase of a *pro indiviso* share in a property. The transaction induces first registration of the share which is being purchased. If the purchaser holds the remaining share in the property on a title recorded in the Register of Sasines, application for voluntary registration of that share may be made to the Keeper;

- a conveyance on marital separation or divorce, *e.g.* a disposition for certain good and onerous causes, certified under exempt instrument category H;

- a conveyance in exchange for taking over financial obligations under a loan, *e.g.* a disposition accompanied by deed of variation of a standard security;

- a conveyance in exchange for other subjects. A contract of excambion is normally treated as containing two transfers for valuable consideration.

In some cases there may be doubt as to whether or not the transfer of title is for valuable consideration. For example, an ostensibly gratuitous disposition may be accompanied by a deed of variation of a standard security, but it may be unclear whether the financial arrangements under the loan are actually being altered. In such circumstances, the Keeper will rely on the applicant or agents to assess whether or not there is valuable consideration. If there is genuine difficulty in making that assessment, the Keeper will normally encourage registration in the Land Register, to avoid the possibility of an inept recording in the Register of Sasines.

Deeds unrecorded at operational date

2.6 Inevitably, just before the commencement date on which an area becomes a Land Register operational area, many conveyancing transactions in that area will be proceeding towards settlement. Just as inevitably, some confusion results, with solicitors in the area being unsure whether the resulting deeds fall to be recorded in the Register of Sasines or registered in the Land Register. The aforementioned list of transactions which induce registration must always be read subject to the qualification in section 2(1)(a), namely, '*in any of the following circumstances occurring* **after** *the commencement of this Act*'. So, even if the transaction meets one of the requirements in paragraph 2.3 it will not necessarily induce registration in the Land Register. The following guidelines may assist:

Delivery of deed prior to commencement date

Where the transaction has been completed by delivery of the deed to the grantee before the commencement date, the registration provisions do not apply. It is therefore competent to complete the real right by recording the deed in the Sasine Register after the commencement date, *i.e.* after the area has become operational. When submitting the writ for recording, the applicant's agent should confirm that delivery took place before the Land Register commencement date.

Delivery of deed on, or subsequent to, commencement date

It follows that where the deed is delivered to the grantee on or after the commencement date, although executed before that date, then, if it falls within any of the categories mentioned in paragraph 2.3 a real right can be obtained only by registration in the Land Register. The submitting agent should confirm, in response to question 14 on the application Form 1, that delivery took place after the Land Register commencement date.

*Proviso: Where long leases, udal tenure, or kindly tenancies are involved, section 2(1)(a) has to be read along with section 3(3). From the commencement date, under section 3(3), a real right in such interests can be obtained only by registration. Prior to the commencement date the tenant can acquire a real right if possession of the subjects follows on delivery. Taking, the grant of a long lease as an example, mere delivery of the lease before the commencement date will not permit the completion of a real right by subsequent recording in the Register of Sasines because, from the commencement date, registration in the Land Register is the sole means of obtaining a real right. The tenant could have obtained a real right without registration if **both** the deed had been delivered and possession of the subjects had been taken before the Land Register commencement date. Where a tenant has such a real right by possession, but after the commencement date wishes to obtain the benefit of the Registration of Leases (Scotland) Act 1857[5], in order, for example, to grant a standard security, then section 3(3) does not operate. The tenant already has a real right and the correct course is to record the lease in the Sasine Register.*

Subjects straddling boundary of operational area

2.7 In terms of section 11(2), where property lies partly within an operational area, the subjects are treated as if they lie entirely within the operational area. No matter how small the part of the subjects lying within the operational area, any of the transactions referred to in paragraph 2.3 relating to the subjects will induce first registration in the Land Register. To take an extreme example, the sale of a 500 hectare farm will still induce first registration even if only one small corner of one field lies within an operational area.

[5]c. 26

Section 11(2) refers simply to *'land which is partly in an operational area'*. It does not explain whether this is limited only to inseparable subjects which straddle the boundary, such as a house built across it, or whether it would cover the case of two properties originally held on separate titles but now treated as a *unum quid; e.g.*, a farm to which fields have been added. The Keeper takes the view that the latter case does come within the ambit of section 11(2), unless the properties are discontiguous in the sense of being separated by other land as opposed to being separated by a road or stream.

It is possible to avoid registration of that part of a property which lies outwith an operational area. For example, if a farm extending to 100 hectares is being sold, with only 1 out of the 100 hectares falling within the operational area, separate deeds could be prepared. An application for first registration of the 1 hectare would then be presented, along with the disposition of the 1 hectare, for registration in the Land Register. The deed relating to the other 99 hectares would be recorded in the Sasine Register. Alternatively, the granter could convey both parts separately in a single deed. This is discussed in further detail in paragraph 2.17.

Voluntary registration

2.8 The combined practical effect of sections 3 and 8(4) is to make registration in the Land Register of any of the transactions specified in section 2(1)(a) essential if a real right is to be obtained. The Act, however, does not limit first registrations to transactions specified in section 2(1)(a) but makes provision for voluntary registration in two different cases:

- Section 2(1)(b) empowers the Keeper to accept for registration an interest in land, lying within an operational area, which is not subject to one of the transactions listed in section 2(1)(a).

- Section 11(1) allows the Keeper to accept applications for voluntary registration in respect of land lying in an area not yet operational.

The following considerations apply to all applications for voluntary registration:

- The Keeper has an absolute discretion to refuse or accept applications for voluntary registration. In practice, he tends to refuse many more applications than he accepts, particularly during times when the workload of the Land Register is especially heavy. Section 25(4) expressly prohibits any appeal against a decision by the Keeper to refuse a voluntary registration.

- Any solicitor considering an application for voluntary registration should write in advance to the Keeper, giving details of the transaction and the reasons why registration is sought.

- Once an interest in land has been registered voluntarily, the whole registration provisions apply to that interest. No further writs relating to that interest may be registered in the Sasine Register.

- If the Keeper grants approval for voluntary registration, the application should be made on a Form 1. The provisions as to identification of the subjects and the production of documents and evidence applicable to a first registration apply in full.

- Full registration fees are normally charged for voluntary registrations, according to the current value of the interests being registered.

- In a case where the Keeper considers it necessary to instruct a special survey in order to complete a voluntary registration, the cost of that survey will be borne by the applicant. The Keeper will not, however, instruct such a survey without first consulting the applicant. If the applicant does not wish to incur the expense of the survey, the application may be withdrawn. Alternatively, but only if the Keeper considers it possible, the application may be completed with an exclusion of indemnity.

- The principal benefit to be gained from voluntary registration is the protection afforded by the indemnity provisions. However, this must be set against the expense of registration, which includes: registration dues; legal and other expenses; production of all necessary documentation; identification of the subjects, *etc.*

Voluntary registration within an operational area

2.9 Keeper does not normally accept voluntary registrations unless there are obvious benefits to him in accepting them. To illustrate:

- Where a builder has a previously recorded title to land which is only now being developed and sold, it would be beneficial to register the estate voluntarily. The house plots subsequently sold would then be registered as transfers of part rather than first registrations. On sales of part, simpler deeds and search procedures can be used. Purchasers need examine only the builder's land certificate, instead of the full progress of titles.

- An application to register voluntarily a *pro indiviso* share in a property, where the remaining *pro indiviso* shares are the subject of an application for first registration, will almost invariably be granted by the Keeper.

- Conversely, voluntary registration of a property whose title history is particularly complicated is likely to be refused if its acceptance would involve a lengthy examination of title, unless there is some significant benefit to the Keeper in accepting it.

Voluntary registration outwith an operational area

2.10 The Keeper seldom accepts applications for voluntary registration of subjects in areas which are not yet operational for the Land Register. He takes the view that, if he were to accept large numbers of voluntary registrations in non-operational areas under section 11(1), both he and the legal profession would soon encounter considerable problems, namely:

- It would quickly become inadvisable for solicitors to embark on property transactions anywhere in Scotland without first establishing (by use of a Form 14) whether or not the particular subjects had already been registered in the Land Register.

- Processing voluntary registrations would create a great deal of extra work for Land Register staff, as the preparatory research which the Keeper carries out in the months before an area becomes operational would not have been done.

In the rare event that the Keeper does choose to accept a voluntary registration of an interest in land lying outwith an operational area, that decision is likely to be a consequence of the following criteria having been met:

- The interest relates to a substantial building development, (*i.e.* a development of at least ten or more individual units).

- The development lies within the area which is next due to become an operational area.

- None of the individual units will have been sold by the builder/developer before the date on which the area becomes an operational area.

Registrable transactions: dealings in registered interests

2.11 While the types of transaction mentioned in paragraph 2.4 do not induce first registration, the registration provisions will apply if they relate to interests which have already been registered (see section 2(3) and 2(4)). Once an interest in land is registered in the Land Register, it follows that any subsequent deed affecting that interest falls to be registered in the Land Register. It is no longer competent to record such a deed in the Register of Sasines. Any such deed presented for recording in the Register of Sasines will be rejected by the Keeper in terms of section 8(4).

What is registrable?

2.12 Section 2(4)(c) allows a much wider range of deeds and other documents to be registered in the Land Register than can be recorded in the Sasine Register. Any deed giving effect to a **transaction** or **event** capable of affecting a registered interest in land can be presented for registration in the Land Register. This category of registrable deeds includes the following deeds, which cannot be recorded in the Register of Sasines:

- a deed of assumption and conveyance containing only a general conveyance or, indeed, a deed of assumption with no conveyance at all;

- a minute of resignation of trustees;

- minutes of meeting appointing new trustees where the statutory provisions as to the continuing infeftment of *ex officio* trustees do not apply;

- a certificate of incorporation on change of name;

- a docket in terms of section 15(2) of the Succession (Scotland) Act 1964[6];

- confirmation in favour of executors.

In many of these examples, the deeds are unlikely to contain any reference to specific properties. However, in terms of section 4(2)(d), the Keeper must reject any deed which relates to a registered interest and accompanies an application for registration if it does not contain the title number. This does not mean that the title number must appear *in gremio* of the deed itself (except where there is a

[6] c. 41

reference description under section 15(1)), but it must be clearly marked on the deed, preferably at the top of the first page. Under no circumstances, however, will the Keeper accept a noting of the title number on the backing of the deed. These comments apply equally to discharges and transmissions of standard securities which usually contain no description of the subjects.

Moreover, an event may be registrable where there is no transaction or deed at all. Examples include:

- the operation of prescription ;

- notification of the death of a co-proprietor holding under a survivorship destination.

In the latter case, the Keeper will register the change in title on production of the land certificate, the death certificate and evidence by way of affidavit that the destination has not been evacuated.

The foregoing paragraphs illustrate those deeds, which under the Sasine system could be used only as links in title, but can, when related to a registered interest, lead to registration in the Land Register. Similarly, section 15(3) provides that, in a dealing with a registered interest, it is no longer necessary to deduce title in a disposition or standard security granted by a party who is uninfeft. Further, by section 3(6), an uninfeft proprietor of a registered interest is not required to complete his title by presenting a notice of title. In either case, all that is required is that sufficient links in title be produced to the Keeper along with the appropriate application Form 2. This is because the Keeper is no longer concerned with registering deeds but with giving effect to them in the Land Register. In only one case is it appropriate to complete title in respect of a registered interest and that is under section 74 or 76 of the Lands Clauses Consolidation (Scotland) Act 1845[7] (compulsory purchase procedure).

The comments in the preceding paragraph relate solely to dealings with a registered interest. An uninfeft proprietor who holds a Sasine title should, before granting a feu (which induces first registration) complete his title in the Sasine Register. Equally, a disposition granted by an uninfeft proprietor, which induces first registration, should include a clause of deduction of title. The Keeper may, however, accept a disposition where the clause of deduction of title has been omitted or contains an error, if the links in title accompanying the application for registration are acceptable to him.

[7] c. 19

As section 2(4)(c) covers only transactions or events capable of affecting a title to an interest in land, missives are generally not registrable. An exception can, in certain circumstances, arise in respect of missives of let or lease. If parties allow a bargain to rest on properly authenticated and stamped missives without executing a more formal document, this can be considered the full equivalent of a lease. Such missives may therefore be registrable providing they meet the requirements of a registrable lease. Overriding interests (defined in section 28 and discussed more fully in Chapter 5) are expressly excluded from the provisions of section 2(4)(c). Servitude rights are included within the definition of overriding interests, but only in connection with the interest of the dominant proprietor over the burdened tenement. A servitude right, therefore, cannot be registered as a burden affecting the servient tenement (although it may be noted on the title sheet of that interest). It is, however, a right in favour of the benefited property, and as such can be registered and appear on the title sheet of that property.

Noting on the Land Register

Noting overriding interests

2.13 In keeping with the intention that the Land Register should be as informative as possible, section 6(4) provides for noting the existence of overriding interests on the title sheet. (See chapter 5 for a detailed discussion on the topic of overriding interests). The interest of a lessee under a short term lease and the interest of a non-entitled spouse within the meaning of section 6 of the Matrimonial Homes (Family Protection) (Scotland) Act 1981[8] are excluded from the noting provision, although both interests are included within the section 28 definition of overriding interests.

Section 6(4)(a) compels the Keeper to note an overriding interest if it is disclosed in any document accompanying the application for registration of the interest which it affects. While this section is mandatory, in the sense that the Keeper must comply with it, section 6(4)(b) gives the Keeper a discretion to note an overriding interest if it comes to his notice by other means. Rule 13 allows for specific application to be made on Form 5 for noting the creation of, or freedom from, an overriding interest. Form 5 need not be used where the request for noting is made in the course of an ordinary application for registration, as provision is made on the application Forms 1, 2 and 3 for a request of that kind.

[8] c. 59

In terms of section 12(3)(h), there is no entitlement to indemnity in respect of loss arising as a result of any error or omission in noting an overriding interest. Indemnity may, however, be payable where the Keeper omits to note, or makes an error in noting, the discharge or freedom from an overriding interest in terms of rule 7.

Noting additional information

2.14 In addition to noting overriding interests, the Keeper, in terms of section 6(1)(g), may enter such additional information in the title sheet as he thinks fit. The general nature of section 6(1)(g) precludes the compilation of a definitive list of the types of information that the Keeper is prepared to note. The most frequent items of information to be noted include: house names, letters from superiors regarding non-enforceability of burdens, letters regarding adoption of roads by local authorities, and the line of boundaries. Similarly, it is not possible to be prescriptive about which types of information the Keeper is unwilling to note. However, in general, the Keeper would not wish to enter in the title sheet information which can be deemed personal to individuals identified in the title sheet. For example, the Keeper would be unwilling to note details of a creditor's obligation to make further advances.

Application to have additional information noted on the title sheet may be made to the Keeper on Form 5 or, if the request is made at the time of a related application, on Form 1, 2 or 3 (as appropriate). In the latter case, details should be supplied in response to the question relating to overriding interests. Application can be made either to include new information or to amend or correct information which is already shown on the title sheet.

Continuing effectiveness of recording In Register of Sasines

2.15 Once an area has become operational, the majority of transactions occurring in that area will lead to registration in the Land Register. Where registration in the Land Register is appropriate, the Keeper is bound to reject any deed submitted for recording in the Sasine Register (section 8(4)). Section 8 provides that recording in the Register of Sasines will continue as regards certain types of deeds despite the subjects pertaining thereto lying within a Land Registration operational area. For those deeds concerned such recording in the Register of Sasines will create a real right or real obligation. Those deeds which fall within the auspices of section 8 and so fall to be recorded in the Register of Sasines are detailed in subsection (2). That subsection identifies three categories, *viz.*;

Section 8(2)(a)
This subsection relates to the recording of deeds under section 143 of the Titles to Land Consolidation (Scotland) Act 1868[9]. Where a deed has been recorded in the Register of Sasines, prior to an area becoming operational, with an error or defect or where there has been an error in the recording of the deed in that Register, recording of the corrective deed will also be in the Register of Sasines, even although the subjects now lie within an operational area.

Section 8(2)(b)
Where a registered interest in land is absorbed into an unregistered interest, the title to which is governed by a deed recorded in the Register of Sasines, recording in that Register of the deed effecting the absorption will be necessary. This is perhaps best illustrated by example. Thus, for instance, suppose A, whose title to 10 acres is recorded in the Register of Sasines, grants a Feu Disposition of 1 acre to B, who in terms of section 2(1)(a)(i) obtains registration of his interest in the 1 acre in the Land Register. Subsequently B agrees to the re-acquisition of the 1 acre by A whom, in turn, decides to effect consolidation of the property and superiority interests in the 1 acre. To achieve this B grants a disposition to A containing a clause of resignation *ad perpetuam remanentiam*. This requires to be presented both for registration in the Land Register, in order that the Keeper can cancel the Title Sheet for the 1 acre, and also for recording in the Register of Sasines, as that is where the higher interest lies.

Section 8(2)(c)
This subsection provides that any deed which is not registrable in terms of section 2(1) to (4) and which prior to the Act commencing was recordable in the Register of Sasines will continue to fall to be recorded in that register if a real right or obligation is to be created or affected. Examples of such deeds include standard securities over an interest in land which is not itself registered in the Land Register, an assignation of such a security if the interest remains unregistered, a gratuitous conveyance, a minute of waiver where neither the superior's nor vassal's title is registered in the Land Register or where the title of only one of them is so registered. In the latter case the deed would require to be registered in both registers.

It should be noted that the provisions of section 8(1) are without prejudice to any other means, other than by registration in the Land Register, of creating or affecting real rights. Thus, for example, it will still be possible to establish a real right in a servitude by possession. However, it will not be possible in an operational

---

[9] c. 101

area to acquire a real right in leasehold subjects, udal property or kindly tenancy without registration as these instances are particularly legislated for in section 3(3). In addition a transaction which would otherwise induce a first registration but which has been completed by delivery of the signed deed before the area has become operational will fall to be recorded in the Sasine Register. Deeds that do not fall into one of the categories outlined above will, if presented for recording in the Register of Sasines, be rejected by the Keeper. This is a mandatory duty imposed on the Keeper by section 8(4).

Ranking

2.16 Section 7 of the Land Registration (Scotland) Act 1979 introduced a change in the law regarding the ranking of deeds. It introduced the rule that, in the absence of any express provision to the contrary, deeds presented on the same day, be that in the Land Register or Sasine Register, would rank equally. The Land Registration (Scotland) Act 1979 (Commencement No 1) Order 1980[10] which brought the 1979 Act into operation as regards registration in the County of Renfrew, applied the provisions of section 7 to the whole of Scotland with effect from 6 April 1981. Previously deeds had ranked according to when they were presented for recording in the Register of Sasines, except that all deeds received in the same post were deemed to be presented and recorded simultaneously.

Section 7 (1) states that the provisions on ranking are without prejudice to any express provision as to ranking in any deed. Ranking clauses are found most commonly in heritable securities affecting the same subjects but do appear in other deeds. Subsection (1) further states that the provisions on ranking are similarly without prejudice to *any other provision as to ranking in, or having effect by virtue of, any enactment or rule of law*', for example the ranking provisions affecting 'discount standard securities' as contained in section 72(5) of the Housing (Scotland) Act 1987.[11]

Section 7 (2) states that ranking of registered interests in land shall be according to date of registration.

Section 7 (3) provides for ranking as between registration in the Land Register on the one hand and the Register of Sasines on the other. A title to a registered interest and a title governed by a deed recorded in the Register of Sasines shall rank according to their *respective dates of registration and recording*'. For example,

[10] 1980 No.1412
[11] c.26

A dispones to B for a valuable consideration 1 acre of his 10 acres which lie within an operational area. However, before B presents his title for registration in the Land Register, A grants a standard security to C over the whole 10 acres. C records his standard security in the Register of Sasines prior to B registering his title in the Land Register. C will rank prior to B in terms of section 7 (3) and that security will be shown in the charges section of B's title sheet. If on the other hand, C presented his standard security for recording in the Register of Sasines after B had registered his title in the Land Register, then the Keeper would reject the deed in terms of section 8 (4) on the basis that part of the security subjects had been registered in the Land Register.

Heritable securities still subsisting at the date of first registration in which creditors acquired real rights by recording in the Register of Sasines will rank in the order of their recording and before heritable securities registered in the Land Register on or after first registration of the interest to which they relate.

Section 7 (4) affirms that *'where the date of registration or recording of the titles to two or more interests in land is the same, the titles to those interests shall rank equally'*. Thus, if A in the above example also conveyed the same one acre, in a separate disposition, to C and both B and C subsequently applied for registration on the same day there titles would, by virtue of section 7(4) rank *pari passu*. The Keeper would not, however, be in a position to grant an unqualified land certificate(s). Indemnity would be excluded as regards B's interest *vis-a-vis* C's title and *vice-versa*.

Registration and recording in respect of one deed

2.17 A transaction which would induce first registration may relate to subjects lying both within and outwith an operational area. Two possibilities exist in this situation: either the subjects comprise two (or more) discontiguous pieces of land lying in two or more registration counties, or they may form a single plot of ground that straddles the boundary of two adjoining counties; the so-called 'straddling plot'.

Straddling plot

The registration implications of the straddling plot have already been discussed at paragraph 2.7. In terms of section 11(2), registration in the Land Register must be sought unless the two areas can be severed, either in separate deeds or as separate subjects within the same deed.

Discontiguous areas

Where the transaction affects two or more discontiguous pieces of land, it is possible to attend to both properties in the same deed. The deed should be endorsed with a warrant of registration for the property within the non-operational area (*i.e.* for recording in the Sasine Register) and, in addition, be submitted with an application for registration in the Land Register for the interest lying within the operational area.

It is preferable, from the Keeper's point of view, for the solicitor to prepare separate deeds. However, there are occasions when the preparation of separate deeds would not be practicable.

When the registered interest is that of the *dominium utile* or a tenant under a long lease, and the superior's or the landlord's title is still recorded in the Sasine Register, a disposition *ad perpetuam remanentiam* or a renunciation of the tenant's interest will lead to registration in the Land Register and a recording in the Sasine Register. Registration in the Land Register is necessary as the transaction affects a registered interest. The deed is recorded in the Sasine Register to show that the lesser interest has merged into the higher interest.

Where an existing, recorded heritable security is secured over property, part of which has been subsequently registered, or is about to be registered, in the Land Register, effect will have to be given in both Registers to any discharge or partial discharge or any deed of restriction which relates to both parts. Thus, in addition to submitting the discharge, *etc.*, along with the appropriate Land Register application form, the solicitor should endorse a Sasine warrant of registration on the deed and enclose a covering letter requesting that the deed be recorded also in the Sasine Register. Where the discharge, partial discharge or deed of restriction relates only to subjects in the Land Register, or only to subjects about to enter the Land Register, there is no need to present the discharge, *etc.*, for recording in the Sasine Register as well.

Transactions relating to registered and unregistered interests

2.18 The solicitor must consider various possibilities when dealing with transactions which affect subjects that straddle the boundary of an operational and a non-operational area. The solicitor must also take care in preparing letters of obligation. Stipulations covering delivery and exhibition of a clear title in missives appropriate to a transaction which falls to be completed by recording in the Sasine Register are not wholly appropriate to a transaction which will also lead to registration in the Land Register. Advice concerning those matters can be found in chapter 8.

The following examples illustrate some of the various possibilities which may arise. They emphasise the wisdom of dealing with composite transactions, where possible, as separate parallel transactions. Attempting to combine such transactions in a single deed tends to increase the risk of serious error. Moreover, a combined recording and registration often leads to unnecessary procedural complications for both the solicitor and the Keeper.

Example 1: The transaction results in a first registration of an unregistered interest and a recording in the Register of Sasines.

Action to be taken concerning:	First registration of an unregistered interest	Recording in the Register of Sasines
Description of the subjects	*The style of description that is appropriate for use in a deed intended for recording in the Register of Sasines will be adequate (e.g. a full bounding description or a statutory reference description).* *The application for registration must contain sufficient information to enable the Keeper to identify the subjects in relation to the ordnance map.*	*The style of description that is appropriate for use in a deed intended for recording in the Register of Sasines will be adequate (e.g. a full bounding description or a statutory reference description).* *The Keeper recommends that the solicitor should provide him with sufficient information to enable him to identify the subjects in relation to the ordnance map, since that makes any future registration in the Land Register much easier.*
Burdens	*A narration of, or statutory reference to, burdens is required.*	*A narration of, or statutory reference to, burdens is required.*
Instructions for registration or recording	*Application for registration should be made on Form 1. This should be accompanied by an inventory Form 4 in duplicate and all other necessary deeds and documents*	*A warrant of registration should be endorsed on the deed.*

| Reports and searches | *A Form 10, and possibly a Form 11 report, should be instructed. Consideration should be given as to whether a P16 report is required.* | *An interim report and subsequently a search for incumbrances in the Register of Sasines and the Register of Inhibitions and Adjudications should be obtained.* |

Example 2: The transaction results in a dealing with a registered interest and a recording in the Register of Sasines.

Action to be taken concerning:	Dealing with a registered interest	Recording in the Register of Sasines
Description of the subjects	*The description of the subjects must be by reference to the title number.* *If the dealing relates to only a part of the registered subjects, the part must be described so that the Keeper can identify it in relation to the ordnance map.*	*The style of description that is appropriate for use in a deed intended for recording in the Register of Sasines will be adequate (e.g. a full bounding description or a statutory reference description).* *The Keeper recommends that the solicitor should provide him with sufficient information to enable him to identify the subjects in relation to the ordnance map, since that makes any future registration in the Land Register much easier.*
Burdens	*No narration of, or statutory reference to, burdens and land conditions is required, unless new burdens or conditions are being created.*	*A narration of, or statutory reference to burdens, is required.*

Instructions for registration or recording	*Application for registration should be made on Form 2, if the dealing is other than a transfer of part.*	*A warrant of registration should be endorsed on the deed.*
	Application for registration should be made on Form 3, if the transaction relates to a transfer of part of the registered interest. In either case, the application should be accompanied by an inventory Form 4 in duplicate and all other necessary deeds and documents.	
Reports and searches	*A Form 12 report, and possibly a Form 13 report, should be instructed.*	*An interim report and subsequently a search for incumbrances in the Register of Sasines and the Register of Inhibitions and Adjudications should be obtained.*

Example 3: The transaction results in a dealing with a registered interest and a first registration of an unregistered interest.

Action to be taken concerning:	Dealing with a registered interest	First registration of an unregistered interest
Description of the subjects	*The description of the subjects must be by reference to the title number.*	*The description should be that appropriate for use in a deed intended for recording in the Register of Sasines (e.g. a full bounding description or a statutory reference description).*

	If the dealing relates to only a part of the registered subjects, the part must be described so that the Keeper can identify it in relation to the ordnance map.	*The application for registration must contain sufficient information to enable the Keeper to identify the subjects in relation to the ordnance map.*
Burdens	*No narration of, or statutory reference to, burdens and land conditions is required, unless new burdens or conditions are being created.*	*A narration of, or statutory reference to, burdens is required.*
Instructions for registration	*An application for registration should be made on a Form 2, if the dealing is other than a transfer of part.*	*Application for registration should be made on Form 1. This should be accompanied by an inventory Form 4 in duplicate and all other necessary deeds and documents.*
	Application for registration should be made on a Form 3, if the transaction relates to a transfer of part of the registered interest.	
	In either case, the application should be accompanied by an inventory Form 4 in duplicate and all other necessary deeds and documents.	
Reports and searches	*A Form 12 report, and possibly a Form 13 report, should be instructed.*	*A Form 10, and possibly a Form 11 report, should be instructed.*
		Consideration should be given as to whether a P16 report is required.

Registration in the Land Register and the Books of the Lords of Council and Session

Simultaneous registration

2.19 It is permissible to submit a writ for registration in the Land Register and request simultaneous registration in the Books of Council and Session (or, more specifically, in the Register of Deeds, which is a constituent register of the Books of Council and Session). The Books of Council and Session are maintained separately from the Land Register by a section of the Registers of Scotland known as the Chancery and Judicial Registers.

In 1998 the Keeper introduced an application form for registration in the Register of Deeds. Although the form is non-statutory, the Keeper urges solicitors to make full use of it. The form has the approval of the Law Society of Scotland's Conveyancing Committee. Use of the form will remove the need for a covering letter, as the completed form will contain all the information that the Keeper will need. However, an applicant who wishes to register in the Books of Council and Session, a deed which accompanies an application for registration in the Land Register should continue to use a covering letter of instruction. The covering letter should state clearly the number of extracts required. Unless the deed is also to be recorded in the Sasine Register, a warrant of registration is not required.

The deed in question will be subjected to a brief, preliminary examination by Land Register staff. If no obvious defects are identified, a copy of the deed is taken and used for purposes of registration in the Land Register. The original is then forwarded to the Chancery and Judicial Registers. The staff of the Chancery and Judicial Registers will subject the deed to another form of examination, this time to ensure its compliance with the registration standards of the Register of Deeds. Provided that examination is satisfactory, the deed will be registered in the Books of Council and Session. The extract(s) will then be issued, normally within 10 working days.

Solicitors should take special care when considering simultaneous registration in the Land Register and the Books of Council and Session. Once a deed has been registered in the Books of Council and Session, it cannot be withdrawn. If a full examination of the copy deed by Land Register staff reveals a serious problem that was not detected by earlier checks, and the original is registered in the Books of Council and Session, it may be difficult to resolve the problem without preparing an entirely fresh deed. The applicant will then have to consider registering the second deed in the Books of Council and Session. In particular, mapping problems will generally be picked up only when the application reaches the later stage of examination.

Separate registration fees will be charged in respect of the registration in each Register.

Subsequent registration

2.20 On completion of registration in the Land Register, all deeds and documents submitted in support of the application for registration are returned to the applicant. Deeds which have been given effect to in the Land Register but which have been retained by the proprietor may be registered in the Books of Council and Session at any time. A deed which contains a consent to registration for execution will not necessarily have been registered in the Books of Council and Session when the application in respect of that deed was given effect in the Land Register. Such a deed should be retained with the land certificate, for, if at some future date it becomes necessary to do summary diligence on that deed, only the principal deed will be acceptable for registration for execution in the Books of Council and Session. A copy of the deed will not suffice.

Where a standard security which has already been registered in the Land Register is later to be presented for registration for execution in the Books of Council and Session, the entire charge certificate should be returned to the Keeper. The Keeper will remove the standard security and register it in the Books of Council and Session. The charge certificate will be re-issued with an extract of the standard security attached.

Chapter 3 - Reports, Searches and Enquiries

Introduction

3.1 Generally, in an operational area a real right can be obtained only by registration of the title to the subjects in the Land Register (section 2(1)(a) and 3(1) and (2) of the Act). Until such registration has taken place, writs which do not induce registration will continue to be recorded in the appropriate division of the Sasine Register unless voluntary registration in the Land Register is accepted by the Keeper. The procedure for searches against subjects in an operational area are discussed in this chapter. It should be noted that the Keeper does not carry out searches in the Register of Charges at Companies House.

This section has been written in the context of the reports provided by the Keeper in terms of the Land Registration (Scotland) Rules 1980[1]. Firms of private searchers produce equivalent reports which can be used; but as these reports are not '*information given by the Keeper in writing*' they do not attract the benefit of the indemnity provided by section 12(1) of the 1979 Act. It is understood, however, that the private searchers provide their own indemnity policy to guarantee their reports. In addition the Keeper will be providing direct access to the Registers under Registers Direct (see paragraph 3.20) and this will enable solicitors, if they choose, to do their own searches and reports. For the avoidance of doubt information provided by the Keeper on screen will be treated as '*information given by the Keeper in writing*' for indemnity purposes.

There are a number of preliminary points which need to be kept in mind when a report or search is required over subjects which lie in an operational area:

- The Sasine Register is invariably some weeks out of date. However, writs presented for recording, unless rejected by the Keeper, will appear in a search made the following day. In cases where the recording procedure has not been completed, *i.e.* by completion of the minute book, the report will still disclose the deed as a 'pending' recording. The time lag between presentment and the completion of the recording process gives the presenter time to withdraw writs. The Keeper will still give solicitors the opportunity to withdraw deeds which require correction. Solicitors will also still be able to withdraw writs on request provided the minute book has not been completed or a Form 10 report has not already been issued in respect of the relevant subjects.

[1] 1980 No.1413

- In operational areas all reports can be brought down to the day before the date of issue of the report. Delay is inevitable, however, if applicants do not use the correct forms or if they complete them incorrectly or they send them to the incorrect DX number.

- Where an interest has been registered in the Land Register, no provision has been made either in the Act or in the Rules for a closing entry to be made in the Sasine Register. Accordingly, once an area has become operational, a search of the minute book of that division of the Sasine Register will not disclose any transfers, whether of the whole or of a part, which have been registered in the Land Register. In practice, however, the Keeper will note this information on the search sheets and, as most sasine searches in operational areas are completed by examining the search sheets, any search in respect of the Sasine Register will disclose transfers of the subjects (including partial transfers) to the Land Register.

- Reports from the Land Register, *i.e.* Form 12 and Form 13 reports, will not merely disclose completed registrations, *i.e.* those in respect of which a title sheet has actually been opened or entries made on an existing title sheet, but will disclose all applications for registration which have been received up to 48 hours preceding the date of issue of the report, providing always that the applications are correctly made. When a report discloses an application for registration the entry will make it clear that the registration process in respect of that application has not yet been completed.

- The part of the indemnity provisions applicable to reports is section 12(1)(d) of the Act. The Keeper is liable to indemnify loss suffered as a result of an error in or omission from a report as regards disclosing:

  - deeds from the parts of the report relating to the Register of Sasines or the Register of Inhibitions and Adjudications; or

  - documents registered or an application for registration from the part of a report relating to the Land Register.

The indemnity cover does not extend to the effect that any deed or document disclosed has on the title to the subjects of the report.

In order that solicitors may rely on the indemnity provisions, stringent care must be exercised in completing the report application form, particularly with regard to the names and addresses of parties to be searched against in the Register of Inhibitions and Adjudications. Any claim may otherwise be refused in terms of section 12(3)(n) of the Act.

Transactions which induce first registration

3.2 As part of the examination of title in transactions which induce first registration, the requirement to ensure that the records are clear of any incumbrances will still apply. However, as the land certificate which is issued on completion of first registration contains all relevant information in respect of the interest registered, a search for incumbrances as such will not be completed. The land certificate itself takes the place of that search. Indeed, any existing search will not have to be examined, as all the relevant information contained in it is contained in the report discussed in the following paragraphs. There are, of course, cases where, although the property lies in an operational area, a completed search for incumbrances in the Sasine Register may still be required. These are discussed in paragraph 3.13.

Form 10 report

3.3 Where a report is required in respect of a transaction which will induce first registration (or in respect of which voluntary registration will be sought), the Rules prescribe a comprehensive form of report covering the Sasine Register, the Land Register and the Register of Inhibitions and Adjudications - the Form 10 report. This report is appropriate whether the search is to be made over the whole subjects described in a recorded deed or over only part of those subjects. Where voluntary registration is sought, it is prudent to ascertain from the Keeper, before making application for a Form 10 report, that an application for voluntary registration will be accepted.

The Form 10 report is divided into three parts:

- A report from the Sasine Register which will narrate:

  1. a prescriptive progress of titles;

  2. a list of undischarged securities recorded within the 40 years prior to the date to which the report is certified, including undischarged securities recorded outwith that period but intromitted with during that period by recorded deed (*e.g.* assignation);

3. a list of discharges recorded within the 5 years to the date of the report; and

4. a list of deeds other than transfers or deeds creating or affecting securities recorded within the 40 year period prior to the date of the report, *e.g.* minutes of waiver, deeds of servitude.

- A report from the Land Register which will disclose whether the interest (or any part of that interest) has been registered and, if so, the title number under which it is registered.

- A report from the Register of Inhibitions and Adjudications against the parties listed by the applicant.

Application for a Form 10 report

Application for a Form 10 report should be made in duplicate. One copy of the application will be returned with the report and should be retained with it. A Form 10 report includes all the relevant entries from the Sasine Register which would be found in a 40 year search, but in a different form. Accordingly, a Form 10 report is not merely a continuation of an existing search, but supersedes it. Any existing search over the subjects should not therefore be sent to the Keeper with the application for a Form 10 report.

It should be borne in mind that a Form 10 report relates only to the property for which an application for first registration will subsequently be made. If that property already has a separate identity in the Sasine Register, no problems should arise. If, however, the first registration will be induced by a sale of a part of a larger area, the Form 10 report will only reveal deeds which affect that part. Deeds transferring or affecting only other parts of the larger area will not be revealed unless it is clear from the sasine minutes that they, in some way, affect the subjects being reported on. It should be noted, however, that this is exactly the situation that pertains when a search for incumbrances in the Sasine Register is ordered over a specific part of a larger area.

To enable the Keeper to issue a Form 10 report the subjects have to be sufficiently described to allow the Keeper to identify them in the Sasine Register and also on the index map. So far as the Sasine Register is concerned, reference to a recorded deed containing a description of the property may be sufficient; but such a reference is not sufficient to enable the Keeper to identify the subjects on the index map. The information which the Keeper will require to search the Land

Register is discussed in chapter 4. In those cases where it is desired to enlist the Keeper's help in comparing legal and occupational boundaries by ordering a Form P16 report, it is recommended that the two reports are ordered together. This attracts the benefit of a reduced fee from the Keeper.

As indicated, a Form 10 report is a report over subjects in respect of which an application for first registration is to be made. If these subjects form the balance of a larger area from which parts have been sold earlier, the report can only be over that balance. Accordingly, if the subjects are to be described by reference to a recorded deed which described the larger area, the report request should narrate the exceptions from that larger area. If *per incuriam* the report request describes only the larger area, the Keeper will contact the agent and draw attention to the exceptions. The exceptions will be added to the description in the report request and the report will be carried out over the balance, *i.e.* the larger area under exception of parts already sold. There will be no mention of the exceptions in the body of the report. This maintains consistency with the principles applied above with regard to a report over an identified part of larger subjects.

The Form 10 report is appropriate for a transaction which will induce first registration either in terms of section 2(1)(a) of the Act or because voluntary registration under section 2(1)(b) is being sought. In the majority of cases, the solicitor will know that the interest has not already been registered; but there may be cases where the solicitor is unaware that registration has taken place or, where on registration of an adjoining property, part of the subjects has been included in that registration. Accordingly, an office copy (see paragraph 3.11) of any appropriate title sheet can be ordered.

Form 11 report

3.4 In registration of title, just as the land certificate takes the place of the completed search for incumbrances, a Form 10 report is equivalent to the uncontinued search plus the interim report on search. Under the sasine system, an interim report is not always instructed; and, when it is, it is usually instructed as nearly as possible to the date of settlement but allowing sufficient time to deal with any unexpected items which might appear in it. It is suggested that the Form 10 report should be obtained at the beginning of the transaction and a continuation of that report (a Form 11 report) obtained at the latest possible moment.

To safeguard against the possibility of the interest (or part of it) having already been registered, it is suggested that the Form 10 report should be obtained before the subjects are put on the market. Any continuation of a Form 10 report must be instructed on a Form 11 which should again be submitted in duplicate. The Form 10 report itself, however, should not be enclosed with this further application as the Keeper retains a copy of the original report. The Form 11 report will automatically include a continuation of the search in the personal registers against those parties named in the application for the Form 10 report. If it is desired to search against additional parties, *e.g.* the purchaser/borrower, these parties should be fully designed in the Form 11 application.

Reports over interests in land registered in the Land Register

3.5 Once an interest has been registered in the Land Register, the land certificate issued in respect of that interest gives a complete picture of the state of the Land Register as at the date to which the land certificate was last updated, this being the date shown on the inside front cover of the land certificate. Neither a search under the Sasine system of recording of deeds nor a Form 10 report is, therefore, appropriate once an interest has been registered under rule 9(3). The land certificate must accompany each application for registration of a dealing in a registered interest, except in the limited number of cases which are set out in rule 18. While, therefore, the land certificate (with the benefit of the rectification and indemnity provisions) may be relied upon as an accurate record as at the date when the land certificate was last updated, there are cases where dealings might have been registered since that date. The Rules provide for alternative methods of updating the information in the land certificate; firstly by submitting the land certificate itself to the Keeper for updating or, secondly, by obtaining a Form 12 report.

Updating land certificate

3.6 Rule 16 provides that the land certificate may be submitted to the Keeper at any time for updating. Application should be made on Form 8 (Rule 16). This facility is more appropriate for use in those cases where there is no current transaction but it is nevertheless desired to check that the information disclosed in the land certificate is up to date. Updating a land certificate is less appropriate where there is a current transaction, as it will take the Keeper longer to update a land certificate than to issue a report from the Land Register. Furthermore, the land certificate, which takes the place of a prescriptive progress of titles, will be required for examination by the purchaser or creditor's solicitor. In the majority of transactions it will be inconvenient for the land certificate to be out of circulation for the time taken by the Keeper to bring it up to date. It should also be noted that, when a land certificate is updated, the Keeper will note any subsisting adverse entries from the Register of Inhibitions and Adjudications.

These entries, however, will only relate to those persons appearing from the title sheet to have an interest in the property. There may be other persons who have acquired an interest since the date to which the land certificate was last updated and of whom the Keeper may not be aware. Any such persons should be disclosed on the Form 8 application.

Form 12 report

3.7 The appropriate method of searching the Land Register in relation to a dealing with a registered interest, is to apply for a Form 12 report. It is strongly recommended that, for the reasons given in the preceding paragraph, in all cases where it is desired to obtain a report during the course of a current transaction covering the period from the date of issue of the land certificate, application should be made for a Form 12 report. Just as the land certificate takes the place of the completed sasine search, a Form 12 report will serve the same purpose as an interim report from the Sasine and personal registers. The report is made against the subjects in or remaining in the title as at the date to which the land certificate was last updated. Where the report relates to the whole of a registered interest, reference to the title number is all that the Keeper requires to identify the subjects.

Where, however, the transaction relates to part only of the registered interest, not only must the title number of the whole be given, but, in addition, that part must be identifiable by the Keeper on the existing title plan. Such identification may be achieved by means of a plan attached to the application, a verbal description or a reference to any approved estate plan.

The report will also cover a search in the Register of Inhibitions and Adjudications. Parties to be searched against should include those parties disclosed in the proprietorship section of the title sheet and any other relevant parties. The names of all parties to be searched against must be included in the appropriate part of the Form 12 application. Attention is drawn to the need for accuracy in completing this part of the form in respect of the names and addresses of the parties to be searched against.

A Form 12 report covers the period from the last date to which the land certificate was updated (shown on the inside cover of the certificate) which is the date to which the title is indemnified, to the date of certification of the report reply form. Where there is no land certificate, because first registration has not been completed, the Form 12 report, in addition to covering the period from receipt of the application for first registration, will also provide a report from the Sasine Register, containing the same information as in the Form 10 report, brought down to the date of first registration.

Details of applications in the course of registration will be included in the report; but it will be stated specifically in these cases that registration has not yet been completed. Disclosure of an incomplete registration in a Form 12 report does not imply any indemnity in respect of that registration.

The application should be sent to the Keeper in duplicate. One copy will be returned with the report.

There are five styles of reply form used by the Keeper in response to an application for a Form 12 report, according to the circumstances:

- Form 12A   used if first registration has been completed for the subjects over which the report has been requested.

- Form 12B   used if first registration has not yet been completed for the subjects over which the report has been requested.

- Form 12C   used if first registration has not yet been completed for the subjects over which the report has been requested and the deed inducing that first registration implements a compulsory purchase.

- Form 12D and 12E used if the subjects over which the report has been requested are in the course of registration as a transfer of part and form part of the subjects in a title (the 'parent title') for which registration has been completed.

Where the subjects of the report form the whole of the subjects in the transfer of part, Form 12D is used.

Where the subjects of the report form part of the subjects in the transfer of part, Form 12E is used.

If registration of the parent title has not been completed, a Form 12B is used in conjunction with either a Form 12D or Form 12E, as appropriate.

As discussed in the following paragraph, provision is also made in the Rules for obtaining a continuation of the Form 12 report.

Form 13 report

3.8 In many transactions affecting registered land, the ordering of a Form 12 report before settlement will be sufficient. There may, however, be circumstances where a continuation of the Form 12 report is required, for example where there is delay in settling the transaction. An application for such a continuation must be made on a Form 13 and the application must be submitted in duplicate. The original Form 12 report should not be sent with the application. The continuation will include an updating of information from the personal registers against those persons searched against in the original Form 12 report. If it is desired to search against additional parties, such as the purchaser/borrower, these parties should be fully designed in the Form 13 application.

Reports over subjects held *pro indiviso*

3.9 As discussed in paragraph 5.52, *pro indiviso* shares will be kept on one title sheet but in some cases separate land certificates will be issued to each *pro indiviso* proprietor. Where a report is required over a *pro indiviso* interest in respect of which a separate land certificate is held, it should be noted that, when a Form 12 report is instructed, the Keeper must be advised on the application form for that report of the date down to which the land certificate was last completed. This date is given on the inside front cover of the land certificate. Where, however, one land certificate has been issued covering all the *pro indiviso* interests (the commonest example of *pro indiviso* ownership is property held in joint names of husband and wife), the Keeper does not require this information.

Other methods of obtaining information from the Land Register

3.10 The principal methods of obtaining information from the registers have already been discussed, namely a Form 10 report where the interest is unregistered but the transaction will induce first registration; or, where the interest has already been registered, a Form 12 report; or, in appropriate circumstances, submission of the land certificate to the Keeper for updating. These latter two methods, are, however, only of use to the holder of the land certificate. Any other party requiring to ascertain the state of the register must either obtain an office copy or apply for a Form 14 report.

Office copy

3.11 While the Land Register is a register of interests in land and not a register of deeds, the Keeper will, in fact, keep on microfiche for each title sheet copies of all deeds or documents referred to in that title sheet. Microfiche copies are also kept of deeds or documents which have induced entries on the title sheet or caused amendments to be made to existing entries. In terms of section 6(5), the Keeper is bound to issue to any person applying, a copy, to be known as an 'office copy', of any title sheet or any part of a title sheet (for example the charges or the burdens section) and of any document referred to in the title sheet. Requests for office copies may be endorsed on a Form 10 report request. However, where a report is not required, or the person ordering the office copy is a third party, application should be made on Form 15. It should be noted that to complete Form 15 it is necessary to know the title number of the relevant interest. If this information is not known to the applicant then application must be made using Form 14.

While an office copy of the title sheet or of the proprietorship section of the title sheet will disclose any subsisting adverse entries from the Register of Inhibitions and Adjudications, it must be stressed that the indemnity in respect of information from the personal registers only covers information relating to those persons who appear to the Keeper from the title sheet to have an interest. There may well be parties of whom the Keeper is unaware, and instructions for a search in the personal registers in respect of such persons may be given on Form 15.

Report to determine if an interest in land has been registered

3.12 Form 14 is an enquiry to discover if particular subjects are registered in the Land Register and can be used to order an office copy of the title sheet of the interest if it has been registered. The form may also be used to instruct a search in the Register of Inhibitions and Adjudications. In cases where the Form 14 report reveals that no registration has taken place, the enquirer may by letter request the Keeper to supply any relevant or specific information which he can provide from the Register of Sasines. A fee will be charged by the Keeper for a Form 14 report, any office copy issued or information provided from the Register of Sasines.

Search over unregistered land in an operational area where first registration is not contemplated

3.13 While a Form 10 report is the appropriate method of searching the Registers in the case of a transaction which will lead to first registration, it is not appropriate to a transaction where the deed still falls to be recorded in the Sasine Register. Conversely, it is not appropriate to instruct the preparation of a search in cases where the transaction will lead to first registration. However there are circumstances where a search will or may require to be continued or prepared as at present although the subjects lie within an operational area:

(a) Where the transaction will not induce first registration, for example, the grant of a standard security over an unregistered interest, a search, or the continuation of an existing search, should be instructed together with, if required, an interim report. There may be cases where the solicitor dealing with a non-registrable transaction will wish to confirm that the interest has not in fact been registered. In such cases application should be made for a Form 14 report.

(b) Where the transaction is a grant of a feu or a long lease and thus itself induces first registration although the title of the superior or landlord will remain unregistered, or where the transaction is a sale of part only of unregistered subjects, the superior, landlord or seller, as the case may be, may wish the existing search for incumbrances to be continued to disclose the transaction. In such cases while the transaction should proceed as one inducing first registration and a Form 10 report will require to be obtained the solicitor may wish to have the search brought down to date as well.

Search over subjects in non-operational area

3.14 There are two occasions when an interest in land outwith an operational area may be registered in the Land Register, namely:

- Where the Keeper accepts an application for voluntary registration of an interest in land lying outwith an operational area under section 11(1); and

- Where subjects lie partly in and partly outwith an operational area, any of the transactions referred to in section 2(1)(a) will induce first registration of the whole subjects (*i.e.* including the part lying outwith the operational area) in terms of section 11(2).

Such occasions call for special consideration.

Voluntary registration under section 11(1)
3.15 The Keeper will accept applications for registration in the Land Register under section 11(1), but only where they relate to substantial developments which lie within the area next to be designated as operational (see paragraph 2.8) It is suggested that where a developer seeks voluntary registration under section 11(1) and already has a recorded sasine title, a Form 10 report should be instructed

prior to an application for registration being submitted. Before application for a Form 10 report is made, it should be ascertained from the Keeper that an application for voluntary registration will be accepted. As interests in land in non-operational areas can, under section 11(1), be registered in the Land Register (albeit that only limited registrations will be accepted), it may be prudent on occasions when dealing with transactions bounded by a new development (which might have been registered) to instruct a Form 14 report from the Land Register to make certain that no part of the subjects has been included in the developer's title sheet in the event of that development having been registered.

Registration under section 11(2) - straddling plots
3.16 In any case falling under section 11(2), whether as a first registration under section 2(1)(a) or as a voluntary registration under section 2(1)(b), a Form 10 report should be instructed. When dealing with transactions relating to subjects in an area not yet operational but lying near the boundary of an operational area, it may be wise to consider obtaining a Form 14 report from the Land Register in case, on registration of a straddling plot, part of the subjects has been included in that registration.

Register of Inhibitions and Adjudications

Transactions inducing first registration

3.17 The application for a Form 10 report includes instructions for a search to be made in the personal registers, and this part of the form should be completed with the full names and addresses of all parties against whom a search is required. There are two practical matters which should be kept in mind:

- If, as is suggested, the Form 10 report is instructed at the commencement of the transaction, care should be taken to ensure that any additional names to be searched against (*i.e.* a purchaser/borrower) are included in the application for a continuation of that report, *i.e.* when applying for the Form 11 report.

- The Form 10 report will list the names of all the parties against whom a report in the personal registers has been instructed. However, the land certificate subsequently issued will not do so, but will only disclose any subsisting entries adverse to the interest being registered. Before issuing the land certificate, however, the Keeper will ensure that all names included in the application for the Form 10 (or Form 11) report are searched against. Any adverse entries found against these names will be investigated by the Keeper even if, *ex facie* of the deeds submitted in support of the application, the party in question is not disclosed as having an interest.

Transactions where the interest is already registered

3.18 The title sheet of each interest in land must include any subsisting entry in the Register of Inhibitions and Adjudications adverse to the interest (section 6(1)(c)). Any such entries will be disclosed in the land certificate of that interest or in an office copy of the title sheet or of the proprietorship section of the title sheet. Similarly, such entries will appear on any Form 12 or 13 report instructed. It should be noted, however, that, as the Land Register reflects the current position of the title and does not give an historical narrative, '*subsisting adverse entry*' means the entry of a diligence recorded in the personal registers which has not expired and in respect of which a discharge or recall has not been recorded. If a diligence has been discharged or recalled neither the diligence nor the discharge will be disclosed.

The Keeper will normally have knowledge only of those parties appearing from the title sheet to have an interest. It is possible that, between the date of the last registration and the date of application for a report, or for an office copy or for the updating of the land certificate, other parties of whom the Keeper may have no knowledge may have acquired an interest in the subjects which may be affected by a diligence recorded in the personal registers. So, while any report instructed, or an updated land certificate, or an office copy of a title sheet or of the proprietorship section of a title sheet, will disclose any subsisting adverse diligence against a person of whom the Keeper has knowledge, if there are any other parties against whom a search should be made, these must be notified to the Keeper. Each of the appropriate forms of application makes provision for so doing.

There is not, of course, any need to instruct specifically a search against persons who will appear from the title sheet to have an interest. A Form 14 report will not, however, disclose any entries in the personal registers unless specific instructions are given for a search in those registers or the report discloses that the interest is registered and the Keeper has been asked in this event to issue an office copy of the title sheet. The form makes provision for instructing a search in the personal registers and can be used to order an office copy.

It is particularly important to remember to instruct the Keeper fully when ordering an office copy or submitting the land certificate for updating. It is probably less likely that the need to search against additional parties will be overlooked where the report is being instructed as part of a current transaction. It should also be remembered that while specific instructions need not be given where the parties' interest will clearly be disclosed from the title sheet, if there has been any change, for example in the address of any of the interested parties, this information should be given to the Keeper.

Applying for reports

3.19 In terms of the Land Registration (Scotland) Amendment Rules 1998[2] which came into force on 1 January 1999, application to the Keeper for a report shall be made on the appropriate form and application for an office copy in terms of section 6(5) of the 1979 Act shall be on Form 15.

A report or office copy may be applied for by fax or electronic mail provided the information which would have been included on an equivalent application using the appropriate form is supplied. A telephone application for a report or office copy may also be accepted, provided the same information is supplied, together with such additional information as the Keeper may require (rule 24).

Registers Direct

3.20 The proposed introduction of a system of direct access to the records maintained by the Agency addresses the twin aims of improving access to public records and helping to reduce the cost to the public of conveyancing in Scotland. Direct access makes the Agency's data bases available to users countrywide and eliminates any need to visit an Agency office or engage the services of a third party to obtain information from the records held by the Keeper.

Logging on to the system is achieved *via* a web browser running on a personal computer equipped with a modem. This gives access to a menu of easily-navigable screens by means of which the user will be able to interrogate the data bases relating to the Land and Sasine Registers, the Register of Inhibitions and Adjudications, the Register of the Books of Council and Session (Deeds) and the Register of Judgments.

Land Register enquiries may be made by examination of the application record (of pending entries for registration) or the title sheet record (for registered properties). Similarly, the Sasine Register offers access to the presentment book (containing pending entries for recording), the minute book (of recorded entries) and the search sheet (a synopsis of all the minute book entries which affect a

[2] 1998 No. 3100

single unit of property). Information from both these registers is accessible by keying in an individual or company name, a property address or via the title or search sheet number (if known). The remaining Registers offer access by either individual or company name or an index reference number.

Electronic access is supported by a customer service centre through which users who do not subscribe to the service may gain access to the system directly as a 'guest user' or be assisted in their enquiry by a member of the Agency's staff. In addition, a call centre allows assisted telephone access for non subscribers. Further information about this service is available from the Keeper.

Application for Registers Direct service

Application for use of the Registers Direct service may be made to the Keeper and should be accompanied by such information as will enable the Keeper to be satisfied that arrangements are in place for the payment of fees incurred. Any user of the service must, when asked, submit such information as will enable the Keeper to be satisfied that this requirement will continue to be met (rule 24A).

Pre-Registration Enquiries section

3.21 Prior to receiving an application for registration, the Keeper is always willing to offer guidance to solicitors on issues relevant to the application. To facilitate the growing number of general enquiries of this nature, a centralised section known as Pre-Registration Enquiries has been established to deal with more complex enquiries. Accordingly, requests for guidance in connection with a forthcoming application for registration should be directed to Pre-Registration Enquiries at the address noted below.

Guidance should be sought from Pre-Registration Enquiries on specific matters of concern stemming from a proposed or actual conveyancing transaction which will induce an application for registration. Guidance offered can include, for instance, views on defects in title, possible exclusions of indemnity, remedial conveyancing or additional evidence that may be required in a given case. It should be noted that the Keeper will answer enquiries about transactions in non-Land Register counties up to six months prior to those counties becoming operational areas.

Pre-Registration Enquiries will not answer hypothetical questions, nor will they undertake a full examination of title. Similarly, guidance of a less complex nature for example, relating to fees, or the appropriate application form, *etc.*, or information in connection with an application already lodged with the Keeper may be obtained from the relevant Customer Services Centre in Edinburgh or Glasgow. Any enquiry relating to a transaction that will take place wholly under the Sasine System should also be directed to either the Edinburgh or Glasgow Customer Services Centre, depending on the county to which the enquiry relates.

Those intending to contact Pre-Registration Enquiries should take note of the following points:

• Pre-Registration Enquiries should be contacted as soon as a particular problem becomes apparent. If contact is delayed until settlement is imminent, the Keeper may not be able to respond to the enquiry within the desired timescale. The Keeper will, if made aware of what stage the transaction has reached, endeavour to provide a response by the settlement date, but can offer no guarantee that he will always be able to do so.

• Enquiries should be made in writing. All relevant details and documentation should be provided as the Keeper will only answer an enquiry when he has all the information necessary to enable him to do so.

Pre-Registration Enquiries may now also be contacted direct on 0845 6070163 or 0131 479 3674 or at Meadowbank House, 153 London Road, Edinburgh EH8 7AU; DX No. 555400, Edinburgh 15 (Fax 0131-479-3675). Correspondence should be clearly marked 'for the attention of Pre-Registration Enquiries'.

Chapter 4 - Maps and Plans in Registration of Title

4.1 In any system of registration of title, the subjects pertaining to the interest registered must be accurately described. Accurate description ensures certainty as to what is or is not covered by the indemnity provisions, and facilitates efficient searching of the Register. A map-based system will fully enable a public land register to fulfil its proper function of providing information about the ownership and identification of registered subjects. As the Register of Sasines is a register of deeds, it does not always provide information about the location and extent of land described in a recorded deed. The system of registration of title brought in by the 1979 Act is map-based.

Ideally, before a system of registration of title is introduced, the whole country should be systematically surveyed. This would, however, be a counsel of perfection and be an expensive and time-consuming exercise. Instead, Scotland has followed the practice in England and Wales; and the recommendation of the Reid and Henry Reports, which provided for registration in successive operational areas, without special survey, has been enacted. The ordnance map is used as a basis for all descriptions of land in the Land Register (see section 6(1)(a)).

Maps and plans prepared by the Keeper

4.2 The Keeper's use of the ordnance map (section 6(1)(a)) allows him to produce, firstly, an index map for all operational areas and, secondly, a title plan and certificate plan for each registered interest.

Between April 1981 and October 1993, the Keeper used paper maps and plans for the first seven operational areas of the Land Register.

Developments in information technology then enabled the Keeper to procure a digital mapping system (DMS) to allow the graphical element of the registration process to be completed electronically. In 1995, Fife became the first area to become operational using the new technology. Maps and plans for the older operational areas have since been converted onto the DMS, allowing the DMS to develop into a comprehensive geographic information system (GIS) for land registration data.

Index map

4.3 One of the advantages of an electronic map-based system is that an index layer is easily prepared. Such an index is much superior to an index of place names as it permits speedier and more accurate searching of the Land Register. In terms of rule 23(a) the Keeper is bound to maintain an index map, based on the ordnance map, of registered interests in land. The first time an application to register an interest in a particular area of land is received the Keeper will prepare a title plan against the backdrop of the latest version of the ordnance map. A paper copy of this plan is provided for use in the land certificate and the original version is held electronically on the Keeper's digital mapping system. The Index Map therefore consists of copies of all registered and pending titles which have been received since a particular County went operational. It is the index map layer of the Keeper's digital mapping system which is the main key to the Land Register.

The index map layer consists of a continuous map on which, as registration proceeds, the Keeper will delineate all interests and note their title numbers. The scale of this map is determined by the base scale of the digital mapbase.

A report can be ordered on Form 14 to ascertain whether or not subjects have been registered in the Land Register and the composite Form 10 report which is appropriate where the transaction induces first registration, contains provision for a similar enquiry. The Keeper can answer such enquiries by reference to the index map.

Title plan and certificate plan

4.4 In the normal course of events, the Keeper prepares a title plan and a certificate plan when he receives an application for registration of an unregistered interest or of the transfer of a part of an already registered interest. ('Transfer' in this context includes the grant of a feu or lease of either the whole or a part of a registered interest). After examination of the titles and other evidence produced, and provided he is satisfied, the Keeper first prepares a title plan which will be stored electronically on the digital mapping system. An authorised copy of the title plan known as a certificate plan will then be prepared. The certificate plan is included in the land certificate issued to the applicant on conclusion of registration. For title plans and certificate plans, the Keeper will use the scale most appropriate for the property in question, normally the largest available Ordnance Survey scale. Generally speaking, for urban property the largest scale (1:1250) will be used, but where the subjects are, for example, a park, football ground or other large open space the plan may be produced to a scale of

1:2500. The title and certificate plan will delineate the property and may also, by use of different colouring or hatching, indicate parts feued or parts let on long lease, parts affected by certain burdens, rights of access or parts of the registered interest which have been conveyed away.

Comparing legal title with the ordnance map

4.5 The advent of the map-based land registration system has highlighted the poor quality of many title deed plans. Whilst these have been capable of being recorded in the Sasine Register where no check is made of their quality or accuracy, the registration process necessitates a much more rigorous examination of property extent. The Keeper's detailed mapping procedures now ensure that legal extents contained in title deeds are considered not only against occupational extents (as defined on the ordnance map) but also compared against adjoining registered properties.

Differences between the legal extent and that which exists on the ground are all too often revealed only at first registration. This situation can cause needless delays for the parties to a conveyancing transaction. Problems with title extents stem from two main failings. The first concerns failure to check that the title extent accurately reflects the situation on the ground. The other concerns the absence of surrounding physical features on the deed plan, which makes it impossible to locate and fix the property on the ordnance map.

Identification of subjects

4.6 Any application for registration must contain sufficient information for the Keeper to identify the subjects by reference to the ordnance map. In terms of section 4(2)(a), an application which does not contain a description sufficient to enable the Keeper to do this will be rejected. In this context 'identify' means locating and delineating the subjects on the ordnance map. As the principal index to the Land Register is the index map, an application for either a report or a registration must contain a sufficient description to allow the Keeper to find the subjects on the index map. The requirements will vary, depending on whether the application is for a report or for registration. They will also vary depending on whether the transaction is one which induces first registration or, if relating to a registered interest, relates to the whole or merely part of that interest. The requirements are therefore discussed below under these separate headings. (See Appendix 1 for detailed deed plan criteria).

Occupational and title boundaries

4.7 There is one more fundamental, practical problem which is inevitable in any transition from a non map-based system of registration of deeds to a system of registration of title, namely the occupational boundaries disclosed on the ordnance map may not always coincide with the legal boundaries disclosed in the title deeds. Under the Sasine system, such discrepancies rarely come to light. However, under registration of title, the Keeper will compare the description of the property as contained in the title deeds with the extent of the property as defined on the ordnance map. Any discrepancy will therefore come to light during the registration procedure. From the purchaser's point of view, it is important that any such discrepancy should be dealt with before the transaction is settled, because the application form for first registration requires the applicant to give the Keeper certain assurances regarding the extent of the subjects. The seller should make sure that any such discrepancy is disclosed at the missives stage. It is therefore recommended that before missives are concluded, solicitors acting for sellers should compare the title description with the property as depicted on the latest ordnance map, and make appropriate qualifications to any acceptance. The problem can also arise with tenement flats in relation to ground pertaining to the flat in question, either exclusively or in common.

Where a discrepancy is disclosed, it may be so slight that the Keeper can complete registration without difficulty by treating the discrepancy as falling within the 'or thereby' principle. Sometimes, however, there is a material discrepancy and the area encompassed by the occupational boundaries, as revealed on the ordnance map, is smaller than and falls wholly within the area described in the title deeds. In these circumstances, the Keeper may register the interest, as defined in the title deeds. However, depending on the results of his investigation and on any supplementary information obtained, the Keeper may exclude indemnity in respect of that part of the subjects outwith the occupational boundaries. The problem is equally serious where the occupational boundaries encompass an area larger than that described in the title deeds. This is because, if the discrepancy is not covered by the 'or thereby' principle, the Keeper may be unable to include the additional area in the title sheet, if there is no deed supporting the application for registration of that area.

The two preceding paragraphs relate to a transaction leading to first registration. Where the transaction relates to an interest which has already been registered in the Land Register, the problem arises only where, on first registration, the ordnance map discloses no, or only some, occupational boundaries and the

Keeper has shown the unmarked boundaries on the title plan by dotted (pecked) lines. In such a case, as occupational boundaries might be shown on the ordnance map at the time of a subsequent dealing, these should be compared as recommended in paragraphs 4.11 and 4.12.

Form P16 report and Form P17 report

4.8 The Keeper is willing, on payment of the relevant fee, to compare a plan and/or a bounding description with the ordnance map and to disclose any discrepancy between the boundaries in the title description or on the title plan and those appearing from the ordnance map to be the occupational boundaries. Application for such a comparison should be made to the Keeper on a Form P16 for subjects that are unregistered, and on a Form P17 for subjects that are already registered and which reflect certain plotted boundaries. It should be remembered, however, that firms of Private Searchers also provide equivalent reports and the solicitor is at liberty to acquire his or her report from whatever source he or she wishes.

Form P16 report - application
4.9 Application for a Form P16 report is most conveniently made at the same time as a solicitor orders a Form 10 report. When submitted together these reports will attract a reduced fee. The Form P16 report must be accompanied by a description sufficient to enable the Keeper to make the comparison between the title description and the boundaries as depicted on the ordnance map. For this purpose the Keeper will accept:

- A copy of a recorded deed plan with boundaries of stated lineal dimensions or boundaries which can be measured from an adequate scale appearing on the face of the plan and, in the absence of a postal address, the position of the property being tied by measurable or stated dimensions to road junctions or other features which are depicted on the ordnance map; or

- Such a recorded deed plan together with a postal address but without the position of the property being so tied to features which are depicted on the ordnance map (note that such a plan would normally be unacceptable for land registration purposes if used as part of a new deed); or

- A written description (extracted from a recorded deed) which includes measurements and refers to adjoining subjects by name or street number and not by the name of the owner, together with a postal address; or

- A new plan that is intended to support an application for registration that complies with the recommended criteria in appendix 1 to this chapter. It is important to note that even where a response is possible within the context of the P16 report, the plan may be rejected as unsuitable for registration purposes.

A plan from which it is not possible to obtain accurate measurements that can be related to adjoining features is inadequate, as is a bounding description in vague terms such as 'bounded on the west by Maggie Thomson's feu'.

Form P16 report - effect
4.10 A Form P16 report is an alternative to a comparison made by the solicitor himself. For avoidance of any doubt a report which discloses that the boundary comparison is satisfactory gives no assurance that, once the full title has been examined and registration completed, there will be no exclusion of indemnity. Where the title and ordnance map descriptions coincide or where any discrepancy is so slight as to appear to the Keeper to be immaterial, no plan will be attached to the report. Where, however, there is a material discrepancy, the Keeper will indicate his interpretation of the discrepancy by means of a plan attached to the report. The possible courses of action open to the Keeper on receipt of an application for registration, if the discrepancy has not been resolved by then, are discussed in paragraph 4.16. In all cases where the Form P16 report discloses a material discrepancy, that report, together with the plan attached to it, must be included with the other deeds and documents submitted with the application for registration even where the discrepancy has, in the interim, been resolved. It is important that Part B. 2. of the application for first registration (Form 1) is completed correctly, particularly where it is asked if the Form P16 report has confirmed that the boundaries of the subjects agree with the relevant detail on the ordnance map. In the event of a discrepancy having been revealed, even if it has subsequently been resolved, the answer here must be 'NO', and the subsequent questions answered to provide the necessary information.

A flow chart explaining the various options open to solicitors arising from an answer 3 to a P16 report can be found in appendix 2 to this chapter.

Form P17 report - application
4.11 Typically such a comparison is only necessary on subsequent dealings of a registered interest where the land certificate plan shows one or more boundaries as pecked (or dotted) lines and the face of the plan bears the following stamp:

The boundaries shown by dotted lines have been plotted from the plans to the deeds. Physical boundaries will be indicated after their delineation on the ordnance map.

Where a Form P17 report is required this should be obtained before missives are concluded.

Whether the transaction in respect of which the report is required relates to the whole or to part only of the registered interest, reference to the title number of that interest will be sufficient to enable the Keeper to compare the pecked boundaries with the ordnance map.

Form P17 report - effect
4.12 This report provides an alternative to a solicitor checking the title boundaries and occupational boundaries in person. If the comparison discloses a material discrepancy, the Keeper will indicate the extent of this on a plan attached to the report. Any application for registration of the dealing must be accompanied by this plan, even if the discrepancy has been resolved in the meantime. It cannot be assumed that the Keeper will not exclude indemnity on registering a dealing. The possible lines of action open to the parties where such a discrepancy does appear and the action likely to be taken by the Keeper are discussed at paragraph 4.20.

Application for Form 10 report

4.13 The Form 10 report covers, in addition to the Register of Inhibitions and Adjudications, both the Sasine and Land Registers. To enable the Keeper to search the Sasine Register, a description by reference to a recorded deed is all that is required. Such a reference, however, will not enable the Keeper to trace the subjects in the Land Register as they must be identifiable on the index map. The following are suggested as guidelines:

- In all cases where there is a postal address, this should be given.

- In all cases where there is a deed plan relative to the subjects, a copy of this should be supplied.

- In some cases where there is no deed plan, a written description from the titles may be sufficient, for example, in established urban property, where the description includes measurements and refers to adjoining subjects by name or street number, rather than by the name of the owner.

- For tenement property a written description will suffice. For example, 'the southmost house on the top flat, 10 High Street, Ayr'. If, however, there is garden ground pertaining solely to that flat, a plan of that ground will be needed.

- If the only way that the subjects can be sufficiently identified is to produce a specially prepared plan, then preferably this should be based on the ordnance map. The scale should not be less than 1:1250 for urban property. Note that if a copy of the ordnance map is used, the question of copyright arises (see 4.23).

Application for registration

Application for first registration (Form 1)

4.14 An application for registration may be rejected if sufficient information is not given to the Keeper to enable him to identify the subjects by reference to the ordnance map (section 4(2)(a)). An application for first registration will be accompanied by the title deeds of the property and, in many cases, the information contained in these deeds will be sufficient to enable the Keeper to identify the subjects. The following guidelines are provided.

1. Even where there is a deed plan, the depiction of the subjects may be no more than a 'floating rectangle' quite unrelated to any identifiable features on the ground. In this case additional information will usually be required to enable the Keeper to locate the subjects precisely by reference to fixed points on the ordnance map.

2. Where a written description is not sufficient to identify the subjects and refers to essential colourings or markings on the plan attached to the deed containing that description, but these colourings or markings are not shown on the plan, such a plan will not be acceptable. This could apply, for example, where the deed containing the description and plan was merely a monochrome extract.

3. Generally, a traditional tenement flat will be sufficiently described by means of a written description; but the Keeper may require a plan showing the area or 'steading' on which the tenement is erected, together with any adjacent ground (*e.g.* back green) over which there are rights and on which there may be small buildings (*e.g.* wash houses). Where any of the adjacent ground

belongs exclusively to the flat, then a plan will almost certainly be required. If the area of any back green or court cannot be identified with certainty, the Keeper will describe in words, in the property section of the title sheet, any relevant right to a back green or court. He will not delineate the back green or court on the plan, and may exclude indemnity as respects the position and/or extent.

4. The Keeper has no authority to be prescriptive on the scale of plan employed for conveyancing purposes. However, as a matter of practice he will make up a title plan for each registered interest in the Land Register using the largest scale of ordnance map available. Accordingly, any deed plan produced from a similar source is unlikely to cause concern. The applicant may present a plan larger than the three ordnance map scales used by the Keeper (1:500 is not an uncommon scale for deed plans) in order to show detail which would not be clear on a smaller scale. The Keeper, depending on what he sees as the title requirements for the title sheet and land certificate, may incorporate a copy of this plan in the title sheet as supplementary to the title plan. Alternatively, the Keeper may prepare an enlarged plan or an insert to show a particular feature. Both these procedures can often help to overcome the lack of sufficient detail on the ordnance map. If the Keeper considers that the detail on the applicant's 1:500 (or such larger scale) plan is unnecessary for the purpose of registration, he will prepare the relevant title and certificate plans at the normal appropriate scale. Any larger scale plan will be subject to the indemnity limitations imposed by section 12(3)(d).

5. Where a plan has to be prepared to enable the Keeper to identify the subjects, it should not be on a smaller scale than 1:1250, 1:2500 or 1:10,000 if the subjects are urban, rural or moorland type properties respectively. In such cases the plan should preferably be based on the ordnance map. It should be remembered that, even with continuous revision by the Ordnance Survey, the latest map information available may not necessarily reflect the situation on the ground.

6. The requirements to identify subjects sufficiently relate not merely to land but also to such other interests in land as salmon fishings or minerals. In the case of minerals which are severed from the lands, sufficient identification may have to include the lands under which the minerals are to be found and, in certain cases, a strata plan. Where minerals are being conveyed as a separate tenement, the registration requirements should be discussed in detail with the Keeper.

7. If any parts of the subjects are affected by particular rights or burdens, sufficient supporting information must be given to allow the Keeper to delineate specific areas on the certificate plan.

8. Where no physical features (fences, walls, hedges, ditches or the like) exist on the ground, the Keeper must be informed, on application for registration, about the dimensions of the land. The boundaries must be related to existing physical detail on the ordnance map so that the property can be clearly and accurately defined. This problem will arise most frequently in the case of new properties on a developing housing estate. The procedures which are available for having a plan of such an estate approved by the Keeper before applications are made to register the house plots are discussed at paragraph 4.37 *et seq.*

Form 1 - (Part B - questions 1-3)

4.15 The Form 1 was revised in 1995 in an effort to speed up the registration process by ensuring that any problems are highlighted and resolved prior to the application being made. In particular, Questions 1-3 of Part B of the Form 1 place greater emphasis on the need to identify the legal extent of a property and compare it with the occupied extent.

Form 1 - Application for first registration

4.16 Frequently the title deeds submitted with the application for registration will contain sufficient information to enable the Keeper to confirm the location, position and extent. If not, the applicant must submit an appropriate, reliable plan. This plan must be drawn to a stated scale and show sufficient existing surrounding detail to allow the Keeper to establish the correct extent of the property in question (See appendix 1 for detailed deed plan criteria).

Even when a deed plan exists in the progress of titles, the Keeper's experience is that discrepancies often arise between the extent shown on the deed plan and that which exists on the latest map information. To avoid such problems delaying the registration process, every attempt must be made to reconcile any differences before the application is submitted.

A solicitor can elect to have an on-site comparison made between the occupied extent and the extent defined in the title deed. Equally, he can choose to use any service which will compare the extent defined in the title deed with the occupied extent as defined on the ordnance map. The Keeper has been providing such a service since the inception of registration of title in Scotland. This is the P16 report service which was introduced at the request of the Law Society of Scotland. All applications for first registration must now provide answers to questions that are designed to ensure that this comparison has been carried out.

Guidance for completion of questions 1-3 Part B of the Form 1

The following guidance is intended to help overcome common problems in relation to the plans-related questions of the Form 1. This is intended to help to ensure that, in future, the correct information is supplied and any necessary investigative work is completed before the application is submitted, thus avoiding unnecessary delays in processing the application.

Question 1 of PART B reads as follows:

1. *Do the deeds submitted in support of this application*   *YES/NO*
   include a plan illustrating the extent of the subjects to
   be registered?

   *If **YES**, please specify the relevant deed and its Form 4 Inventory number:*

   *If **NO**, have you submitted a deed containing a full*   *YES/NO*
   bounding description with measurements?

   *If **YES**, please specify the deed and its Form 4 Inventory number:*

N.B. *If the answer to both the above questions is **NO** then, unless the property is part of a tenement or flatted building you must submit a plan of the subjects properly drawn to a stated scale and showing sufficient surrounding features to enable it to be located on the ordnance map. The plan should bear a docquet, signed by the person signing the Application Form, to the effect that it is a plan of the subjects sought to be registered under the attached application.*

It should be noted that a full bounding description is one with measurements which will allow the extent of the subjects to be identified on the ordnance map. It is insufficient that the subjects are stated (for instance) to be 'bounded on the north by land owned by John Thompson and on the south by the High Street'. A full bounding description requires the dimensions, orientation and a description of the features themselves for all the property boundaries.

It is important that the land depicted should accurately reflect the title deeds and be in the possession of the applicant (substantiated by relevant title deeds or otherwise). In particular the response to question 3 of the Form 1 (see below) takes on extra significance in such cases.

The Form 1 states that the need for a plan or full bounding description of the individual property does not apply in the case of tenement or flatted buildings. However, it is still necessary for the extent of the tenement steading to be identifiable from the deed plans or descriptions lodged in support of the application.

Question 2 of PART B reads as follows:

2. *Is a Form P16 Report issued by the Keeper confirming that*   **YES/NO**
the boundaries of the subjects coincide with the Ordnance
Map being submitted in support of this Application?

If **NO***, does the legal extent depicted in the plans or descriptions*   **YES/NO**
in the deeds submitted in support of the Application cohere with
the occupational extent?

If **NO***, please advise:*

(a) the approximate age and nature of the occupational boundaries, or

(b) whether, if the extent of the subjects as   **YES/NO**
    defined in the deeds is larger than the
    occupational extent, the applicant is prepared to
    accept the occupational extent as viewed, or

(c) whether, if the extent of the subjects   **YES/NO**
    as defined in the deeds is smaller than the
    occupational extent, any remedial action has been taken.

Care should be taken to ensure that an affirmative answer to the first part of this question is given only if '*the boundaries of the subjects coincide with the ordnance map*', *i.e.* the P16 response was an answer 2. An answer 1 or 3 from a P16 report requires the response **NO**.

Equally, an affirmative answer to that part should only be given where '*a Form P16 report issued by the Keeper*' has been obtained, not when another method of comparison has been used.

In all cases, if a P16 report is available, it should be submitted with the application, regardless of the answer given.

If a comparison on the ground or using a report service other than the Keeper's has revealed that the legal extent and occupational extent do cohere then the second part of the question can be answered **YES**.

If the answer is **NO** then it is important that matters at 2 (a), (b) and (c) are carefully considered and answered.

Clearly if a discrepancy exists, then the situation must be properly investigated and remedied before the application for registration is made. It is recommended that a site visit be undertaken to ensure full awareness of the scale and background of the problem.

If the legal extent as depicted in the plans or descriptions in the title deeds does not cohere with the occupational extent, then information regarding the approximate age and nature of the occupational boundaries must be given.

If the extent of the property as defined in the deeds is found to be larger than the occupational extent and the occupational extent is contained wholly within the legal extent, verification that the applicant is willing to accept the smaller extent must be given. On the other hand, if the legal extent is less than that occupied, or any part of the occupied extent falls outwith the legal extent, then evidence of any necessary remedial action must be included with the application. Investigations in this regard will be largely dependent on the reliability and usefulness of the supporting information. For instance, if a recorded deed plan which contains no surrounding detail is to be used to establish a particular extent, it will often prove difficult if not impossible to identify exactly where any discrepancy lies.

Question 3 of PART B reads as follows:

3. *Is there any person in possession or occupation*   *YES/NO*
   of the subjects or any part of them adversely to the
   interest of the applicant?

   *If **YES**, please give details:*

If a discrepancy is evident, it is likely that a comment will be required in addition to the response to question 3.

If remedial conveyancing is necessary, much will depend on the circumstances surrounding the problem. Advice is available from the Keeper's Pre-Registration Enquiries Section.

Problems with plans

4.17 The Keeper has encountered recurring problems in relation to plans submitted in support of applications. As the registration of title system is fundamentally plan-based, the quality of the plans annexed to title deeds and the references to those plans are of crucial importance to initial acceptability of an application and its subsequent progress through the system. Appendix 1 to this chapter offers further guidance on the Keeper's requirements in the preparation of deed plans and will hopefully help to eradicate similar problems in the future.

Application for Form 12 report - registered interest

4.18 An application for a Form 12 report presents no problems of identification when the anticipated dealing is with the whole of the registered interest, as reference to the title number is all that is required. If, on first registration, the subjects have been delineated by the Keeper by pecked lines, a Form P17 report may be ordered. Where the dealing is with part only of the registered interest, the applicant or the applicant's agent must provide not only the title number of the whole but, in addition, a description or plan of the part sufficient to enable the Keeper to identify the part on the existing title plan, *viz*;

Transfer, feu or lease of whole of registered interest
4.19 No plan need be annexed to a transfer which relates to the whole of the subjects registered. This applies even in cases where the transfer is a grant of feu or lease of the whole subjects. The subjects will be described in the deed as *'the subjects registered under title number(s) (. . .)'* (Rule 25 and Schedule B). The title number itself is sufficient information for the Keeper.

Transfer, feu or lease of part of registered interest
4.20 When the Keeper receives an application for registration of a transaction which relates to part only of a registered interest, he will, where the transaction is a sale of part, or the grant of a feu or lease of a part, require sufficient information to enable him to identify the part, so that he can amend the title plan of the registered interest to show the part sold, feued or leased, and in addition prepare a new title plan for that part. Even where the transaction is not a transfer but is, for example, the grant of a standard security relating to part only of a registered interest, or a deed of conditions creating burdens which affect a part

only, the Keeper will require sufficient information to enable him to delineate on the title plan that part of the registered interest so affected. The following guidelines are applicable in every case:

- If a new plan is not specifically prepared, a copy of the certificate plan contained in the granter's land certificate may be used. This copy, with the part delineated neatly and accurately thereon, supplemented by lineal boundary measurements, will be acceptable to the Keeper. No written description is necessary. The lineal measurements are required because the paper on which the copy is made may contract or expand in the copying process. If the applicant uses a copy of the certificate plan, questions of copyright will arise (see 4.23).

- If the part is already clearly defined on the certificate plan (for example it is tinted pink in distinction to the remaining land in the title sheet which is tinted blue) no plan is required and the description of the part as 'the part tinted pink on the land included in the land certificate' will be taken as adequate for the purposes of Note (a) to Schedule B of the Rules and will, for the Keeper's purposes, be sufficient identification.

- If the applicant does not make use of the certificate plan but instead prepares a new plan, the advice given in appendix 1 hereto should be adhered to. If a plan, other than a copy of the certificate plan, is attached to the deed giving effect to the dealing, it should show not only the land affected by that dealing, but also sufficient adjacent detail to enable the position of the part affected to be ascertained on the title plan of the granter's property. If need be, dimensions should be used to indicate accurately the extent of the plot tying its position in with existing, adjacent detail.

- A plan presented to the Keeper in terms of the preceding sub-paragraphs will not be acceptable if it is declared to be demonstrative only. Such a plan must be taxative, although it is acceptable if measurements are qualified by the words 'or thereby'.

Application for Form 14 report

4.21 The guidelines suggested in paragraph 4.13 with reference to an application for a Form 10 report apply equally here. However, this form of enquiry will very often be used by a third party with little or no information about the property in question. In that situation, especially in the absence of a postal description, a plan indicating the subjects in respect of which information is sought will have to be submitted with the application.

Ordnance Map

Scales

4.22 Of the map data produced and maintained by Ordnance Survey, those on the following scales will be used by the Keeper, namely:

1:10000	mountain and moorland areas;
1:2500	villages, small towns and rural areas;
1:1250	cities and larger towns.

Copying ordnance maps (copyright)

4.23 As the ordnance map is the cornerstone of the Scottish system of registration of title, there will be occasions when solicitors will wish to make copies of ordnance maps. To do so without permission is a breach of crown copyright. Information about licences to allow copying can be obtained from:

ORDNANCE SURVEY
CUSTOMER SERVICES DIGITAL HELP DESK
Telephone: 01703 792773   Fax: 01703 792324
E mail: dighlpdesk@ordsvy.gov.uk

Title plans prepared by the Keeper are prepared by him under licence. It is also a breach of crown copyright to copy title plans, unless a licence has been obtained from Ordnance Survey. The licences mentioned above will, however, cover such copying.

Copying (distortion)

4.24 Because of optical distortion or paper shrinkage, copies made on most office copying machines are not completely accurate reproductions. Where the copy is required for illustrative purposes, these inaccuracies may not matter. In other circumstances, however, because of the small scale, the inaccuracies can be material; scaling alone on such copy plans, unsupported by specific measurements, should not be relied upon.

Digital mapping

4.25 The mapping element of land registration is supported by a digital mapping system which allows the extent of each registered title to be fixed against the backdrop of the ordnance map. To ensure no overlaps in titles are introduced, an index layer detailing each individual title is also maintained. This record also provides the necessary link between each registered parcel and the corresponding title sheet.

Access to this index map can be pursued *via* the title number, a postal address, national grid co-ordinates or through reference to a plan. This is done using a street gazetteer based on the Ordnance Survey's Address Point product and following the principles of BS 7666 which promotes standards for geographical referencing of spatial datasets.

The map-base itself comprises OS Land-Line© vector map data which is the most detailed large scale mapping for Great Britain. Geographical features are represented as vector data (point and line) and supplied in complete tiles which are edge matched to allow seamless work across map edges.

Land-Line© line maps are continually revised by Ordnance Survey and currently the Keeper is supplied with monthly batches of significantly changed maps. The term 'significantly changed maps' refers to complete map tiles which have had the equivalent of 20 units of change occur since the last version of that map was supplied to the Keeper. (1 unit is equivalent to 1 house and its fences or equivalent amount of change).

New versions of maps can be obtained from Ordnance Survey if the Keeper requires to instigate a specific check survey of an area or feature in order to investigate a discrepancy between the map and the extent to be registered, or when he is aware that new detail which is required has been surveyed and is available but has not yet crossed the 20 unit threshold.

On receipt of a new version of a map, the Keeper will compare it with the version of the map currently being used and verify where change has occurred. The effect of such change will then be considered against the extents of any registered titles. If necessary, remedial action will be taken to ensure the registered extent is correctly depicted against the revised backdrop of the ordnance map.

The 'or thereby' rule

4.26 The ordnance map is a map of scientific accuracy but is nevertheless subject to the limitations of scaling. On the 1:1250 scale map, 1 millimetre on the map is the equivalent of 1.25 metres on the ground. It is possible to scale to 0.23m on a 1:1250 map, to 0.46m on a 1:2500 map and to 1.83m on a 1:10,000 map. Plotting boundaries to any greater degree of accuracy is not possible on those scales.

These limitations in scaling are, however, covered in section 12(3)(d) which provides that *'there shall be no entitlement to indemnity in respect of loss where the loss arises as a result of any inaccuracy in the delineation of boundaries shown in a title sheet, being an inaccuracy which could not have been rectified by reference to the ordnance map, unless the Keeper has expressly assumed responsibility for the accuracy of that delineation'.*

This exclusion of indemnity to cover the limitations in scaling does not introduce a new concept into Scottish conveyancing as under the Sasine system boundary or area measurements are normally qualified by the phrase 'or thereby'. If anything, section 12(3)(d) removes to some extent the previous uncertainty as to what is or is not covered by those qualifying words. Subject to the Keeper's statutory obligation to include a statement as to the area of any land which appears to him to extend to two hectares (4.942 acres) or more in extent (section 6(1)(a)), the Keeper when preparing title plans will not usually include either boundary or area measurements. In some cases, however, he will do so for example, to expand a description where details of a particular boundary will not be clear from the title plan, or to tie down the location of particular subjects in relation to a fixed point on the ordnance map. Where measurements are included, it may be thought that the Keeper is assuming responsibility for the accuracy of these measurements in terms of section 12(3)(d). This is not so, however, as each land certificate provides that lineal measurements are to be read subject to the qualification 'or thereby' and to the limitations of scaling excluded from indemnity under section 12(3)(d). Such measurements are therefore subject to the limitations of scaling. Indemnity in respect of any area measurement which the Keeper has to include in terms of section 6(1)(a) is expressly excluded by section 12(3)(e).

Boundaries

Position and length

4.27 The ordnance map depicts, by black lines, the boundary features on the ground. However, these physical 'occupational' boundaries are not necessarily the same as the legal boundaries disclosed in the title deeds. In some cases, the boundary feature may have been deliberately erected some distance away from the legal boundary. This may occur, for example, where the true boundary is the centre line of a burn or river or, as is the case with railway property, where the boundary fence is normally erected a specified distance within the title boundary. In other cases, the boundary feature may have been quite simply erected in the wrong position. In the case of new property or the subdivision of an existing unit, physical boundaries, or some of them, may not be disclosed on the ordnance map at all. When preparing title plans, the Keeper will compare the boundaries as depicted on the ordnance map with (where the property is unregistered) any plans, title descriptions and other evidence submitted or (where the interest is registered) the existing title plan. The following situations can arise:

1. The legal boundaries coincide exactly with those indicated on the ordnance map. The Keeper will delineate the boundaries of the registered land by red edging or tinting within the black lines on the ordnance map.

2. There is such a small discrepancy between the information supplied to the Keeper about the boundaries and the relevant black lines on the ordnance map that the Keeper decides to ignore it on the 'or thereby' principle. Again, the Keeper will delineate the boundaries of the registered land by red edging or tinting within the black lines on the ordnance map.

3. There is a discrepancy so large that the Keeper cannot ignore it. He may exclude indemnity from part of the subjects, in terms of section 12(2), and will generally identify that part by means of colouring or hatching on the certificate plan.

4. The subjects are not depicted on the ordnance map at all, for example on first registration of a new house plot. In such a case, the Keeper may delay processing the application until such time as the ordnance map is updated if the pace of development is such as to suggest that the necessary 20 units of change have occurred. Alternatively, he may plot the subjects and depict the boundaries by pecked lines. A note will be added to the face of the plan in the following terms:

'The boundaries shown by dotted lines have been plotted from the deeds. Physical boundaries will be indicated after their delineation on the ordnance map'.

If, at some suitable time in the future, the ordnance map shows the physical boundaries, updated plans will be prepared. Where subjects are not depicted on the ordnance map, the evidence which the Keeper will require must include boundary measurements. The evidence must also include sufficient additional information to enable him to determine the location of the subjects with reference to some fixed points shown on the ordnance map.

5. Where, in respect of some of the boundaries, reference to the ordnance map shows no physical boundaries, the Keeper will show those boundaries on the title plan by pecked lines as in 4 above, and, for the remaining boundaries for which physical boundaries are disclosed, proceed as (in 1 to 3) above.

Survey instructed by the Keeper

4.28 The discrepancy in situation 3 above, between the deed plan or other evidence presented to the Keeper and the ordnance map, may be too large for the Keeper to resolve. He may then instruct a survey by the Ordnance Survey in order to establish the true position as regards the physical boundary. The expense of any such survey is borne by the Keeper, unless the registration is a voluntary one in either an operational or non-operational area. The Keeper may, however, seek recompense for the cost of any survey which subsequently proves the ordnance map to be correct and which confirms the discrepancy has arisen through incomplete or erroneous information supplied in support of the application for registration.

If there is a physical object such as a wall or fence close to a boundary, but not itself forming the legal boundary (for example, a railway fence), it will be helpful if the applicant so informs the Keeper. Such information can be useful and may avoid an unnecessary survey or exclusion of indemnity.

Where indemnity is excluded

4.29 If the applicant, after receipt of the land certificate, is dissatisfied with exclusion of indemnity, he has a right of appeal to the Lands Tribunal in terms of section 25. In practice, the Keeper will not proceed to issue a land certificate containing an exclusion of indemnity without first consulting the applicant. Prescription may of course operate in favour of the applicant as regards the part from which indemnity has been excluded (section 10). In some cases, remedial conveyancing or a Section 19 Agreement may resolve matters. Where a boundary discrepancy comes to his notice, the Keeper will not take it on himself to make any approach to the neighbouring proprietor.

Line of boundary in relation to a physical object

4.30 On first registration of subjects, the Keeper may indicate either by means of blue letters and arrows, or by a black arrow, the line of the boundary in relation to the physical object, as disclosed in the relevant deed accompanying the application. If the boundary is indicated by the arrow and lettering method, the title sheet will disclose the line of the boundary thus: 'A - B, centre line' or 'C - D, inner face', *etc.* As regards the black arrow method, an arrow drawn through the boundary will indicate that the centre line is stated in the title deeds to be the line of that boundary. If the line is stated to be the outside face of the physical boundary, the arrow will be drawn outwith the delineation of the subjects being registered and pointing towards the appropriate black line on the title plan. If the line is the inside face, the arrow will be drawn within the delineation of the subjects being registered and pointing towards that boundary. Each method merely confirms what the title states to be the part of the physical object forming the boundary.

Where an applicant wishes confirmation that the titles of adjoining subjects agree with his or her title regarding the part of the physical boundary which forms the mutual boundary, the Keeper will, if he can, provide such confirmation on payment of a fee. The fee will cover the expenses of the Keeper's examination of the title sheet of the adjoining property, or, if the adjoining subjects are not in the Land Register, the relevant Sasine Register volumes.

If the Keeper is able to confirm that there is agreement as to the line of the boundary, a suitable note will be added to the property section of the title sheet or, if the black arrow method is used, then a black bar will be added to the arrow. If, however, the information does not coincide, no note will be added in the case of the former method, and as to the latter method, no bar will be added and the arrow will indicate the situation as disclosed in the applicant's title deeds. The Keeper will not, however, inform the adjoining proprietor that there is disagreement as to the line of the boundary in relation to the physical boundary feature as disclosed in the relevant titles.

Boundary references excluded from indemnity

4.31 Boundary references are expressly excluded in each land certificate from the indemnity provisions. Confirmation that there is agreement as to the line of a boundary does no more than confirm that the titles of the adjoining properties agree as to the part of the physical object which forms the boundary. The Keeper does not guarantee that the existing physical object, depicted on the ordnance map, is the object referred to in the titles. For instance, the titles of the adjoining subjects may agree that the mutual boundary is the centre line of a hedge, whereas the black line on the ordnance map indicates a wall which may have been built wholly on the land of the adjoining proprietor. The wall may have been erected immediately adjacent to the hedge which has since withered or been removed. Also, Ordnance Survey criteria dictate that, in the case of two parallel boundaries on the ground lying within a metre of each other, the more 'robust' of the two will be reflected on the ordnance map. If the boundaries lie at a greater distance, both will be shown unless one is particularly dilapidated or withered.

Updating boundary information on plans

4.32 There are times when the Keeper has to delineate boundaries on the title plan by pecked lines because, at the time of first registration, either there are no physical boundaries on the ground or the ordnance map does not show any. On receipt of a subsequent application for registration of a dealing, or if a land certificate is submitted for updating the Keeper will compare the title plan with the most up-to-date edition of the ordnance map. If it is found that the physical boundaries are depicted on the ordnance map and coincide with the boundaries shown on the title plan by pecked lines, or that any discrepancy falls within the 'or thereby' concept, a new title plan will be prepared. On this new plan, the boundaries which were shown by pecked lines will be shown by black lines. The Keeper will attach a new plan to the land certificate. The superseded certificate plan, marked as cancelled, will be returned with the land certificate so that the new plan can be checked.

In some cases, there will be a material discrepancy disclosed between the legal boundaries, i.e. the pecked lines on the title plan, and the physical boundaries depicted on the updated ordnance map. The discrepancy may be deliberate (*e.g.* where a fence has been erected by design well within a boundary) but may also arise because the boundary feature has been erected in the wrong place.

In the two examples considered below, it is assumed that, on first registration, A's property and B's property, which were two adjoining plots on a developing building estate, were shown by pecked lines on their respective title plans because the ordnance map then showed no physical boundaries for their properties. On first registration, both properties were registered without exclusion of indemnity because the deed plans submitted in support of the original applications disclosed no discrepancy. It is further assumed that the discrepancy has been noticed by the Keeper when processing an application for registration of a dealing with A's property, or dealing with a request to update A's land certificate, or a request by A to confirm that the boundaries, as shown by pecked lines on the title and certificate plans, conform to the physical boundaries depicted on the ordnance map.

Whenever the Keeper discovers a material discrepancy the matter will be drawn to the proprietor's attention, giving time for it to be resolved under rules 11 and 12. The Keeper will not make any direct approach to the adjoining proprietor.

Where a boundary line, as depicted by a pecked line on the title plan, does not coincide with the physical boundary, as shown on the ordnance map, this indicates that the physical boundary has been erected either within or outwith the legal boundary. The following examples illustrate the options open to the proprietor and the resultant action by the Keeper.

Example 1 - The fence (y-z in Figure 1 below) has been erected within A's legal boundaries.

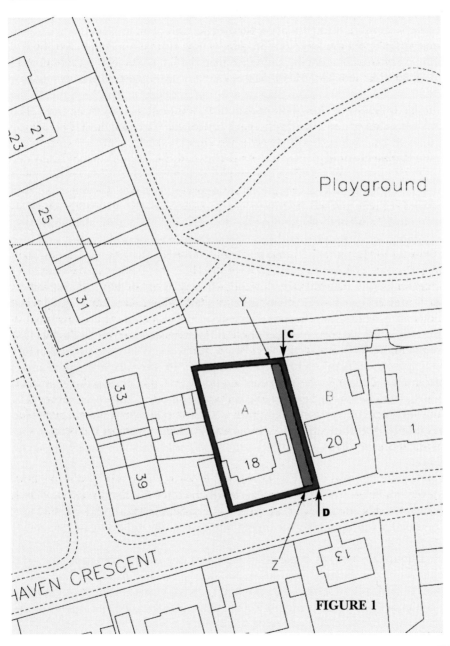

FIGURE 1

A, on being contacted by the Keeper, has three options.

Option 1: A intimates that no action will be taken.

Option 2: A informs the Keeper that a fence has recently been erected, or it is proposed that a fence be erected, on the line of the east legal boundary (the pecked line C-D in Figure 1).

Option 3: A agrees with his neighbour B that, although the fence has not been erected on the line of the legal boundary (the pecked line C-D in Figure 1), they now wish the fence (y-z in Figure 1) to form the legal boundary between their properties. As the size of the strip of ground between the fence and the legal boundary is considerable, the Keeper would take the view that an agreement between A and B in terms of section 19 is not appropriate in this situation. Accordingly A dispones the strip to B by formal deed.

In response to Option 1, the Keeper will substitute for the title plan a new plan showing the physical boundaries (one of which is the fence y-z) delineated in black and will show the legal extent of the property by red delineation (see Figure 1). The fact that the line of A's east legal boundary will remain shown by a pecked line does not prejudice A. Provided A remains in possession of the blue area in Figure 1, A's real right thereto will remain unchallengeable in spite of the fact that the area is outwith A's apparent boundary fence.

In response to Option 2, the Keeper will substitute a new plan as for Option 1. The new fence is not yet shown on the ordnance map but, when it is revealed by a future revision, the Keeper can substitute for the title plan a further new plan showing the physical boundaries in black and the legal extent of the property by red delineation.

In response to Option 3, the Keeper will prepare new title plans for both properties. The blue area in Figure 1 will be incorporated in B's title and, for both properties, the boundaries as indicated on the ordnance map will be shown.

Example 2 The fence (y-z in Figure 2 below) has been erected outwith A's legal boundaries.

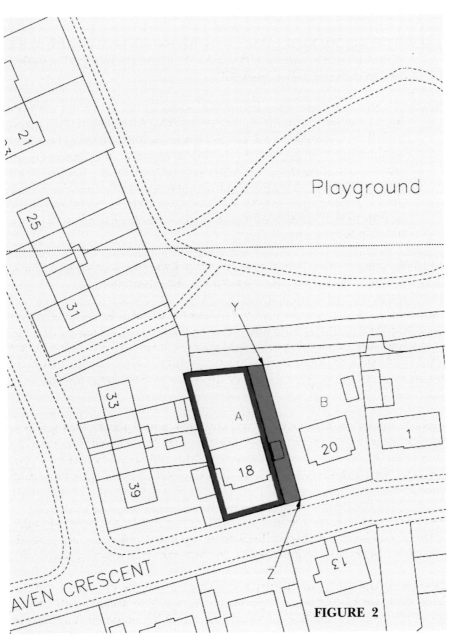

FIGURE 2

A, on being contacted by the Keeper has four options.

Option 1: A intimates that no action will be taken.

Option 2: A informs the Keeper that a fence has recently been erected, or it is proposed that a fence be erected, on the line of the east legal boundary (the pecked line C-D in Figure 2).

Option 3: Investigation shows that the strip of ground between the fence and the legal boundary is within the registered title of neighbour B. A agrees with B that, although the fence has not been erected on the line of the legal boundary (the pecked line C-D in Figure 2), they now wish the fence (y-z in Figure 2) to form the legal boundary between their properties. The size of the strip of ground is considerable. The Keeper would take the view that an agreement between A and B in terms of section 19 is not appropriate in this situation. Accordingly B dispones the strip to A by formal deed.

Option 4: A prepares a disposition a non domino of the blue area in Figure 2 and submits it in support of an application for registration.

In response to Option 1, the Keeper will substitute for the title plan a new plan showing the physical boundaries (one of which is the fence y-z in Figure 2) but will not include the blue area in Figure 2 within the red delineation by which he will show the legal extent of the property. Even if A continues to possess the blue area, A cannot, without further action, become the owner (see the responses below to Options 3 and 4).

In response to Option 2, the Keeper will substitute a new plan as for Option 1. The new fence is not yet shown on the ordnance map but, when it is revealed by a future revision, the Keeper can substitute for the title plan a further new plan showing the physical boundaries in black and the legal extent of the property by red delineation.

In response to Option 3, the Keeper will prepare new title plans for both properties. The blue area in Figure 2 will be incorporated in A's title and, for both properties, the boundaries as indicated on the ordnance map will be shown.

In response to Option 4, the Keeper will wish to investigate in some detail the available evidence of title to and possession of the blue area. Details of any negotiation between A and B as to ownership should be submitted. The Keeper may refuse the application if he considers it is *'frivolous or vexatious'* (see section 4(2)(c). Alternatively, the Keeper may add the blue area to A's title plan but exclude indemnity in respect of it. The exclusion of indemnity, which will be inserted in the proprietorship section will disclose B's prior title to the blue area.

Since B already has a fully indemnified title which includes the blue area, that area will remain in B's title sheet without exclusion of indemnity, but A's competing interest will be disclosed by the insertion of A's unindemnified title to the blue area in the proprietorship section of B's title sheet. The blue area will be identified on B's title plan. The overlap between the titles will be shown on the index map.

A request (on a Form 8) to update B's land certificate or a request for a Form 12 report will reveal A's competing title to the blue area and B will have the opportunity of judicially interrupting A's possession. A successful challenge will lead to the Register being restored to the position prior to the registration of A's *a non domino* title.

If, however, prescription runs in favour of A an application by A may be made to the Keeper, supported by the necessary evidence, for removal of the exclusion of indemnity. The Keeper will remove the exclusion of indemnity from A's title sheet, remove the blue area from B's title plan and the reference to it from the proprietorship section of B's title sheet and amend the index map accordingly.

An updated land certificate will be issued to A. The Keeper will call in B's land certificate and amend it as well (Rule 17(2)).

4.33 The foregoing examples illustrate a couple of simple boundary discrepancies of the kind that may never have come to light at all under the Sasine system. Under registration of title, however, material discrepancies of this kind will come to light sooner or later. Material discrepancies can, of course, affect more than one boundary and, indeed, may have a cumulative effect on a number of properties. Where this kind of problem arises, the Keeper's advice should be sought.

Guarantee of boundaries

4.34 The provisions of the Act contain no specific mention of guarantee of title or boundaries. The terms of section 12, however, in effect do guarantee that the Keeper will indemnify against loss suffered because he has rectified or refused to rectify the Register (section 12(1)(a) and (b)), or because *'there is an error or omission in any land or charge certificate or in any information given by the Keeper in* *writing ...'* (Section 12(1)(d)). The Keeper does not guarantee that a property boundary will remain forever inviolate. A proprietor requires to maintain possession, actual or civil (*e.g.* through a tenant). Prescription can operate against a registered proprietor who is not in possession. Where this happens it is possible for the Register to be rectified against the registered proprietor (section 9(1) and (3)).

In the unlikely event that the land certificates for two adjoining properties erroneously include the same ground, the Keeper is unable to guarantee that the boundaries will not be altered. The Register will require to be rectified and whoever can prove loss attributable to the rectification may be entitled to indemnity. The proprietor who can prove possession (not prescriptive possession) will prevail. So too, anyone is entitled to be indemnified who can prove loss because the Keeper, as regards the registered land, wrongly locates it (*e.g.* he registers 6 High Street, Renfrew, instead of 8 High Street, Renfrew) or, in registering 6 High Street, Renfrew, includes a part of 8 High Street, Renfrew, or wrongly measures boundaries on the ordnance map (section 12(1)(d)).

Reference has already been made in paragraph 4.26 to the limitation of indemnity provided for in section 12(3)(d). If rectification is ruled out, indemnity may be payable, where the registered proprietor suffers loss by reason of any inaccuracy in the boundary shown on the title plan, being an inaccuracy which is greater than that which can be explained by the limitations of scaling on the ordnance map. In paragraph.4.31 it is stated that the information as to the exact line of a boundary given by the two methods already mentioned is outwith the indemnity provisions. This is so, for, while this is information which would fall within the terms of section 12(1)(d), each land certificate specifically excludes indemnity in respect of that information.

Description of registered interest

4.35 Under the Sasine system, the majority of properties are described either by a written description alone, or by a written description supplemented by a plan which is usually declared to be demonstrative only and not taxative. Rarely is a description based on the plan alone. Under registration of title, however, the converse will be the case; the title plan will be the principal means of identifying the subjects. In most cases, any written description in the property section of the title sheet will be limited to a simple statement of the postal address, together with a note of any incidental rights pertaining to the property. Occasionally, however, the Keeper may feel that a more elaborate written description is required to amplify the title plan. In the case of a tenement flat, description by plan alone is not appropriate. The title sheet of a tenement flat will contain a written description, for example 'the north house on the first flat above the ground or street flat of the tenement ...' and the title plan will show the solum of the tenement and any adjacent ground (*e.g.* a back green) over which there are common rights, provided this common ground can be identified (see also paragraph, 4.19 and 4.20).

In some cases, the ordnance map which is appropriate for the particular subjects may not be of sufficient scale to identify clearly parts of those subjects. The Keeper may then include on the title plan, as an insert, a section based on one of the larger ordnance scales to show that detail, or he may prepare a separate title plan on an even larger scale. For example, the title plan of a farm may be based on the 1:10,000 scale, the farm buildings being shown on an insert based on the 1:1250 scale. Indeed, the Keeper may even, by way of supplementing the title plan, copy an existing plan from an earlier title deed and include this in the title sheet. It should be remembered, however, that, unless the Keeper assumes responsibility for the accuracy of any such larger scale plan or existing deed plan, the exclusion of indemnity discussed in paragraph 4.26 above will apply. Furthermore, the exclusion of indemnity relates to the limitation of scaling from the ordnance map and the fact that a greater degree of accuracy can be obtained from a larger scale does not extend the scope of the Keeper's indemnity (see also paragraphs 4.19 and 4.20).

Builders' developments

4.36 Where an application for registration of a transfer (including a feu or long lease) of part only of a registered interest is submitted to the Keeper, the part must be sufficiently described to enable the Keeper to identify the part. This is, firstly, so that the new title and certificate plans of the part can be prepared and, secondly, so that the title and certificate plans of the registered interest can be amended. The most common example of a transfer of part is the disposal by a builder or developer of the individual units on a building estate or development. When the first applications for registration of the separate units are received, the title plan of the building estate will show no more than the open site. However, the Keeper requires not only a detailed description of each unit, but also sufficient additional information to enable him to accurately locate that unit within the estate. Indeed, these requirements arise at an earlier stage in the transaction, for the Keeper cannot issue a Form 12 report in respect of such a transfer unless the application for that report contains similar information. It should be noted that the application for the Form 12 report must relate to the interest about to be registered (*i.e.* the individual unit) rather than to the whole interest contained in the builder's title sheet.

Approved estate layout plans

4.37 To overcome these problems and to ensure that transfers out of a developing estate and the subsequent registration of the individual interests are dealt with simply and smoothly, the Keeper operates a system of approved layout plans. Experience has shown that the majority of builders find the approved layout plan system to be of considerable benefit, to themselves and to house purchasers. Basically, what is required is that before any disposals have taken place out of the development, the builder submits a layout plan of the development to the Keeper. Once the plan has been approved by the Keeper, subsequent conveyancing and registration procedures are much simplified.

Benefits of approved layout plan

4.38 The benefits of the approved layout plan may be summarised as follows:

- Discrepancies between the boundaries of the registered interest (*i.e.* the building estate) and of the proposed development can be resolved by the builder and the Keeper before individual purchasers become involved.

- There is no need to prepare detailed descriptions of each unit to enable the Keeper to issue Form 12 reports and office copies of the title plan. The unit concerned is sufficiently identified by reference to the plot number on the approved plan.

- While each deed of transfer must contain a conveyancing description appropriate to a transfer of part of a registered interest and not merely a reference to the plot number shown on the approved plan, these descriptions can be greatly simplified by using an excerpt from the approved plan as the deed plan. The excerpt should be clearly marked as being an excerpt from a plan approved by the Keeper and the date of approval should also be noted.

- Purchasers' solicitors can accept an approved layout plan as conclusive evidence that the individual plot does indeed form part of the subjects contained in the builder's title sheet.

- From the builder's point of view conveyancing procedures should be simpler and delays in settlement less likely.

- The Keeper benefits by the saving in time and cost involved in repetitive examination of individual plans submitted with applications for reports and, where an excerpt of an approved layout plan is used as the deed plan, by the saving in time in checking the description in that deed.

Circumstances in which application may be made

4.39 Application for approval of an estate layout plan may be made at any time after the builder's interest has been registered in the Land Register. In any event, approval must be sought before the Keeper receives the first application for registration of a transfer of an individual unit.

The scheme does not operate where the builder's title is still in the Sasine Register even although the individual transfers will induce first registration in the Land Register. However, because of the many benefits, it is suggested that builders and developers should consider applying for voluntary registration where their titles are still in the Sasine Register, either under section 2(1)(b), if the subjects lie within an operational area, or under section 11(1), if the subjects lie within an area which is soon due to become operational.

In those cases where the builder proposes to develop the estate in phases, approval may be sought for separate layout plans for each phase. Where a layout plan is approved for part only of a registered interest, the Keeper may exercise his right in terms of rule 8 to split the title sheet of that interest.

Approval may be sought whether it is intended to dispose of the individual units by sale, feu or long lease.

The scheme is not limited in any way to new residential development but applies equally to other types of development, *e.g.* industrial, commercial, mixed, flatted properties. It is also appropriate to developments which relate to existing property which is being refurbished and then split into separate units. The scheme applies to any development consisting of 10 or more units.

Application for approval

4.40 Application for approval should be made at the earliest possible time, by letter to the Keeper. The title number of the builder's interest should be quoted and two copies of the estate layout plan submitted. The builder's land certificate must accompany the application if the interest has already been registered.

The plan must:

- show sufficient detail to enable the position of the intended development to be related to the boundaries of the land in the registered title or to other detail shown on the title plan.

- be drawn to a stated scale. The scale normally used is 1:500 but, if the development is regular in pattern, a scale of 1:1250 may prove satisfactory. Plans marked 'demonstrative only' are not acceptable.

- clearly define the extent of each plot or property and show the number or other reference identifying it. Where the individual property comprises two or more parcels (*e.g.* a house plot with a separate garden, garage, parking area, refuse-bin space or storage site) each parcel must be distinguished on the estate layout plan by means of a different number.

After approval, one copy of the plan marked as officially approved will be returned to the applicant. The other copy will be retained by the Keeper.

Departure from approved plan

4.41 If a builder intends to depart from an approved plan, the Keeper should be notified immediately, the approved plan should be returned to the Keeper and two copies of the amended plan submitted for approval. The substitution of an amended approved plan cannot affect purchasers' interests which have already been registered in the Land Register but may mean that Form 12 reports already issued but not yet followed by registration will be inaccurate. Similarly, deed plans prepared on the basis of an approved plan may no longer be correct. Since the Keeper will not at this stage be able to advise purchasers of the altered plan, the builder should do so and, where necessary, obtain correct Form 12 reports and prepare a new deed plan. It is recommended, therefore, that where a transaction has proceeded on the basis of an approved plan, purchasers should, at settlement, obtain confirmation that the builder has not departed from the approved plan. Until the amended plan has been approved, any subsequent application for a Form 12 report must provide a property description which will enable the Keeper to identify the subjects and locate them on the builder's title plan.

Surveys of developing estates are made by Ordnance Survey at frequent intervals and the Keeper's plans are then revised to show all new buildings, fences, roads and other physical features. If it becomes apparent that a builder has departed from the features shown on the plan approved by the Keeper, approval will be immediately withdrawn. This may affect reports already issued. It will certainly delay the issue of further reports as applications for these will require to describe the individual subjects in a way which will enable the Keeper to identify and locate them on the builder's title plan. Withdrawal of approval of the approved plan cannot, of course, affect interests already registered.

Reference to approved plans

4.42 Where reference is made to a plot number on an approved plan, *e.g.* in missives or in an application for a Form 12 report, the date of approval should always be specified. Similarly, where an excerpt from an approved plan is used as the deed plan (and it is recommended that such an excerpt should be used in each case) the plan should be docqueted in the following terms:

This is an excerpt from (copy of) the estate layout plan approved by the Keeper on (...).

Deposit of land certificate

4.43 In terms of Rule 9(3) each application for registration must be accompanied by the relative land certificate. In a developing building estate it would be quite impracticable if the builder's land certificate had to be available on the one hand for examination by each individual purchaser and, on the other hand, for submission to the Keeper with each individual application for registration. The builder's land certificate should therefore be deposited with the Keeper who will advise the builder of a deposit number which applicants for registration can quote when applying for registration (Form 3) instead of producing the builder's land certificate. Under the Sasine system, it is common practice to order a number of sets of Sasine extracts of the builder's title for exhibition to each purchaser and, under registration of title, a number of office copies of the builder's title sheet should be ordered by the builder for this purpose. It will be remembered, however, that as and when each individual interest is registered, the builder's title sheet (and title plan) will be amended to reflect the transfer. Later office copies will, therefore, show more up-to-date information than office copies ordered at the commencement of the development. In cases where it is anticipated that the number of office copies required will increase as the development proceeds, there is merit in ordering these at intervals rather than at the commencement of the development.

Metrication

4.44 Since 1969, land measurements based on the metre, the millimetre and the hectare have increasingly replaced those based on the imperial system. Accordingly, all new map data produced by the Ordnance Survey is in metric form. Metric measurements are already standard in the Land Register, with the Agency undertaking conversions of imperial measurements at the time of registration when appropriate.

A revised European Union Council Directive[1] promotes a general policy, which became effective on 1 October 1995, of phasing out units of measurements which are incompatible with the international (metric) system of measurements. The directive requires legal and official recognition to be given to the metric system, with recognition being withdrawn from the imperial system of measurements except for transitional arrangements or recognised exemptions.

Scope of directive

4.45 The directive is not confined to trade; it covers 'economic purposes' and 'administrative purposes' among others. The directive is of obvious relevance to conveyancers because it prescribes the units of measurement in which lineal and area extents in new conveyancing descriptions of land and property must be expressed.

The validity of documents which use units of measurement not authorised by the directive is in question. Subject to authoritative guidance, the only safe way to proceed is to assume that a document which is subject to the new directive, but does not comply therewith, will be void or at least voidable. Therefore it is necessary to ensure that the documents comply with the directive. As the Keeper cannot guarantee that documents which fail to comply with the directive will be acceptable for recording in the Sasine Register or registration in the Land Register, care must be taken to ensure that new measurements are always expressed in units authorised by the directive.

Effect of directive

Units of measurement
4.46 For conveyancing and registration purposes, the rule is that the primary indicator of measurement of length, depth, height or area in new (not existing) property descriptions must be metric, not imperial. As is explained later, the acre is permitted to be used as a primary indicator for land registration purposes only. It will also be permissible to show imperial units as supplementary indicators of measurement.

Existing measurements, however expressed, are not affected by the directive. So there is no need for a conveyancer to convert an existing property description into metric units. It is only new measurements which need to be expressed in units of measurement authorised by the directive. Since 1 October 1995 the

[1](80/181/EEC, amended by 85/1/EEC and 89/617/EEC)

requirement for any new contract or transaction in land which will lead to an application for registration in the Land Register, a recording in the Sasine Register or a submission to the Registers of Scotland for associated purposes in respect of a newly defined area, is that metric measurements must be used to define the property in question. This is true even for a contract which was entered into before 1 October 1995 but has still to be implemented.

The yard, foot and inch are statutorily defined as being 0.9144 metre, 0.3048 metre and 0.0254 metre respectively. Accordingly, any existing imperial measurement can easily be converted to metric units. Alternatively, the extent can be remeasured. It is preferable to use metric units from the outset in respect of new descriptions.

Exceptions to the metric rule
4.47 The acre: The directive allows the acre to be used in perpetuity for land registration purposes. Fractions of an acre must be expressed in decimal points. Note, however, that in the Land Register the Keeper is statutorily obliged to convert the measurement of any property which extends to 4.942 Acres (2 hectares) or more into the metric equivalent in hectares.

Supplementary indicators to primary units of measurement
4.48 The directive also allows an imperial measurement to be used as a supplementary indicator to a metric measurement. But the metric measurement must precede the imperial unit, and the supplementary indicator (which may be conveniently placed in brackets) must be in characters no larger than the metric indicator. The directive does not authorise the expression of a length, depth, height or area in imperial units followed by the metric equivalent.

Effect on previous deed descriptions and plans
4.49 Measurements in existing descriptions of land are not affected by the directive. Hence existing particular descriptions using imperial units of measurement, and descriptions by reference to such particular descriptions, will continue to be acceptable in writs describing the same land and recorded in the Register of Sasines and presented with applications for first registration in the Land Register.

The directive only applies when a new identification requires to be drawn, typically upon the creation and first sale of a building plot.

However, the application form for first registration (Form 1) now obliges both the selling and purchasing solicitor to ensure that the property sought to be registered can be both accurately identified on the ordnance map, and that the legal title agrees with the present situation on the ground.

These requirements mean that in some cases new deed plans will need to be prepared. It should be borne in mind that all dimensions in such plans should be metric even although previous descriptions or plans may have used imperial units. Extracts or copies of plans from earlier deeds used to support a Form P16 application to compare a bounding description with the ordnance map do not require to have any imperial dimensions converted to metric. However, the Agency's replies to these requests will use metric units of measurement.

Implications for Registers of Scotland

Textual records
4.50 There will be no wholesale substitution of metric measurements for existing imperial measurements in any of the registers maintained by the Keeper.

Dimensions for all new applications, or updates to existing registrations, will be in metric units irrespective of the date of the document from which they are extracted, or indeed the form in which they appear. Where an earlier deed has expressed a dimension in imperial units, then a supplementary indicator may be included in the entry if circumstances merit it.

Where possible, conversion of the imperial unit will be done without any approximation.

Where passages from deeds are reproduced verbatim, any references to units of measurement will continue to be reproduced unchanged.

When a copy of an earlier deed plan with imperial units is incorporated in a title sheet, no conversion of the measurements shown thereon will be undertaken.

Title plans
4.51 As with the textual element of the Land Register, there will be no wholesale substitution of metric measurements for imperial measurements already disclosed on title plans. Dimensions on new filed plans, or added to existing ones, will be shown in metric units. If it becomes necessary to add metric dimensions to an existing title plan which already carries imperial measurements, the latter may be converted to metric at the Keeper's discretion.

NOTE: Further information and advice on the Directive is available from the Department of Trade and Industry, Consumer Affairs Division, 1-19 Victoria Street, London SW1H 0ET (Tel: 0171 215 0334 Fax: 0171 215 0315).

APPENDIX 1

Recommended criteria for preparation of plans attached to deeds for conveyancing

- A scale and the orientation of north must be shown. A drawn or bar scale is to be preferred, because it allows distortion from any subsequent photocopying to be identified.

- The Keeper produces title plans using 1:1250, 1:2500, and 1:10,000 base scale ordnance survey mapping for properties falling in urban, rural, and mountain and moorland areas respectively. Deed plans drawn for properties in these areas should be adequate for the corresponding scale - but see below.

- If the scale of the most suitable map is insufficient to reflect the necessary detail, an inset plan at a larger scale may be used. Situations will invariably arise when even the 1:1250 scale map cannot provide enough detail, in which case plans at 1:500 are the preferred option.

- Scales based on the imperial system (*e.g.* 1 inch to 8 feet) are no longer acceptable.

- The plan must not be stated to be 'demonstrative only and not taxative'.

- The plan must contain sufficient surrounding established detail (*e.g.* fences, houses, road junctions *etc.*) to enable its position to be fixed with accuracy on the ordnance map.

- Where it is necessary for any measurement to be shown on the plan, metric units must be used to two decimal places.

- Where measurements are deemed necessary, then the dimensions shown on the plan ought to agree, as far as possible, with the scaled measurements.

- A plan employing dimensions which are simply a perimeter measure are incapable of being accurately plotted or proven. Dimensioned plans must therefore include proof measurements which may consist of:

  - cross/diagonals;

  - angles at each change of boundary direction; or

- local or national grid co-ordinates of boundary changes supported by tape checks along each boundary; or

- any other form of independent check which is capable of proofing the survey.

- The property forming the transaction must be clearly indicated by means of suitable graphic references (*e.g.* edging, tinting, hatching).

- Exclusive and shared areas must be properly differentiated and referenced as above and consistent with the text of the deed.

- Undefined boundaries (*i.e.* where no physical boundary exists) must be accurately fixed to existing detail by metric measurements shown on the plan.

- Where buildings, pathways, *etc.*, require to be referenced on the plan to reflect shared or common interests they must be shown in the correct position relative to other surrounding detail.

- Boundaries should be identified by description (*e.g.* centre line of wall, outer face or inner face of hedge, *etc.*).

- Details of how, by whom, and when the survey was completed. Information as to the currency of the survey detail and whether or not it relates to the as-built positions or merely the proposed layout should also be noted.

- Extracts from proposed development plans must not be employed if the property involved physically exists.

Guidance for Resolution of P16 Answer 3

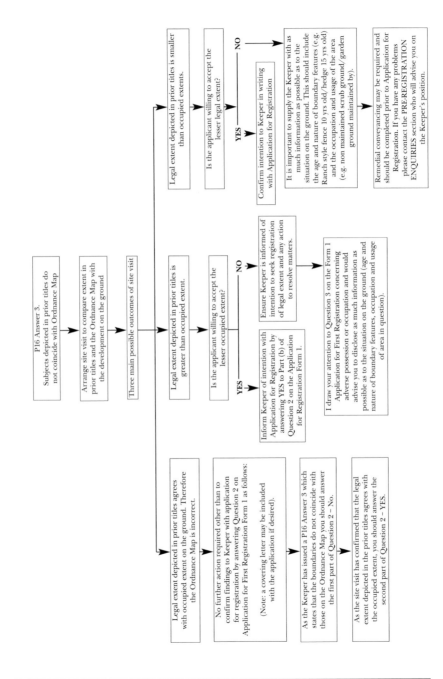

P16 Answer 3.
Subjects depicted in prior titles do not coincide with Ordnance Map

Arrange site visit to compare extent in prior titles and the Ordnance Map with the development on the ground

Three main possible outcomes of site visit

Legal extent depicted in prior titles agrees with occupied extent on the ground. Therefore the Ordnance Map is incorrect.

No further action required other than to confirm findings to Keeper with application for registration by answering Question 2 on Application for First Registration Form 1.

(Note: a covering letter may be included with the application if desired).

As the Keeper has issued a P16 Answer 3 which states that the boundaries do not coincide with those on the Ordnance Map you should answer the first part of Question 2 – No.

As the site visit has confirmed that the legal extent depicted in the prior titles agrees with the occupied extent, you should answer the second part of Question 2 – YES.

Legal extent depicted in prior titles is greater than occupied extent.

Is the applicant willing to accept the lesser occupied extent?

YES ——— NO

Inform Keeper of intention with Application for Registration by answering YES to Part (b) of Question 2 on the Application for Registration Form 1.

Ensure Keeper is informed of intention to seek registration of legal extent and any action to resolve matters.

I draw your attention to Question 3 on the Form 1 Application for First Registration concerning adverse possession or occupation and would advise you to disclose as much information as possible as to the situation on the ground (age and nature of boundary features, occupation and usage of area in question).

Legal extent depicted in prior titles is smaller than occupied extents.

Is the applicant willing to accept the lesser legal extent?

YES ——— NO

Confirm intention to Keeper in writing with Application for Registration

It is important to supply the Keeper with as much information as possible as to the situation on the ground. This should include the age and nature of boundary features (e.g. Ranch style fence 10 yrs old/hedge 15 yrs old) and the occupation and usage of the area (e.g. non maintained scrub ground/garden ground maintained by).

Remedial conveyancing may be required and should be completed prior to Application for Registration. If you have any problems please contact the PRE-REGISTRATION ENQUIRIES section who will advise you on the Keeper's position.

Chapter 5 - Application for Registration

Introduction

5.1 Unlike the Sasine Register, the Land Register is not a register of deeds; it is a register of interests in land. While the Keeper, as a matter of practice, keeps a microfiche or imaged copy of each previously unrecorded deed or document that induces or affects an entry in the title sheet, it is the effect of the deeds and documents submitted rather than the deed itself that is registered. Deeds that induce registration or that affect an already registered interest do not require a warrant of registration unless they must also be recorded in the Sasine Register. Instead rule 9(1) provides for the use of application forms.

An application for registration typically consists of:

- the appropriate application form;

- the deed to which the application relates;

- the appropriate remittance in respect of the registration dues;

- other documents and evidence that may be required to support the application; and

- an inventory (Form 4) in duplicate.

The documents and evidence required for the various types of application are discussed more fully in chapter 2. They must be listed on the Form 4, Inventory of Writs.

Application forms

5.2 Rule 9(1) prescribes three different forms of application for registration of interests in land: Forms 1, 2 and 3. Rule 9(2) provides for a statutory form of inventory, Form 4, which must accompany such applications

Rule 13 prescribes a form to be used for noting (in contrast to registering) some matter on the title sheet. Form 5 may be used, for example, for a noting of a house name of registered subjects, or for noting the existence of (or freedom from) an overriding interest. A Form 4 inventory must accompany a Form 5 application.

Forms 1, 2 and 3 do not need warrants of registration. The first page of each form (Part A) is designed to provide the Keeper with both the authority to register the interest and the information that he needs to enter the application on the Application Record. Part B requires answers to various questions which are intended to elicit essential pieces of information.

The Part B questions are not exhaustive, and in some cases the Keeper may ask for additional information before completing registration.

In terms of rule 9, an application for registration must be made by the person in whose favour the real right will be created or affected by registration. The application form must be signed by the applicant or the applicant's solicitor. By signing the application form, the applicant or the applicant's solicitor certifies that the information given in the form is correct. In that sense, the form is rather like an insurance proposal form. During a conveyancing transaction, the prudent solicitor acting for the grantee will always adjust the terms of the application form with the granter's solicitor.

By section 4(3), the date of receipt of an application by the Keeper becomes the date of registration. Except where the application is rejected or withdrawn, this priority of registration will not usually be lost merely because the Keeper requests further information. The position is different where the application form is unsigned. The Keeper's view is that his receipt of an unsigned application (even one supported by all necessary documents and evidence) is not receipt of an application at all. The Keeper will therefore return the unsigned application. In such a case (assuming that there is no other reason for refusal), the date of registration will not be the date of receipt of the unsigned form but the later date on which a properly signed application form is received by the Keeper. Where an application is not accompanied by a remittance for the appropriate registration dues, the application will be rejected by the Keeper and returned to the submitting agent.

Land Register application Forms 1 to 15 and Forms P16 and P17 are available on disk from the Keeper. The software package enables agents to reproduce the aforementioned forms electronically, so helping to streamline procedures for submitting Land Register applications. The forms are printed from disk onto single sheets of A4 paper. In order to comply with section 8 of the Requirements of Writing (Scotland) Act 1995[1], the system encodes a unique electronic identifier on each sheet of the application form where it comprises more than one sheet.

[1] c.7

Such a unique identifier is essential as it ensures the separate sheets of an application form can be linked together in such a unique way as to ensure there can be no doubt the information contained in the form and the answers to the questions relate to the same application. In the absence of such a unique electronic identifier the application form will not be acceptable to the Keeper.

It is in everyone's interest that all applications should enter the Application Record as soon as possible, and certainly on the day that they are received by the Keeper. All applications entered in the Application Record but not yet reflected in the title sheet will be disclosed in reports from the Land Register. A report will therefore show the position in the Land Register up to the date to which the Application Record is complete; usually this will be the day before the issue of the report. Failure to complete the application form and, in particular, to answer the relevant questions accurately and after proper enquiry can lead to unfortunate consequences for an applicant. Neither the Keeper nor the court has any general powers to rectify the Land Register against the registered proprietor in possession. But, in terms of section 9(3)(a)(iii), the Keeper may exercise a power of rectification where an inaccuracy has been caused wholly or substantially by the fraud or carelessness of the proprietor in possession. This could clearly cover an inaccurately completed application form. Indemnity may also be denied (section 12(3)(n)).

In many instances, whether on first registration or where the interest has already been registered, two application forms will be required. For example, where property is being purchased and the purchaser is also granting a standard security, two separate applications are needed; one in respect of the disposition and the other in respect of the standard security. Where the disposition induces first registration, the appropriate forms are Form 1 and Form 2. Where the disposition conveys the entirety of a registered interest, separate applications must be made on Form 2 for the disposition and the standard security.

In only one case will the Keeper give effect to a deed which is not accompanied by the appropriate application form. That is where on a sale an existing heritable security is being discharged and the discharge is submitted along with the application for registration of the purchaser's interest. In the latter case a fixed registration fee applies. (Fees payable in respect of registration of title are determined from time to time by the First Minister. Details of the 'fixed fee' can be found in the current 'Fees in the Registers of Scotland Order').

First registration - Form 1

5.3 Application for first registration should be made on Form 1. This form is similar in layout and content to the application Forms 2 and 3, but in addition contains two further Schedules; one for heritable securities and one for burdens. In listing outstanding heritable securities or burdens, there is no need to list the relative deeds using a standard conveyancing reference, or to set the burdens out at length. It is quite sufficient to refer to the writs by reference to their number on the Form 4 that must be submitted along with the application.

For example, the Schedules of the Form 1 submitted for the transaction illustrated in paragraph 5.5 would be completed as follows:

Schedule of heritable securities *etc.*

1. Standard security No. 5 of Form 4

Note that No. 9 of Form 4 should not be listed as it is not an outstanding standard security; it has yet to be registered.

Schedule of burdens

1. Instrument of sasine	No. 1 of Form 4.
2. Feu charter	No. 2 of Form 4.
3. Feu disposition	No. 3 of Form 4.

Form 1 is appropriate for any first registration of an unregistered interest and must be used whether the application follows one of the transactions listed in section 2(1)(a) or is an application for voluntary registration under either section 2(1)(b) or section 11(1).

If an application for first registration is accompanied by a new heritable security or any dealing other than those mentioned in paragraph 5.5 a separate application for registration of the security or other dealing must be made on the appropriate form, either Form 2 or Form 3.

Interest already registered - Forms 2 and 3

5.4 There are two forms for use where the transaction for which registration is sought relates to an interest which has already been registered. Form 2 should be used where the application will vary or amend an existing title sheet. Form 3 should be used where the application will require the opening of a new title sheet.

Where the application relates to part only of the registered interest, it will normally be necessary to furnish the Keeper with an accurate scaled plan. This will enable him to identify the part on the ordnance map. The general rule in registration of title is that anything entered in the title sheet affects the whole subjects in the title sheet unless there is any express statement to the contrary. For example, where the application relates to a standard security over part only of the registered interest,the part in question, except where a verbal description is appropriate, *e.g* a tenement flat, will require a separate plan reference for identification purposes in the relevant entry in the title sheet.

Form 2 is appropriate where the transaction is, for example:

- the transfer (whether for valuable consideration or not) of the whole of the registered interest, but not a grant of a feu or lease;

- the creation of a standard security, liferent or incorporeal heritable right whether over the whole or a part only of the registered interest;

- a deed of conditions whether over the whole or a part only of the registered interest; or

- any transmission or discharge of a heritable security whether secured over the whole or a part only of the registered interest;

- an application to remove an indemnity exclusion note.

Form 3 is appropriate where the transaction is, for example:

- the transfer (whether for valuable consideration or not) of a part only of the registered interest; or

- the grant of a feu or long lease whether of the whole or a part only of the registered interest.

Inventory of writs - Form 4

5.5 The Inventory of Writs (Form 4) should be completed in duplicate and submitted with the following types of application:

- application for first registration (Form 1)

- application for registration of a dealing (Form 2)

- application for registration of a transfer of part of a registered interest in land (Form 3)

- application for noting of overriding interest or entry of other information (Form 5)

- application for rectification of register (Form 9).

The Form 4 should list all the deeds and other documents relative to the application. This should be done even when, at the time of submitting the application, not all the deeds listed are available for production to the Keeper. For example, on first registration, writs referred to for burdens should be listed even although the seller has yet to pass them to the purchaser for exhibition to the Keeper. This applies also where the purchaser is aware that the Keeper has already examined the writs referred to for burdens and will not require to see them again.

Those writs actually included with the application should be clearly indicated on the Form 4 with the letter 'S' (an abbreviation for the word 'submitted'). Those which are not enclosed, but will be submitted later, should be marked as 'To follow' on the Form 4. Such deeds must be submitted within 60 days of receipt of the application.

An example of a completed Form 4 in a simple house purchase transaction involving a loan from an institutional lender on first registration might look as follows:

Item No	Please mark "S" against writs submitted	Writ	Particulars of writ	
			Grantee	Date of Recording
1		Instrument of Sasine	Green	3 May 1814
2		Feu Charter	Black	4 June 1938
3	S	Feu Disposition	Smith	10 Feb. 1939
4	S	Disposition	Sand	3 Mar. 1973
5	S	Standard Security	County B/S	3 Mar. 1973
6	To follow	Confirmation	Sand's Exors of No.5	1 Apr. 1998
7	S	Discharge		
8	S	Disposition	Brown	
9	S	Standard Security	National B/S	
10	To follow	Feuduty redemption receipt		
11	S	Affidavit (Matrimonial Homes Act)		

In this example it is assumed that:

- the first two writs are burdens writs relating to a building development which have already been examined by the Keeper;

- while the seller intends to produce the confirmation (item 6) it is not yet available;

- the redemption of the feuduty is being processed and the redemption receipt, (item 10) will in due course be obtained and submitted to the Keeper; and

- one beneficiary succeeded to the deceased's estate, who, instead of completing title, instructed Stuart's executors to sell. Under the terms of the Matrimonial Homes (Family Protection) (Scotland) Act 1981[2] that transaction could be construed as a dealing of the entitled spouse. Evidence regarding the non-entitled spouse would therefore be required.

The Form 4 also serves as an acknowledgement and should be submitted in duplicate. The Keeper will return one receipted copy to the applicant.

Where a transaction gives rise to two separate applications, as in the example above, *i.e.* one application for the disposition (item 8) and another application for the standard security (item 9), separate application forms are required, but it is unnecessary to complete two inventories. One Form 4 (in duplicate) will suffice for both, even where separate solicitors are acting. If each solicitor requires an acknowledgement from the Keeper, an additional copy of the Form 4 should be enclosed along with a note of the name and address of the solicitor to whom the extra acknowledgement should be sent.

In some instances, there may already exist with the title deeds an inventory of writs in a suitable form for submission with the application. The Keeper will not object if the existing inventory is photocopied and attached to the Form 4, provided the photocopy is legible.

Noting on the Land Register - Form 5

5.6 Reference is made in chapter 2 to noting additional information on the title sheet and, more particularly, noting the existence of, or freedom from, an overriding interest. When a proprietor wishes the Keeper to note a matter on the Register, application should be made on Form 5. Although the Keeper is not

---

[2] c.59

bound to give effect to any such application (sections 6(1)(g) and 6(4)(b)(ii)), he will usually comply. The application should be accompanied by the land certificate and such documents as are necessary to support the application, together with a completed Form 4 in duplicate.

In practice, except in the case of the noting of an overriding interest, the Keeper is seldom asked to note any additional information (for which a fee is chargeable), except as part of an application for the registration of a dealing. In this latter case, a Form 5 is unnecessary as each application form allows the applicant to ask the Keeper to note additional matters. Although the forms refer specifically to overriding interests, they can be used to notify other information, *e.g.* a change of street name. In this case the local authority's notification should be submitted along with the other evidence supporting the application for registration. The Keeper is under a duty in terms of section 6(4)(a) to note an overriding interest where any of the documents supporting the application for registration discloses the existence of that interest.

Application for land or charge certificate to be made to correspond with title sheet - Form 8

5.7 In terms of rule 16(1) and (2), an application can be made to the Keeper for a certificate of title (*i.e.* a land or charge certificate) to be made to correspond with the relevant title sheet. Application is made on Form 8 and a fee is chargeable. On receipt of a Form 8 application, the Keeper will search the Application Record for details of any outstanding applications which have still to be reflected in the title sheet, and for any entries which have yet to be reflected in the land certificate. A search is also undertaken of the Register of Inhibitions and Adjudications (the ROI, also known as the Personal Register).

If no alteration is required and the ROI search is clear, the inside cover of the certificate is stamped with the new date and the certificate is returned to the ingiving agent. Where new information contained in the Application Record is to be incorporated, a new set of pages is bound into the certificate. If the Keeper discloses adverse ROI entries, appropriate notes, excluding indemnity in respect of loss arising from reduction, *e.g.* (a) of any dealing struck at by the inhibition or (b) resulting from sequestration, will be endorsed on the relevant certificate.

Registration and recording

5.8 In all cases where it is desired not only to register in the Land Register but also to record the deed inducing that registration in the Sasine Register, the appropriate application for registration should be made in the terms discussed in paragraph 2.17.

In addition, a warrant of registration should be endorsed on the deed and a Form CPB2 completed requesting that the deed also be recorded in the appropriate Division of the Sasine Register. The terms of Part III of the Fees in the Registers of Scotland Order 1995[3] apply where a deed is simultaneously recorded and registered as above.

The appropriate method of searching the Registers in such a transaction is discussed in chapter 3.

Certificate of value for registration fee

5.9 The fees payable in respect of registration of title are determined from time to time by the First Minister in accordance with section 25 of the Land Registers (Scotland) Act 1868[4], as amended by section 23 of the 1979 Act. As the fees for registration are based on an *ad valorem* scale, each application form contains, at box 10 of Part A on the front page, space for the insertion of the value which must be completed even if there is no consideration or the sum secured is not stated.

Documents and evidence

5.10 In terms of section 4(1) the Keeper is required to accept an application for registration if it is accompanied by such documents and other evidence as he may require to examine. The precise nature of the documents and other evidence which the Keeper will require to examine will depend on two general factors:

- The type of application: whether for first registration of an interest; for registration of a dealing with a registered interest; or for transfer of part of a registered interest.

- The exact nature of the transaction.

The documentation and evidence required in connection with the three most common types of application are discussed in the following paragraphs.

Documentation to be submitted with an application for first registration

5.11 An application for first registration should be accompanied by the following:

- All deeds and documents necessary to establish the validity of the title.

[3]1995 No. 1945 (s.142)
[4]c.64

- Any deeds and documents containing information about matters which the Keeper is required, in terms of section 6(1) and (2), to enter in the title sheet.

- Any deeds and documents containing information about matters which the applicant asks the Keeper, in terms of section 6(3), to enter in the title sheet.

- Any documents or other evidence relating to any overriding interest which the applicant wishes the Keeper to note in the title sheet in terms of section 6(4).

- Where appropriate, sufficient additional information to enable the Keeper to identify on the ordnance map the subjects, or any part of them, affected by any of the matters to be entered or noted in the title sheet in terms of section 6(1) to (4).

In practical terms the documentation to be submitted includes:

1. *Application forms*. An application Form 1 in respect of the deed inducing registration. A separate application Form 2 is required for every other deed presented for registration.

2. *Inventory*. An inventory (Form 4) in duplicate. The inventory must list all relevant documents, whether submitted or not.

3. *The relevant fee*. The fee payable in respect of an application for first registration must be pre-paid. If it is not, the Keeper will reject the application and return it to the submitting agent.

4. *The deed(s)being presented for registration*. The document by which the transaction is effected.

5. *Prescriptive progress*. A sufficient progress of title, including any relevant supporting links in title.

   Note: Questions 10 and 11 of Part B of the application Form 1 provide a caveat to the above. Question 10 is applicable where the deed inducing first registration is in implement of the exercise of a power of sale under a heritable security; question 11 is applicable where the deed inducing first registration is a general vesting declaration or a notice of title pursuant to a compulsory purchase order. Both questions ask whether the statutory procedures in connection with such transactions have been complied with. If the question can be answered in the affirmative then no evidence of compliance with the necessary statutory procedures need be supplied to the Keeper. Where doubt remains about answering in the affirmative, or a negative answer is appropriate, all available evidence should be submitted to the Keeper with the application.

6. *Deeds containing rights and burdens, etc*. All deeds outwith the prescriptive progress which create, vary or discharge rights, burdens or conditions affecting the subjects. This is subject to what is narrated in paragraph 5.13 below.

7. *Outstanding heritable securities*. All outstanding heritable securities and all transmissions, restrictions and discharges of outstanding securities.

8. *Identification of the subjects*. The documents submitted in support of an application must contain sufficient information to enable the Keeper to identify the subjects on the ordnance map. Thus a deed containing a full description of the property should be submitted; as should any deed containing a deed plan. Alternatively, the agent should submit sufficient additional information which will enable the Keeper to make such identification.

9. *Form P16 report*. If a P16 report has been issued by the Keeper, it should be submitted regardless of the answer given.

10. *Matrimonial Homes evidence*. All the necessary consents, renunciations or affidavits in terms of section 6 of the Matrimonial Homes (Family Protection) (Scotland) Act 1981[5], as amended. (See Rule 5(j) of the Land Registration (Scotland) Rules 1980[6].)

11. *Any other relevant documentation*. Examples include ground burden redemption receipts, letters from the superior, etc.

Note: If any correspondence has been entered into with the Keeper prior to an application being lodged, both the initial enquiry and the reply should be submitted.

Documentation not to be submitted with an application for first registration

5.12 The Keeper often receives a number of deeds and documents which are not required in respect of an application for first registration. The following deeds and documents need not be submitted:

- Heritable securities for which final discharges have been recorded in the Sasine Register; and transmissions and discharges of such securities.

[5]c.59
[6]1980 No. 1413

- Any search for incumbrances.

- Building warrants, completion certificates and letters about planning permission.

- Matrimonial Homes affidavits from the purchaser on the granting of a standard security.

Circumstances under which common titles should be submitted

5.13 Before any county becomes an operational area, a team of the Keeper's staff commence new area preparation by searching the Register of Sasines for that county to identify areas of land (research areas) which have been, or are likely to be, divided into several units of property and which may be subject to common burdens. Such areas generally comprise a building development or a feuing estate.

When compiling research areas the common burdens deeds will be examined. So, on first registration of any properties affected, the Keeper will not normally require to examine any deeds prior to the foundation deed. There are occasions however, where the Keeper will require, on first registration, to examine the prior titles to an area of ground notwithstanding the fact that it fulfils the criteria of a research area:

- The area of land may have been developed subsequent to the initial search to identify potential research areas in that county.

- An area's potential as a research area may not have been realised at the initial search stage.

- Deed plans may not be available or, as plans are not colour copied, obtainable only in black and white. Prior to the commencement of copying writs by photography in 1934, plans were not copied unless a duplicate plan was ingiven. Even then plans were still not copied if they exceeded certain dimensions. Although attempts are made by the new area preparation staff to obtain the original deed plan in those circumstances it is not always possible to trace the original deed.

In practice it is suggested that a solicitor, when dealing with a property which forms part of a development comprising ten or more units, should proceed on the basis that the Keeper will not require to see common titles or common burdens writs. These common writs should, however, still be listed on the Form 4.

When dealing with a property which does not form part of a development comprising ten or more units the common titles must be submitted to the Keeper on first registration. Once examined, the Keeper will stamp such deeds 'Examined'. Solicitors should note that only the original deed, as opposed to National Archives of Scotland (formerly Scottish Record Office) copies or simple photocopies, will be so stamped. Any common deed stamped in such a way need not be re-submitted in connection with any other application for first registration. Such deeds must, however, be listed on the Form 4.

Documentation to be submitted with an application for dealing with a whole registered interest

5.14 An application for registration of a dealing with a registered interest should be accompanied by:

1. *Application forms.* A separate application Form 2 will be required for each deed or document presented for registration.

2. *Inventory.* An inventory (Form 4) in duplicate. The inventory must list all relevant documents, whether submitted or not.

3. *The relevant fee.* The fee payable in respect of an application for registration of a dealing with a registered interest must be pre-paid. If it is not, the Keeper will reject the application and return it to the submitting agent.

4. *Land and charge certificates.* The relevant land certificate and any relevant charge certificate. The charge certificate should only be produced in cases where the transaction is a dealing with a heritable security over registered subjects.

Note 1: In terms of rule 9(3), the certificate of title must always be produced to the Keeper with any application for registration of a dealing affecting a registered interest unless, in terms of rule 18, the applicant can show good cause for failure to produce it. For the purposes of rule 18, good cause includes situations where the certificate has been lost or destroyed or is otherwise unobtainable or, in the case of a land certificate, is held by a heritable creditor.

Note 2: In terms of rule 9(3) the charge certificate must be submitted to the Keeper along with any application for registration of a dealing with a registered heritable security. Except on good cause shown, the land certificate should also be submitted along with the application even if the debtor's interest is not directly affected by such a dealing. This requirement is to enable the land certificate to be updated to reveal the effect of the dealing. The fact that the land certificate is in the hands of a prior creditor is good cause for not submitting it to the Keeper.

5. ***The deed(s) being presented for registration.*** The document by which the transaction is effected.

6. ***Progress of title.*** A sufficient progress of title, including any relevant supporting links in title. If there is no qualification in the existing proprietorship section of the land certificate, then the only progress of title required is that from the date to which the land certificate is certified.

   Note: Similar considerations to those set out in the Note item 5 of paragraph 5.11 apply where the deed inducing registration of the dealing is, (a) a transfer of the subjects proceeding on the power of sale provisions in a security deed, or (b) a general vesting declaration or notice of title pursuant to a compulsory purchase order.

7. ***Matrimonial Homes evidence.*** All the necessary consents, renunciations or affidavits in terms of section 6 of the Matrimonial Homes (Family Protection) (Scotland) Act 1981, as amended. (See rule 5 (j) of the Land Registration (Scotland) Rules 1980.)

8. ***Any other relevant documentation.*** Any other relevant documentation and evidence containing new information about any matter already entered in the title sheet or which will lead to a new entry in the title sheet. Examples include ground burden redemption receipts, superiors' letters, *etc.*

   Note: If any correspondence has been entered into with the Keeper prior to an application being lodged, both the initial enquiry and the reply must be submitted.

Documentation to be submitted with an application for a transfer of part of a registered interest

5.15 An application for registration of a transfer of part (T.P.) of a registered interest should be accompanied by:

1. ***Application forms.*** A Form 3 is required for the deed which induces the transfer. Any other deed being registered (for example, standard security, deed of restriction, *etc.*) should be accompanied by a Form 2.

2. ***Inventory.*** An inventory (Form 4) in duplicate. The inventory must list all relevant documents, whether submitted or not.

3. **The relevant fee.** The fee payable in respect of an application for a transfer of part of a registered interest must be pre-paid. If it is not, the Keeper will reject the application and return it to the submitting agent.

4. **Land certificate.** The land certificate for the major area (known as the parent title) should always be lodged with the T.P. application, assuming it has been issued by the Keeper. This will allow the Keeper to reflect in the parent title land certificate that a transfer or removal has taken place. In any developing building estate it will probably be impossible for the developer's land certificate to be lent to all the purchasers of houses in the estate at the time they require it to register their individual interests. In these circumstances the developer's land certificate should be placed on deposit with the Keeper who will provide the developer with an office copy of the title sheet, including the title plan, free of charge. The office copy can then be produced to purchasers for the purpose of examination of title and the drafting of conveyances.

5. **Charge certificate.** If there is a standard security over the parent title there is no need to submit the charge certificate until the standard security is discharged.

6. **The deed being presented for registration.** The document by which the transaction is effected.

7. **Plan.** The deed inducing a transfer of part will normally include a plan of the subjects being conveyed.

8. **Progress of title.** A sufficient progress of title, including any relevant supporting links in title. If there is no qualification in the existing proprietorship section of the land certificate, then the only progress of title required is that from the date to which the land certificate is certified.

   Note: Similar considerations to those set out in the Note to item 5 of paragraph 5.11 apply where the deed inducing the transfer of part is a transfer of the subjects proceeding on, (a) the power of sale provisions in a security deed, or (b) a general vesting declaration or notice of title pursuant to a compulsory purchase order.

9. **Matrimonial Homes evidence.** All the necessary consents, renunciations or affidavits in terms of section 6 of the Matrimonial Homes (Family Protection) (Scotland) Act 1981, as amended. (See rule 5(j) of the Land Registration (Scotland) Rules 1980.)

10. *Any other relevant documentation*. Any other relevant documentation and evidence containing new information relating to any matter already entered in the title sheet or which will lead to a new entry in the title sheet. Examples include ground burden redemption receipts, superiors letters, *etc*.

Note: If any correspondence has been entered into with the Keeper prior to an application being lodged, both the initial enquiry and the reply must be submitted.

Return of deeds and documents

5.16 All deeds and documents submitted in support of an application for registration will be returned, on completion of registration, to the agent who originally presented them, on behalf of the applicant. If the deeds and documents are to be returned to a party other than the original presenting agent, written authorisation to that effect, signed by the original presenting agent, will be required.

Before returning the deeds and documents submitted to him, the Keeper will make copies of those of which he may require to issue office copies in terms of section 6(5), or which may be required as evidence of his authority for a particular entry in the title sheet.

Following registration of the applicant's title the land certificate supersedes the title deeds. The limited circumstances in which it is necessary to retain Sasine titles once an interest has been registered is discussed more fully in chapter 8.

Correction or rejection of application

5.17 In terms of section 4(1) and (2), the Keeper has power to reject an application for registration in the Land Register if the application does not comply with the provisions of those sub-sections. However, in many cases, rather than reject an application out of hand, the Keeper will make use of the provisions of section 4(3)(b).

Section 4(3)(b) provides that where an application is not accepted by the Keeper because:

- it is not accompanied by sufficient evidence or information under section 4(1); or

- it cannot be identified by reference to the ordnance map in terms of section 4(2)(a); or

- a deed accompanying the application and relating to a registered interest does not bear the title number of the registered interest in terms of section 4(2)(d);

It may, if not otherwise rejected by the Keeper or withdrawn by the applicant, be accepted by the Keeper once these provisions have been met. In this event, the date of registration remains the date on which the application was first received by the Keeper. In terms of rule 11, the Keeper may return to the applicant for amendment any document relating to the application. It is thus possible for a component part of an application to be returned for amendment without the entire application being rejected and losing its original date of registration.

Where a deed is returned for amendment because it does not bear the title number, it is usually not necessary to have a new deed prepared to incorporate the title number *in gremio*. It is quite sufficient if the title number is clearly marked on the first page of the deed in question, preferably at the top but certainly not on the backing. The only case in which a new deed should be prepared is the case of a description by reference to the title number, under section 15(1), where the title number was given incorrectly.

If the Keeper is not satisfied with the documents and evidence submitted in support of an application he can, instead of rejecting the application, request additional information from the applicant or, where appropriate, instruct a survey of the subjects. In such a case, there will inevitably be a delay in the completion of that registration, but, because of the composition of the Register, the delay will affect only the title sheet or sheets relevant to the application. The Register itself will not be disrupted as would the Register of Sasines by a similar delay.

It is undesirable, however, that there should be undue delay in the completion of registration. Rule 12 provides that, if the applicant fails to comply with a request from the Keeper to supply additional evidence or information or to amend a document in terms of rule 11 within 60 days of such request the Keeper may complete registration, subject to exclusion of indemnity, or reject the application.

Failure to submit documents and evidence

5.18 The Keeper must accept an application if it is accompanied by such documents and other evidence as he may require. The applicant's solicitor will obviously want to submit sufficient evidence to ensure that a fully indemnified land certificate is issued by the Keeper. The onus, however, is on the submitting agent to ensure that he meets the Keeper's requirements as set out in the preceding paragraphs. In practice, it is not uncommon for deeds and documents to be omitted from applications for registration or to be marked 'to follow' on the Inventory Form 4. This is acceptable on certain occasions, the most common being when there is good cause to believe that the Keeper has already examined a common burdens deed. The Keeper will, however, requisition from the submitting agent such deeds and documents which he requires to examine in order to complete the registration process. The submitting agent will then be allowed a period of up to 60 days to comply with the requisition. No reminder will be sent. If an agent fails to make a satisfactory response to a requisition within the 60 day period the Keeper is empowered under rule 12 either to complete registration, subject to exclusion of indemnity, or to reject the application.

Similarly, any deed or document returned to the agent in terms of rule 11 for amendment must be returned to the Keeper within 60 days. Failure to do so may result in the application being rejected or completed subject to an exclusion of indemnity.

The following paragraphs offer guidance on the action the Keeper will take concerning certain particular omissions.

Identification on the ordnance map
5.19 As the Land Register is a map based system it is intrinsic to its integrity that the subjects in any application for first registration or transfer of part must be identifiable on the ordnance map. It follows, therefore, that any application for registration which cannot be so identified either because there are no plans or extent deeds readily available or inadequacies exist with those that are, should not be accepted. However, section 4(3)(b) provides for the saving of the registration date where the application although not initially acceptable because the subjects cannot be identified on the ordnance map, but without being rejected, is subsequently accepted by the Keeper. In view of this the Keeper will accept most applications irrespective of problems with identification and allow the applicant up to 60 days to provide sufficient evidence to enable him to identify the subjects.

Incomplete or incorrect title number in deed submitted with an application for registration
5.20 The omission of the title sheet number from a deed which relates to a registered interest in land and is executed after the interest has been registered is unacceptable in terms of section 4(2)(d). However, in terms of section 4(3)(b) the Keeper will accept such an application and allow the applicant 60 days to add the title number. Incorrectly quoted title numbers fall into the same category, but where the incorrectly quoted number has led to an application registered against the wrong title sheet, the application will be cancelled. The agent will require to resubmit the application, the registration date being the date of receipt of the re-presented application.

Land certificate not submitted

5.21 Rule 18 allows for circumstances where a certificate of title need not be submitted with an application for registration. Notes 1 and 2 to item 4 of paragraph 5.14 looks at this issue in detail. In practice the most common occasion where the certificate of title need not be submitted is where a land certificate is held by the creditor and a sale is not pending.

Applications for registration of dealings with whole (other than improvement grants, second securities, *etc.*) where the submitting agent has not provided the Keeper with good cause in terms of rule 18 as to why the certificate of title has not been submitted, could be rejected by the Keeper. However, in view of the difficulties which do arise in obtaining certificates of title, the Keeper has agreed to give submitting agents a limited time to produce them. A requisition will be issued by the Keeper and, if after 30 days the requisition has not been complied with, the application will be cancelled.

Superiority/mixed fee applications

5.22 The Keeper has had particular problems with the identification of superiority/mixed fee titles in the past and this being the case, and notwithstanding section 4(3)(b), the Keeper is not prepared to accept an incomplete application of such titles nor allow any problems to be sorted out at a later date. Before the Keeper is willing to accept such an application, he must be able at minimum to establish the extent of the area to be registered and also the extents of the various individual feus and leases. The overall extent of any large estate/superiority or mixed fee title must therefore be identifiable; and in view of the potential risk to the Keeper's indemnity an application of this nature will not be accepted for registration unless identification can be made.

Identification of the extents of the individual feus and leases is the responsibility of the submitting agent. This will usually mean providing the Keeper with copies of the feus and leases and also identifying them on a plan where appropriate. As the Keeper may have registered some of the individual feus and leases previously, a check of the Land Register will confirm those feus and leases the Keeper still requires to see. If the Keeper has not seen the feus or leases previously and they are not submitted with the application, the application is likely to be rejected.

Matrimonial Homes evidence

5.23 The Keeper is required by rule 5(j) to insert in the proprietorship section of the title sheet:

'a statement that there are in respect of the interest in land no subsisting occupancy rights, in terms of the Matrimonial Homes (Family Protection) (Scotland) Act 1981, of spouses of persons who were formerly entitled to the interest in land, if the Keeper is satisfied that there are no such subsisting rights'.

If no evidence, or insufficient evidence, is submitted to satisfy the Keeper that there are no subsisting occupancy rights in the subjects of the application, then the Keeper will insert in the title sheet a note to the effect that no evidence has been produced to the Keeper or that the evidence is deficient in some manner. No further enquiry will be made by the Keeper.

Discharge(s) of outstanding securities/charges

5.24 *First registration or dealing with whole.* If there is an outstanding charge, the discharge or deed of restriction will not be requisitioned and the outstanding charge will be disclosed on the title sheet. If the discharge or deed of restriction is marked 'to follow' on the Form 4 and is not presented as an application by the time the Keeper undertakes legal examination of the application, the application will be completed showing the outstanding charge.

Transfer of part. If an outstanding charge exists against the parent title sheet, the discharge or deed of restriction will not be requisitioned and the outstanding charge will be disclosed on the title sheet for the part. If the discharge or deed of restriction is marked 'to follow' on the Form 4, and is not presented as an application by the time the Keeper undertakes legal examination of the application, the application will be completed showing the outstanding charge.

Adverse entry in the Register of Inhibitions and Adjudications

5.25 An adverse entry found to be still outstanding at the time of registration, will be disclosed in the title sheet and indemnity will be excluded in respect thereof. Where doubt exists as to the relevance of the entry in the Register of Inhibitions and Adjudications to the parties in the application, the Keeper will contact the submitting agent for clarification.

No certificate of registration of charge for limited company standard security

5.26 In view of the fact that the time limit for registration of a charge in the Companies Register is 21 days from the date of registration, the Keeper allows 60 days for production of the certificate of registration of the charge. If the certificate is not produced within the 60 days period, registration will proceed with an appropriate exclusion of indemnity. The Keeper will not revert to the submitting agent.

Stamp duty

5.27 If a deed is incorrectly stamped or, on the face of it, should have been stamped, the Keeper will submit the deed to the Inland Revenue for marking. If stamp duty is payable the deed will be returned to the agent who will be given 60 days to have the deed stamped. Failure to do so will result in cancellation of the application.

Simplification of deeds relating to registered interests

5.28 Once an interest in land has been registered subsequent deeds relating to that interest will no longer be framed in the same way and with the same clauses as deeds presented either for recording in the Sasine Register or for first registration. Section 15 relates solely to registered interests and seeks to simplify deeds in four ways:

(1) Description of subjects

By virtue of section 15(1) there is no place in registration of title neither for a description of lands by general name nor for descriptions by statutory reference. Section 15(1) provides that it shall be sufficient in a description of land in respect of a registered interest if it is described by reference to the title number of the registered interest. Rule 25 and schedule B further amplify this.

If the whole of an interest in land is being dealt with the reference to the title number (*i.e.* the number of the title sheet) is sufficient on its own. Schedule B suggests the interest be described as '*the subjects registered under Title Number(s) ...*'. It is suggested that the description should also include a brief postal address, as this could be useful as a 'signpost' if inadvertently there is a transposition of numbers within the title number.

For a conveyance or other deed dealing with a part only of the lands comprised in a registered title, in other words a transfer of part, the description of the part conveyed or otherwise dealt with will effectively comprise two parts. Firstly, the part being dealt with will have to be identified. This will almost invariably require reference to a plan showing figured dimensions for the boundaries. The description will then go on to narrate that the subjects form '*part of the subjects registered under title number ...*' (see note (a) to schedule B). Alternatively, schedule

B provides that the subjects can be described by exception: '*All and whole the subjects registered under Title Number(s) ... with the exception of ...*'.

Note (b) to schedule B makes provision for the situation whereby several subjects are registered under the one title number and it is desired to specify one or more of them. In such instances the subjects can be distinguished by referring to, for example, '*the subjects (first) registered under Title Number ...*' or say '*the subjects (first) and (third) registered under Title Number ...*'.

(2) Burdens and conditions
For those deeds presented either to the Sasine Register or submitted as part of an application for first registration, burdens and conditions require to be set out at length or alternatively, if subsequent to their constitution, be entered by reference to the deed wherein they were made real by recording in the Register of Sasines. Where subjects have been registered in the Land Register there is no necessity in any subsequent deed relating to that registered interest to insert or refer to the burdens and conditions which appear in the title sheet. Section 15(2) provides that any deed relating to a registered interest in land shall import for all purposes '*a full insertion of the real burdens, conditions, provisions or other matter*' affecting that interest. Burdens and conditions that are being created subsequent to first registration will have to be entered at length in the deed which seeks to establish them.

(3) Clause of deduction of title
Where the granter of a registered interest in land is not the infeft proprietor the Keeper requires evidence, as per section 4(1), that the granter is in right of the interest. The Keeper will require to examine the links in title which connect the granter with the last infeft proprietor. No clause of deduction of title is however necessary in the disposition in favour of the applicant. It is sufficient that the links in title be produced to the Keeper. In such an instance the disposition will be as valid as if it had contained a clause of deduction of title.

Similarly, by virtue of section 3(6) a notice of title is unnecessary where the subjects have already been registered. The applicant who wishes to complete his title by registration need only submit to the Keeper the links in title between himself and the party last infeft, along with the relevant application form. It should be noted that this facility does not apply to completion of title under section 74 or 76 of the Land Clauses Consolidation (Scotland) Act 1845[7].

[7] c.19

(4) Assignation of obligations/rights of relief
Section 50 of the Conveyancing (Scotland) Act 1874[8] provided for an assignation, in the form of schedule M thereto, of any obligation or right of relief (such as from feuduty) the title to which does not pass under the general assignation of writs clause in a disposition and so requires repeated specific assignation in each successive transmission. Under land registration, if the Keeper's examination of title on first registration reveals an assignation in terms of section 50 and schedule M of the 1874 Act, he will enter the terms of the obligation or right of relief in the title sheet. Thereafter, by virtue of section 15(4), it will be unnecessary in any deed relating to that interest in land to include such an assignation or to narrate the series of writs by which the granter of the deed became entitled to enforce the obligation or exercise the right.

Outstanding heritable security

Keeper's obligation to disclose security in title sheet
5.29 If at the time of an application for first registration the interest is burdened by a heritable security recorded in the Register of Sasines, that heritable security will be entered in the charges section of the title sheet unless the application is accompanied by a valid discharge or deed of restriction disburdening the interest of the security. The entry in the charges section will also reflect the effect of any subsequent recorded deeds affecting the heritable security; for example, an assignation of the creditor's interest under the security. The entry of the recorded security in the charges section discloses that the security subjects are burdened by an *ex facie* security deed. Although there is no need for a creditor's interest in an existing standard security recorded in the Sasine Register to be registered in the Land Register when the security subjects are themselves registered, it is essential that the security appears as a charge in the land register.

Failure to disclose security in title sheet
If the Keeper were to omit an existing heritable security from a title sheet, the creditor under the security would not be able to enforce it against the registered proprietor unless the Keeper is able to rectify the omission under section 9. If the Keeper cannot rectify the title sheet, the creditor will have a claim for indemnity against the Keeper.

Registration of creditor's interest
Although there are good reasons for doing so, there is no compulsion that a creditor's interest in an existing recorded heritable security be registered when the security subjects are themselves registered. An unregistered security however,

[8] c.94

is subject to any defects which may have existed prior to registration of the security subjects. Since the Keeper has neither received the certification which an applicant would be required to make on an application form nor examined documents or other evidence required to support such an application, no charge certificate will be issued. No indemnity will attach to the creditor's interest except where the Keeper has failed to note the existence of the security in the title sheet and is unable to rectify the omission.

To obtain the full benefit of the indemnity provisions under the Act, the creditor's interest must therefore be registered. Such an application is competent, however, only if the security subjects are already registered, or if an application for registration is pending it is subsequently completed. Application should be made on Form 2 whether the existing security relates to the whole or to a part only of the registered interest. The effect of the registration of a recorded heritable security is that the creditor obtains the full benefit of the Keeper's indemnity provisions and a charge certificate is issued.

Even if the decision is made not to register the creditor's interest, subsequent transactions involving the security interest may make registration of the creditor's interest necessary; for example, to give effect to a subsequent variation of the security.

An example of this situation arises where the proprietor of a half share in subjects sells that share to the proprietor of the other half; *e.g.*, on divorce when one spouse acquires the other's share in the matrimonial home. The disposition of the half share, if for value, will induce a first registration and in these circumstances the Keeper will almost invariably encourage voluntary registration of the other half share. If the spouses had previously granted a standard security the creditor will usually require the spouse acquiring the whole property to undertake the other spouse's personal obligation under the security, normally by way of a variation of the standard security. If such an application is submitted to the Keeper (*i.e.* half compulsory, half voluntary) accompanied by a recorded standard security granted by the previous proprietors and a variation thereof in the terms above-mentioned, the creditor's interest under the security will have to be registered. Accordingly, separate application forms should be submitted for both the standard security and the variation.

Standard registration dues are payable for the registration of a recorded heritable security, but, where the application for registration of the recorded security accompanies the application for registration of the security subjects, the reduced fee for heritable securities accompanying transfers will apply.

Discharge of outstanding heritable security

5.30 As part of a transaction which induces first registration, an existing standard security (*i.e.* one recorded in the Sasine Register) may have to be discharged. Strictly speaking, the discharge should be recorded in the Sasine Register and also listed on the Form 4 accompanying the application for first registration.

However, there is no need to present the discharge for recording in the Sasine Register (and consequently to endorse a warrant of registration on it). On completing first registration the Keeper will give effect to the discharge, provided it is submitted with the application for first registration and is included in the Form 4 inventory accompanying that application. Similarly, if the interest secured is already registered, on a subsequent sale, a separate application for registration of an accompanying discharge need not be lodged, provided the discharge is submitted along with the application for registration of the purchaser's interest and is listed on the Form 4.

The foregoing practice applies equally to a deed of disburdenment, a discharge of an *ex facie* absolute disposition or a reconveyance which relates only to the subjects about to be registered. If, however, the security being discharged includes subjects additional to those for which the application is being made, further action is required. If the additional subjects are registered, application for registration of the discharge is necessary in order to give effect to the discharge in the title sheet(s) of those additional subjects. If the additional subjects are held on a Sasine title, the discharge will have to be recorded in the Sasine Register as well. Another example of the latter situation is a partial discharge and deed of restriction.

Links in title

5.31 An application for registration must, in terms of section 4(1), be accompanied by all relevant unrecorded supporting documents such as links in title. Where the interest in land is already registered in the Land Register it is only necessary to submit mid-couples or links between the uninfeft proprietor of that interest and the registered proprietor. Conversely, an application for first registration should be accompanied by all relevant links in title within the progress of title. Links in title should be produced to the Keeper whether or not there is a clause of deduction of title in the deed or a subsequent notice of title. Sections 3(6) and 15(3) make notices of title and clauses of deduction of title unnecessary in relation to a registered interest, provided sufficient links in title are produced to the Keeper. Although those sections do not apply to a transaction leading to an application for first registration, the Keeper will not insist on a clause of deduction of title or notice of title provided (1) satisfactory links between the uninfeft proprietor and the person last infeft are submitted and (2) the uninfeft proprietor is granting neither a feu writ nor long lease.

If satisfactory links in title are not produced to the Keeper the ingiving agent will be given the opportunity to obtain these and submit them for examination. It should be noted however, that if the Keeper requisitions such links and they are not forthcoming, the application will either be rejected in terms of section 4(1) or proceed to registration but with indemnity being excluded in respect of the absence of the relevant link(s) in title. Where a midcouple is likely to be relevant to other applications (for instance, a certificate of incorporation on change of name relating to a development company or the deeds and documents transferring the undertaking of a former building society on conversion to plc status), the Keeper will enter details of the link in title into the record of common links which he maintains. The common links index is simply a catalogue of those links in title common to more than one title. Its purpose is to aid the registration process by removing the need to submit common links in title on every occasion. It must be stressed that unless it is certain that a link in title has previously been examined by the Keeper, such documentation should always be submitted in support of the application to which it relates.

The remainder of this section looks at a number of common transactions involving the grant of deeds by uninfeft proprietors and highlights the evidence which should be submitted to the Keeper in support thereof.

Executry conveyancing

Conveyance by executor(s)
5.32 Where a person vest in heritable property has died and the property is subsequently being conveyed, the Keeper will require to examine either the confirmation appointing the executor or a certificate of such confirmation which includes a description of the property.

In testate succession, as an alternative to the confirmation or certificate of confirmation, the Keeper may accept the will itself if it contains a general conveyance to the executor(s). If the will is to constitute the link in title it should be accompanied by the death certificate of the testator. In addition, the Keeper may seek assurance that the will so founded on constitutes the last will and testament of the deceased and had not been subsequently revoked.

In terms of section 17 of the Succession (Scotland) Act 1964[9] the title of a person who has acquired in good faith and for value from an executor or from a person deriving title from an executor, for example a beneficiary, is not open to challenge. Section 12(3)(j)(i) of the 1979 Act extends similar protection to the Keeper; no indemnity will be payable to a beneficiary who suffers loss in respect of any title granted by an executor, the validity of which is unchallengeable by virtue of section 17 of the 1964 Act. Accordingly, where subjects have been conveyed for value and the application form does not, in answer to any of the questions in Part B, give any indication of bad faith, the Keeper will not require assurance, such as sight of the will, that the executor has conveyed to the person so entitled. The converse applies where a gratuitous transfer has been made by an executor and has not been followed by a transfer for value. In those circumstances the Keeper will require assurance that the executor has conveyed to the person entitled. In testate succession, a copy of the deceased's final will should be lodged with the application. Where the deceased died intestate the Keeper will require proof of the identity of the heir; for example a family tree sworn to by the executor.

Conveyance by beneficiary or person entitled to succeed
5.33 A beneficiary or person entitled to succeed to the heritable property of the deceased can dispose of the property by using the confirmation (or certificate of confirmation) with a docket endorsed as a link in title. The docket acts as the conveyance of the property to the beneficiary or person entitled to succeed. In any such transaction the Keeper will require to examine both the confirmation (or certificate of confirmation) and the docket.

The method in use prior to the 1964 Act by which a legatee could convey the deceased's property using the will as the link in title was never expressly ruled incompetent by the 1964 Act. A reference to the then four Professors of Conveyancing in 1966 failed to resolve the question of whether or not it was still competent to deduce title through a will. Two formed the view that it was incompetent to use the will whilst two opined that it was still competent but recommended that confirmation be used instead.

In light of this uncertainty, the Keeper will not insist that confirmation be used in every case. However, in the absence of confirmation, the Keeper requires to be satisfied that there is no risk of challenge to the title before he will proceed on the will and issue a title with no exclusion of indemnity in that respect. The evidence required will depend on the individual circumstances of the transaction, but in every case the will itself and the death certificate of the deceased must be

[9] c.41

submitted along with an assurance that the will is the last will and testament of the deceased. In addition, the terms of the will must clearly and unambiguously support the legatee's claimed entitlement. For example, a will which bequeaths the deceased's house to the eldest daughter would not, without further evidence of the identity of the eldest daughter, be acceptable to the Keeper.

Trusts and trustees

Conveyance by trustee(s)
5.34 Section 12(3)(j) provides that there shall be no entitlement to indemnity in respect of loss suffered by (a) a beneficiary under a trust in respect of any transaction purported to be connected with the trust estate and entered into by its trustees or any title granted by them in purported implement of the trust or (b) a person in respect of any interest transferred to him by trustees in purported implement of trust purposes. Accordingly, the Keeper need not check that the trustees have acted in accordance with the trust. The Keeper will, however, wish to examine the original trust deed to ensure it was properly executed and that it conveyed the property to the trustees. In addition, if the current trustees are different from those named in the trust deed, the Keeper will wish to examine the links, for example deeds of assumption, minutes of resignation *etc.*, between the old and the new trustees.

Conveyance by ex officio trustees
5.35 Clubs and similar organisations often take title in the name of designated office-bearers as trustees for the club, for example, disposition by A to B as chairman, C as secretary and D as treasurer and their successors in office as trustees for X Club, *etc.* Unless the club or organisation has changed its constitution since it acquired title, the Keeper would expect any conveyance by the club or organisation to be granted by the present holders of those offices as trustees. Where the present office-bearers differ from those named in the original title, the Keeper will require to examine evidence (for example, minutes of meetings, *etc.*) of the appointment or election of the present office-bearers. If the club has changed its constitution to allow holders of other offices to act as trustees, the Keeper will require evidence of the change of constitution in addition to evidence of election of the present office-bearers.

Company transactions

Conveyance by company in receivership
5.36 Where a deed has been granted by a receiver there must be submitted in support of the application for registration not only the instrument of

appointment of the receiver but also the floating charge itself. The Keeper requires to examine the floating charge in order to determine that it has been validly constituted and is sufficient in its terms to create a fixed charge over the property in question on crystallisation.

Where a receiver has applied to the court under section 61(1) of the Insolvency Act 1986 for authority to sell subjects free of a particular security, or diligence, a copy of the court's authorisation must be submitted to the Keeper before the relevant security or diligence can be omitted from the title sheet.

Sharp v Thomson: Keeper's response
5.37 The House of Lords decision in the case of Sharp v Thomson[10] prompted the Keeper to review his attitude to applications for registration involving sales by receivers. The Keeper recognises that a purchaser of heritage from a receiver may be at risk of having his or her title defeated by a person holding on a previously delivered but unregistered conveyance. The Keeper also recognises that the risk may pass to him if he proceeds to register the purchaser's title without exclusion of indemnity.

The Keeper considers that the risk of a latent unregistered disposition surfacing once registration has been completed is too small to justify a policy of blanket indemnity exclusion for all sales by receivers. Accordingly, an application for registration of a conveyance by a receiver will not result in an exclusion of indemnity solely because of the risk that an unregistered disposition may come to light. Nevertheless the Keeper expects that a purchaser acting in good faith will make appropriate enquiries of the receiver. If the receiver's response to those enquiries is less than satisfactory, or point to some difficulty or anomaly, the purchaser should seek the advice of the Keeper's Pre-Registration Enquiries Section (see chapter 3) before proceeding to settle the transaction. Pre-Registration Enquiries will take a measured view of the circumstances and consider the risk to the Keeper's indemnity.

The above comments apply equally to applications for registration that involve sales by liquidators or trustees in sequestration. They also apply to any application for first registration where a conveyance by a receiver, a liquidator, or a trustee in sequestration is included in the progress of titles.

Conveyance by company in liquidation
5.38 Where subjects are being conveyed by a company in liquidation the Keeper will require to examine evidence of the appointment of the liquidator. Where a

[10] 1997 SCLR 328

company is in voluntary liquidation the resolution, passed by the company, to wind-up the company, will comprise the appropriate link in title. In cases of compulsory winding-up the court order should be submitted.

Change of company name
5.39 Where a company transacting with property has changed its name since the original acquisition, the Keeper will require to examine a certified copy certificate of incorporation on change of name.

Bankruptcy

Conveyance by trustee in sequestration
5.40 Although a heritable proprietor who has been sequestrated remains infeft in the property, the trustee in sequestration becomes personally vest in the property as the debtor/bankrupt's successor, by virtue of the act and warrant issued by the court confirming the trustee's appointment or election. The Keeper will, therefore, require to examine the act and warrant should the trustee either complete title to or sell the bankrupt's heritable estate.

Realisation of bankrupt's estate
5.41 Section 39 of the Bankruptcy (Scotland) Act 1985[11] (as amended) provides for the realisation of the bankrupt's estate, including the sale by the trustee in the sequestration of the bankrupt's heritable estate. The section provides that the trustee should comply with certain rules and procedures. However, section 39(7) of the 1985 Act provides that the validity of the title of any purchaser shall not be challengeable on the grounds that there has been a failure to comply with a requirement of section 39. Accordingly, in a sale governed by section 39, the Keeper will not seek any specific assurance that the trustee has acted in accordance with the provisions of that section.

Disposal of bankrupt's family home
5.42 It is unlikely to be apparent to the Keeper whether the trustee in sequestration is selling the bankrupt's 'family home' (as defined in section 40(4) of the 1985 Act) or some other heritable property covered by the terms of section 39(7) of said Act. Therefore, in an application for registration where a trustee in sequestration is selling or disposing of a dwellinghouse belonging to the bankrupt the Keeper will require evidence that the terms of section 40 have been complied with. The Keeper will accept the following:

---

[11] c.66

- the consent of the bankrupt's spouse or former spouse, as appropriate, in terms of section 40(1)(a) of the 1985 Act; or

- the consent of the bankrupt, as appropriate, in terms of the aforementioned section 40(1)(a); or

- an order of the court granting the trustee in sequestration authority to dispose of the bankrupt's family home; or

- written confirmation that the subjects of sale are not the bankrupt's family home.

The Keeper will not require evidence in terms of the Matrimonial Homes (Family Protection) (Scotland) Act 1981[12] (as amended) in connection with a sale by a trustee in sequestration. Such a transaction is not a voluntary dealing by the entitled spouse.

Expiry of sequestration

5.43 Section 54(1) of the 1985 Act provides for the automatic discharge of the debtor/bankrupt on the expiry of 3 years from the date of sequestration. Section 14 (4) of the aforementioned Act does however permit the trustee to renew the sequestration and provision is made for recording the memorandum of renewal in the Register of Inhibitions and Adjudications before the expiry of the initial 3 year period. In the absence of such a renewal attention is drawn to the terms of section 44(4)(c) of the Conveyancing (Scotland) Act 1924.

Transactions by bankrupts: acquisitions prior to discharge

5.44 Where an application for registration of property acquired by the bankrupt after the date of sequestration and prior to the date of discharge is made on behalf of the bankrupt, the Keeper requires written confirmation from the submitting agent that the bankrupt has informed the trustee in sequestration of the acquisition and that the trustee is content for title to be taken in the name of the bankrupt. In terms of section 15(8) of the 1985 Act, the bankrupt has a duty to inform the trustee in sequestration of the acquisition, and in terms of section 15(9) may be guilty of a criminal offence if this is not done.

If such confirmation from the submitting agent is forthcoming the Keeper will proceed with the application. However, the limitations which sequestration place

---

[12]c.59

upon the bankrupt's ability to transact with the property will be reflected in the proprietorship section of the title sheet by the insertion of a note in terms similar to the following:

'In terms of section 32(6) of the Bankruptcy (Scotland) Act 1985, the interest of said X in the subjects in this Title is vested in the trustee in sequestration on the estate of said X. The title of the said X is subject to the following entry in the Register of Inhibitions: (details of CCI)'

Gratuitous alienations and unfair preferences
5.45 The Keeper will not exclude indemnity from a title on the grounds that a deed could at some later stage be challenged as a gratuitous alienation or unfair preference unless he is alerted in the application for registration to the insolvency or possible insolvency of the party granting the deed. Should a deed be challenged as a gratuitous alienation or unfair preference, protection is afforded to the Keeper under section 12(3)(b).

Transactions involving a company

5.46 For the purposes of paragraphs 5.46 to 5.50, a company is one that is registered under the Companies Acts. (The definition includes an overseas company re-registered under Part XXIII of the Companies Act 1985[13].) Where a company is a party to a deed creating or dealing with an interest in land and application is made to register that interest, the Keeper requires certification of certain matters concerning the company. The certification allows the Keeper to decide if the application is acceptable and the interest can be registered without exclusion of indemnity. The applicant must answer the following questions in the application forms: questions 6 and 7 on Form 1, questions 2 and 3 on Form 2 and questions 4 and 5 on Form 3, *viz*;

Where any party to the deed inducing registration* is a Company registered under the Companies Acts

Has a receiver or liquidator been appointed?　　　　　　　　　**YES/NO**

If **YES**, *please give details:*

If NO, has any resolution been passed or court order made for the winding up of the Company or petition presented for its liquidation?　　　　　　　　　**YES/NO**

If **YES**, *please give details:*

[13]c.6

Where any party to the deed inducing registration* is a Company registered under the Companies Acts can you confirm

(a) that it is not a charity as defined in section 112 of the Companies Act 1989 and   **YES/NO**

(b) that the transaction to which the deed gives effect is not one to which section 322A of the Companies Act 1985 (as inserted by section 109 of the Companies Act 1989) applies?   **YES/NO**

*Where the answer to either branch of the question is **NO**, please give details:*

* Note 1: the phrase 'deed inducing registration' in Form 1 is replaced by the word 'dealing' in Forms 2 and 3.

Note 2: The Keeper shares the view of most commentators that sections 35 and 35A of the Companies Act 1985 have effectively abolished the ultra vires doctrine in its external aspect. The only exceptions are where the company is a charity or where the transaction is one to which directors or their associates are parties (section 322A applies in the latter case). Question 7 is designed to elicit the information that either of the exclusions applies.

If the Applicant can answer NO to both branches of question 6 and YES to both branches of question 7 then, assuming the remainder of the application is found to be in order, the interest will be registered without exclusion of indemnity.

Unfortunately, there is often a delay between the date of certification (that is, the date when the applicant signs the application for registration) and the date when the Keeper receives the application. It is the Keeper's usual practice, which he reserves the right to alter, to ignore a delay that does not exceed 10 days. However, if the delay exceeds 10 days, the Keeper will normally insist that the applicant should renew the certification.

Occasionally, an applicant will give other answers to the relevant questions than those indicated above. It does not necessarily follow that the Keeper will reject the application. His staff will consider the answers carefully and may ask the applicant to reply to further questions or provide further evidence. Depending on the outcome of this interchange, the Keeper may be able to complete registration under exclusion of indemnity.

The Keeper's sole source of knowledge of a receivership or liquidation is the information given in answer to the questions shown above. So, at other times, *e.g.* when issuing an office copy [or a report] or updating a land or charge certificate, the Keeper will not know about any subsequent appointment of a receiver or liquidator, or the commencement of a winding up. Obviously, the Keeper cannot disclose such details if he does not have them. While the Keeper has a statutory duty under section 6(1)(c) to draw attention to sequestrations, he has no such duty as regards receiverships, *etc.*, except where they come to his attention in an application for registration.

Standard securities by companies

5.47 The effect of section 410 of the Companies Act 1985 is twofold:

- Confirmation of the date of registration in the Land Register of a standard security by a company is essential to ensure that the statutory provisions in relation to registration in the Register of Charges are complied with.

- This requirement to register in the Register of Charges impacts on the Keeper's indemnity.

Confirmation of date of registration
5.48 Where the standard security relates to an existing registered interest, the Keeper should be able to confirm the date of registration on the working day following receipt of the application. Where the standard security accompanies an application for first registration, the Keeper should normally be able to confirm the date of registration within a few days. However, if application forms are completed incorrectly or insufficient information is supplied in support of the application, delay is inevitable.

The applicant should **not** request confirmation in a separate letter. Instead, at the top of the first page of the application form (Form 2), the applicant should write or type, in red block capitals, the words 'CONFIRMATION OF REGISTRATION IS REQUIRED'. Where the loan transaction accompanies the application to register the debtor's interest in the property, the application form relative to the registration of the debtor's interest should be similarly marked.

Where any item, *e.g.* a link in title, is missing, the Keeper should be able to confirm the date of registration. However, he will exclude indemnity unless the link is produced before the registration process is completed. If there is doubt as to the extent and location of any part of the subjects in respect of which the company or the lender is seeking registration, again the Keeper will exclude indemnity unless satisfactory evidence is produced. In these cases, despite the fact that the Keeper has confirmed the date of registration, completion of the registration process will be delayed for a reasonable period under rule 12 so that matters potentially attracting exclusion of indemnity may be resolved.

Some time may elapse before a solicitor can provide sufficient evidence to persuade the Keeper to issue a guaranteed title. Such delay does not, however, jeopardise the confirmed date of registration. By section 4(3), this remains the date on which the Keeper receives the application for registration. Even if the company is put into liquidation before matters are resolved, the company's real right and the lender's real right in security date from the date of registration, except where an application is withdrawn before registration is completed.

Flaws such as failure to execute the deed inducing registration or to sign the application forms are fatal. These will be noticed when the application is received and no entry will be made in the Application Record. Faulty documents will be returned to the applicant for correction. Registration will date from the date of re-presentment.

Exclusion of indemnity
5.49 At the time of registration of the standard security in the Land Register, particulars will not yet have been registered in the Register of Charges in accordance with section 410 of the Companies Act 1985. The applicant should of course attend to registration in the Register of Charges within the requisite 21-day period, as soon as he receives the Keeper's confirmation of the date of registration in the Land Register. The Registrar of Companies will duly issue a certificate of registration of charge. Unless the certificate of registration of charge is exhibited to the Keeper within 30 days of receipt of the application, the charge certificate issued by the Keeper will be endorsed with an exclusion of indemnity in the following terms:

> *'Indemnity is excluded in terms of section 12(2) of the Land Registration (Scotland) Act 1979 in respect of any loss which may result from failure to register the above Standard Security in accordance with section 410 of the Companies Act 1985.'*

If where indemnity has been excluded it subsequently transpires that the standard security has been registered in the Register of Charges timeously, the Keeper will accept a request to delete the exclusion of indemnity. The request should be made on a Form 5 (Application for Noting on the Register), accompanied by the certificate of registration of charge, the land certificate, the charge certificate and a Form 4 Inventory in duplicate.

Major ownership schemes

5.50 For the removal of doubt, it has been confirmed by the Registrar of Companies that standard securities granted by company nominees over retained *pro indiviso* shares under major ownership or shared equity schemes are regarded as securities by the development companies themselves. The provisions of section 410 of the Companies Act 1985 as to timeous registration in the Register of Charges and the Keeper's requirements outlined in the foregoing paragraphs therefore apply.

Transactions by corporate bodies other than companies

5.51 Where any party to a deed which creates or deals with an interest in land is a corporate body (other than a company registered under the Companies Acts), the Keeper requires certification as regards the following questions which appear as questions 8(a) and (b) on Form 1, questions 4(a) and (b) on Form 2 and questions 6 (a) and (b) on Form 3:

> *Where any party to the deed inducing registration* is a corporate body other than a Company registered under the Companies Acts*
>
> *(a) Is it acting intra vires?* **YES/NO**
>
> > *If **NO** please give details:*
>
> *(b) Has any arrangement been put in hand for the dissolution of any such corporate body?* **YES/NO**
>
> > *If **YES** please give details:*

* Note: the phrase 'deed inducing registration' in Form 1 is replaced by the word 'dealing' in Forms 2 and 3.

If the applicant can answer YES to part (a) and NO to part (b), then, if the application is otherwise in order, the Keeper will register the interest without exclusion of indemnity, subject to the previous comments about the need for possible re-certification.

Pro indiviso proprietors

5.52 In all cases involving *pro indiviso* proprietors it is the Keeper's practice to open only one title sheet, in terms of rule 8, for the property in which the *pro indiviso* interests subsist. For the Keeper to open separate title sheets for each *pro indiviso* interest would result in tremendous duplication and unnecessary effort.

- Where the *pro indiviso* proprietors hold on one title, only one land certificate will be issued unless each *pro indiviso* proprietor requests otherwise. For example, a disposition by A to B and C will, unless B and C request otherwise, result in the issue of only one land certificate.

- On a subsequent transfer of one of the *pro indiviso* shares a separate land certificate will be issued to the transferee. For example, on the transfer of B's *pro indiviso* share to D, D would receive a separate land certificate.

- Where the *pro indiviso* proprietors hold on separate titles, separate land certificates will be issued to each proprietor, unless there is evidence that the contrary should be the case. For example if C sold to E, and D sold to F, separate land certificates would be issued to E and F. However, if E and F were spouses only one land certificate will be issued, unless E and F request otherwise.

No matter how many land certificates are issued for each *pro indiviso* share, each will be a complete copy of the title sheet.

When a separate land certificate is held for a *pro indiviso* share, any application for a Form 12 report must contain a note of the last date to which the land certificate has been brought down. This date can be found in the inside front cover of the land certificate.

When a *pro indiviso* share is held as an adjunct to other property, for example, a share in a backgreen, no title sheet will be opened for the *pro indiviso* share. It will be registered simply as a pertinent in the title sheet of the main subject.

At a meeting of the Joint Consultative Committee of the Law Society and Registers of Scotland in November 1997, it was agreed the Keeper should continue with his policy of discouraging solicitors from submitting, for recording or registration, feu deeds of *pro indiviso* shares. The Committee noted that doubts exist as to the competency of feuing *pro indiviso* shares, as they are, by their nature, indivisible from the other parts of the same property; but acknowledged there was an absence of clear authority in point. Accordingly, until such time as the matter has been judicially decided the Committee agreed the Keeper could not refuse to accept such deeds.

Long leases

What is a long lease?

5.53 A long lease is defined in section 28(1). The requirements are that:

- it must be executed in accordance with the provisions of section 3 of the Requirements of Writing (Scotland) Act 1995[14]; and

- its term must exceed 20 years or be capable of being renewed, without any subsequent express or implied agreement, so that its total duration exceeds 20 years.

In addition to the above, for a lease to be registrable a rental must be stipulated.

Acquiring a real right

5.54 The law relating to the completion of a real right in a long lease by the lessee depends on the location of the subjects. If the lease relates to subjects lying outwith an operational area it is still possible to acquire a real right by possession or recording in the Sasine Register. Once an area has become operational, however, section 3(3) stipulates that a real right in a lessee's interest in a long lease can only be obtained by registration of that interest in the Land Register. The same law applies to udal tenure and kindly tenancies.

Section 3(3) does not affect the standing of a lessee who has acquired a real right by possession or recording in the Sasine Register prior to the commencement date for an area becoming operational. If, for instance, a lessee under a long lease recorded in the Sasine Register grants a standard security over the leasehold subjects after the area has become operational, the standard security will fall to be recorded in the Register of Sasines in order to complete the creditor's real right (section 8(2)(c)). Similarly, if at the commencement date a tenant has a real right by possession and subsequently wishes to grant a standard security, both the lease and the standard security may be recorded in the Sasine Register. What section 3(3) does mean, is that an incoming lessee, whether by assignation for value, gift, or succession, can obtain a real right only by registration in the Land Register. This would apply, even where the assignation had been completed before the commencement date, if the assignee had not entered into possession or obtained infeftment before that date. Once a lessee's interest has been registered, all subsequent dealings with that interest require to be registered in the Land Register.

[14]c.7

The interest of a lessee under a long lease, who has acquired a real right by possession, is also included in the definition of an overriding interest (section 28(1)), and, until that interest falls to be registered by virtue of section 2, it may be noted on the landlord's title sheet under section 6(4).

Termination of a long lease

Expiry of original term
5.55 When a long lease comes to the end of its duration the Keeper, upon receiving notice of such, will cancel the title sheet relating to the lessee's interest and will, under rule 17, call in the land certificate for cancellation. The Keeper will also delete the lease from the schedule of leases on the landlord's title sheet. Although there is no requirement placed on the landlord to advise the Keeper at the time of the termination of a long lease it is recommended that, as a matter of practice, the landlord should do so. Unless the Keeper receives such notice no action will be taken in respect of the lease, as the possibility remains that the lease may have continued by tacit relocation.

Notice that a long lease has terminated by efflux of time should be accompanied by an application Form 2. Evidence that the lease has terminated and not been continued by tacit relocation should also be submitted; for example, a copy of the notice to quit sent to the tenant.

Renunciation/irritancy of long lease
A long lease may also come to an end during its term, either by renunciation or on operation of irritancy provisions. The registration procedure to be followed in these circumstances is discussed in paragraph 5.66 under the title absorption of interests. Details of the evidence which requires to be submitted can be found in the following paragraphs.

Where a lease has come to an end by reason of an irritancy provision the extract decree of declarator of irritancy should be submitted to the Keeper in support of a Form 2 application. In addition, unless the tenant is willing to remove from the premises voluntarily, a court decree of extraordinary removing should be submitted. In the absence of such a decree evidence that the tenant has voluntarily vacated the premises must be submitted before the tenant's interest will be removed from the register. The Keeper will also have to be satisfied that any provisions in the actual lease governing irritancy have been met. For instance, it is not unusual to see clauses stipulating that notice of irritancy be given to heritable creditors.

Where a tenant voluntarily renounces the lease with the agreement of the landlord, evidence of such renunciation should be submitted in support of a Form 2 application. Evidence will generally consist of a formal deed of renunciation. Discharges of outstanding heritable securities should also be submitted.

Tenant unilaterally renounces lease

It is not uncommon, especially where businesses fail, for a tenant to simply walk out of the lease, and in practice, the subjects. In such circumstances the correct procedure is for the landlord to seek to irritate the lease. Accordingly, the above comments on irritancy apply.

Confusio

Where the landlord acquires the interest of the tenant or *vice versa* there is a presumption that *confusio* operates to extinguish the lease, unless the proprietor acts in such a way as to rebut that presumption. Application can be made to the Keeper to give effect to the *confusio*. The registration procedure is discussed in paragraph 5.66 under the heading absorption of interests.

Extension of a long lease

5.56 If on expiry of the original term, the lease is renewed for a further period in excess of 20 years, the minute of extension or renewal is registrable in terms of section 2(4)(c). Application should be made on Form 2 to ensure the lessee's continuing real right.

Description of leasehold subjects

First registration

5.57 Where a first registration is induced by the grant of a long lease or by the transfer of the tenant's interest in such a lease the subjects let should be described in accordance with existing practice. In addition, however, the Keeper must be able to identify the subjects on the ordnance map.

Lease of the whole registered interest

Neither the Act nor the rules prescribe a form of long lease over a registered interest. However, rule 25 and schedule B (description of a registered interest in land) apply to such a lease.

In the grant of a long lease over an interest in land already registered the subjects let should be described as follows:

'All and Whole the subjects (insert postal address if appropriate) registered under Title Number(s) (   ).'

Lease of part of registered interest
Where the lease relates to part of a registered interest, the part let should be described in sufficient detail (preferably by reference to a plan) to enable the Keeper to identify the part on the ordnance map. The guidelines set out in paragraph 4.20 apply and if, therefore, the part affected is not already separately described in the title sheet it should be described in accordance with these guidelines. Thus, the subjects let should be described as:

'being part of the subjects registered under Title Number(s) (   )'.

Alternatively the part affected may be described as follows:

'All and Whole the subjects (insert postal address if appropriate) registered under Title Number(s) (   ) with the exception of (   ).'

The excepted part should be described in accordance with the guidelines laid down in paragraph 4-20.

If the part affected is separately described in the title sheet of the whole interest, then a further detailed description is not required and the part may be described using either of the following methods:

'All and Whole the subjects (insert postal address if appropriate) (First) registered under Title Number (   ).'

'All and Whole the subjects (insert postal address if appropriate) marked (   ) on the plan of Title Number (   ).'

Where individual rights are to be granted these must be clearly described. Equally, where the benefit of existing rights is not to pass to the tenant these should, where necessary, be specifically excluded.

Dealing with a lease being a registered interest
Once the tenant's interest has been registered in the Land Register that interest should be described in any assignation, renunciation or standard security simply by reference to the title number under which the lease is registered:

'All and Whole the subjects (insert postal address if appropriate) registered under Title Number(s) (   ).'

Dealing with part of a lease being a registered interest
In the case of a dealing which relates to part only of the tenant's interest, the part should be described in a similar fashion to a lease of part of a registered interest.

Landlord uninfeft

5.58 While section 3(6) dispenses with the need for an uninfeft proprietor of a registered interest to expede a notice of title, the Keeper will not be able to register the interest of a tenant under a lease granted by an uninfeft proprietor without exclusion of indemnity. The landlord should procure himself infeft before the lease is submitted.

Short term leases

5.59 A short term lease is not defined in the Act but is a lease which is not a long lease as defined above. The interest of a lessee in a short term lease is, however, included in the definition of an overriding interest (section 28(1)), but, as overriding interests are excluded from the registration provisions in section 2, the interest cannot be registered in the Land Register. Further, by special exclusion in sections 6(4) and 9(4) the noting of short leases in the Land Register is not permitted. Short term leases will not, therefore, be disclosed in the Land Register under any circumstances.

Leases of shootings and fishings

5.60 Following the Opinion of Lord Davidson in Palmer's Trustees v. Brown[15] to the effect that a long lease of shootings qualified as a probative lease of 'lands and heritages in Scotland' within the meaning of section 1 of the Registration of Leases (Scotland) Act 1857[16], and could, therefore, be registered under that Act in order to make it binding upon singular successors of the landlord; the Keeper will accept for registration any lease of shootings which meets the usual statutory requirements for registration.

The same principle applies in the case of a lease of trout fishings. Such leases will, therefore, also be accepted for registration provided they meet the same statutory requirements.

[15] 1988 SCLR 499
[16] c.26

Applications for registration following a compulsory acquisition

5.61 Where the deed inducing registration in the Land Register is a general vesting declaration or a notice of title following on a compulsory purchase order, the applicant should answer question 11 on Form 1, question 7 on Form 2 and question 9 on Form 3.

The applicant should, where possible, certify that all necessary statutory procedures such as the service of the various notices, *etc.* required have been carried out. A **YES** answer relieves the Keeper of any need to make further enquiry or seek an affidavit from the acquiring authority that all statutory procedures have been complied with.

If a **NO** answer is given, the applicant must provide full details so that the Keeper can consider whether a fully indemnified title can be issued.

Tenement properties

5.62 Applications for registration in respect of individual flats within a tenement can give rise to a number of specialties that should always be kept in mind. Some of these are examined in the following paragraphs, along with a few of the more common problems encountered when dealing with applications involving tenement property.

Description of flatted property

5.63 Section 4(2)(a) provides that an application must contain sufficient material to enable the Keeper to identify the subjects on the ordnance map. With non-flatted properties the Keeper will normally expect a plan, and often one is annexed to the foundation deed for the particular property. With tenements or flatted properties the situation is somewhat different. Here the foundation deed for the particular flat may only provide a written description such as 'northmost house on third or top floor entering by the common close numbered 20 High Street, forming part of the tenement 18 to 22 High Street erected on the steading of ground extending to 550 square yards more particularly described in and disponed by and delineated in blue on the plan annexed to ...'. Such a written description, with its reliance on compass directions is, in light of the two Beneficial Bank[17] cases, likely to be acceptable to the Keeper. Other written descriptions may not be. Attention is drawn to paragraph 6.67 where this matter is dealt with in more detail.

[17]Bennett v Beneficial Bank 1995 SLT 1105, Beneficial Bank v McConnachie (IH) 1996 SC 119, 1996 SLT 413.

However, because the title to the flat will invariably carry with it rights in common to parts of the steading on which the tenement is erected or even exclusive rights to garden ground, bin shelters or the like, the Keeper will need to identify the location and extent of the steading. He will therefore require to see the foundation deed for the steading as well. The usual method of describing tenement property in a title sheet is to red-edge the extent of the steading on the title plan and to describe the flat in words in the property section, adding that it lies 'within the land edged red on the title plan'. If there are common or exclusive rights to things such as bin shelters which are capable of identification and delineation on the title plan, this is done. If the description is insufficient to admit of this, these rights are set out in writing in the property section, again with a reference that they lie 'within the land edged red on the title plan'. In some cases of extremely poor descriptions, it may be necessary to exclude indemnity in respect of the location or extent of such pertinents or rights.

Rights and burdens

5.64 The nature of a tenement means that the rights and obligations of the owners of the individual flats can be very much interdependent. In the majority of instances the break-off writs for individual flats in a tenement will narrate what is owned exclusively and what is to be held in common. Similarly, burdens as regards upkeep and the basis on which liability is to be apportioned between individual flats will also be detailed. In some instances such rights and burdens will be contained in a deed of conditions, with the subsequent break-off writ simply making express reference thereto as regards both the rights which are conveyed and the burdens which apply. The Keeper will reflect in the title sheet those rights and burdens contained in or duly referred to in the break-off writ for the flat in question. The Keeper does not, however, examine the titles to the other flats within the tenement to ensure that there is consistency across the board with regard to rights and burdens. It remains the duty of a solicitor acting in the purchase of a flat in a tenement to check the titles for the other flats to ensure ensure consistency in the apportionment of maintenance obligations *etc.*

Where titles to tenement property are silent as regards the ownership and maintenance of some or all of the common parts pertaining thereto, the common law of the tenement will resolve which flat owners have rights in the common parts and maintenance obligations in respect thereof. Notwithstanding the fact that such rights are not explicitly narrated in past titles nor appear in the land certificate, section 3(1)(a) provides for such rights to pass *sub silentio* and vest in the registered proprietor. Such common law rights in tenement property are, by virtue of section 28(1), overriding interests, and as such can affect a tenement in one of three possible ways:

1. No rights and maintenance burdens have been imposed in any of the respective titles of those individual flats comprising the tenement. In such circumstances the common law of the tenement will affect the titles of those flats without the necessity of any reference thereto in the title sheet of each individual flat.

2. Rights and maintenance burdens relating to the tenement have been comprehensively imposed in all of the respective titles of those individual flats comprising the tenement. The rights and obligations will be entered in the title sheet upon registration of each flat and will bind the registered proprietor accordingly.

3. Rights and maintenance burdens relating to the tenement have been imposed in the titles of some flats but not in all. Thus, in reflecting the deeds submitted with the application, some title sheets will contain rights and maintenance burdens affecting the tenement, whereas other title sheets will be silent in this regard. As far as maintenance obligations are concerned, the proprietors of those flats whose title sheets remain silent will be able to rely on the common law of the tenement, regardless of whether this contradicts what has been stated in the title sheets of other flats within the tenement. For instance, if they are not the top floor proprietors then under the common law of the tenement no liability will exist as regards maintenance costs in relation to the roof. The other title sheets may narrate that maintenance costs in relation to the roof have to be split equally between all flats in the tenement. However, the proprietors of those flats will be subject to the right of the other proprietors to apply the common law of the tenement, and may therefore be required to pay more than just the equal tenemental share specified in the title sheet for maintenance of the roof. Nor will the Keeper be liable to indemnify those proprietors, since section 12(3)(h) protects the Keeper against any claim for loss arising in respect of any error or omission in the noting of an overriding interest.

The Keeper's duty is to reflect in the title sheet those rights and burdens which have been explicitly narrated in the titles and supported by positive prescription. He will not attempt to interpret what may be implied by the common law of the tenement.

If deeds are inconsistent between flats or if they are completely silent as regards the rights and maintenance obligations incumbent on individual flat owners it is, of course, open to the proprietors of flats within the tenement to record/register a deed of conditions or minute of agreement defining the common parts and liability for common repairs. Such a deed will be acceptable to the Keeper provided that it is granted by all the proprietors of the various properties within the tenement and contains the consent of their respective heritable creditors, if any. However, the Keeper will not guarantee the enforceability of the provisions of such a deed (see section 12(3)(g)).

Attic conversions - encroachment into roof space

5.65 Where title deeds are silent as to roof space each top floor proprietor has, in terms of the common law of the tenement, a right to the roof and the space between the ceiling and the roof beams in so far as directly above their property. In tandem with such a right to the roof and roof space, top floor proprietors are also responsible for maintaining the portion of the roof above their flat. The Keeper is frequently asked what his position would be in the event the top floor proprietor builds into the roof space. The answer depends on both the nature of the conversion and what is narrated in the deeds subsequent to the attic conversion, as illustrated in the following examples:

- If the property description continues to refer merely to (*e.g.*) 'the northmost house on the third or top floor', *i.e.* with no mention of the attic conversion, then no problem arises as far as the Keeper is concerned. The description in the title sheet will simply reflect the progress of titles and will neither specifically exclude nor specifically include the attic space. It will be for the parties themselves, whom failing the courts, to take a view as to whether the title is habile to include the roof space.

- If the property description makes specific reference to the attic conversion (*e.g.* 'the northmost house on the top and attic floors'), the Keeper will reflect this description in the title sheet. However, subject to the exception noted below, he will exclude his indemnity as regards the reference to the attic floor to the extent that no right therein has been explicitly conveyed by the prescriptive progress of titles. The Keeper's practice is merely to reflect the exact terms of, and not to interpret or improve upon, the titles presented in support of the application for registration. The Keeper takes the view that reflecting the common law of the tenement in the property section of a title sheet, when that law has not been expressly stated in the titles, amounts to interpretation. For instance, the Keeper is not in a position to determine whether the attic conversion has been built solely in the roof space applicable to the flat for which registration is sought. The situation is compounded should dormer windows have been built. By its very nature a dormer window invades the airspace above the actual tenement. That airspace belongs, at common law, to the proprietor(s) of the solum. Even where the title deeds alter the common law position so that airspace is the common property of all proprietors within the tenement, the top floor proprietor will still lack the outright ownership which is required for a permanent encroachment.

- There is, however, one circumstance in which the Keeper will reflect the roofspace conversion in the property section of the title sheet without exclusion of indemnity. That is where the other proprietors within the tenement either consent in the deed with the effect of renouncing any interest they may have in the roof space or otherwise convey their interests to the top floor proprietor. (The consent of affected heritable creditors is, of course, also required). Similarly, if an extension is built on common ground the Keeper will expect to see evidence of the consent of the remaining proprietors within the tenement. Such evidence should take the form of a conveyance, either individually or collectively, by them in favour of the party so encroaching, of their interest in the common ground encroached upon. The consent of their respective heritable creditors, if any, should be included.

Absorption of interests (consolidation)

5.66 Sections 2(1)(a)(iv), 2(4)(a) and (b) and 8(2)(b) provide for the absorption of one interest by another. In this context, absorption means the merging of two fees. Common examples are the consolidation of property with superiority or the termination of a lease otherwise than by expiry of its natural term. The methods of giving effect to the absorption of one interest by another vary, according to whether either or both of the interests are registered or unregistered. During the transitional period, while the Register of Sasines and the Land Register co-exist in an operational area, the lower fee (*i.e.* the *dominium utile* or the tenant's interest) is absorbed into the higher fee (*i.e.* the superior's or landlord's interest), in whichever Register is appropriate for the higher fee.

Absorption is one of the few situations in which there is a departure from the basic concept of section 2, namely, that only a transfer for valuable consideration will induce first registration. If the higher fee is registered in the Land Register and the lower fee is not, absorption requires registration of the lower fee in the Land Register, even if there is no transfer for valuable consideration.

If the higher fee is recorded in the Sasine Register, the deed effecting the merger is recorded in that Register, whether or not there is a transfer for valuable consideration. Even if the lower fee is already registered, the deed effecting the merger is recorded in the Sasine Register and the title sheet for the lower fee is cancelled. This is the only situation in which an interest is removed from the Land Register and returned to the Sasine Register. As well as recording the deed effecting the merger in the Sasine Register, the applicant should submit an application for registration, in terms of section 2(4), to permit the Keeper to give effect to the merger in the Land Register. This is achieved by closure of the title sheet for the lower fee.

Where a transfer merely vests an interest in a person already infeft in a higher or lower fee without effecting a consolidation or merger, the normal rules regarding registration in the Land Register or recording in the Sasine Register will apply. However, if subsequent consolidation is a possibility, consideration should be given to effecting the consolidation as part of the transfer, because in certain circumstances the Keeper will abate the registration fee when the same deed is registered and recorded at the same time.

The following examples offer some illustration of the registration implications of the most common types of absorption.

Disposition with minute of consolidation annexed

1. Higher fee disponed for value. Granter's title in Sasine Register. Title to lower fee in Sasine Register.

Implications for registration in Land Register:

- The transaction induces first registration of the higher fee in terms of section 2(1)(a)(ii). The two fees are consolidated in the Land Register, even though the grantee's title is recorded in the Sasine Register.

Procedure:

- Preferably, two applications for registration should be submitted: one on Form 1 in respect of the disposition and the other on Form 2 in respect of the minute of consolidation. However, as the applicant in both cases is the same, the Keeper is prepared to accept application on Form 1 only, provided there is a clear instruction on the Form 1 that he should give effect to both the disposition and the minute of consolidation.

- The Keeper requires to examine the prescriptive progress of titles and all other relevant deeds and documents relating to each fee. These must be submitted and listed on the Form 4 accompanying the application(s).

2. Higher fee disponed for value. Granter's title in Sasine Register. Title to lower fee in Land Register.

Implications for registration in Land Register:

- The transaction induces first registration of the higher fee in terms of section 2(1)(a)(ii). The two fees are consolidated in the Land Register.

Procedure:

- Preferably, two applications for registration should be submitted: one on Form 1 in respect of the disposition and the other on Form 2 in respect of the minute of consolidation. However, as the applicant in both cases is the same, the Keeper is prepared to accept application on Form 1 only, provided there is a clear instruction on the Form 1 that he should give effect to both the disposition and the minute of consolidation.

- The land certificate for the lower fee must be submitted. No deed is recorded in the Sasine Register.

3. Higher fee disponed but not for value. Granter's title in Sasine Register. Title to lower fee in Sasine Register.

Implications for registration in Land Register:

- The transaction does not induce first registration and the two fees are consolidated by recording the disposition in the Sasine Register.

Procedure:

- The lower fee being in the Sasine Register, no action other than recording the deed in the Sasine Register is necessary.

4. Higher fee disponed but not for value. Granter's title in Sasine Register. Title to lower fee in Land Register.

Implications for registration in Land Register:

- The transaction does not induce first registration and the two fees are consolidated by recording the disposition in the Sasine Register.

- The lower fee being registered in the Land Register, the title sheet is cancelled (see section 8(2)(b)).

- A creditor who has registered a standard security over the lower fee will be prejudiced by the cancellation of the title sheet. The standard security will no longer relate to a registered interest, and the Keeper's indemnity will no longer apply. Attention is drawn to paragraph 6.77.

Procedure:

- An application Form 2, along with the land certificate, should be submitted to enable the Keeper to give effect to the transaction in the Land Register and close the title sheet. It should be noted, either on the application form or on a separate covering letter, that a purpose of the application is to effect consolidation.

- It is essential that the description in the deed complies with Sasine Register requirements, as consolidation will be effected in the Sasine Register.

5. Higher fee disponed, either for value or not for value. Granter's title in Land Register. Title to lower fee in Sasine Register.

Implications for registration in Land Register:

- The consolidation is given effect to in the Land Register. Though the grantee's title is recorded in the Sasine Register, the consolidation effects the transfer of the lower fee to the Land Register.

Procedure:

- Preferably, two Form 2 applications for registration should be submitted: one in respect of the disposition and the other in respect of the minute of consolidation. However, as the applicant in both cases is the same, the Keeper is prepared to accept application on a single Form 2 only, provided there is a clear instruction on the Form 2 that he should give effect to both the disposition and the minute of consolidation.

- The Keeper requires to examine the prescriptive progress of titles and all other relevant deeds and documents relating to each fee. These must be submitted and listed on the Form 4 accompanying the applications.

6. **Higher fee disponed, either for value or not for value. Granter's title in Land Register. Title to lower fee in Land Register.**

Implications for registration in Land Register:

- The consolidation is given effect to in the Land Register only.

Procedure:

- Preferably, two Form 2 applications for registration should be submitted: one in respect of the disposition and the other in respect of the minute of consolidation. However, as the applicant in both cases is the same, the Keeper is prepared to accept application on a single Form 2 only, provided there is a clear instruction on the Form 2 that he should give effect to both the disposition and the minute of consolidation.

- Both land certificates must be submitted. No deed is recorded in the Sasine Register.

Note: Examples 1 to 6 above equally apply mutatis mutandis to the acquisition by a tenant in a registered or recorded lease of the landlord's interest.

7. **Lower fee disponed either for value or not for value. Granter's title in Sasine Register. Title to higher fee in Sasine Register.**

Implications for registration in Land Register:

- None.

Procedure:

- Consolidation is effected by recording the disposition in the Sasine Register (see section 2(2)).

8. Lower fee disponed, either for value or not for value. Granter's title in Sasine Register. Title to higher fee in Land Register.

Implications for registration in Land Register:

- The transaction induces first registration of the lower fee and consolidation is effected in the Land Register (see section 2(1)(a)(iv)).

Procedure:

- Preferably, two applications for registration should be submitted: one on Form 1 in respect of the disposition and the other on Form 2 in respect of the minute of consolidation. However, as the applicant in both cases is the same, the Keeper is prepared to accept application on Form 1 only, provided there is a clear instruction on the Form 1 that he should give effect to both the disposition and the minute of consolidation.

- The land certificate for the higher fee must be submitted.

- No deed is recorded in the Sasine Register.

9. Lower fee disponed, either for value or not for value. Granter's title in Land Register. Title to higher fee in Land Register.

Implications for registration in Land Register:

- Consolidation is effected in the Land Register (see section 2(4)(a) and (b)).

Procedure:

- Preferably, two Form 2 applications for registration should be submitted: one in respect of the disposition and the other in respect of the minute of consolidation. However, as the applicant in both cases is the same, the Keeper is prepared to accept application on a single Form 2 only, provided there is a clear instruction on the Form 2 that he should give effect to both the disposition and the minute of consolidation.

- Both land certificates must be submitted.

10. **Lower fee disponed, either for value or not for value. Granter's title in Land Register. Title to higher fee in Sasine Register.**

Implications for registration in Land Register:

- Consolidation is effected by recording the disposition in the Sasine Register.

- The title sheet for the lower fee is cancelled (see section 8(2)(b)).

- A creditor who has registered a standard security over the lower fee will be prejudiced by the cancellation of the title sheet. The standard security will no longer relate to a registered interest, and the Keeper's indemnity will no longer apply. Attention is drawn to paragraph 6.77.

Procedure:

- An application Form 2, along with the land certificate, should be submitted to enable the Keeper to give effect to the transaction in the Land Register and close the title sheet. It should be noted, either on the application form or on a separate covering letter, that a purpose of the application is to effect consolidation.

- It is essential that the description in the deed complies with Sasine Register requirements, as consolidation will be effected in the Sasine Register.

Note: Examples 7 to 10 would apply equally to:

- *a disposition with a clause of resignation ad perpetuam remanentiam; and*

- *a renunciation of a lease.*

Separate minutes of consolidation

11. **Titles to higher and lower fees both registered in the Land Register.**

Implications for registration in Land Register:

- Consolidation is effected in the Land Register.

- The title sheet for the lower fee is cancelled.

Procedure:

- Application for registration is made on an application Form 2.

- Both land certificates must be submitted.

12. Titles to higher and lower fees both recorded in the Sasine Register.

Implications for registration in Land Register:

- None.

Procedure:

- Consolidation is effected by recording the memorandum of consolidation in the Sasine Register.

13. Title to higher fee in the Land Register. Title to lower fee in the Sasine Register.

Implications for registration in Land Register:

- Consolidation is effected in the Land Register.

Procedure:

- Application for registration is made on an application Form 2.

- The land certificate for the higher fee must be submitted.

- The Keeper requires to examine the prescriptive progress of titles and all other relevant deeds and documents relating to the lower fee. These must be submitted and listed on the Form 4 accompanying the application.

- No deed is recorded in the Sasine Register.

14. Title to lower fee in the Land Register. Title to higher fee in the Sasine Register.

Implications for registration in Land Register:

- Consolidation is effected by recording the memorandum of consolidation in the Sasine Register.

- The title sheet for the lower fee is cancelled (see section 8(2)(b)).

- A creditor who has registered a standard security over the lower fee will be prejudiced by the cancellation of the title sheet. The standard security will no longer relate to a registered interest, and the Keeper's indemnity will no longer apply. Attention is drawn to paragraph 6.77.

Procedure:

- An application Form 2, along with the land certificate, should be submitted to enable the Keeper to give effect to the transaction in the Land Register and close the title sheet . It should be noted, either on the application form or on a separate covering letter, that a purpose of the application is to effect consolidation.

- It is essential that the description in the deed complies with Sasine Register requirements, as consolidation will be effected in the Sasine Register.

*Note: Examples 11 to 14 above apply equally **mutatis mutandis** to the acquisition by the landlord of the tenant's interest in a registered or recorded Lease.*

Consolidation by prescription

15. Higher fee in Sasine Register. Lower fee in Land Register.

Implications for registration in Land Register:

- Provided the superior's title is habile to cover the property, prescriptive possession can enable consolidation to be effected in the Sasine Register.

Procedure:

- The superior must apply to the Keeper on an application Form 2 for cancellation of the title sheet pertaining to the *dominium utile* interest.

- The application must be supported by sufficient documents and evidence to satisfy the Keeper that he may give effect to the consolidation. The nature of the documents and other evidence will tend to vary depending on the particular circumstances of the application but will include the superior's title and properly sworn affidavits in support of the superior's claims of uninterrupted possession.

16. Higher fee in Land Register. Lower fee in Land or Sasine Register.

Implications for registration in Land Register:

- None. (Where the higher fee is registered in the Land Register, consolidation by prescription will no longer operate. This is as a result of sections 6(1)(b) and 10.)

Explanation:

- In terms of section 6(1)(b), the Keeper must enter in a title sheet the nature of the interest in land (*i.e,* whether it is *dominium directum* or *dominium utile*). The title sheet in respect of a superiority interest will disclose that it relates to the superiority. Such a title cannot be a foundation for consolidation by prescription, as it is restricted to the superiority. Even if the superior acquires right to the *dominium utile* and both titles are registered in the Land Register, prescription will not effect consolidation. The interest covered by each title sheet will be limited to the *dominium directum* and *dominium utile* respectively. Also, prescription in relation to registered interests only operates where indemnity has been excluded. There would be no such exclusion in these title sheets. It therefore follows that consolidation can only be effected by minute of consolidation.

- In terms of section 10, for prescription to operate in relation to an interest registered in the Land Register, possession must be founded on registration of that interest subject to an exclusion of indemnity. If the superior was to prescribe a title to the *dominium utile* by possession, founded on registration of an a *non domino* title to the *dominium utile*, such a title still could not be used as a foundation for consolidation by prescription. As previously mentioned, the title sheet would be restricted to the *dominium utile*.

- When the superior becomes vest in the *dominium utile* by virtue of prescription, the only means through which the two interests can be consolidated is a minute of consolidation. Any application for registration of a minute of consolidation in the Land Register would have to be accompanied by evidence in support of the superior's prescriptive possession of the *dominium utile*.

Overriding interests

5.67 There has always been a number of rights in, or restrictions over, heritable property in Scotland which did not require the recording of a deed in the Sasine Register to make them real rights, or, where real right is not a strictly correct description, to make them run with the lands. The most obvious example is that of a servitude. Although, 'overriding interest' is not a term of art familiar to the Scottish conveyancer, the use of the term in the context of registration of title is not introducing any new concept into Scottish conveyancing; the expression is merely a convenient label for those 'real' rights or restrictions which may affect a given property but which, under present procedures, a search in the Sasine Register may not disclose. Section 3(1), therefore, by providing that the effect of registration in the Land Register is to vest a real right in the registered proprietor *'subject only to ... any overriding interest whether noted under that section* (section 6) *or not'* is doing no more than stating for registered land what is the present position for land held on a Sasine title.

Definition of overriding interest

5.68 The expression 'overriding interest' is defined in section 28(1). It lists fourteen types of overriding interest. Overriding interest means, subject to sections 6(4) and 9(4), *'in relation to any interest in land, the right or interest over it of*

1. *the lessee under a lease which is not a long lease;*

2. *the lessee under a long lease who, prior to the commencement of the Act, has acquired a real right to the subjects of the lease by virtue of possession of them;*

3. *a crofter or cottar within the meaning of section 3 or 28(4) respectively of the Crofters (Scotland) Act 1955[18] or a landholder or statutory small tenant within the meaning of section 2(2) or 32(1) respectively of the Small Landholders (Scotland) Act 1911[19];*

4. *the proprietor of the dominant tenement in a servitude;*

5. *the Crown or any government or other public department, or any public or local authority under any enactment or rule of law, other than an enactment or rule of law authorising or requiring the recording a deed in the Register of Sasines or registration in order to complete the right or interest;*

[18]c.21
[19]c.49

6.   *the operator having a right conferred in accordance with paragraph 2, 3 or 5 of Schedule 2 to the Telecommunications Act 1984[20] (agreements for execution of works, obstruction of access, etc.);*

7.   *a licence holder within the meaning of Part 1 of the Electricity Act 1989[21] having such a wayleave as is mentioned in paragraph 6 of schedule 4 to that Act (wayleaves for electric lines), whether granted under that paragraph or by agreement between the parties;*

8.   *a licence holder within the meaning of Part 1 of the Electricity Act 1989 who is authorised by virtue of paragraph 1 of Schedule 5 to that Act to abstract, divert and use water for a generating station wholly or mainly driven by water;*

9.   *insofar as it is an interest vesting by virtue of section 7(3) of the Coal Industry Act 1994[22], the Coal Authority;*

10. *the holder of a floating charge whether or not the charge has attached to the interest;*

11. *a member of the public in respect of any public right of way or in respect of any right held inalienably by the Crown in trust for the public;*

12. *the non-entitled spouse within the meaning of section 6 of the Matrimonial Homes (Family Protection) (Scotland) Act 1981[23];*

13. *any person, being a right which has been made real, otherwise than by the recording of a deed in the Register of Sasines or by registration; or*

14. *any other person under any rule of law relating to common interest or joint or common property, not being a right or interest constituting a real right, burden or condition entered in the title sheet of the interest in land under section 6(1)(e) of the Act or having effect by virtue of a deed recorded in the Register of Sasines,*

    but does not include any subsisting burden or condition enforceable against the interest in land and entered in its title sheet under section 6(1) of the Act.'

The right of a lessee under a long lease, who has acquired a real right by possession prior to the commencement of registration of title in the area in which the leasehold property is situated is an overriding interest. It is subject to the noting provisions in section 6(4) (see below). Such an interest is also an interest

[20]c.12
[21]c.29
[22]c.21
[23]c.59

in land and is, once the area becomes an operational area, subject to the provisions for registration following a registrable transaction under section 2(1)(a)(v). In those circumstances therefore, where the tenant's interest is assigned, whether or not for value, the assignee will obtain a real right only by registering his or her interest in the Land Register.

The overriding interest described in category 13 above is designed to catch any right not otherwise specifically mentioned as included in the term 'overriding interest'. For example, the registration of title pilot scheme for the Parish of Renfrew revealed a number of areas, title to which still lay with the original charter of erection of the Royal Burgh. Consequently, such areas were still in the ownership of the Burgh whose title was complete though unrecorded, being prior to 1681 when the Burgh Registers of Sasines were constituted. The Burgh therefore, had a prior and overriding interest to any other registered interest relating to those areas and not obtained directly or indirectly from the Burgh.

Common law rights in tenement property are overriding interests unless they have been altered by the agreement of the parties concerned (see 14 above). Three possible scenarios can arise:

- No rights and maintenance burdens have been imposed in any of the respective titles of those individual flats comprising the tenement. In such circumstances the common law of the tenement will affect the titles of those flats without the necessity of any reference thereto in the title sheet of each individual flat.

- Rights and maintenance burdens relating to the tenement have been comprehensively imposed in all of the respective titles of those individual flats comprising the tenement. The rights and obligations will be entered into the title sheet upon registration of each flat and will bind the registered proprietor accordingly.

- Rights and maintenance burdens relating to the tenement have been imposed in the titles of some flats but not in all. In reflecting the deeds submitted with the application, some title sheets will contain rights and maintenance burdens affecting the tenement, whereas other title sheets will be silent in this regard. Those flats whose title sheet remains silent will be able to rely on the common law of the tenement, regardless of whether this contradicts what has been stated in the title sheets of other flats within the tenement. For instance, if they do not comprise a top floor flat then, under the common law of the tenement no liability will exist for maintenance costs in relation to the roof. The other title sheets may narrate that maintenance costs in relation to the roof have to be split equally between all flats in the tenement. However, this is subject to the overriding interest of the other flats to apply the common law of the tenement. The other flats will therefore be free of all maintenance costs concerning the roof whereas those flats whose title sheet is not silent will be required to pay more than just the equal tenemental share specified in the title sheet. Nor will the Keeper be liable to indemnify those proprietors. Section 12(3)(h) protects the Keeper against any claim for loss arising in respect of any error or omission in the noting of an overriding interest.

Noting overriding interests on the Land Register

5.69 Ideally, the Land Register should disclose all rights, burdens and restrictions which run with the lands. However, it was considered that to require registration of all interests which have been included in the definition of overriding interests, in order to make them run with the lands, would be both impractical and seriously disruptive to the introduction of registration of title into any given area. Section 2 of the Act, therefore, provides that overriding interests are not registrable. In addition, section 3(2) stipulates that the provisions regarding the creation of real rights by registration, instead of recording, are without prejudice to any other means of creating real rights.

Although not registrable, section 6(4) provides for noting the existence of overriding interests, subject to two exceptions, on the title sheet. The exceptions are:

- Short term leases. Although leases not within the definition of long leases (see section 28(1)) are overriding interests, they are not, in terms of section 6(4), capable of being noted on the title sheet. Short term leases (*i.e.* those for 20 years or less with no facility for extension) will not appear in the Land Register under any circumstances.

- The interest of a non-entitled spouse under section 6 of the Matrimonial Homes (Family Protection) (Scotland) Act 1981. Although an overriding interest, it is likewise excluded from noting on the title sheet. However, where the property appears likely to fall within the definition of 'matrimonial home', the Keeper will endorse the title sheet with a statement on whether or not he is satisfied that the property is not affected by the occupancy right of the spouse of any previous proprietor within the 5 year prescriptive period under the 1981 Act.

The remaining overriding interests are capable of being noted on a title sheet. Section 6(4) details the circumstances in which an overriding interest can be noted on the register. These are as follows:

- The Keeper must note an overriding interest if it is disclosed in any document accompanying an application for registration of the interest which it affects (section 6(4)(a)). For example, if on registration of a heritable security by a limited company, the security deed, in addition to creating a fixed security, contains a floating charge, the Keeper would have to note the existence of the floating charge. He would do this in the charges section of the title sheet. The Keeper would not, however, have to trace and then note the charge on any other title sheets of that limited company's properties, but, as an overriding interest, the charge would still affect those other properties.

- The Keeper may note an overriding interest if application is made to do so (section 6(4)(b)(i)). For example, if a servitude right is granted over a registered interest it is, so far as that interest is concerned, an overriding interest; and either the benefited or burdened proprietor may, by making application on Form 5, request the Keeper to note the servitude on the title sheet of the property burdened by the overriding interest.

- The Keeper may note an overriding interest if it is disclosed in any application for registration (section 6(4)(b)(ii)). For example, if on the grant of servitude mentioned above, application is made by the proprietor of the dominant tenement, for registration of the servitude as a right benefiting that interest, the Keeper may, on processing that application, note the existence of the servitude right on the title sheet relating to the servient tenement.

- The Keeper may note an overriding interest if it otherwise comes to his notice. For example, if two adjoining proprietors jointly grant a servitude right in favour of a third, and one of those proprietors applies to have the overriding interest noted on the title sheet of his or her property, under section 6(4)(b)(iii) the Keeper may also note the overriding interest on the title sheet of the co-granter.

Noting an overriding interest when it is disclosed in an application for registration or otherwise comes to the Keeper's attention is authorised by section 9(3)(a)(i). This specifically permits rectification of the register against the proprietor in possession where the purpose is to note an overriding interest or to correct any information relating to an overriding interest.

Effect of noting

5.70 As explained above overriding interests require neither the recording of a deed in the Sasine Register nor registration in the Land Register to make them 'real' and so run with the land. It follows, therefore, that the sole purpose of noting an overriding interest in the Land Register is publication of an already existing right, thereby ensuring that the Land Register contains as much relevant information as possible.

Applying for noting

5.71 Neither the Act nor the Rules place any restriction on who may apply for noting. Application for noting may be made by any person whose interest will be served by the noting. Consequently, the noting of an overriding interest may take place without the consent or even the knowledge of the burdened proprietor.

Form 5 is prescribed for use where application is being made for the noting of an overriding interest on the title sheet. In addition, application Forms 1, 2 and 3 make similar provision. If, therefore, the request for noting is made at the same time as an application for registration, either on first registration or of a dealing, a separate Form 5 is not required.

Discharge of, or freedom from overriding interests

5.72 While section 6(4) only makes provision for noting overriding interests, a discharge of an overriding interest may be noted on the Register in terms of section 6(1)(g). This provides that the Keeper shall enter on a title sheet *'such other information as the Keeper thinks fit to enter in the Register'*. Application for noting the discharge of, or freedom from, an overriding interest should be made on Form 5 and must be accompanied by such documents or other evidence as are necessary to support the application.

Rule 7 provides that, where, an overriding interest is discharged by probative deed, the Keeper must, subject to what is stated in the following two paragraphs, enter particulars of that deed in the burdens section of the title sheet if the following pre-requisites are met:

- The discharge relates to an overriding interest which has either been recorded in the Sasine Register or noted on the title sheet.

- The applicant requests that the particulars of the discharge are so noted.

The aforementioned provisions do not apply where the overriding interest is a floating charge. In this case, the discharge or memorandum of satisfaction will be given effect to by simply removing the original entry.

In the case of a servitude, particulars of a probative discharge will be noted, whether or not the original grant was recorded in the Sasine Register or noted on the title sheet and regardless of whether the applicant requests it. This is to cover the case of a servitude, constituted by prescriptive possession but subsequently discharged by probative writ.

Indemnity provisions

5.73 In terms of section 12(3)(h) indemnity is not payable for loss arising in respect of any error or omission in noting an overriding interest. This is so even where the Keeper must note an overriding interest in terms of section 6(4)(a). Indemnity may, however, be payable where the Keeper has omitted to note, or has made an error in noting, the discharge or freedom from an overriding interest in terms of rule 7.

Although no indemnity attaches to the noting of an overriding interest, the Keeper will not note an overriding interest unless satisfied that it has been validly created.

Defects in prior recorded titles

5.74 Registration of title allows the Keeper discretion to ignore minor technical defects in deeds submitted as part of an application for registration. In deciding whether to treat any defect in prior titles as technical in nature the Keeper will take into account the following:

1. Does the defect wholly invalidate the deed?

2. If the deed is not wholly invalidated, is the intention of the deed clear?

3. Should the Keeper choose to ignore the defect, what risk would this pose to his indemnity?

Where the defect wholly invalidates the deed the Keeper will not exercise his discretion and ignore the defect. The applicant would, therefore, have to consider the possible options available. These include:

- Re-recording of the deed under section 143 of the Titles to Land (Consolidation) (Scotland) Act 1868[24].

- Obtaining a corrective deed.

- Application to the court under section 8 and 9 of the Law Reform (Miscellaneous Provisions) (Scotland) Act 1985[25] for rectification of the deed where it fails to accurately express the common intention of the parties.

- Should the applicant choose to take no action, and, notwithstanding the defect, the application for registration is acceptable to the Keeper, indemnity will likely be excluded as regards said defect.

Which of the above options will be appropriate will depend on the particular circumstances relating to each individual defective deed. Where the defect does not wholly invalidate the deed, the Keeper will give due consideration to points 2 and 3 above in determining whether to ignore the defect. As each defective deed will be considered individually, it is inappropriate to provide examples of defects in title which the Keeper may be willing to overlook.

Defects in clause of deduction of title

5.75 Sections 3(6) and 15(3) render notices of title and deductions of title unnecessary in relation to a registered interest, provided sufficient links in title are produced to the Keeper. These sections do not, however, apply to a transaction leading to a first registration. Nevertheless, provided that satisfactory links between the uninfeft proprietor and the person last infeft are submitted along with the application for registration, the Keeper will not insist on a notice of title or a clause of deduction of title being inserted in the conveyance. Similarly, if there is a defective clause of deduction of title in the prescriptive chain, the Keeper will not insist on a corrective deed if satisfactory links in title are submitted with the application for first registration.

Defectively stamped deed

5.76 In terms of section 14 of the Stamp Act 1891[26] a deed cannot be used for any purpose unless it is duly stamped. A deed which has not been duly stamped cannot therefore be accepted by the Keeper in support of an application for registration.

[24]c.101
[25]c.73
[26]c.39

Defects in completion of application forms

5.77 In terms of rule 9 every application for registration of an interest in land must be made on the appropriate application form:

- First registration - Form 1

- Dealing (other than a transfer of part) - Form 2

- Transfer of part - Form 3

If there is no application form, or if the application form has not been signed or duly completed, the application will automatically be rejected by the Keeper. A duly signed and completed application form is vital because it is the Keeper's authority to register the transaction or event in respect of which the application is made. An application for registration must be made by the party in whose favour the real right will be created or who will otherwise benefit from the registration. The application form must be signed by the applicant or the applicant's solicitor.

In completing the application form the applicant is required to make a number of certified statements. It is important that the application form is completed accurately as failure to do so may affect not only the validity of the registration, but also the power of the Keeper or the court to rectify the register, and the Keeper's liability for indemnity. For example, suppose that part of the subjects an applicant seeks to register is, in fact, possessed by another party, but this information is not disclosed to the Keeper in response to the relevant question in the application form. (*'Is there any person in possession or occupation of the subjects or any part of them adversely to the interest of the applicant?'*) The Keeper proceeds to register the subjects without excluding indemnity in respect of said part. A declarator from the courts in favour of the other party would allow that party to seek rectification of the register. Because the registered proprietor would not be a proprietor in possession, the terms of section 9(3) of the Act would allow the Keeper to rectify the register against that proprietor; and, as section 12(3)(n) provides that there is no entitlement to indemnity where the claimant by his fraudulent or careless act has caused the loss, the fraudulent or careless certification would preclude a successful claim on the indemnity.

Completion of registration

Return of documents and issue of certificate

5.78 On completion of registration the Keeper will return to the presenting agent all deeds, documents and other evidence which were submitted in support of the application for registration. The Keeper will also issue a land certificate and, if appropriate, a charge certificate. Only if the presenting agent gives written authority will the documentation be returned to the applicant or another party.

Certificate of title

5.79 Rule 2 defines 'certificate of title' as including 'a land certificate and a charge certificate'. The statutory provisions which relate to certificates of title are to be found in sections 5 and 6 and in rules 14 to 19. The forms of a land certificate (Form 6) and a charge certificate (Form 7) are prescribed by rules 14 and 15 respectively. The Keeper authenticates certificates of title by the Seal of the Land Register.

Land certificate

5.80 The land certificate is a copy of the title sheet and contains all the information entered in the title sheet as at the latest date shown on the certificate. If the interest has already been registered in the Land Register, the Keeper will, in respect of any subsequent application to register a dealing affecting the whole or part of that interest, amend the title sheet to give effect to the application. The land certificate must be produced in any application to transfer the property or to secure the first charge over the property. The charge certificate must be submitted in any application affecting the charge detailed in the charge certificate. In all other cases the circumstances of the dealing will dictate whether or not the certificates of title should be produced. The Keeper's authority to order production of a certificate of title for amendment or cancellation is governed by rules 17 and 18. Where production of a certificate of title is necessary, it will be amended to bring it into line with the amended title sheet.

Where the dealing is a transfer of part the Keeper will open a new title sheet in respect of that part, and amend the existing title sheet to remove the interest being transferred. On completion of registration, the existing land certificate, duly amended, will be re-issued in addition to the land certificate for the part transferred.

The following paragraphs illustrate that the rules on the issue of land certificates are not entirely inflexible.

Combination and division of title sheets

5.81 Rule 8 gives the Keeper power to combine two or more title sheets into one, or, to divide a title sheet into two or more title sheets. The Keeper will, however, always consult the agent for the applicant or the registered proprietor before embarking on either course of action. If the agent raises a strong argument against combining title sheets (or dividing a title sheet, as the case may be), the Keeper will proceed only in exceptional circumstances. For example, if a proprietor acquires additional property, the Keeper may insist on adding it to the proprietor's existing title sheet rather than opening a new title sheet. On the other hand, a title sheet may become so voluminous as to make the resulting land certificate impossibly bulky. In such a case, the Keeper may decide to split the title sheet, and consequently the land certificate, into smaller, more manageable parts. Similarly, if several deeds of conditions are prepared, each relating to a different part of a large area contained in one title sheet, a separate title sheet may be prepared for each part.

Certificate for scheme title

5.82 The Keeper offers a facility which is available to anyone acquiring property piecemeal for redevelopment or other purposes. By arrangement with the Keeper, an applicant may indicate on a plan the extent of an area which the applicant is proposing to acquire by a series of transactions. The Keeper will then register each application for registration of a component part under one title number but he will delay issuing a land certificate until the whole area has been acquired. The land certificate eventually issued will reflect the complete acquisition and include a plan of the whole area and rationalised rights and burdens. If at any time prior to completion, documentary evidence is required from the Keeper as to a part only of the larger area, he will issue an office copy in respect of that part. Indeed, if redevelopment or sale of a part of the area is contemplated, land certificates can be obtained for specified parts.

Deposit of land certificate with Keeper

5.83 The land certificate relating to a developing estate should be deposited with the Keeper. This matter is discussed in detail in paragraph 4.43.

Charge certificate

5.84 Unlike the land certificate the charge certificate does not contain all the information on the title sheet. Instead, the charge certificate contains only details of the heritable security secured over an interest in land and discloses other information relating to that security; for example, any prior or *pari passu* securities affecting the interest. In addition the principal security is attached to the charge certificate.

A charge certificate is issued in respect of any deed entered in the charges section and falling within the definition in section 28(1) of 'heritable security'. This section adopts the definition of heritable security contained in section 9(8)(a) of the Conveyancing and Feudal Reform (Scotland) Act 1970[27], *i.e.*, any security capable of being constituted over any interest in land by a disposition or assignation of that interest in security of a debt. Since November 1970, however, it has only been possible to create a heritable security by means of a standard security. Accordingly, a charge certificate will only be issued in respect of a registered standard security.

A charge certificate is not, however, issued in respect of a deed entered in the charges section in terms of rule 6(1)(b), that is to say a deed which charges the interest with a 'debt' as defined in section 9(8)(c) of the 1970 Act which is not constituted by way of a standard security. Examples include a notice of payment of improvement grant and an absolute order or other statutory charge. In such cases the deed creating the charge will be stamped 'registered' by the Keeper to denote that registration has been given effect to, before it is returned to the applicant.

Note: Debt is defined in section 9(8)(c) of the 1970 Act as '... any obligation due, or which will or may become due, to repay or pay money, including any such obligation arising from a transaction or part of a transaction in the course of any trade, business or profession, and any obligation to pay an annuity or ad factum praestandum, but does not include an obligation to pay any feuduty, ground annual, rent or other periodical sum payable in respect of land, ...'.

If there is an outstanding, recorded heritable security at the time of first registration, that heritable security will be disclosed in the charges section of the title sheet of the security subjects. However, no charge certificate will be issued unless the creditor applies for registration of the security. The effect of registration of the outstanding security is discussed in paragraph 5.29.

---

[27] c.35

Combined charge certificates

5.85 The Keeper's normal practice is to issue a separate charge certificate for each heritable security secured over an interest. Where a heritable security is secured over more than one interest a separate charge certificate will be issued in respect of that heritable security for each interest. If, however, a creditor in several securities over the same interest, or a creditor in a heritable security over several interests, does not want to hold separate charge certificates, the Keeper will, on request, combine these into a single charge certificate.

Office copies

5.86 Although the Land Register is a register of interests in land and not a register of deeds, the Keeper will, in fact, keep on microfiche for each title sheet copies of all previously unrecorded deeds or documents referred to in that title sheet or which have induced entries on the title sheet or caused amendments to be made to existing entries. By section 6(5) the Keeper is required to issue, to any person who applies, a copy, known as an 'office copy', of any title sheet, or part thereof (for example, the charges or burdens section) or of any document referred to therein. The affixation of the Agency's seal, without any signature, constitutes proper authentication of an office copy.

Evidential status

5.87 An office copy enjoys privileged evidential status. Section 6(5) declares that its contents shall be accepted for all purposes as sufficient evidence of the contents of the original. Consequently, an office copy does not require any other form of certification by the Keeper, nor, in any court proceedings, does it require the appearance of a member of the Keeper's staff, to attest to its status. To reinforce this point office copies now include the undernoted certificate:

> *'This office copy has been issued in terms of section 6(5) of the Land Registration (Scotland) Act 1979, which provides that it shall be accepted for all purposes as sufficient evidence of the contents of the original.'*

An office copy, because of its privileged evidential status, is of considerable use with development titles. It can be used to expedite the progress of simultaneous transactions where, if there were only one land certificate available, purchasers would be delayed in their examination of title.

Factors governing issue of office copy

5.88 The practical implications of section 6(5) are that the Keeper can only issue an office copy of a deed or document if that deed or document has been referred to in the title sheet. The Keeper's position is that an office copy of any other deed or document cannot be issued even if that deed or document forms part of an application for registration and has been microfilmed. This view appears to be given credence by the opinion of the Lord President in the case of *Short's Trustee v Keeper of the Registers of Scotland*[28] wherein he states that

> *'there is an important difference ... as to the amount of information to which a person dealing on the faith of the two registers (the Land Register and the Register of Sasines) has access. Provision is made by section 6(5) of the 1979 Act for the issuing by the Keeper to any person applying of a copy of the title sheet or of any document referred to in a title sheet on the Land Register. But there is no provision enabling a party to obtain access to any of the deeds which would have been required to be searched had they been registered in the Sasine Register'*

It follows that the Keeper cannot normally issue an office copy of a deed inducing an entry in, say, the property or proprietorship section of the title sheet, because the entry merely reflects the effect of the deed as distinct from referring to it. Exceptionally, the deed may be specifically referred to in, for example, an exclusion of indemnity, or elsewhere in the title sheet as in the case of a feu disposition referred to for burdens in the burdens section. If that is the case, it can then be copied. It should be noted that when a deed or document that has been the subject of an application for registration but which does not appear on a title sheet is required by in connection with a court action, the Keeper will likely co-operate in releasing the document without the need for a specific commission and diligence of the document.

Office copies may not be issued until registration is completed and the title sheet available. Thus a request for an office copy of a deed or document lodged with a pending application, for example a standard security, will be rejected. Until the application has been completed the deed cannot be described as being referred to in the title sheet.

If the interest under the title sheet has been returned to the Sasine Register consequent upon a disposition *ad remanentiam* or, say, the termination of a lease, an office copy cannot be issued because after de-registration the title sheet no

---

[28]1994 SCLR 135 at page 139 D - F

longer exists. That said, a copy of the information contained in the title sheet immediately prior to de-registration is available.

For the level of fee payable in respect of an office copy see the relevant fee order.

Application for office copy

5.89 In terms of rule 24 application for an office copy should be made on Form 15. To complete Form 15 it is necessary to know the title number of the relevant interest. If this information is not known it can be ascertained by making application on a Form 14 to determine whether or not the interest has been registered.

Office copies and the register of inhibitions and adjudications

5.90 An office copy of the title sheet or of the proprietorship section of the title sheet will disclose any subsisting adverse entries from the Register of Inhibitions and Adjudications. However, it must be stressed that, because of the effect of section 12(3)(k), the indemnity in respect of information from that Register only covers information relating to those persons who appear to the Keeper from the title sheet to have an interest. There may well be parties of whom the Keeper is unaware. Accordingly, instructions for a search in the Register of Inhibitions and Adjudications, against such parties, may be given on Form 15.

Quick copies

Factors governing issue of quick copies

5.91 Whereas an office copy can be provided only where the application has been completed and the title sheet made up, quick copies of deeds can be issued while the application is still in the process of registration. The Keeper will issue quick copies of deeds still in the process of registration upon request by any party, provided only that the deed can be regarded as public, *i.e.* that no question of confidentiality attends it. A deed will be considered public if, upon completion of the application, it is referred to in the title sheet or if it has already appeared in a public register or has been issued by a public authority.

Requests for copies of Sasine recorded deeds which have been submitted with an application can be made to the Keeper.

For the level of fee payable in respect of a quick copy and a certified office copy see the relevant fee order.

Evidential status

5.92 It should be noted that a quick copy does not afford the same privileged evidential status as an office copy. However, if requested, the Keeper will certify on the quick copy deed that it is a true copy of the original.

Chapter 6
1979 Act - Interaction With Substantive Conveyancing Law

6.1 It has been noted that substantive conveyancing law has not altered with the inception of the 1979 Act, but it is true to say that it has been necessary for the Keeper to consider carefully how to give effect to the range of substantive private law issues that have arisen in the context of land registration. The approach the Keeper has taken has been built up and developed since the first County, Renfrew, became operational in 1981. Through consultation with the Joint Consultative Committee of the Keeper and the Law Society of Scotland, and the Society's Conveyancing Committee, the Keeper has been able, through discussion and debate to arrive at a view on the many and novel issues that have arisen over the years affecting registration. The aim has been to agree on an approach to registration that takes into account the underlying legal position on title whilst ensuring that the system is workable in practice. The statutory indemnity provisions are a major consideration in this connection. The sections in this, the largest chapter of the book, examines those areas of the law where the Keeper has taken strategic policy decisions that inform his approach to registration and explain the rationale for policy.

Prescription

6.2 The existence of registered titles containing an exclusion of indemnity, and competing titles, ensures that the role prescriptive possession plays in the Sasine system, continues to be of importance under registration of title. To clarify the application of prescription within the Land Register, section 10 of the Act amended section 1 of the Prescription and Limitation (Scotland) Act 1973[1]. That section now reads:

'1. (1) If in the case of an interest in particular land, being an interest to which this section applies,-

(a) the interest has been possessed by any person, or by any person and his successors, for a continuous period of ten years openly, peaceably and without any judicial interruption, and

(b) the possession was founded on, and followed (i) the recording of a deed which is sufficient in respect of its terms to constitute in favour of that person a title to that interest in the particular land, or in land of a description habile to include the

---

[1] c.52

particular land, or (ii) registration of that interest in favour of that person in the Land Register of Scotland, subject to an exclusion of indemnity under section 12(2) of the Land Registration (Scotland) Act 1979,

then, as from the expiration of the said period, the validity of the title so far as relating to the said interest in the particular land shall be exempt from challenge.

(1A) Subsection (1) above shall not apply where-

(a) possession was founded on the recording of a deed which is invalid ex facie or was forged; or

(b) possession was founded on registration in respect of an interest in land in the Land Register of Scotland proceeding on a forged deed and the person appearing from the Register to be entitled to the interest was aware of the forgery at the time of registration in his favour.'

Section 1(1)(b)(ii) applies only where there is an exclusion of indemnity. In the vast majority of registered titles indemnity will not be excluded. Where the Keeper issues a land certificate to an applicant without excluding indemnity, and the applicant is in possession of the whole subjects, the applicant's title is immediately valid and unchallengeable (unless one of the circumstances specified in section 9(3) of the Act applies). This places the title in the same position it would be in if fortified by ten years positive prescription on a Sasine title under the 1973 Act. This is the case whatever the quality of the title prior to registration.

Exclusion of indemnity

6.3 Where indemnity has been excluded, and the exclusion relates to a matter which can be cured by prescriptive possession, the applicant's title can, in due course, be fortified by positive prescription under section 1(1) of the 1973 Act as amended. At the conclusion of the ten or twenty year period, whichever is appropriate, the applicant may apply to the Keeper to have the exclusion removed. The application should be accompanied by evidence that possession has been open, peaceable and without judicial interruption throughout the prescriptive period. An explanation of the evidence acceptable to the Keeper, where *a non domino* titles are involved, is contained in the following paragraphs.

Dispositions a non domino

6.4 Dispositions *a non domino* are a useful device for founding prescriptive possession and so, in time, making good a lack of title which cannot otherwise be made good without inordinate expense and/or difficulty. It may be used, for example, when property has been in the same family for generations and unrecorded links in title were either not created or have been lost. It is sometimes used to regularise boundary problems, or where a proprietor of land seeks to acquire an adjoining strip of waste land but cannot trace the owner. The Keeper will not, therefore, stand in the way of registration of a legitimate disposition *a non domino*.

Although the majority of dispositions *a non domino* clearly serve a legitimate purpose, the Keeper recognises that there is scope for misuse. They might be utilised by persons seeking to obtain control of property clearly belonging to other people. Such dispositions *a non domino* will be viewed by the Keeper as, at best, speculative in purpose and possibly as frivolous or vexatious. Speculative dispositions *a non domino* will be rejected by the Keeper, in terms of section 4(2)(c).

Dispositions accepted by the Keeper for registration will result in an exclusion of indemnity being entered in the title sheet as regards the part of the interest that is *a non domino*. Possession for the prescriptive period will entitle the proprietor to apply for rectification of the Land Register and to have the exclusion of indemnity note removed. Such an application should be made on Form 2 and accompanied by satisfactory evidence as to the nature of the possession. The evidence the Keeper will require to examine will depend on the particular circumstances of each application. At the very least the Keeper will require affidavit evidence to the effect that there has been continuous, open and peaceable possession for the ten year prescriptive period, and that without any judicial interruption. In some circumstances it may suffice to accept affidavits from the party(ies) exercising possession; in others, additional affidavits from neighbouring proprietors may also be required. In yet other circumstances the Keeper may not be content with affidavit evidence and may insist, for example, that a declarator from the court in support of the application is obtained.

Further discussion of the above issues is to be found in an article published in the *Journal of the Law Society of Scotland*[2], and it is recommended that this be read in conjunction with this section.

---

[2] 1997 JLSS 72

Competing titles

6.5 A title which has been recorded in the Sasine Register and which has been fortified by prescription, or a title registered in the Land Register, without exclusion of indemnity, will not necessarily remain forever inviolate and unchallengeable. A title registered without exclusion of indemnity can be subject to competition from another title recorded in the Sasine Register or registered in the Land Register with exclusion of indemnity. Possession on the competing title, for the period of positive prescription, can operate to fortify the competing title. It then prevails over the original registered title to the effect of depriving the proprietor under that title of his interest.

Competing title in the Register of Sasines

6.6 Where, at the time of first registration of the title in the Land Register, a competing title exists in the Sasine Register, the Keeper's action will depend on whether or not the competing title comes to his notice.

(a) If the Keeper is unaware of the competing title the interest will be registered without any exclusion of indemnity in that respect.

(b) If the Keeper is aware of the competing title, the applicant will be entered in the proprietorship section of the title sheet as the registered proprietor. However, where the competing Sasine title ranks prior to the registered title the Keeper will exclude indemnity. Where the competing Sasine title does not rank prior to the registered title, the registered proprietor's entry will be qualified by a note containing details of the competition in title. Factors which the Keeper will consider include the response given to question 3, Part B, of the application Form 1, concerning adverse possession.

An applicant who is aware of a competing title should disclose it to the Keeper when completing the application form. Failure to do so may prevent the applicant from relying on the protection afforded to registered proprietors by section 9(3). Because of the terms of rule 21(2) the Keeper will not intimate the existence of the competing title to the Sasine proprietor. In the circumstances outlined at (a) and (b) above, prescription will operate as follows:

Registered proprietor

6.7 In case (a) there will be no exclusion of indemnity as regards the competing title. The registered proprietor has, therefore, no need of positive prescription. In case (b), if the registered proprietor's interest has been registered without exclusion of indemnity, the same will apply. If, on the other hand, indemnity is excluded, prescriptive possession will fortify the title and enable the applicant to seek rectification of the register by having the exclusion of indemnity removed.

Sasine proprietor

6.8 If the Sasine proprietor can prove prescriptive possession, then, in either case (a) or (b), it is the Sasine proprietor who will be entitled to seek rectification against the registered proprietor. The registered proprietor, although holding a registered title, is not in possession and thus not afforded the protection of section 9(3). If loss can be demonstrated the registered proprietor may be entitled to indemnity, but not if section 12(3)(a) applies. In rectifying the Land Register in either case (a) or (b), the Keeper will remove the area, for which a competition in title exists, from the existing title sheet. If the Sasine proprietor is at that time seeking to register adjoining property, the Keeper will incorporate the removed interest in that registration. In no circumstances will the disputed area, having once appeared in the Land Register, be merely deleted and allowed to revert to the Sasine title. If necessary the keeper will open a new title sheet in question showing the sasine proprietor as registered proprietor.

Competing title in the Land Register

6.9 Competition can equally arise between two registered interests. Where that occurs indemnity will be excluded in respect of one of the interests. If indemnity has not been excluded in respect of the prior registration, then it follows the Keeper must exclude indemnity in respect of the later registration. In terms of rule 21(2) the Keeper is precluded from intimating the competition in title to the proprietor of the previously registered subjects. The Keeper will reflect the competition in title in the prior registered title sheet. It follows that any pre-registration report over the registered interest will reveal the competing title. In the circumstances outlined above, prescription will operate as follows:

Registered proprietor without exclusion of indemnity

6.10 The registered proprietor who holds without exclusion of indemnity has no need of prescription at all. The title is good as long as the registered proprietor retains possession of the subjects. In a competition, the registered proprietor can, as proprietor in possession, seek to have the register rectified against any competitor. The registered proprietor does not need to prove possession of the subjects for any given period, only that the registered proprietor is in possession. On rectification, the competitor's name will be removed from the proprietorship section of the title sheet.

Registered proprietor with exclusion of indemnity
6.11 If it is the competitor, holding under an exclusion of indemnity, who can subsequently prove prescriptive possession, the register can be rectified against the proprietor who holds under no exclusion. This is possible because the latter proprietor is not in possession and thus not afforded the protection of section 9(3). In this case, the Keeper should be able to resist a claim for indemnity by the excluded proprietor under section 12(3)(a).

Warrandice

6.12 The accuracy of the Land Register and of any information provided therefrom by the Keeper in exercise of his statutory functions is guaranteed and backed by the statutory indemnity provisions. This does not mean that the protection afforded to a grantee or lessee by the traditional grant of warrandice, whether it be express or implied, is no longer necessary. There are two compelling reasons why warrandice continues to be of importance under registration of title:

1. Section 12(3) excludes various issues from the indemnity provisions in the Act; but these may be covered by warrandice.

2. The Keeper may register an interest in the Land Register and exclude indemnity either in whole or in part as regards that interest. For example, where doubt exists about title to part of the interest, the Keeper may, while registering the whole interest, exclude indemnity for that part. If the disponee is subsequently evicted from that part, no claim will lie against the Keeper; but the disponee may well have a claim under warrandice against the seller.

It is apparent then that a purchaser, under land registration, will still require warrandice to be granted by the seller. Equally, as the following examples illustrate, the seller must consider carefully the terms of any warrandice to be granted.

- Where a seller's interest is subject to an exclusion of indemnity, and the property is subsequently conveyed either with an express unqualified grant of warrandice, or where absolute warrandice is implied, the purchaser may be successful in pursuing a claim against the seller.

- Paragraph 3 of the general information on the inside back cover of each land certificate states that 'Lineal measurements shown in figures on title plans are subject to the qualification "or thereby". Indemnity is excluded in respect of such measurements'. Assume that the seller of a registered interest grants a conveyance of that interest with warrandice in statutory form and the subjects are described by reference to the title number. The title plan of the interest contains measurements to which paragraph 3 applies. These measurements, so far as the Keeper and the seller are concerned, will be read with the familiar qualification 'or thereby' and applied to the description by paragraph 3. However, paragraph 3 protects the Keeper against any inaccuracy in these measurements which could not be ascertained from the ordnance map. (The limitations of accuracy of the ordnance map are discussed in Chapter 4.) The seller, on the other hand may not have this protection and, standing the present authorities 'or thereby' could imply a higher degree of accuracy[3].

- Care should also be exercised in any case where the Keeper has, in terms of section 6(1)(a), entered the area of the subjects in the title sheet (*i.e.* where it extends to 2 hectares or more). In terms of section 12(3)(e), any such statement by the Keeper is excluded from indemnity, but a seller of subjects so described may wish to exclude any such statement of area from warrandice.

Qualifications to warrandice

6.13 The Keeper will always consider the quality of warrandice, whether express or implied, which is afforded to the grantee under and in terms of the deed being presented for registration. Whereas a title founded on a disposition *a non domino* with simple warrandice will attract an exclusion of indemnity, a title founded on a disposition where no consideration is passing and with fact and deed warrandice, will not lead to an exclusion of indemnity provided the title is otherwise in order. Thus an omission of or qualification to warrandice does not automatically lead to an exclusion of indemnity from the registered title. The Keeper may be prepared to exercise discretion concerning the alleged defect. In addition some exceptions from warrandice may prove to be overriding interests.

Warrandice and subrogation

6.14 Where a purchaser has, on eviction, the choice of proceeding under the indemnity provisions or of pursuing a claim under warrandice, the purchaser is likely to choose the former. However, section 13(2) allows the Keeper to be subrogated to the rights of the purchaser. As a condition of being indemnified

[3]*Griffen v. Watson*, 1962 S.L.T. (Sh. Ct.) 74)

the claimant may be required, in terms of section 13(3), to assign to the Keeper any rights of relief available, which would include any grant of warrandice in the claimant's favour.

Operation of warrandice in Sasine and Land Registers

6.15 The following paragraphs examine the application of warrandice to deeds inducing first registration or dealings with a registered interest against the background of a number of possible situations and, at the same time, contrast that approach with the traditional obligation of warrandice in a conveyance to be recorded in the Sasine Register.

In each of the following examples it is assumed that the grant of warrandice is in the statutory form introduced by section 8 of the Titles to Land Consolidation (Scotland) Act 1868[4], i.e. 'and I/we grant warrandice'.

The typical situations in which a total or partial, actual or constructive eviction occurs, giving rise to a claim, can be summarised against a hypothetical transaction. Examples 1 to 10 are based on A, the proprietor of a landed estate, disponing 10 acres of it to B. The transfer is effected by a disposition containing a particular description and a plan, with a grant of warrandice in statutory form. The setting for example 11 is that of a conveyance by A to B of a tenement flat. All eleven examples will explore whether on registration in the Land Register, with or without exclusion of indemnity, B is in any different a position vis-à-vis A than under the Sasine system.

Example 1 - Prior recorded title to part of the subjects

B discovers that C, a neighbour, has a prior recorded title from A, which either:

(a) takes the form of a bounding title with a particular description which includes about 1 acre of B's 10 acre plot on a valid progress of title ; or

(b) is a title with an indeterminate, non-bounding description on which C has possessed, within the meaning of the Prescription and Limitation (Scotland) Act 1973[5], 1 acre of B's 10 acres for more than 10 years.

[4]c.101
[5]c.52

Outcome under Sasine system

As far as affecting the disputed 1 acre, there is a clear conflict between B's title and C's title under (a) above, and between title and possession under (b). C could challenge B's title *quoad* the disputed 1 acre on proof of personal prior infeftment or infeftment and possession. Alternatively, C could exclude B from possession of the disputed 1 acre. In either event, if C's right is established, B would have a claim under warrandice against A the original disponer.

Outcome under land registration

Under (a) above, C has the prior express infeftment on a valid progress of titles and therefore C's title is bound to prevail over B's. If C is in possession of the 1 acre, B's application for first registration will be erroneous if B claims possession of the whole 10 acres since in reality possession of 9 acres only can be claimed. If this is not noticed at first registration and a land certificate covering the whole 10 acres is issued to B without exclusion of indemnity, the Register could be rectified against B by removal of the 1 acre from B's title sheet.

Because B's application for first registration contained a statement to the effect that no other party was in possession of the disputed 1 acre, no claim could be made against the Keeper by virtue of section 12(3)(n), even though the Keeper had not excluded indemnity. The disposition by A to B would, however, convey the whole 10 acres and contain warrandice in statutory form. In those circumstances B would have a claim against A *quanti minoris* in exactly the same way as under the Sasine system.

If under (a) above C had the prior infeftment from A on a valid progress of titles to the 1 acre but was not in possession, C's prior infeftment should prevail against B's disposition. The Keeper would note C's title on B's title sheet and exclude indemnity in respect of the 1 acre. However, if the Keeper fails to notice C's prior Sasine title to the disputed 1 acre, then B's application for first registration would not be erroneous because B would correctly claim to have possession of the whole 10 acres. In that case, the Keeper would issue a land certificate without exclusion of indemnity. B would then immediately be beyond challenge at the instance of C, or anybody else, since B has a title without exclusion of indemnity and possession of the whole property. As the innocent proprietor in possession, B is invulnerable under section 9(1) and is not affected by any of the special provisions of section 9(3).

If B's title is made invulnerable by the issue of the land certificate, then no question of a claim arises and, in that situation, A is saved from a claim under warrandice at the instance of B by the provisions of the Act.

Where (b) above applies, C, in order to establish a valid competing claim, must show possession; mere prior infeftment by itself would not suffice. Therefore, under (b), the application for registration by B would always be incorrect in so far as B claimed possession of the whole 10 acres. The Keeper would resist any claim for compensation by B and could rectify the Register against B for the benefit of C, the proprietor in possession. B would have a valid claim under warrandice against A which would be unaffected by the actings of the Keeper at first registration.

If, in contrast, the Keeper, on the application for first registration, noticed C's competing title and registered B's title with an exclusion of indemnity in respect of the 1 acre, that would not by itself give rise to a claim under warrandice at the instance of B against A. The mere threat of eviction (in the guise of the exclusion of indemnity) does not by itself give rise to a claim and actual eviction is necessary (see *Clark v. Lindale Homes Limited*[6]). However, it would be prudent for B to intimate the potential claim to A by reference to the exclusion of indemnity. B would have to await events before it became clear whether or not the claim was to be made good. In all such cases where indemnity is excluded in the land certificate, there can be no claim for compensation against the Keeper. In this situation B would have a valid claim against A under warrandice if B was later evicted on rectification of the Register.

Example 2 - Prior recorded title to dominium utile only of part of the subjects

B having taken delivery of the disposition of 10 acres then discovers that D has a valid and unchallengeable title by feu charter to the *dominium utile* of one of B's 10 acres. B was unaware of this at the date of delivery of the disposition. In the previous example, B's title to 1 acre failed in a competition with C. In this example, B's title to the whole 10 acres remains unimpaired but, *quoad* 1 acre he has the *dominium directum* only and is excluded from the *dominium utile* by the earlier recorded feu charter in favour of D.

Outcome under Sasine system
Notwithstanding the technical difference between this example and example 1, B's claim is substantially the same as in example 1.

Outcome under land registration
The main differences between this example and example 1 on first registration are as follows:

---

[6] 1994 S.L.T. 1053

- The Keeper is unlikely to overlook the presence of the feu charter; though that remains a possibility with older descriptions.

- Where the feu charter comes to the Keeper's attention, he will not register B's title to 10 acres with exclusion of indemnity in respect of the disputed 1 acre (as in example 1); instead he will register B's title to 10 acres, but will reflect in B's title sheet the feu to D, thus restricting B's title *quoad* 1 acre to *dominium directum* only.

- It is unlikely that D would not be in possession in contrast to the possibility of non-possession by C in example 1.

Under example 1, registration with exclusion of indemnity did not itself create a claim under warrandice. However, in this example, registration of a title to 10 acres, but with 1 acre registered as *dominium directum* only, following on a conveyance of the whole 10 acres with no exclusion from warrandice would automatically imply eviction of B from the 1 acre feu. This would automatically give rise to a claim under warrandice by B against A. There would be no claim against the Keeper.

In contrast, if the Keeper failed to notice the feu charter to D and registered B as proprietor of the *dominium utile* of the whole 10 acres, D could apply for rectification of the Register on the grounds that B was not in possession. The Register would be rectified by amending B's title sheet to show B as proprietor of the *dominium directum* only as regards the 1 acre. Whether or not B would have a claim against the Keeper would depend on the circumstances and whether section 12(3)(n) was applicable. If B did not have a claim against the Keeper, a claim would normally be available against A under warrandice.

Example 3 - Minerals reserved from title

B, having taken delivery of the disposition, discovers that minerals are reserved from the title. B was unaware at the date of delivery of this reservation. The reservation is not referred to in the disposition in favour of B.

Outcome under Sasine system
Although there is no direct authority on this point, on general principle it would seem that the lack of the minerals in the title is a partial eviction, or partial failure of the ostensible title from the centre of the earth to the sky, which may entitle the disponee B to a claim under warrandice *quanti minoris*.

Outcome under land registration

By virtue of section 12(3)(f) no claim as regards the omission of minerals from the title sheet could be made against the Keeper except in the unlikely event of the Keeper having expressly certified that minerals were included in the title. B's claim would lie against A, *quanti minoris*.

Example 4 - Property subject to recorded lease

B, having taken delivery of the disposition, discovers that 1 acre of the property is subject to a recorded lease.

Outcome under Sasine system

The position is identical in principle to the resulting position in example 2 above. B would, therefore, have a claim under warrandice against A.

Outcome under land registration

The existence of a recorded lease produces exactly the same result as the existence of a recorded feu charter in example 2.

Example 5 - Property subject to unrecorded lease

B, having taken delivery of the disposition, discovers that 1 acre of the property is subject to an unrecorded lease.

Outcome under Sasine system

The authorities[7] suggest that unrecorded leases do not found a claim under warrandice, at least if they are unexceptional in the type of property in question. If, however, the conveyance to B included a reference to 'entry and actual physical possession' of the subjects disponed it may be that, in such circumstances, physical possession is warranted by the ordinary warrandice clause in which case the existence of a lease would be a breach of warrandice. No authority exists on this point.

Outcome under land registration

Unrecorded leases are overriding interests under (a) or (b) of the definition of overriding interests in section 28 and are excluded from the indemnity provisions (see section 12(3)(h)). Therefore, in all cases, if there is a claim based on a clause which provides for physical possession, it would be a straightforward claim by B against A under warrandice unaffected by first registration or the terms of the land certificate.

[7]see *Lothian and Border Farmers Limited v. McCutcheon*, 1952 S.L.T. 450

Example 6 - Property subject to servitude

The property turns out to be subject to a servitude which is not disclosed in the missives nor is apparent from the examination of title.

Outcome under Sasine system
If the servitude is onerous there is no doubt that this founds a claim under warrandice. Just how onerous the servitude has to be is not clear from the reported cases and, indeed, if the opinions delivered in *Welsh v. Russell*[8] are to be followed, the level required may not be hard to achieve. Whatever the rule may be, there are clearly any number of cases where the existence of a material servitude will found a claim. It would seem to make no difference whether the servitude is constituted by recorded or unrecorded deed, by implication or by prescription. In any of these circumstances B, if the servitude passes the onerousness test, would have a claim under warrandice against A.

Outcome under land registration
In so far as affecting the servient tenement, servitudes are overriding interests and may or may not be noted by the Keeper. Whether noted or not, B as the owner of the servient tenement would have no claim against the Keeper if and when the servitude was constituted. B may, however, have a claim against A under warrandice, if and when the owner of the dominant tenement establishes the right. Failure to note a servitude on the title sheet does not in any way invalidate the servitude right. The servitude remains enforceable at the instance of the dominant owner. The noting of a servitude on the title sheet does not, of itself, constitute the servitude right and so would not, of itself, amount to a constructive partial eviction. To found a claim under warrandice, the dominant owner would have to constitute the right against B as servient owner and that would be the event which would trigger the warrandice claim.

Example 7 - Real burdens

A real burden has been constituted by some earlier recorded deed but is not referred to in the disposition in favour of B.

Outcome under Sasine system
On general principle B would have a claim under warrandice against A, but to be successful eviction or threatened eviction would have to be proved.

---

[8] 1894 21 R 769

Outcome under land registration

A real burden in an earlier recorded deed, to be effective against B as registered proprietor, would have to enter the title sheet. Otherwise, by its omission, the burden is effectively discharged and B's title disburdened thereof (unless circumstances exist by which the Keeper is able to rectify the title sheet to disclose the omitted real burden). The creditor in that real burden may be able to claim for compensation against the Keeper for omitting the burden. If, on the other hand, the burden was not disclosed in B's disposition but was included in the title sheet, B would have a claim against A under warrandice if loss could be proved.

Example 8 - Heritable security

Outstanding heritable security over the land to which the purchase of said land had not been made subject.

Outcome under Sasine system

The heritable security would constitute partial eviction and so found a claim under warrandice by B against A.

Outcome under land registration

B's position is exactly the same as with the real burden in example 7.

Example 9 - Common interest

Could an emergent right of common interest affecting B's property found a claim under warrandice? In both the Sasine and Land Registers the answer would appear to be no, since common interest arises primarily by operation of law in certain standard situations, and the warrandice rule is that the granter does not warrant against loss arising from the nature of ownership or burdens natural to the disponee's right. Common interest would seem to come under that exclusion in all cases.

Example 10 - Incorporeal rights

In the disposition by A to B, an incorporeal right (for example salmon fishings, servitude rights of access, drainage *etc.*) is conveyed as an addendum. It later transpires that B does not get a valid title to such incorporeal rights or that the right has been extinguished, for example by the negative prescription.

Outcome under Sasine system

The entitlement to the incorporeal right would be warranted by the warrandice obligation in common form. B would, therefore, have a claim against A under warrandice.

Outcome under land registration

The position on first registration would seem to be the same as the position under the Sasine system so far as incorporeal rights are concerned. However, where property is conveyed by A to B with the benefit of a pre-existing servitude right, for example of access to the property, A warrants the validity of that right of access under the normal warrandice obligation in the disposition. If B then registers the title, the benefit of the right of access may be entered in the property section of the title sheet on registration. Under section 12(3)(l), the Keeper, by entering the benefit of the right in the title sheet, warrants that the right of access was originally duly constituted for the benefit of B's property. The Keeper does not warrant that the right of access has not, in the interim, been extinguished by the negative prescription.

If the right of access has been so extinguished, B would have no claim for compensation against the Keeper; but a claim may be available against A under warrandice.

Example 11 - Common property

Outcome under Sasine system

This example involves the case of a tenement. The conveyance to B takes the form of a disposition of the ground floor flat with the front ground and the ground at the back. In terms of that title, B would expect to be subject only to the common interest of the upper proprietors in maintaining the stability of the tenement. But, an earlier recorded disposition of an upper flat in that tenement conferred a right of common property on the disponee in, *inter alia*, the *solum* of the tenement and the front and back ground. This would undoubtedly qualify B's apparent exclusive right to the *solum* and front and back ground. Clearly, in that case, B would have a claim under warrandice.

If, in a similar situation, the disposition to B was silent on the ownership of the solum of the tenement and the front and back ground, the normal implication of a ground floor conveyance is that it carries to the disponee the same exclusive rights to the solum and to the front and back ground. However, these implied rights would be qualified and limited by the prior infeftment of the upper floor proprietor. On general principle, it would seem that B may be entitled to claim under warrandice.

In the converse case, B takes a conveyance of an upper flat, together with a right in common to the *solum* of the tenement and front and back ground, and possibly a right in common to the roof. B would have a claim under warrandice if it subsequently turns out that the front and back ground had previously been conveyed exclusively to the ground floor proprietor, either expressly or by implication; or that the top flat has been conveyed without reference to a right in common to the roof. By virtue of the prior infeftment of the ground floor or top floor proprietor with exclusive rights in the front and back ground or the roof respectively, B would be excluded from the ostensible *pro indiviso* share of these assets and to that extent would have a warrandice claim.

Outcome under land registration

Common property is an overriding interest unless created by recorded or registered title. For practical purposes, rights of common property are invariably so created. If B's title to a flat in a tenement is registered with some incidental right, such as a joint right to the backgreen which turns out to conflict with some prior recorded title (for example, a title to the ground floor flat with exclusive rights to the backgreen), B's registered title would prevail over the title of the ground floor proprietor. However, this would occur only if B can show that following upon registration, and before the ground floor proprietor sought rectification of the Register, B is exercising this right, and in so doing, is in the position of being a *'proprietor in possession'* for the purposes of section 9(3): B's title could not then be rectified by deleting the joint right claimed.

In the converse case, where B does not exercise the purported joint right in the backgreen, the matter of proprietor in possession for the purposes of section 9(3) would not apply. B's title could be rectified to delete that joint right. In that event, no claim could be made against the Keeper, indemnity being excluded under section 12(3)(n); but a claim would be available against the disponer under warrandice.

Transfer of the registered interest in whole or in part

6.16 Whatever the contractual position at the missives stage may be, there is no doubt that when the purchaser or the purchaser's solicitor takes delivery of the disposition, either party will have examined the land certificate. By the date of the delivery of the disposition, therefore, the purchaser must be held to be aware of all matters included in the land certificate and accordingly, to be personally barred from any subsequent claim under warrandice in respect of any matter appearing in the land certificate, for example an onerous burden, a noted servitude, or an outstanding heritable security.

In the context of the eleven examples outlined above, the warrandice position on the transfer of the registered interest in whole or in part is the same as on first registration.

Destinations

6.17 In terms of rule 5(d) the Keeper shall disclose in the proprietorship section of the title sheet *'the destination, if any, to which the interest in land is subject'*. A distinction is drawn between general and special destinations. A general destination ('to A and his (or her) executors and assignees') is implied by law and is therefore not shown in the title sheet. Conversely, a special destination will be entered in the proprietorship section of the title sheet as it regulates and determines the proprietor's right and title to the registered interest. In order to avoid any misunderstanding or misinterpretation of the intention or meaning or effect of the wording, the Keeper will generally enter the special destination exactly as it appears in the deed. However, some special destinations can pose particular problems as evidenced in the following paragraphs.

It is common when a couple buy a house in joint names for the title to be taken to 'A and B, equally between them and to the survivor of them'. Such a destination gives each party a half *pro indiviso* share in the property. If one dies before the other without evacuating the special destination by *inter vivos* or, where competent, *mortis causa* deed then that person's half *pro indiviso* share falls to the other automatically. In that event the Keeper will not issue a fully indemnified title to the survivor, or a person deriving title from the survivor, unless he is satisfied that the destination has not been evacuated. In these circumstances the Keeper will require to examine the death certificate, and evidence that the destination was not evacuated. Documentary evidence of this latter nature is not easy to produce. For instance, even if a testamentary writing which does not evacuate the destination is produced, that in itself is not conclusive evidence that there is no other writing, testamentary or *inter vivos*, which does evacuate the destination. It is for that reason that the Keeper requires written assurance that no such document exists. Such assurance can take the form of an affidavit by the seller or a letter from the applicant's solicitor.

Difficulties can also arise where it is claimed that the special destination has been evacuated unilaterally by of one of the parties subject to the special destination. It may be, for instance, that the special destination contained in the deed has created a contractual arrangement between the parties. Consequently, it may not be possible for the destination to be evacuated by unilateral action. Similarly, it may be unclear whether the terms of the deed purporting to evacuate the destination are habile to do so[9]. Situations such as these are not ones which the Keeper can easily determine. For that reason the Keeper will take a cautious approach when faced with a destination which purports to have been evacuated and may request that parties with

[9]For a detailed analysis of these and other issues concerning the evacuation of special destinations see *Destinations* by G.L. Gretton, 1989 JLSS 299

an interest in the destination consent to the evacuation. Alternatively, the Keeper may recommend that matters be resolved in court by way of an action of declarator.

If a couple holding title under an equally and survivor destination part, it is common for the separation agreement or divorce settlement to provide that one party will convey his or her half share to the other. If this is done by a disposition by A to B of A's half share, the destination as regards A's half share is evacuated. However, it will remain operative in respect of B's half share. In the event of B predeceasing A without evacuating the destination, that half share will revert to A. In those circumstances the special destination in respect of B's original half *pro indiviso* share will be reflected in the title sheet. Should B subsequently wish to evacuate the destination affecting the original half *pro indiviso* share, similar problems to those detailed in the preceding paragraph may be encountered. The accepted solution is for both *pro indiviso* proprietors to convey their respective interests, thus evacuating the special destination.

Adverse entries in the Register of Inhibitions and Adjudications

6.18 In terms of section 6(1)(c) and rule 5(h) the Keeper is bound to enter in the proprietorship section of any title sheet a subsisting entry in the Register of Inhibitions and Adjudications ('ROI') adverse to the registered interest. The Keeper will note subsisting adverse entries in the title sheet only when the title sheet is initially created or subsequently updated. If adverse entries in the Personal Register are not subsisting they will not appear in the title sheet. So, if a five year search in the Personal Register reveals a notice of letters of inhibition, letters of inhibition and discharge of that inhibition, they will not appear on the title sheet as there is no subsisting adverse entry.

By section 44(3)(a) of the Conveyancing (Scotland) Act 1924[10] an inhibition prescribes after 5 years. As a result, on receipt of an application for registration, the Keeper will search the ROI for the five years prior to the date of registration against the parties to the transaction and any parties notified to the Keeper as having an interest in the subjects. Should that search disclose a subsisting adverse entry which appears to be relevant to the title sheet, the Keeper will inform the submitting agent that the entry(ies) will be disclosed in the title sheet and indemnity excluded in respect thereof unless written evidence that the entry(ies) is/are not relevant is produced.

Similarly, when an ROI search is instigated in response to a request for an office copy of a title sheet and subsisting adverse entries are found, these will be

[10] c.27

disclosed in the title sheet in the same way as subsisting adverse entries revealed at the time of an application for registration. In terms of section 12(3)(k) the Keeper is not liable in indemnity for loss where he omits to disclose, in an office copy, an adverse entry affecting any person whose entitlement to the registered interest is not disclosed in the register nor otherwise known to the Keeper .

Indemnity will be excluded in respect of an adverse entry disclosed in a title sheet. Failure to do so would prejudice the inhibiting creditor because the provisions of section 9(3)(b) would prevent the court ordering rectification of the Register in implement of a decree of reduction obtained by the inhibiting creditor. This in turn could lead to a claim on the Keeper's indemnity by the inhibiting creditor. An indemnity exclusion note in terms similar to the following will therefore be entered immediately after the adverse entry:

> 'Indemnity is excluded in terms of section 12(2) of the Land Registration (Scotland) Act 1979 in respect of any loss arising from the reduction of any dealing following the above inhibition (or, as a result of the above abbreviate petition for sequestration, etc.).'

It may be necessary to enter a similar note in the charges section and the charge certificate.

An adverse entry with an attendant indemnity exclusion note may be removed from the title sheet once the adverse entry has lost its force and effect. This may arise, for instance, following registration of the discharge of the inhibition in the ROI or on the operation of prescription after expiry of the five year period without a renewal notice being registered. Any entry with an indemnity exclusion note will, however, remain on the title sheet until the Keeper receives and processes an application to remove it. The application should be accompanied by satisfactory evidence that the inhibition is spent. The Keeper may, depending on the time that has elapsed since the inhibition expired, require an affidavit by the registered proprietor or inhibitee certifying that no action for reduction of the title had commenced prior to the expiry of the inhibition.

It is not uncommon for persons named in the ROI to be designed 'whose present whereabouts are unknown'. This lack of a substantive address poses an added difficulty for the Keeper when assessing whether or not an entry is adverse to the registered interest. Where such an entry matches the name of one of the parties being searched, the Keeper will contact the agent applying for registration. The Keeper will require written assurance from both agents to the transaction certifying that they have satisfied themselves from their enquiries that the party disclosed in the ROI is not a party to the transaction. Without such assurance the Keeper will disclose the adverse entry in the title sheet and indemnity will be excluded.

Debtor selling property

6.19 An inhibition affects only property over which the debtor has a power of disposal at the time the inhibition is registered. Consequently, if the debtor has entered into binding missives of sale prior to the date of registration of the inhibition, the inhibition will not bite at the property in the missives as the debtor had already contracted to sell them. It may be unclear, from the deeds and documents submitted in support of an application for registration, whether or not an inhibition affects the transfer. In those situations the Keeper will require sight of the missives to satisfy himself on whether or not the inhibition strikes at the current transaction.

Debtor purchasing property

6.20 An inhibition does not apply to property acquired by the debtor after the date of registration of the inhibition. So, where delivery of the deed conveying heritable property to the debtor takes place after the registration of the inhibition, that property is not affected by the inhibition. (The Keeper takes the view that the date of delivery of the deed will usually be the date of settlement of the transaction.) It may be unclear from the deeds and documents submitted in support of an application for registration whether or not an inhibition bites at the transaction. In such circumstances the Keeper will require evidence of the date of settlement of the transaction. Such evidence could, for example, take the form of a declaration of the date of settlement, signed by both the purchaser's and seller's agents. Conversely, an inhibition registered in the ROI after the date of settlement will strike at any future voluntary deeds or dealings by that purchaser affecting the subjects, and as such must be disclosed on the title sheet. Indemnity will be excluded in respect thereof.

Standard security

6.21 Where a proprietor is inhibited, the inhibition may affect not only a future transfer of the property but also any heritable securities granted by the proprietor after the date of registration of the inhibition. Conversely, if the debtor is inhibited subsequent to the granting of the standard security, the inhibition will have no impact on the standard security. Where it is unclear if a standard security is affected by an inhibition the Keeper will look to the date of settlement of the loan transaction. The Keeper will generally equate the date of settlement of the loan transaction with the date of encashment of the loan cheque. So, where uncertainty exists, the Keeper will require written confirmation of the date of encashment of the loan cheque. If the inhibition was registered before the date of settlement of the loan transaction, the heritable security will be struck at by the inhibition.

Where the standard security is affected by the inhibition a note, excluding indemnity as a result of the inhibition noted in the proprietorship section, will be added after the entry for the security in the charges section of the title sheet. A similar note will be entered in the charge certificate. Where the security is not affected by the inhibition noted in the proprietorship section, the Keeper will insert a note to that effect below the entry for that security in the charges section. The note will run as follows:

> *'The above standard security is not affected by the letters of inhibition registered ... (notice whereof was registered ...) referred to in the proprietorship section.'*

No such note will be added where it is clear from the face of the title sheet that the security is not struck at by the inhibition.

Sub-sale

6.22 In the case of *Leeds Permanent Building Society v. Aitken Malone & Mackay*[11] it was held that the right of the purchaser under missives is moveable and does not become heritable until the disposition is delivered to the purchaser. Consequently, when faced with a sub-sale by which B acquires a personal right to heritable property under missives and then, without taking title, sells the subjects on to C (by means of a disposition by the infeft proprietor, A, with the consent of B), the Keeper will not disclose in C's title sheet an inhibition against B. This is regardless of whether the inhibition was registered either before or after the date on which missives were concluded between A and B.

Inhibitions and receivership

6.23 The law concerning inhibitions and sales by receivers is not entirely clear (see for example *The Law of Inhibition and Adjudication* by GL Gretton[12], chapters 11 & 12). It appears settled that a receiver cannot sell free from an inhibition against the company which granted the floating charge, where the inhibition was registered prior to the creation of the floating charge. However, the law is unsettled on whether an inhibition registered after the creation of the floating charge but before its crystallisation impacts on the receiver's authority to sell. On general principles the floating charge should prevail over the inhibition on the basis that the security established thereunder was created prior to the inhibition. Any transfer by the receiver cannot therefore be said to be voluntary on the part

[11]1986 SLT 338
[12]Gretton, GL: *The Law of Inhibitions and Adjudication*, 1996, 2nd edition, Butterworths/Law Society of Scotland, Edinburgh

of the debtor company. However, section 61 of the Insolvency Act 1986[13] indicates that it would be appropriate in such a situation for the receiver to obtain the creditor's consent or the court's sanction to sell.

In light of the above the Keeper will take a cautious approach to prevent a claim on his indemnity from an inhibiting creditor. Where an inhibition has been registered before conclusion of missives between the receiver and the purchaser, the Keeper will disclose the inhibition and exclude indemnity in respect thereof in the title sheet of the purchaser, unless the inhibition is discharged or restricted appropriately, or the receiver sells with the consent of the inhibiting creditor, or the court, under section 61, authorises the sale of the subjects free from the inhibition.

Sequestration

6.24 Section 14(1) of the Bankruptcy (Scotland) Act 1985[14] provides that the clerk of the court shall forthwith after the date of sequestration send a certified copy of the court order, either awarding sequestration or granting warrant to cite the debtor, to the Keeper for registration in the ROI. Registration under section 14(1) has the effect of an inhibition as from the date of sequestration, and so will be disclosed in the title sheet with attendant exclusion of indemnity if it affects the registered interest therein.

Discharge of the debtor under sequestration happens automatically on the expiry of three years unless the trustee in sequestration or creditor applies for deferment. However, discharge of the debtor does not terminate the sequestration. It is only when the trustee is discharged that the sequestration will formally end. Accordingly, if the Keeper receives an application for registration following on the sale of property by an apparently undischarged bankrupt, with no evidence that the sequestration is at an end, the application will not proceed without exclusion of indemnity unless the Keeper receives evidence that the trustee consents to the sale or that both the debtor and permanent trustee are discharged. Evidence of the latter will comprise the certificates of discharge for both the debtor and the trustee issued by the Accountant in Bankruptcy. Such evidence is required both before and after the expiry of the three year period.

Sequestration and prior inhibitions

6.25 By section 31(2) of the 1985 Act the actings of the trustee in sequestration are not affected by prior inhibitions against the debtor. The trustee in

[13] c.45
[14] c.66

sequestration can therefore sell free of any prior inhibition against the debtor, and the purchaser's title sheet will not disclose such prior inhibitions as adverse entries. Equally, if the trustee should make up title to the debtor's property, the title sheet will not disclose prior inhibitions against the debtor. However, where the debtor had taken title subject to an inhibition against a previous proprietor, that inhibition will be disclosed on the title sheet as an adverse entry so long as it remains extant and indemnity will be excluded in respect thereof.

Liquidation and prior inhibitions

6.26 In terms of section 185(1)(a) of the Insolvency Act 1986 an inhibition registered within 60 days before the commencement of winding-up proceedings is equalised along with other diligences. The liquidator can sell heritable property belonging to the company free of such inhibitions and they will not be disclosed as adverse entries in the purchaser's title sheet.

The situation with inhibitions registered before the 60 day period is less clear (see, for example, Gretton: *The Law Of Inhibition and Adjudication*, chapter 11). Some commentators (see for instance, *Palmer's Company Insolvency In Scotland*[15], chapter 4) argue that liquidators can sell free of any prior inhibition against the company, whilst others are less certain. Gretton for example (see above reference) discusses the possibility that a distinction can be made between a voluntary and a compulsory winding-up, arguing that the latter cannot be held to be a voluntary act of the company and so prior inhibitions against the company cannot be effective. Since all such views must remain speculative until the matter is clarified by legislation or settled by the courts, the Keeper is obliged to adopt the prudent line that all prior inhibitions registered against a company before the 60 day period are effective, and so require to be disclosed as adverse entries with attendant exclusion of indemnity. This is the case whether the winding-up is compulsory or voluntary.

Administration orders and inhibitions

6.27 Prior inhibitions are effective in the face of an administration order (see Gretton, chapter 12) and will therefore be disclosed as adverse entries with attendant exclusion of indemnity in the purchaser's title sheet unless the inhibition is discharged or the administrator obtains the consent of the court to sell free of the inhibition.

---

[15]*Palmer's Company Insolvency in Scotland*, ed. Bennett, D.A 1993, W Green/Sweet & Maxwell, Edinburgh

Where a company is already subject to an administration order, a new inhibition against the company is not competent without leave of the court or the consent of the administrator - section 11(3)(d) of the 1986 Act. It follows that inhibitions registered without leave or consent as aforementioned are unenforceable and so will not be treated as adverse entries by the Keeper. It is not always possible, however, for the Keeper to ascertain the status of such an inhibition without obtaining a statement from the administrator as to the efficacy of the inhibition. So, where the administrator is transacting with the company's property in the face of such an inhibition, a statement from the administrator should accompany the application for registration explaining whether or not leave of the court or the administrator's consent was obtained in respect of the registration of the inhibition. Only then will the Keeper be able to determine whether or not the inhibition should be classed as an adverse entry.

Matrimonial Homes (Family Protection) (Scotland) Act 1981[16]

6.28 The interest comprising an occupancy right of a non-entitled spouse, within the meaning of section 6 of the 1981 Act, is included within the definition of overriding interest in section 28(1) of the 1979 Act. Although classed as an overriding interest, the right is one of the exceptions to the noting provisions contained in section 6(4) of the 1979 Act. It is, therefore, not capable of being noted on the title sheet. It does not follow, however, that occupancy rights are of no relevance in land registration.

Section 6(1) of the 1981 Act allows, in certain circumstances, for the subsistence of an occupancy right of a non-entitled spouse beyond the divestiture of the entitled spouse. To ensure vacant possession, a purchaser must find out if an occupancy right of a non-entitled spouse subsists. Since a title sheet discloses only the current registered proprietor, it is not possible to identify from it details of former proprietors. To avoid the need to retain and refer to a progress of titles for that purpose after registration, rule 5(j) requires the Keeper, if he is satisfied that there are no such subsisting rights, to insert in the proprietorship section of the title sheet a statement that:

> *'there are in respect of the interest in land no subsisting occupancy rights, in terms of the Matrimonial Homes (Family Protection) (Scotland) Act 1981, of spouses of persons who were formerly entitled to the interest in land.'*

The Keeper will insert the above statement only if an application for registration is supported by evidence that no occupancy rights of spouses of former

[16] c.59

proprietors exist. In order to be satisfied that there are no such subsisting rights, the Keeper will require to see one of the documents listed in paragraph 6.29 below. Technically, in the case of a first registration, documentation is required in respect of every person, other than the applicant, who has been entitled to the interest since the coming into force of the legislation on 1 September 1982. In the case of a dealing with a registered interest, documentation is required in respect of the proprietor disclosed in the land certificate and any person, other than the applicant, who was subsequently entitled to the interest.

The above-mentioned statement regarding occupancy rights under the 1981 Act entered in the title sheet is in respect of persons who were formerly entitled to the subjects. The Keeper gives no such assurances as respects the current registered proprietor and consequently does not require sight of any documentary evidence for the applicant. It therefore follows that when applying to register a dealing that is not a transfer of the property, no evidence under the 1981 Act need be produced to the Keeper.

The term 'entitled' in rule 5(j), considering the terms of the Act, is not necessarily synonymous with having a recorded or registered title. The Keeper will therefore require to see one of the documents listed in the following paragraph, in respect of all persons who have had a right to the interest, whether completed by infeftment or not. Since rule 5(j) refers only to 'persons who were formerly entitled to the interest in land' the Keeper considers that the occupancy rights of spouses of persons permitted by the proprietor to occupy the home, for example a tenant, or a beneficiary under a trust which directs the trustees to hold the subjects on the beneficiary's behalf, are excluded.

Evidence Keeper will require to examine

6.29 The documents the Keeper will require to examine (hereinafter referred to as 'matrimonial homes act evidence') are:

- a consent by the non-entitled spouse to the dealing by the entitled spouse;

- an affidavit by the entitled person that there is no non-entitled spouse; or, an affidavit by the entitled person that the subjects of sale are not a matrimonial home in relation to which a spouse of the entitled person has occupancy rights;

- a duly stamped renunciation of the occupancy right by the non-entitled spouse;

- a written assurance that the dealing implements a binding obligation entered into before 1 September 1982 (the date when the legislation came into force);

- an order of the court dispensing with consent, in terms of section 7 of the 1981 Act;

- evidence of the death of the entitled spouse;

- a written assurance that the dealing implements a binding obligation entered into by the entitled spouse before marriage; or

- as regards a sale by an executor, one of the documents referred to in paragraph 6.40.

If the Keeper is satisfied with the matrimonial homes act evidence submitted to him, he will enter in the proprietorship section of the title sheet the statement referred to in paragraph 6.28 above, indicating that there are no subsisting occupancy rights in the subjects. Should appropriate matrimonial homes act evidence not be submitted, the Keeper will insert a statement, noting the deficiency in evidence which has prevented him inserting an unqualified statement. For example:

> 'The Keeper is satisfied that there are in respect of the subjects in this title no occupancy rights in terms of the Matrimonial Homes (Family Protection) (Scotland) Act 1981, of spouses of persons who were formerly entitled to the said subjects, except AB (design) who ceased to be entitled on ... and in respect of whose entitlement no evidence of the non-existence of an occupancy right has been produced to the Keeper.'

A qualified statement entered in a title sheet is not an exclusion of indemnity, as the existence or not of an occupancy right only affects the right to vacant possession and does not affect title. Such a qualified statement indicates that sufficient evidence of the absence of occupancy rights has not been produced to the Keeper. It does not necessarily imply that an occupancy right exists.

Although an occupancy right is an overriding interest, section 12(3)(h) of the 1979 Act does not apply to a statement in terms of rule 5(j), so the full indemnity provisions apply to such a statement. Where sections 6(3)(e) and 8 of the 1981 Act have not operated, and the consent *etc.*, is not valid, the occupancy right will prevail over that of the grantee in the dealing. In such an event an unqualified statement in terms of rule 5(j) may give the registered proprietor a claim for indemnity against the Keeper.

Prescription of occupancy rights

6.30 The new section 6(3)(f) of the 1981 Act, introduced by the Law Reform (Miscellaneous Provisions) (Scotland) Act 1985[17], provides that the occupancy right of the non-entitled spouse will prescribe if it remains unexercised for a

[17]c.73

continuous period of five years after the termination of the entitled spouse's entitlement. Prescription will not start to operate if the non-entitled spouse remains in occupation. This means that one cannot necessarily ignore transactions which took place more than five years prior to first registration. However, the Keeper is normally prepared to take a pragmatic view where question 9 in application Form 1 (which asks whether all the necessary matrimonial homes act evidence has been submitted) is answered in the affirmative.

Removal of qualified statement

6.31 Where the Keeper has inserted a qualified statement, he will remove the qualification on the subsequent submission to him of satisfactory evidence that the occupancy right has terminated. Such evidence can take a variety of forms and includes:

- evidence that the requirements of section 6(3)(f) of the 1981 Act have been met. The evidence which the Keeper requires is an affidavit from each proprietor during the five year period to the effect that no non-entitled spouse of the person named in the note in the title sheet exercised an occupancy right during the deponent's period of ownership;

- evidence of the termination of the relevant marriage after the occurrence of the dealing, either on divorce or the death of either spouse. Evidence of termination of the marriage before the occurrence of the dealing, except by the death of the entitled spouse, is not satisfactory evidence because the entitled spouse might have remarried;

- evidence of the death of the entitled person whether or not that person was married.

Should the evidence not submitted to the Keeper at the time of the application become available, it may be submitted in support of an application to have the qualified statement removed.

Evidence

6.32 Since the advent of the 1981 Act there have been a number of frequently recurring situations in which the Keeper has been asked to state what evidence, in terms of the 1981 Act, would satisfy him that no occupancy rights subsist. Those common situations and the evidence, if any, the Keeper would expect to see are set out in the following paragraphs.

Married couple

6.33 If A and B are married to each other, they are both entitled spouses within the meaning of the 1981 Act. If either separately disposes of his or her half share the Keeper would require to examine a deed or minute of consent or a renunciation of occupancy rights by the other in respect of that share. If both dispose of their shares jointly no consents or renunciations are needed.

Termination of marriage by divorce

6.34 An occupancy right ends on the termination of the marriage. Nevertheless, except where the marriage is terminated by the death of the entitled spouse, evidence of termination of the marriage is not acceptable where the marriage terminated before the occurrence of the dealing. The reason for this is that the entitled spouse might have remarried and created another occupancy right. Where the marriage was terminated by divorce before the dealing, the appropriate matrimonial homes act evidence is an affidavit that there is no non-entitled spouse. If the marriage terminated after the dealing, the Keeper may accept a decree of divorce as evidence that no occupancy rights subsist.

Multiple entitlement

6.35 Section 6(2)(b) provides that the term *'entitled spouse'* does not include a spouse who is *'entitled to occupy a matrimonial home along with an individual who is not the other spouse'*. This means that if A and B hold title jointly but are not married to each other then either or both can dispose of their interest without any need for consents, renunciations, or affidavits, even if they are married to other people. Accordingly, no evidence need be supplied to the Keeper. With regard to section 8, which deals with the interests of heritable creditors, the Keeper applies the same practice to sales by heritable creditors in virtue of the power of sale provisions contained in a heritable security granted in their favour by (*e.g.*) a cohabiting couple.

Body corporate

6.36 It is self-evident that no occupancy right can arise out of the entitlement of a body corporate as such a body cannot have a spouse. No evidence need be supplied to the Keeper in respect of the entitlement of such a body.

Landlord and tenant

6.37 A landlord in terms of a long lease has a registrable interest in the subject matter of the lease but, because of the existence of the lease the landlord is not entitled to occupy the property. The spouse of a landlord cannot, therefore, have an occupancy right in the subjects. In the event of the landlord's interest being sold, although no consent, renunciation, or affidavit *etc.* need be forwarded to the Keeper, the Keeper will require written assurance from the agent that the subjects are subject to a subsisting lease and that the landlord, therefore, cannot occupy them. Such an assurance is necessary because on the sale and subsequent registration of the landlord's interest it will not necessarily be apparent to the Keeper that there is a subsisting lease of the subjects. Even if the Keeper can find out that there is a lease, he has no way of knowing if the lease still subsists. It may well have been renounced or abandoned which would entitle the landlord to occupy the subjects and so give rise to a potential occupancy right for the spouse.

The position is different with a tenant under a long registrable lease. As a tenant is both entitled to occupy the property and has an interest which is capable of registration, on a disposal of that interest the possibility of an occupancy right existing must be covered by the submission of the appropriate matrimonial homes act evidence to the Keeper.

Liferent and fee

6.38 A fiar, under a liferent and fee title, has a registrable interest in the property but, because of the existence of the liferent, cannot occupy the subjects. On disposal of the property, with the consent of the liferenter, no matrimonial homes act evidence need be supplied to the Keeper for the fiar. The position is different for the liferent. As the liferenter has both a registrable interest and a right to occupy the subjects, matrimonial homes act evidence will be required.

If the liferent was renounced some time before the conveyance of the subjects but after the commencement date of the 1981 Act, the Keeper will require to examine the appropriate matrimonial homes act evidence in respect of both the liferenter and the fiar. In this case the liferenter had an interest up to the time of the renunciation of the liferent, from which point the fiar became entitled to occupy the property.

Trustees

6.39 Where property is held by trustees there can be no occupancy right of a spouse of any of the trustees because the trustees are not entitled to occupy the property as individuals. No evidence need therefore be supplied for the trustees. Nor will the Keeper require evidence in connection with a sale by a trustee in sequestration. The Keeper's view is that such a transaction is not a voluntary dealing by the entitled spouse. Appropriate evidence, in terms of section 40 of the Bankruptcy (Scotland) Act 1985[18], will, however, have to be produced to the Keeper.

Death of entitled spouse/ conveyance by executors

6.40 An occupancy right terminates on the death of the entitled spouse. Although in terms of section 14 of the Succession (Scotland) Act 1964[19], the whole estate of the deceased person vests in the executor for the purposes of administration, it is generally held that for all other purposes property vests as at the death of the testator in the person entitled to succeed. It is therefore possible for that person to become an entitled spouse in terms of the 1981 Act when a house vests on the death of the testator. If the person entitled to succeed, instead of completing title, instructs the executor to sell, that transaction could be construed as a dealing of the entitled spouse. If, on the other hand, an executor is directed by a testamentary deed to sell a house forming part of the estate, or requires to sell to meet the debts of the deceased or to distribute the estate in appropriate shares, there is no question of the transaction being a dealing of an entitled spouse. Similarly, if more than one person is entitled to succeed then no occupancy right capable of enforcement against third parties is created.

When a sale by an executor leads to an application for registration the Keeper will require to examine one of the following documents:

- a written assurance that more than one person was entitled to succeed to the house;

- a written assurance that the sale was not instructed or requested by the person entitled to succeed (for example where the executor requires to sell to meet the debts of the deceased); or

- one of the documents referred to in paragraph 6.29 above.

Incapacity of seller - curators bonis

6.41 Where an individual has become *incapax*, the established practice is for the court to appoint a curator bonis to handle that person's interests. The Keeper's practice is to accept that a sale by a curator bonis is not a dealing of the *incapax*

[18]c.66
[19]c.41

to which section 6 of the 1981 Act applies. In such a case, the Keeper is prepared to enter the usual unqualified statement regarding occupancy rights in the title sheet without seeing documentary evidence in one of the forms provided for in section 6(3)(e) of the 1981 Act.

Power of attorney

Consent/renunciation
6.42 The view of the Law Society's Conveyancing Committee, as reported in the Law Society Journal[20], is that a power of attorney may be used for the purposes of execution of a consent or renunciation by a non-entitled spouse if the power of attorney *'confers express power on the attorney to sign a form of consent or renunciation of occupancy rights'*. The Keeper adheres to this view in practice.

Affidavit
The Law Society Conveyancing Committee, in the same above-mentioned report, stated *'that a power of attorney cannot be used for the purpose of an affidavit under section 6(3)(e) or section 8(2) of the Act as the grantor of such an affidavit is making a sworn or affirmed statement that a certain state of affairs exists'*. The Keeper does not accept affidavits running in the name of a seller but signed on the seller's behalf by an attorney.

Mental incapacity of the seller since granting the power of attorney
The Keeper may be prepared to exercise discretion if the seller is unable to make a sworn statement through becoming *incapax* since granting the power of attorney. Before doing so the Keeper would have to be satisfied on two points:

1. That there is good reason why the evidence cannot be obtained in proper form. If this is because the seller is unable to understand and make a sworn statement, the Keeper would expect to see a letter from the seller's doctor giving some indication of the nature of the problem, confirming the seller is unable to understand and make the relevant sworn statement and noting the length of time the person has been *incapax*.

2. That there is no risk of the seller being married. If, for example, the seller was recently widowed and was already *incapax* before his or her spouse died, there is clearly no risk that remarriage could have taken place; but if the seller has been widowed for a number of years, or was never married, the Keeper would look for assurances that there was no non-entitled spouse. Such assurances should normally take the form of affidavits from one or more people who have had close and regular contact with the seller throughout the relevant period.

[20] 1983 JLSS 466

Physical incapacity of seller

6.43 If the seller is suffering a physical incapacity such that it would not be possible to sign the affidavit the Keeper will accept an affidavit executed in terms of section 9 of the Requirements of Writing (Scotland) Act 1995[21]. In such cases, the Keeper recommends that the *'relevant person'* for the purposes of section 9 should be a different individual from the notary public who receives the sworn statement.

Affidavit sworn/affirmed in foreign country

6.44 An affidavit under the 1981 Act which has been sworn/affirmed in a foreign country will be acceptable to the Keeper in the following circumstances:

- It will be acceptable if it is sworn in the presence of a person authorised by the law of the country in question to receive sworn statements, and supported by evidence that the person before whom it is sworn is duly authorised. Such evidence should take the form of an apostille or legalisation, as appropriate.

- It will also be acceptable if sworn in the presence of a UK diplomatic official acting in the country in question and authorised under section 6 of the Commissioners for Oaths Act 1889[22].

- If sworn in England, it will be acceptable if it is sworn in the presence of a solicitor licensed to practise there, since all English solicitors are *ex officio* commissioners for oaths by virtue of section 81 of the Solicitors Act 1974[23].

Gift of heritage

6.45 The protection from challenge afforded to a purchaser in good faith who is in receipt of an affidavit or consent or renunciation, by section 6(3)(e) of the 1981 Act does not extend to a donee who has acquired the property by way of gift. Nevertheless, the Keeper will insert the usual unqualified statement with regard to occupancy rights in the title sheet if one of the documents referred to in paragraph 6.29 above is submitted to him.

Grant of/power of sale in standard security

6.46 The statement regarding occupancy rights under the 1981 Act entered in the title sheet is in respect of persons who were formerly entitled to the subjects. The Keeper gives no such assurances in respect of the interest of the current

[21] c.7
[22] c.10
[23] c.47

registered proprietor and consequently does not require sight of any documentary evidence for the applicant. As such, neither the granting of a standard security nor the subsequent granting of any deed of variation would necessitate the submission to the Keeper of any matrimonial homes act evidence. The only circumstances in which the Keeper would require to examine an affidavit granted in respect of a standard security or related deed is in the event of a sale by the creditor under the power of sale procedure. The Keeper's requirements in this respect will depend on whether the standard security was recorded or registered before or after 1 January 1991.

Prior to the coming into force of the Law Reform (Miscellaneous Provisions) (Scotland) Act 1990[24] creditors could only gain protection in terms of section 8 of the 1981 Act if the documentation was produced *'before the granting of the loan'*. So, if the standard security was recorded or registered before 1 January 1991, the Keeper, in addition to examining an affidavit or consent or renunciation in respect of the granting of the standard security, will require an assurance that the document was produced to the creditor *'before the granting of the loan'*. The effect of the 1990 Act was to remove the stipulation. If, therefore, the standard security was recorded on or after 1 January 1991 no such assurance will be required. The law is unclear as to whether a further advance under a standard security constitutes a dealing under the 1981 Act. Until such time as it is judicially decided that section 8(2) or 8(2)(A) of the 1981 Act applies to further advances, the Keeper will not require to examine a further affidavit, consent or renunciation, in respect of such further advances, in relation to applications for registration proceeding upon powers of sale.

Matrimonial home

6.47 The definition of matrimonial home found in section 22 of the 1981 Act includes *'any garden or other ground attached to and usually occupied with or otherwise required for the amenity or convenience of the house etc.'*. It follows that if such an adjunct is disposed of separately from the house the Keeper will require to examine the necessary matrimonial homes act evidence.

Time-Lapse

6.48 In any situation where there is a time-lapse between the granting of a deed under the 1981 Act and the date on which a party ceases to be 'entitled' to the subjects, the question must arise as to whether the deed in question is still the

[24]c.40

appropriate evidence. The Keeper reserves the right to judge each case on its merits, taking into account such factors as the length of time that has elapsed, the wording of the affidavit, consent, or renunciation, the extent to which the requirements of good faith afforded by section 6(3)(e) of the 1981 Act appear to have been met, and the nature of the certification by the purchaser's agent in response to the questions in Part B of the application form.

Ex facie absolute dispositions

6.49 Although by section 9 of the Conveyancing and Feudal Reform (Scotland) Act 1970[25] it is no longer competent to create a security by way of an *ex facie* absolute disposition, existing ones remain valid until discharged or enforced by the creditor. Those that survive cannot simply be treated, for land registration purposes, in the same manner as their successor, the standard security. The following paragraphs illustrate the registration implications for transactions involving *ex facie* absolute security deeds.

Transfer of an ex facie absolute proprietor's interest
The transfer for value of an ex facie absolute proprietor's interest would, where the subjects lie in an operational area, induce first registration. Application for registration should be made on Form 1. The creditor will be entered as registered proprietor in the proprietorship section of the title sheet. However, the entry will be qualified by a note to show the security nature of the title. The Keeper does not guarantee that the person disclosed in the note as the granter or consentor in the *ex facie* absolute deed is the person presently in right of the reversionary interest.

Transfer of reversionary proprietor's interest
The accepted view is that the reversionary proprietor's interest under an ex facie absolute disposition is an interest in land as defined in section 28. It follows that a transfer of that interest for value will induce a first registration in the Land Register in terms of section 2(1)(a).

Where the transaction affecting the reversionary interest is not a transfer but is, for example, the grant of a further security, then that deed will fall to be recorded in the Register of Sasines, unless the reversionary interest has already been registered in the Land Register.

If the creditor's interest has been registered in the Land Register, any transaction affecting the reversionary interest also falls to be registered in the Land Register.

[25] c.35

Discharge or reconveyance of ex facie disposition

If the creditor's and the reversionary proprietor's interests remain in the Sasine Register, any discharge or reconveyance should be recorded in that Register. Such recording may be dispensed with if the discharge or reconveyance is granted as part of another transaction which induces first registration, and the discharge or reconveyance is presented along with the application for registration of that transaction. A separate application form in respect of the discharge or reconveyance is required.

If either the creditor's or the reversionary proprietor's interest has been registered in the Land Register, the discharge or reconveyance must be registered in that register.

Adjudication

Adjudication in execution

6.50 A decree of adjudication (in execution) does not by itself give the adjudger an absolute title to the subjects as the debtor can purge the debt at any time during the legal, thereby nullifying the effect of the decree. On registration of such a decree in the Land Register, the proprietorship section of the title sheet will therefore continue to show the debtor as proprietor but a further entry will be made also showing the adjudger as proprietor. However, there will be an exclusion of indemnity in respect of the latter entry to reflect that the adjudger's title is a decree of adjudication subject to the legal. An entry will also be made in the charges section of the title sheet in respect of the security aspect of the decree, to establish its ranking in relation to other securities.

If, on the expiry of the legal, the adjudger obtains and registers a decree of declarator of expiry of the legal, the entry relating to the former registered proprietor will be removed from the title sheet and the exclusion of indemnity will be removed from the adjudger's entry. The entry in the charges section will also be deleted.

If no declarator of expiry of the legal is registered, since the adjudger's title is subject to an exclusion of indemnity, prescription will operate in favour of the adjudger from the date of expiry of the legal if prescriptive possession can be proved from that date. The long negative prescription can, of course, operate in favour of the proprietor if the adjudger neither registers a decree of declarator of expiry of the legal nor completes the adjudger's right by prescriptive possession. The long negative prescription commences on the date of expiry of the legal.

Adjudication in implement

Unlike a decree of adjudication in execution a decree of adjudication in implement immediately gives the adjudger an absolute title. Consequently, when an application is made to register a decree of adjudication in implement, this event is treated in the same way as a sale or transfer of the subjects. The entry relating to the former registered proprietor is deleted and replaced with an entry giving full particulars of the adjudger as the person entitled to the interest.

Application for registration of decree

In either of the above cases, application for registration should be made on Form 2 and the decree submitted in support of the application. As it is unlikely the adjudger will hold the land certificate, this is an instance where the applicant need not produce a land certificate with the application for registration. The Keeper may use his powers under rule 17 to require the holder to exhibit the land certificate to him.

After registration, where the adjudication is in execution, the amended land certificate will be returned to the holder and a land certificate will also be issued to the adjudger. Where the adjudication is in implement, the Keeper will issue the amended land certificate to the adjudger, now shown as the registered proprietor, unless the land certificate was originally obtained from a prior heritable creditor in which case the amended land certificate will be issued to that creditor.

Servitudes

6.51 In the context of the 1979 Act (section 28(1)), a servitude is both an *'interest in land'* and, in relation to the servient tenement, an overriding interest. This means that in relation to the interest of the benefited proprietor, the owner of the dominant tenement, it can be registered, but in relation to the interest of the servient tenement it can only be 'noted' (the circumstances in which noting can take place are detailed in section 6(4)(a) and (b). Furthermore, since overriding interests, with the exception of long leases, are not interests for which a title sheet can be opened in terms of section 5(1)(a), a servitude can only be registered as a pertinent of the dominant tenement. Obviously such registration can only be effected if the dominant tenement is itself a registered interest. Equally, a servitude can only be 'noted' if the servient tenement is a registered interest. Where a deed of servitude is granted and one or other of the dominant or servient tenements is registered, it is advisable to record the deed in the Sasine Register as well as seeking registration or noting in the Land Register to ensure that both interests are covered.

The Keeper's statutory duty

6.52 In terms of section 3(1)(a), registration in the Land Register vests a real right in the registered proprietor. This real right is not only to the interest in land but also to *inter alia* any servitude, express or implied, forming part of the interest. Express servitudes, such as those contained in a deed or grant of servitude or referred to in a conveyance, will appear in the property section of the title sheet if they are revealed by the Keeper's examination on first registration and supported by a valid prescriptive progress of title. Implied servitudes, such as those constituted by implied grant and fortified by prescription, will on registration transfer to the registered proprietor but will not be reflected in the title sheet. It is not necessary that they appear in the title sheet as their existence is continued by the operation of section 3(1). Conversely, the real right arising on registration of the servient tenement is subject to the dominant tenement's servitude whether that is noted or not on the servient tenement's title sheet because of section 28(1). Section 3(2) recognises the continuing role of possession in relation to servitudes within areas operational for land registration (and by implication the continuing efficacy of section 3(2) of the Prescription and Limitation (Scotland) Act 1973)[26].

Section 6(1)(e) provides that the Keeper is required to enter in the title sheet *'any enforceable real right pertaining to the interest'*. Whilst this sub-section makes no distinction as to the method of constitution of a real right, and thus a servitude right, the Keeper will only enter such a right if he is satisfied that it has been properly constituted. If the Keeper is not satisfied that a servitude right has been properly constituted he is not likely to consider it enforceable. The Keeper will therefore require to examine evidence of its constitution before he will include the servitude right in the property section of the title sheet. Section 4(1)(a) authorises the Keeper to set the standard of evidence required. It provides that *'an application for registration shall be accepted by the Keeper if it is accompanied by such documents and other evidence as he may require ...'*. The nature of that evidence is considered in the following paragraphs.

Servitudes and plans

6.53 For the avoidance of doubt, servitudes which are properly constituted and carried with the prescriptive progress need not be shown on a deed plan in order for the servitude to be included in the title sheet. In such instances reference to the servitude will be included in the property section without a reference on the title plan.

---

[26]c.52

Implied servitudes

Previous practice

6.54 Notwithstanding the comfort afforded by statute to servitude rights which have been constituted either by implied grant or by possession alone, the Keeper has been asked to enter such servitude rights in the property section of the title sheet. Previously the Keeper would ask for supporting evidence that the servitude had been properly constituted and the evidence supplied would take the form of affidavits. The Keeper then entered the servitude, excluding indemnity in respect of the servitude if the affidavit evidence did not cover the whole of the necessary prescriptive period.

The dangers of affidavit evidence

6.55 Affidavit evidence submitted to the Keeper with respect to a dominant tenement represents a one sided version of events. There is little or no risk for deponents by either being selective or exaggerating the position. There is also scope for more innocent misrepresentation by the deponent of the position on the ground. On numerous occasions the Keeper has been the recipient of subsequent contrary evidence from proprietors of putative servient tenements to the effect that no servitude had ever been constituted. The Keeper would then find himself in the middle of a dispute that he had no power to resolve. In addition his indemnity could be at risk should it transpire the affidavit evidence was less than accurate.

Limitations on rectification

6.56 Experience has shown that rectification - which in practice is limited to subsection 9(3)(a)(iii) where *'the inaccuracy has been caused wholly or substantially by the fraud or carelessness of the proprietor in possession'* - to remove or amend an inaccurate entry of a servitude right is not a viable option in the majority of cases. The Keeper would have to show that the applicant was, or ought to have been, aware that the right had not in fact been properly constituted. Clearly however, a purchaser may not be in a position to know if affidavits accepted in good faith are false or inaccurate. Registration of a servitude right with full indemnity therefore has the practical effect of sterilising the putative servient proprietor's right of challenge. Whilst the Keeper may then be liable in indemnity to the proprietors of the putative servient tenement this is far from the ideal solution.

Limitations of an exclusion of indemnity

6.57 Excluding indemnity in respect of a servitude predicated on affidavit evidence does not resolve matters satisfactorily. An exclusion of indemnity would not prevent the proprietor of the putative servient tenement from making representations to the Keeper challenging the inclusion of a servitude in the title sheet. When faced with contrary evidence, unless the proprietor of the putative dominant tenement rescinds his servitude right, the Keeper may be placed in an invidious position. He lacks both the judicial powers and any sort of procedural framework necessary for dealing fairly and effectively with such situations. The refusal by the Keeper to make any such decision is likely to embroil him in litigation which is, or ought to be, truly a dispute between neighbours. Moreover, the expense of such litigation may be visited on the Keeper who, by his administrative action, has put the proprietor of the servient tenement in the position of vindicating his right.

Current policy

6.58 In view of the dangers inherent in making decisions based on possibly unreliable affidavit evidence the Keeper felt compelled to review his policy. From the end of 1997 he decided that he would not alter, by his own administrative action, the footing upon which a servitude right rests. Rather, the onus of establishing that a servitude right has been properly constituted will fall to the party who seeks to have its constitution declared. Accordingly, subject to the one exception outlined in the following paragraph, the Keeper will include a servitude right in a title sheet only where it has been constituted by express grant by the owner of the servient tenement, or by Act of Parliament, or is supported by the production of a declaratory court decree. In cases prior to the end of 1997 where a servitude right, said to have been constituted by implied grant or possession alone, has been entered in the title sheet of the putative dominant tenement, but subject to exclusion of indemnity, the Keeper will review the position at the end of the prescriptive period, if requested to do so. As part of that review he will consider evidence advanced to justify removal of the exclusion of indemnity.

Servitudes a non domino

6.59 Clearly there are occasions when, notwithstanding the best efforts of practitioners to discover the identity of the owner of a servient tenement so that formal conveyancing to obtain a servitude right can take place, no such owner can be traced. In such circumstances, where the solicitor is not content to rely on the terms of section 3(1)(a) and instead seeks to have a servitude right expressly referred to in the title sheet the Keeper may be prepared to accept a servitude which is granted *a non domino*. Registration of an *a non domino* servitude interest will be accompanied by an exclusion of indemnity note in the title sheet for the prescriptive period: twenty years in terms of section 2(1) of the Prescription and Limitation (Scotland) Act 1973. It is emphasised that where the owner of a servient tenement can be identified the Keeper will not accept registration of a servitude right on an *a non domino* basis.

Discharge of a servitude

6.60 Although a servitude may be effectively discharged by acquiescence or other informal means, the Keeper will not remove a servitude right from a title sheet unless presented with a formal discharge/renunciation of the servitude right by the party entitled to grant such, or a court order extinguishing the servitude right.

Servitudes and indemnity

6.61 In order to disclose the existence of a servitude right in a title sheet, the Keeper, on registration, must be satisfied that the servitude has been validly constituted. In terms of section 12(3)(l), the Keeper will not indemnify the proprietor of the dominant tenement if a servitude subsequently turns out to be unenforceable. A servitude may be lost by non-use or other supervening event and the Keeper cannot investigate every case to find out whether or not a servitude subsists.

Indemnity is payable to the proprietor of the dominant tenement only in respect of a claim relating to the validity of the constitution of a servitude. If the Keeper makes an error in the land certificate on that point, the proprietor of the dominant tenement who suffers loss through the error may be entitled to indemnity. The restrictions imposed by section 12(3)(l) apply only to the proprietor of the dominant tenement. As far as the servient tenement is concerned, a servitude right is an overriding interest. In terms of section 12(3)(h), no indemnity is therefore payable to the servient proprietor for any error or omission in the noting of the servitude in the title sheet for the servient tenement.

Public rights of way

6.62 In terms of section 28(1)(g) the right of a member of the public in respect of any public right of way is, in relation to any interest in land, an overriding interest over it. As such, a public right of way can therefore be noted on the title sheet and referenced on the title plan if any of the circumstances detailed in sub-sections (4)(a) and (b) of section 6 apply, and the Keeper receives sufficient evidence as to its constitution and precise location.

Evidence of constitution should take the form of a court declarator, proof of entry on a local authority rights of way register or a formal agreement involving the proprietor of the land over which the public right of way exists. In the latter case, the Keeper will also need to be satisfied that the subject matter of the agreement is in fact a public right of way rather than a servitude right of access.

On several occasions the Keeper has been presented with evidence of an apparent public right of way which on closer inspection has proved to be no more than a servitude. Whilst servitudes and public rights of way have similar characteristics, they are far from identical. The distinction between them is important not only in terms of constitution and enforcement of the right, but also from the point of view of extinguishing the right. Specific requirements exist as to the establishment of a public right of way, *viz.* public *termini*, appropriate use for prescriptive period, definite route (see *Rhins District Committee of Wigtownshire County Council v. Cuninghame*[27]); and the Keeper will wish to ensure these are met. Similarly, in order for the Keeper subsequently to remove a public right of way from a title sheet he will require either a court declarator stating that the right is no longer extant or evidence that a specific statutory provision, such as occurs under planning and compulsory purchase legislation, has closed the right of way.

As with other overriding interests, the fact that a public right of way is not noted in a title sheet does not imply the non-existence of that right.

Power Of Attorney

6.63 Where a deed pertinent to an application for registration is executed under power of attorney the Keeper will require to examine the power of attorney or a certified copy. The view of the authorities (for example Halliday, *Conveyancing Law and Practice*[28], Volume 1, Chapter 13) is that powers of attorney are construed strictly and that all powers required should be specifically expressed since nothing more will be implied. Halliday notes in particular that special powers must be conferred on an attorney to enable him to sell or dispose or otherwise transact with heritable property (*e.g.* to execute a standard security or a consent or renunciation under the Matrimonial Homes (Family Protection) (Scotland) Act 1981[29], as amended). A power of attorney submitted in support of an application for registration must, therefore, contain specific authorisation for the transaction to which the deed executed thereunder relates. Further discussion on powers of attorney in the context of the Matrimonial Homes (Family Protection) (Scotland) Act 1981 can be found at paragraph 6.42.

Agreement As To Common Boundary

6.64 Section 19 came into operation on the passing of the 1979 Act. Where the titles to adjoining subjects disclose a discrepancy as to a common boundary, this

---

[27](1888) 15R (H.L.) 68
[28]Halliday, JM: *Conveyancing Law and Practice*, 2nd edition 1996-7, ed. IJSTalman, W Green, Edinburgh
[29]c.59

section provides a simple mechanism for resolving the matter. The expense of a conveyance is avoided. Under the terms of the section, the proprietors can come to an agreement about the boundary and execute a plan showing its location (section 19(1)). Where the titles to both interests are held by virtue of deeds recorded in the Register of Sasines, the agreement should take the form of a deed and plan, which can be recorded in that register. This will bind singular successors and other parties with an interest in the land (*e.g.* secured creditors) (section 19(2)).

In the situation where the adjoining properties are both registered, no deed is required. A plan showing the agreed boundary line, and bearing a docquet executed by both proprietors referring to the agreement, will enable the Keeper to make the appropriate amendments to the register. A Form 2 application should be submitted for each affected title. Again, singular successors *etc.* will be bound (section 19(3)).

Where one interest is registered and the other is held on a Sasine title, a deed and plan should be presented with appropriate applications in respect of both registers.

The following example illustrates when section 19 might provide a remedy:

The Keeper has issued a P16 report comparing the boundaries of certain subjects as shown on a deed plan with the ordnance map. The deed plans for the two adjacent properties differ as to the location of one of the boundaries. A site inspection is arranged and confirms that the Ordnance Survey map correctly delineates the occupied extent, this being less than the legal title. However, the deed plan for the adjoining subjects also includes the ground in question. The verbal descriptions in the title deeds for both subjects indicate that they bound each other. The section 19 procedure provides a possible solution. The adjoining proprietors can agree to accept the current occupied extents or they can fix their common boundary at any point within the overlap.

As noted, the section 19 procedure applies only when a comparison of the titles to adjoining lands discloses a discrepancy as to the common boundary. It does not apply when the title boundaries adjoin but there is a discrepancy between title and occupation. In that situation, remedial conveyancing (*e.g.* a contract of excambion) would be necessary. Equally, the section 19 procedure should be used only to regularise a situation that has already arisen, not where the adjoining proprietors simply wish to adjust the position. Nor should the procedure be used as the alternative to taking title *a non domino*. Confusion does sometimes arise as to the circumstances in which a section 19 Agreement is appropriate. Solicitors who intend to use the procedure in an individual case are therefore encouraged to seek the advice of the Keeper's Pre-Registration Enquiries Section.

Standard Securities

Descriptions in standard securities

6.65 The decision in *Bennett v. Beneficial Bank plc*[30] highlighted the need for property descriptions in standard securities to comply with the provisions of Note 1 to Schedule 2 of the Conveyancing and Feudal Reform (Scotland) Act 1970[31], *viz*:

> *'The security subjects shall be described by means of a particular description or by reference to a description thereof as in Schedule D to the Conveyancing (Scotland) Act 1924 or as in Schedule (G) to the Titles to Land Consolidation (Scotland) Act 1868.'*

A property description that does not comply with those provisions will render the standard security void.

The First Division of the Inner House of the Court of Session later pronounced upon the same issues in the case of *Beneficial Bank plc v. McConnachie*[32]. The court upheld *Bennett* and made further observations, *viz*:

- The requirement of a particular description was for a description that would make it unnecessary for the creditor to refer to extraneous matters such as the state of possession or the title of the proprietor. Thus the description must both identify the security subjects and also define their extent.

- A postal address was not, in general terms, sufficient to constitute a particular description as it would not identify the boundaries of the subjects. In the *McConnachie* case, the court had been invited to decide the validity of a standard security granted over a mid-terraced villa house with adjoining ground described as:

'The Property: The Heritable subjects known as 57 LONGDYKES ROAD, PRESTONPANS IN THE COUNTY OF EAST LOTHIAN.'

The court held that such a description did not constitute a particular description. It did, however, suggest that a postal address could, in exceptional circumstances, constitute a particular description if the address contained all

[30] 1995 S.C.L.R. 284 (O.H.)
[31] c.35
[32] 1996 S.C.L.R 438 (I.H.)

that was needed to identify the boundaries. The example given by the court was that of a small offshore island, the name of which constituted its postal address.

- Tenement flats received special mention, with a distinction being drawn between upper flats and ground floor flats. For upper flats, the traditional or common law description (*e.g.* 'northmost house on the second flat of the tenement entering by the common close 10 High Street') could be sufficient both to identify the flat within the tenement and to delineate it. For ground floor flats, the traditional or common law description would not always be competent. If, for example, a ground flat had been extended, some amplification of the description would be required.

The implications of the decisions in the above cases for standard securities submitted with an application for first registration are as follows:

Non-flatted properties
6.66 Only for a very small number of non-flatted properties, such as small offshore islands, will a description premised solely on the property's postal address be acceptable. Even then it will depend upon the particular circumstances, such as whether the island is owned as a single unit. For the majority of non-flatted properties a description based solely on the postal address will not be acceptable to the Keeper. Instead, the description should comply with the requirements stipulated by virtue of Note 1 to Schedule 2 of the 1970 Act otherwise the standard security will be unacceptable for registration in the Land Register or recording in the Register of Sasines.

Flatted properties
6.67 The Keeper will accept, without exclusion of indemnity, a standard security over a tenement flat which relies on a common law description, provided the common law description meets the criteria set out in the following paragraph. This applies equally to ground floor flats and upper floor flats.

For a common law description in a standard security over a ground or upper floor flat to be acceptable to the Keeper, the description must make reference to fixed and unchanging compass directions (for example, 'northmost'). Such usage is well established in conveyancing practice. By contrast, flats described by reference to general and changing directions such as 'left' and 'right' will be unacceptable, as they are based on the subjective viewpoint of a person climbing the tenement stairs. Such references are potentially misleading, since a flat which is on the right side when seen from the street may be on the left side when seen from the stairs. Examples of what is/is not acceptable to the Keeper are given below.

Acceptable descriptions

- The northmost west facing second floor flat 1 Registers Terrace, Anytown.
- The northmost of two second floor flats 1 Registers Terrace, Anytown.
- The northmost second floor flat 1 Registers Terrace, Anytown.

Unacceptable descriptions

- Top flat right 1 Registers Terrace, Anytown.
- TFR 1 Registers Terrace or 3FR 1 Registers Terrace, Anytown.
- 3F2 1 Registers Terrace, Anytown.
- Flat 4/1 Registers Terrace, Anytown.

If the description of a tenement flat in a standard security does not comply with the requirements stipulated in this paragraph, the standard security will not be accepted for registration/recording.

Existing registered property

6.68 The above comments do not apply to a standard security over registered subjects. Section 15(1) Act and rule 25 and Schedule B of the 1980 Rules provide for the interest over which the security has been granted to be described by reference to the title number of that interest; *i.e.*

> '*ALL and WHOLE the subjects known as 10 London Road, Glasgow, registered under Title Number GLA 12345 ...*'

However, where a standard security relates to a part of a registered interest (*e.g.* where it accompanies an application for registration of a transfer of part), the implications are the same as for a standard security granted at the time of first registration, except that a reference to the title number of that larger interest is also required.

Power of sale

6.69 In dealing with an application to register a purchaser's title following on the exercise of a power of sale by a heritable creditor under a standard security recorded in the Sasine Register, the Keeper will exclude indemnity in the purchaser's title sheet if the description of the security subjects does not comply with the requirements stipulated in the foregoing paragraphs. The note excluding indemnity, which will appear in the proprietorship section of the title sheet, will run in terms similar to the following:

Note: Indemnity is excluded in terms of Section 12(2) of the Land Registration (Scotland) Act 1979 in respect of any loss arising as a result of the Standard Security, by AB in favour of CD, recorded GRS (...) ..., being declared or found to be invalid because the description of the security subjects contained therein does not comply with the requirements of Note 1 to Schedule 2 to the Conveyancing and Feudal Reform (Scotland) Act 1970, said Standard Security being the link in title of said CD who disponed the subjects in this Title as heritable creditors in possession to [said] EF [the current proprietor(s) [or] former proprietor(s) within the prescriptive period] by Disposition registered ... .

The exclusion note may be removed after the operation of ten years prescription, subject to production of satisfactory evidence of unchallenged possession.

Alternatively, it may be possible to take remedial action and rectify the standard security under sections 8 and 9 of the Law Reform (Miscellaneous Provisions) (Scotland) Act 1985[33], and so avoid an exclusion of indemnity or have it removed before the expiry of ten years.

In applications to register a purchaser's title following on the exercise of a power of sale under a standard security, for which the Keeper has already issued a fully indemnified charge certificate, the title will be registered without an exclusion of indemnity in respect of the description of the security subjects in the standard security for which the charge certificate was issued. This will apply even where the description of the security subjects does not comply with the requirements set out in the foregoing paragraphs.

Even date references
6.70 It is inadequate to use the description by reference *'and registered in the Land Register of even date with the registration of these presents'* in standard securities submitted with foundation dispositions or feu dispositions at first registration or with transfer of part applications. Section 29, which substitutes in the conveyancing statutes reference to the Land Register for references to the Register of Sasines, does not apply to this form of reference description which is no longer available for a registered interest. Nor, if the standard security is to be registered along with the purchasers/borrowers interest, can a section 15(1) reference to the title number be used as a title number has not yet been allocated. Instead, the standard security should repeat the full particular description contained in the disposition or feu disposition. If that description is dependant upon a plan, a copy of the plan must be annexed to the standard security. Reference cannot be made to the plan annexed to the disposition.

[33]c.73

Other security deeds

6.71 The above considerations apply not merely to standard securities but also to deeds of restriction or disburdenment, and to combined partial discharges and deeds of restriction (see Forms C and D of Schedule 4 to the 1970 Act).

Deduction of title

6.72 Section 15(3) of the 1979 Act dispenses with the need to deduce title in a standard security where the granter is the uninfeft proprietor of an interest registered in the Land Register. Sufficient links in title must, however, be produced to the Keeper along with the application for registration.

Exercise by creditor of power of sale

6.73 The Land Registration (Scotland) Rules 1988[34] introduced the following question to the Application Form 1:

Where the deed inducing registration is in implement of the exercise of a power of sale under a heritable security

Have the statutory procedures necessary for the proper exercise of such power been complied with?   **YES/NO**

Similar questions were also introduced to application Forms 2 and 3.

The inclusion of this question is intended to obviate the need for the Keeper to examine documentary evidence in relation to the exercise of a power of sale under a heritable security. Such evidence will already have been examined by the submitting solicitor and answering this question in the affirmative on the application form avoids the duplication of such examination by the Keeper. If the submitting agent is satisfied that the statutory procedures necessary for the proper exercise of the power of sale have been complied with, the question should be answered in the affirmative.

If the question is answered in the affirmative, the Keeper will normally rely on that certification and not seek to examine the power of sale documentation. The power of sale documentation need not be submitted in support of the application; should it be submitted, the Keeper will not examine it.

If the question is answered in the negative, such power of sale evidence as is available should be submitted in support of the application for registration. The

[34]SI 1988 No. 1143

submitting solicitor should also specify which provisions of the Conveyancing and Feudal Reform (Scotland) Act 1970[35] have not been complied with. While a negative answer draws the Keeper's attention to a perceived defect, it will not necessarily lead to an exclusion of indemnity. The Keeper will examine such evidence as there is in the light of the full circumstances surrounding the application, and will consider whether he is at risk in issuing a fully indemnified title.

Question 10 of Part B of the application Form 1 relates only to the current transaction. It follows that if an earlier transaction within the prescriptive period was in implement of the exercise of a power of sale under a heritable security, the appropriate documentary evidence should be submitted in support of the application for registration. If the documentary evidence, or part of it, is no longer available, that fact should be drawn to the Keeper's attention in response to Question 13.

Ranking of standard securities

6.74 In terms of section 7(2) of the 1979 Act, titles to registered interests will, subject to section 7(1), rank according to the date of registration of those interests. Consequently, standard securities will rank in the date order in which they are entered in the charges section of the title sheet. Section 7(3) provides for ranking as between registration in the Land Register on the one hand and recording in the Sasine Register on the other. The section stipulates that ranking will be according to the respective dates of registration and recording. Thus, heritable securities still subsisting at the date of first registration for which creditors acquired real rights by recording in the Register of Sasines will rank in the order of their recording and before heritable securities registered in the Land Register on or after the date of first registration of the interest to which they relate.

Section 7(1) provides that the statutory ranking provisions may be overridden by either a deed which contains express provisions as to ranking, such as a standard security with a ranking clause or a separate ranking agreement, or any provision as to ranking regulated by statute or rule of law. An example of the latter would be a 'discount security' under the Housing (Scotland) Act 1987[36] which, in terms of section 72(5) thereof, ranks immediately after any standard security granted in security of a loan for the purchase or improvement of the former local authority house.

The Keeper will reflect any properly constituted ranking clause or agreement by means of a footnote to the entry relating to each security in the charges section of the title sheet. For example:

[35] c.35
[36] c.26

Note: The above standard security ranks postponed to [or prior to or pari passu with] the standard security in Entry X.

Alternatively, if the ranking provisions are of a complex nature or contained in a separate ranking agreement, the footnote will simply reflect the existence of the ranking. For example:

Note: The above standard security contains ranking provisions affecting the standard security in Entry X.

Where the subjects over which a standard security is being granted are burdened by another heritable security which, because of its earlier date of recording or registration, will rank prior to that standard security, Note 5 to Schedule 2 of the Conveyancing and Feudal Reform (Scotland) Act 1970 provides that there should have been inserted before the warrandice clause in the deed, the following clause:

'But the security hereby granted is subject to [the prior security deed]'

The warrandice clause will, in turn, be amended to reflect the presence of such a clause.

The Keeper takes the view that such a qualification to warrandice is no more than a warning to the creditor in the new standard security that a prior security exists. It is not regarded as affecting the ranking of the securities. Consequently if two standard securities are received on the same date, one of which contains a *'subject to'* clause, they will be treated as ranking *pari passu*. The Keeper's view is based on his reading of Note 5 to Schedule 2 which distinguishes between the situation where a standard security is described as being *'subject to'* another heritable security, and the situation where a ranking clause is required. Whilst there is no case law directly in point, support for the Keeper's stand can be found at paragraph 57-30 of J. M. Halliday's *Conveyancing Law and Practice in Scotland*[37] (2nd edition, Greens 1997).

Standard securities by limited companies

6.75 See paragraphs 5.47 *et seq.* for a comprehensive discussion of this topic.

Standard security over standard security

6.76 This is an extremely rare occurrence and solicitors intending to register such a deed should contact the Pre-registration Enquiries Section to discuss the application.

[37]Halliday, JM: *Conveyancing Law and Practice,* 2nd edition 1996-7, ed. IJSTalman, W Green, Edinburgh

Feudal Relationship

6.77 By virtue of section 2(1)(a)(iv), an unregistered interest in land becomes registrable on a transfer whereby it is absorbed into an already registered interest. This is so whether or not there is valuable consideration. By 'absorption' is meant consolidation of two fees in the feudal chain by separate or endorsed minute or by disposition with a clause *ad perpetuam remanentiam*, or the merger of leasehold interests, *e.g.* a renunciation by a tenant in favour of the landlord. Where the higher fee is already registered in the Land Register and the proprietor acquires by disposition *ad rem* the subjacent fee, title to which is recorded in the Register of Sasines, the absorption must be given effect to in the Land Register.

Section 2(2) states that section 2(1)(a)(ii) is inapplicable where the interest transferred is to be absorbed into an unregistered interest. So, in this case, if there is a disposition *ad rem*, even one for valuable consideration, it is not registrable in the Land Register if the superior's interest is not registered there. Section 2(4)(a) covers any transfer of a registered interest incuding those cases in which such an interest is absorbed into another registered interest in land. A disposition *ad rem* of a registered interest to the proprietor of the higher registered interest is a dealing with a registered interest in land and is thus registrable. Section 2(4)(b) ensures that any absorption by a registered interest in land of another registered interest in land shall also be registrable.

In practical terms, where section 2(4) applies, the part absorbed is removed from the title sheet of the lower interest. If the whole of the lower interest is absorbed, the title sheet is cancelled. The title sheet of the higher interest is amended by removing any reference to the lower interest as burdening the higher one.

Where a registered interest is absorbed by an interest the title to which is recorded in the Register of Sasines, a real right may be obtained only by recording the absorption in that register. In such a case, the disposition *ad rem* or minute of consolidation should be presented with applications for joint registration in both the Land Register and the Register of Sasines. The deed must contain an adequate description and bear a warrant of registration. The Keeper will cancel the relevant title sheet. This does not, however, apply where absorption results from the operation of prescription (see section 8(2)(b)). (The question of absorption is discussed in more detail in paragraph 5.66.)

Third party rights

6.78 Where consolidation has taken place, one might assume that the conditions in the original feu deed no longer subsist. But when giving effect to an application involving the merger of two fees, the Keeper must consider whether the feu deed has created, either expressly or by implication, a *jus quaesitum tertio*. The subject of third party rights is somewhat complex and although it is not possible to be prescriptive about the many scenarios that may arise where there may be third party rights subsisting, the approach the Keeper takes is to enter in the burdens section of the appropriate title sheet any burdens which in his view may still subsist and be enforceable at the instance of a third party. The preamble to the entry in the burdens section will make it clear that the conditions have been entered notwithstanding the consolidation of the interests. It should be noted though that the Keeper does not guarantee that such burdens are subsisting or enforceable. The content of burdens in the deeds submitted will be carefully examined and a cautious approach will be taken when editing these. This is because once a burden has been omitted from the title sheet experience shows that it is unlikely that the proprietor of the dominium utile interest will consent to its being reinstated in the title sheet. The burden, effectively, will be lost in all time coming (see section 3(1)(a) of the Act). Burdens are of course capable of being discharged, waived or varied at the instance of the party entitled to enforce them, or application may be made to the Lands Tribunal for an order. In the case of *Brookfield Developments Limited v. the Keeper of the Registers of Scotland*[38], certain alleged burdens in a title sheet were declared by the tribunal not to subsist and they were ordered to be struck out.

Effect of consolidation on existing standard security

6.79 Where there are standard securities over the *dominium directum* and/or the *dominium utile* prior to consolidation being effected and these are not discharged by the creditor, it is normal practice for these to be considered as affecting the consolidated fee thereafter. It can be helpful if the creditor indicates consent by executing any minute of consolidation. Existing charge certificates would require to be submitted to reflect any change in title number on consolidation.

Grant by uninfeft proprietor

Minute of waiver
6.80 On occasion the Keeper has been asked to accept a minute of waiver by a party not yet infeft in the appropriate fee. For example, a new local authority

---

[38] 1989 SCLR 435

might be put to the expense of making up title to an extensive superiority vested in a predecessor council in order simply to grant a waiver in respect of one small piece of land. While there is no specific provision for such a grant in section 3 of the Conveyancing (Scotland) Act 1924[39], the Keeper may in certain circumstances adopt a pragmatic approach and give effect in the Land Register to a deed of waiver containing a suitable clause of deduction of title.

Non enforcement of conditions - letters from superiors
The Keeper will make an entry in the title sheet in respect of those burdens which are considered to subsist. Occasionally superiors' letters are submitted to the Keeper confirming that the particular burden or condition will not be enforced. Such letters do not bind singular successors; but the Keeper will note the existence of such correspondence in the burdens section if it is brought to his attention.

Feu grant by uninfeft proprietor
When a feu writ is granted by an uninfeft proprietor, the vassal will obtain title by registration, but no valid real right is obtained. It is incompetent to deduce title in a feu writ, so a clause of deduction does not provide a remedy. However, accretion operates to validate the feu writ retrospectively when the superior completes title. Under registration of title, if the deed inducing registration is a feu writ by an uninfeft proprietor, the Keeper will exclude indemnity in respect of the lack of infeftment. The Keeper will inform the applicant, who will be given the opportunity to put matters right. This will normally mean that the superior should complete title by recording a deed in the Sasine Register or submit a Form 2 application with the appropriate links in title to update the title sheet for the superiority interest. The Keeper will hold the application relating to the vassal's interest in abeyance until he is notified that the superior has completed title. It should be noted that the *onus* is on the solicitor for the vassal to advise the Keeper when this has been done. The Keeper will then issue a title to the feu retaining the original date of registration and without exclusion of indemnity.

If however the applicant does not wish to proceed as above, the Keeper will issue a title containing an exclusion of indemnity in respect of the granter's lack of title to feu. The title may subsequently be validated by prescriptive possession. An application for removal of the exclusion of indemnity may therefore be made at the end of the prescriptive period. Such an application should be supported by affidavit evidence from the proprietors of the ground in question during the prescriptive period, to the effect that they have possessed the property openly, peaceably and without judicial interruption.

[39]c.27

Similar considerations apply in the case of a lease granted by a landlord who is uninfeft.

Redemption of feuduty and other annual payments

6.81 Feuduty and certain other annual payments such as ground annual, skat, standard charge and stipend are burdens on the title rather than charges. It follows that the Keeper will enter them in the burdens section of the title sheet.

Subject to the restrictions on rectification in section 9(3), any subsisting obligation revealed in an application form or in supporting documents for payment of any of these sums will be entered in the burdens section. This applies whether the obligation is to pay the whole sum or an apportioned share. In the latter case the apportioned amount and the original sum will both be shown. In general, if the documents in an application for registration indicate that an obligation for payment subsists but the applicant certifies on the application form that no annual payments are exigible, the matter will be referred back to the applicant. Where a deed executed after 1 September 1974 purports to create a new feuduty, ground annual *etc.* the obligation to pay will not be inserted either in the burdens section of the title sheet for the burdened property or in the property section of the title sheet for the benefited subjects. Where a burden of payment was created before that date, the Keeper will disclose the obligation unless satisfactory evidence of redemption is produced. For feuduties, such evidence may take the form of a redemption receipt, or a letter from the superior confirming that the feuduty has been redeemed.

Even where question 5(d) in Part B of the application Form 1 (about whether any recurrent monetary payments are exigible from the subjects) has been answered in the negative, the Keeper has found it difficult to obtain from applicants the necessary redemption receipts *etc.* The Keeper has therefore adopted the policy of accepting such certification at face value and of not requisitioning the supportive evidence, provided the annual payment is one to which section 5 of the Land Tenure Reform (Scotland) Act 1974[40] applies.

Exceptionally it will be noted that an extract order has been recorded by the superior. Such recording is, on the face of it, evidence that some difficulty exists and the Keeper will therefore seek further information. If no satisfactory explanation is forthcoming the Keeper will show the fact that the redemption money is payable in respect of redeemed feuduty in terms of section 5 of the Land Tenure Reform (Scotland) Act 1974 as a burden on the title. If section 5 of

[40]c.38

the 1974 Act does not apply (*e.g.* where the payment is an informally apportioned feuduty), the Keeper will include details of the payment in the burdens section unless he is presented with evidence of formal allocation or voluntary redemption.

Over feuduties etc.

6.82 The redemption provisions of the 1974 Act relate only to the payment of feuduty *etc.* from the interest transferred for value. So, while the immediate feuduty may have been redeemed, the over-feuduty may remain payable.

Although not bound in terms of section 6(3) of the 1979 Act to enter in the title sheet particulars of an over-feuduty or over-rent, the Keeper may do so if it comes to his notice. In terms of section 12(4)(a) of the 1979 Act a refusal or omission by the Keeper to enter into a title sheet any over-feuduty or over-rent exigible in respect of a registrable interest does not of itself preclude a claim on the indemnity.

Foreshore

6.83 Foreshore is in the unusual position of being both *regalia majora* and *regalia minora*. Whereas certain rights in foreshore (*regalia majora*) cannot be alienated, for example the right of the public for navigation and fishing, the Crown can divest itself of the property in foreshore (*regalia minora*). Title to foreshore can thus be made by direct grant from the Crown. The Crown Estate Commissioners are the custodians of the property held by the Sovereign in right of the Crown. Being *regalia minora* it is possible that titles, other than those derived from the Crown, may include foreshore. Such titles require to be fortified by 20 years uninterrupted possession (Prescription and Limitation (Scotland) Act 1973[41], section 1(4)). The evidence that the Keeper will require to examine in respect of foreshore will therefore depend from where the title has derived.

Where title to foreshore is derived from a Crown grant the Keeper, in the absence of any indications of adverse possession, does not require to examine any other evidence in fortification of the title. In the absence of such an express grant from the Crown the Keeper will require evidence that the grant of foreshore by any other party has been supported by 20 years uninterrupted possession, as per the above. The Keeper has no concluded view as to what evidence of possession would suffice, though he notes that the evidence would have to relate to acts consistent with a right of property and go beyond mere exercise of the rights of the public. Similarly, any such acts would have to be referable to the title relied upon and not to some lower right such as, for example, a servitude. In the

[41]c52

absence of such evidence or if the evidence produced is inadequate the Keeper will exclude his indemnity as regards the right to foreshore.

Effect of exclusion of indemnity

6.84 Where the Keeper proposes to exclude his indemnity because of lack of evidence of prescription having fortified the title to foreshore, or rights in foreshore, he is obliged, in terms of section 14(1), to inform the applicant for registration. If the applicant agrees to the exclusion of indemnity the Keeper need take no further action other than issuing a land certificate bearing the exclusion. If the applicant requests the Keeper not to exclude indemnity the Keeper is bound, in terms of section 14(1)(b), to notify the Crown Estate Commissioners that he has been so requested.

Section 14(2) details the steps the Crown Estate Commissioners must take if they wish to challenge the applicant's title to the foreshore, or rights in the foreshore. On receipt of the notification sent to them by the Keeper the Crown Estate Commissioners have one month in which to give the Keeper written notice of their interest and three months in which to inform the Keeper in writing that they are taking steps to challenge the title. If the Commissioners observe this procedure the Keeper must continue to exclude indemnity in respect of the foreshore either until the operation of prescription, coupled with evidence of possession, permits the Keeper to remove the exclusion or until such time as it appears to him that the Commissioners are no longer taking steps to challenge the title or that their challenge has been unsuccessful.

Kindly Tenancies

6.85 One of the aims in introducing registration of title was to make the Land Register as comprehensive as possible. To that end, the number of interests to which a real right can be perfected without registration has been reduced in those parts of Scotland which are now operational areas of the Land Register. In this regard, it used to be possible to obtain a real right to land held under a kindly tenancy without recording a deed in the Sasine Register. Kindly tenancies survive only in four villages (Hightae, Smallholm, Heck and Greenhill), collectively called the Four Towns of Lochmaben, in Dumfriesshire. (For a fuller description of kindly tenancies, see the *Stair Memorial Encyclopaedia*[42], Vol. 18, Para. 72.) Since the former county of Dumfries became a Land Register operational area on 1 April 1997, completion of title to a kindly tenancy can now be effected only by registration (section 3(3)).

[42]*Stair Memorial Encyclopaedia: The Laws of Scotland,* 1993, Law Society of Scotland/Butterworths, Edinburgh

The position is that any kindly tenant who did not obtain a real right in and to his interest prior to 1 April 1997 can obtain a real right only by registration in the Land Register. Further, even where a real right was obtained prior to 1 April 1997, an incoming kindly tenant (whether by transfer for value, or on a gratuitous transfer, or by succession) can obtain a real right only by registration. This applies even where the transfer had been completed prior to 1 April 1997, if the incoming kindly tenant had not entered into possession or had not recorded his deed in the Sasine Register before that date.

A kindly tenant whose title was made real before 1 April 1997 is not immediately affected by the introduction of registration of title to the county of Dumfries (although, as indicated above, an incoming kindly tenant is affected). Should a kindly tenant with a recorded title in the Sasine Register now wish to grant a standard security, the standard security must be recorded in the Sasine Register in order to complete the creditor's real right (section 8(2)(c)). Similarly, if the kindly tenant has obtained a real right by possession prior to 1 April 1997 and now wishes to grant a standard security, the creditor will obtain a real right following the recording of the title and the standard security in the Sasine Register.

Udal Tenure

6.86 Registration of title will be introduced to Orkney and Shetland on 1 April 2003, according to the current Land Register extension programme. Until then, it remains possible to perfect a real right to land held under udal tenure without recording a deed in the Sasine Register. Udal tenure, a form of allodial tenure peculiar to Orkney and Shetland, derives from old Norse law and survives to the present day, though many owners feudalised their holdings by obtaining charters from the Crown. When Orkney and Shetland become operational areas of the Land Register, a real right will be obtained only by registration (section 3(3)). Thereafter, the position will be much the same as for kindly tenancies, as described in the three preceding paragraphs, the only difference being the commencement date.

Liferents

6.87 Proper conventional liferents are registrable interests; legal and beneficial or trust liferents are not.

A liferent is registrable only if the interest over which it is created is registered in the Land Register (section 2(2) and (3)). A separate title sheet is not opened for a liferent (section 5(1)) and no certificate of title is issued in respect of it (section 5(2) and (3)).

A proper liferent existing at the time of first registration will be noted on the title sheet. Otherwise, the interest being registered would no longer be subject to the liferent. Where a real right has already been established, there is no need for the liferenter to apply for registration.

The liferent will be noted in the proprietorship section of the title sheet, though not as a proprietorial interest in the subjects in the title but rather as a burden on the subjects. Should the liferenter wish his interest to be shown as a proprietorial interest, an application in the name of the liferenter should be made on Form 2. The fixed registration fee will be charged.

When a liferent is created over a registered interest, the liferenter's interest must be registered to secure a real right. In terms of rule 9, an application to register a liferent interest should be made on an application Form 2.

The creation of a liferent over a registered interest may be revealed to the Keeper in an application for registration affecting the registered interest (*e.g.*, where the liferent is created by reservation in a disposition or where a destination in a disposition is to A in liferent and B in fee), without an application being made to register the liferenter's interest. In that situation, the Keeper will note on the title sheet the creation of the liferent, but the liferenter will not obtain a real right until the interest is registered.

On termination of a liferent disclosed in a title sheet, application should be made to the Keeper for registration of the termination. If no other dealing is contemplated, an application may be made on Form 2, accompanied by evidence of termination. Where the liferent terminates on the death of the liferenter, a death certificate or an affidavit will be acceptable to the Keeper as sufficient evidence of termination.

If a transfer of the fiar's interest is contemplated, the evidence of termination may accompany the application for registration of the transfer. There is no need for a separate application as regards the termination of the liferent.

Where the liferent terminates on renunciation, a formal renunciation or a consent by the liferenter to a conveyance of the subjects will be required, unless the liferent is alimentary in nature. A renunciation of an alimentary liferent by the liferenter is not competent. However, in terms of section 1(4) of the Trusts

(Scotland) Act 1961[43], the court can revoke or vary an alimentary liferent. The Keeper would expect to have sight of an order from the court before removing an alimentary liferent from a title sheet.

Minerals

6.88 The Henry Report did not recommend that mines and minerals which already existed as a separate tenement should be included in the scheme for first registration. The report did, however, provide for the registration of minerals severed from the surface after the registration of the lands. The 1979 Act does not differentiate. An interest in mines and minerals transferred as a separate tenement for valuable consideration in an operational area requires registration to establish a real right. The problems associated with identification are the same in each case. The applicant must be able to identify the surface lands under which the minerals being transacted with are situated and, where necessary, provide evidence by plan identifying the strata. The position as regards minerals under lands being registered can be less than clear; and the prior titles may not provide much assistance. For example, the existence of old, unrecorded mineral leases might not have been brought to the attention of the Keeper at the time of first registration. Such leases would be overriding interests.

Where titles do make reference to minerals the Keeper enters the details in the property section of the title sheet (*e.g.* 'with minerals' or 'the minerals are excepted'). If the title sheet is silent as to minerals there is a rebuttable presumption that the minerals are included on the principle *a caelo usque ad centrum* (from the sky to the centre of the earth). There is, however, no guarantee that minerals are included in the title.

General rule

6.89 As a general rule a conveyance of land will, in the absence of an express provision to the contrary, carry any minerals under the surface. In common with most general rules, however, this one is subject to exceptions. Once the minerals interest is severed from the interest in the land, usually by reservation in favour of the granter of a feu or disposition of the surface, the minerals become a separate tenement. Minerals must therefore be specifically included in any subsequent disposition by the person to whom they were reserved if they are to be carried by such a disposition (unless they were reserved in a feu and the subsequent disposition of superiority was drawn in the true feudal manner, the significance of which is explained below).

[43]c.57

Exceptions to general rule

6.90 By an Act of the Scots Parliament of 1424[44], gold and silver form part of the regalia and are vested in the Crown. By a series of more recent statutory provisions, coal, mines of coal and associated minerals were vested in the British Coal Corporation, and petroleum and natural gas in the Crown. Any reference to minerals in any conveyance or in any title sheet must therefore be construed as not including those minerals vested in public bodies. The Keeper will therefore omit from the title sheet any specific reference in a deed to any of the minerals vested in a public body.

Attention is drawn to the article 'Minerals and the Land Register'[45] which contains a discussion of the effects of the Coal Industry Act 1994[46] (the 1994 Act). With effect from 31 October 1994, the interest of the British Coal Corporation in unworked coal and coal mines vested in a new body called the Coal Authority by virtue of the 1994 Act. The interest of the Authority remains an overriding interest. However, under the 1994 Act, coal can return to private ownership and any conveyance or long lease of coal by the Authority will induce registration as infeftment will be required to obtain a real right.

Another exception to the general rule is that a conveyance in the form set out in Schedule A or Schedule B to the Lands Clauses Consolidation (Scotland) Act 1845[47] does not carry minerals unless they are expressly included. This is true also of any of the deeds which may be used as an alternative to a schedule conveyance in a compulsory acquisition, namely a notarial instrument, notice of title or general vesting declaration.

Reservation of minerals

6.91 A conveyance by feu writ or disposition will, of course, only carry minerals *sub silentio* if the minerals are in the title. It has been common practice for centuries, especially in feus, for the granter of a deed to reserve the minerals and the right to work them. A mineral reservation is often included in a deed even where the granter has no title to the minerals. It is, therefore, often extremely difficult to discover where the title to minerals lies. Where the titles are silent as regards minerals the title sheet also will be silent, and there will be no indemnity in respect of minerals. Where there is a reservation of minerals the reservation will be disclosed on the title sheet in the manner described below.

[44] c.13
[45] 1996 JLSS 266
[46] c.21
[47] c.17

It is not unknown for a mineral reservation to be followed by an express inclusion of minerals in a subsequent deed. That subsequent deed may serve as a foundation for prescription to the minerals and the Keeper may in such a case insert both a mineral reservation and an express inclusion of minerals followed by an exclusion of indemnity in the title sheet. Note, however, that the 1994 Act prevents prescription operating against the right of the British Coal Corporation or the Coal Authority, although a purchaser from either body is not so protected and nor is the Keeper. In order to prevent misunderstanding, therefore, the Keeper will add a note along the lines of the following to the property section of title sheets which either relate to minerals or include minerals in terms which may be construed as implying that coal may be included and there has been no grant by the Coal Authority to confirm that interpretation:

'Note: Notwithstanding any other terms of this title, no interest in coal or allied minerals is included in the subjects in this title.'

Inclusion of minerals in title sheet

6.92 A proprietor whose title is silent as regards minerals, but who nonetheless considers he owns them, may be dissatisfied with a title which does not give a fully indemnified title to minerals, and ask the Keeper to expressly include them. An application may also be received for registration of a title to minerals alone. On some occasions a deed submitted as part of an application may contain an express inclusion of minerals qualified by a phrase such as 'so far as vested in us' or 'so far as we have right thereto'. In this situation the Keeper will usually omit the minerals from the title sheet unless it can be demonstrated from the progress of deeds submitted with the application that the minerals have carried. Where this is clear the Keeper will further expect evidence of possession of the mineral interest otherwise it is likely there will be an exclusion from indemnity expressed in the title sheet in appropriate terms.

Exclusion of indemnity

6.93 Where the title sheet is silent about minerals there is no guarantee that the minerals are included in the title. It follows that there can be no indemnity for loss in respect of an interest in mines and minerals where the title sheet does not expressly disclose that such an interest is included in the registered interest in land. There is statutory provision for this exclusion at section 12(3)(f) of the Act. The Keeper is also empowered by section 12(2), on registration of an interest in land, to exclude, in whole or in part, any right to indemnity in respect of anything appearing in, or omitted from, the title sheet. This power is frequently used in relation to the failure by applicants to provide the Keeper with sufficient evidence to demonstrate title to, and possession of, the minerals for the prescriptive period. Evidence of possession would normally include evidence that the minerals had been worked during the relevant period or take the form of a court declarator. As regards the former, the existence of a mineral lease has been accepted as sufficient evidence as have documents produced that point quite clearly to the ongoing working of minerals. The Keeper is not prescriptive about the evidence that he will accept in order for a fully indemnified mineral title to be granted. In the event that it cannot be established that sufficient prior legal title exists and/or no evidence of possession can be produced, the Keeper will exclude indemnity. In this event, the following notes are typically entered in the proprietorship section of the title sheet as appropriate:

> 'Note: As regards the minerals specified in the property section of this title indemnity is excluded in terms of section 12(2) of the Land Registration (Scotland) Act 1979 in respect that no prescriptive progress of legal title to minerals prior to the disposition by ... to ... registered [date] has been produced to the Keeper.'

> 'Note: As regards the minerals specified in the property section of this title indemnity is excluded in terms of section 12(2) of the Land Registration (Scotland) Act 1979 in respect that evidence that the above-named proprietor's legal title has been vindicated by uninterrupted and unchallenged possession for the prescriptive period has not been produced to the Keeper.'

Note that exclusion notes of the latter type do not simply expire after ten years in the absence of challenge. Further discussion regarding this aspect is to be found in the article mentioned above.

Not unnaturally, an applicant may not be satisfied with a land certificate bearing an exclusion of indemnity even if the exclusion affects only the minerals. In certain circumstances (*e.g.* where no third party rights are involved) the Keeper may be able to issue a land certificate which is silent as to minerals; or it may be possible to make up a separate title sheet for the minerals interest and issue a separate land certificate for the minerals containing any necessary exclusion of indemnity relating exclusively to them. Any application which may lead to the express inclusion of minerals in a title sheet, whether or not it is followed by an exclusion of indemnity, is examined rigorously by the Keeper. Similarly any case involving a request for the removal of an existing exclusion of indemnity in respect of minerals (see below) is investigated thoroughly before a decision is taken.

Effect of consolidation of fees

6.94 It is not uncommon for the proprietor of the *dominium utile* of land to also acquire the superiority. The proprietor may or may not subsequently consolidate the two fees. This is sometimes resorted to by builders and developers as a means of getting rid of conditions which hamper the development of the surface land. If the minerals were reserved in the original feu their current position can be unclear.

If the disposition of the superiority is drawn in the true feudal fashion, that is, it conveys the lands without stating that it is the superiority that is being conveyed, and the indication that it is superiority is gleaned from the fact that the rents and feuduties are assigned and the feu rights are excepted from warrandice, then that disposition can be held to have conveyed the minerals. This is because it is a disposition of the granter's whole right in the subjects under exception of the feu rights granted by him. As the minerals were reserved to the superior in the feu deeds, and it is only the rights granted in the feus which are excepted, then the disposition carries the minerals. Conversely, if the minerals are excepted in the feu deed, and the subsequent disposition of the superiority states *in gremio* that it is a disposition of the superiority of the subjects in the feu deed, then, as the minerals were excepted from the feu deed, the inference is that they are excepted from the disposition of superiority. In other words, if the disposition of superiority actually says *in gremio* that it is a disposition of superiority, the minerals must be expressly conveyed if they are to be carried by the disposition.

There is, however, a school of thought that maintains that if the disposition of superiority contains some such phrase as 'together with my whole right title and interest in and to ...' the effect is that this is sufficient to carry the minerals even without a specific reference to them. In such cases, when a builder who has acquired both the property and superiority comes to sell individual house plots, the Keeper may experience difficulties in deciding what to do about minerals in the title sheets. If the minerals are not carried by the disposition of superiority, then, even if the two fees are consolidated, the Keeper will still show the mineral reservation in the title sheet. If there is doubt as to whether the minerals have been carried it is the Keeper's view that it is better to include the reservation in the title sheet. If the minerals have been carried by the disposition of superiority but no consolidation has followed, if any subsequent conveyance of the whole or part of the subjects refers only to the *dominium utile* title then severe doubts must exist as to whether the conveyance carries the minerals or not.

Because of these doubts and difficulties, in any case where the documents and evidence submitted reveal that the minerals were reserved in a feu and the superiority has subsequently come into the possession of the proprietor of the *dominium utile*, the question of whether the minerals should be shown as reserved or not requires careful consideration.

Three rules

6.95 The preceding paragraphs give some idea of the problems surrounding the whole question of minerals. However, the matter can be simplified by applying the following three rules:

1. If the documents and evidence are silent as to minerals the title sheet will normally be silent as to minerals.

2. If the documents and evidence reveal a straightforward mineral reservation with no complicating factors, that reservation will be included in the title sheet in the manner outlined below.

3. If there are complicating factors the Keeper may call for further evidence before reaching a decision on how to reflect the position.

Reservation of minerals - practical examples

6.96 A reservation of minerals is an exception from the subjects in the title sheet rather than a burden on them. However the terms of a minerals reservation clause may not only except the minerals but also create burdens on the minerals title which are rights in favour of owners of the surface subjects; for example, restrictions on how the minerals are worked, compensation for damage to the surface, obligations of support *etc*. Similarly the minerals reservation clause may create burdens on the surface subjects which are rights in favour of the mineral owner; for example, rights to sink shafts, erect pit head gear *etc*. For practical purposes therefore, only a brief reference to the mineral reservation is made in the property section and the full text of the mineral reservation clause is set out in the burdens section. The mineral reservation is entered in the property section by means of a note along the lines of the following:

> '*Note: The minerals are excepted. The conditions under which the minerals are held are set out in the [name of deed] in entry [number] of the burdens section.*'

The note is adapted as necessary to cater for circumstances of the kind narrated in the following paragraphs.

If the documents and evidence reveal that there is more than one mineral reservation (for example the over superior and the superior may both have reserved the minerals in the respective feus) then both reservations are inserted in the title sheet and the note is adapted to show both deeds containing the reservations.

Where the mineral reservation applies only to part of the subjects in the title sheet, that part is separately referenced on the title plan and the note is adapted accordingly. For example:

'Note: The minerals under the part tinted [blue] on the title plan are excepted. The conditions under which these minerals are held ... etc.'

Occasionally a mineral reservation relates only to certain specified minerals, not to all minerals under the surface. In such a case the note will refer only to those specified minerals. For example:

'Note: The fireclay between the millstone grit and blue clay layers under the part tinted [yellow] on the title plan is excepted. The conditions under which the fireclay is held ... etc.'

There may be cases where the minerals are excepted but the deed does not narrate any conditions under which they are held. Here all the Keeper can do is show that the minerals are excepted. In this case a note is inserted that states simply 'the minerals are excepted'.

Coal

6.97 From 1 July 1942, when coal and allied minerals became vest in the Coal Commission (the predecessor of the National Coal Board *et al*) under the Coal Act 1938[48], up until the Coal Industry Act 1994[49] ('the 1994 Act') conveyancers were able to proceed on the basis that, whatever other minerals might pass and regardless of what was narrated in earlier titles, coal was virtually always excluded from a title. As regards a registered title, the interest in coal of British Coal was an overriding interest. The 1994 Act has removed that certainty.

Under the 1994 Act the entire interest of British Coal Corporation in unworked coal and coal mines vested in the Coal Authority on the restructuring date of 31 October 1994. In so far as coal remains vest in the Coal Authority no problems will arise for the 1994 Act makes provision for that to be classed as an overriding interest. However, one of the principal aims of the 1994 Act is to facilitate the

[48]c.52
[49]c.21

return of coal to the private sector and this carries considerable implications for land registration. The most obvious result will be registration in the Land Register, for the first time, of unworked coal as a separate interest in land, and of long leases of coal. That is because the purchaser, or lessee under a long lease, of a coal interest from the Coal Authority will require to take infeftment in order to complete a real right.

This creates potential problems with existing registered titles which purport to be to the whole minerals, and with titles which specifically include the whole minerals along with the surface land but do not exclude coal from those minerals. The traditional assumption that the private surface owner does not own the coal will therefore become increasingly untenable. Similarly it will become progressively more difficult for an inquirer to determine whether the reason why coal is included in the property description in a title sheet is due to the fact the terms of the title date from pre-nationalisation days or because title to coal has been acquired from the Coal Authority. Where the former applies, the title insofar as it relates to coal is and will remain ineffective to the extent that the 1994 Act provides that no one shall be able to acquire an interest or a right adverse to the title of the British Coal Corporation or Coal Authority by virtue of prescription.

Thus, in order to ensure the Land Register does not mislead anyone or create a potential competition in title, the Keeper will add coal interest exclusion notes to the property sections of all title sheets (a) which are either created or updated with effect from 31 October 1994 or after; (b) which either relate to minerals or which specifically include minerals in terms which allow the conclusion to be drawn that coal is or may be included; and (c) where there has been no grant by the Coal Authority to justify that interpretation. The exclusion note will run in terms similar to the following:

> 'Note: Notwithstanding any other terms of this title, no interest in coal or allied minerals is included in the subjects in this Title.'

Conclusion

6.98 Handling applications involving title to minerals, including coal, is inherently problematic. The Keeper is always happy to discuss the evidential requirements pertaining to any particular case (especially as regards possession, normally by working, of minerals for the prescriptive period). Queries, preferably in writing in the first instance, should be directed to the Pre-Registration Enquiries Section.

Natural Water Boundaries

6.99 Subjects which have as one of their boundaries a natural water feature, such as a river, loch or the sea, present additional considerations for the Keeper and the submitting solicitor both at the time of first registration and subsequently. Such considerations include two related issues, namely identification of the actual position of the natural water boundary and *alluvio*.

The problem with natural water boundaries

6.100 References in a deed to a natural water feature can take many forms. Where it is a river the boundary is commonly stated to form the *medium filum* but it can, for instance, be the near or far river bank. Similarly, with the sea the boundary could be stated to be the foreshore or low or high water mark of ordinary spring tides or some other feature. In other cases the actual position will not be defined, rather the deed will simply narrate that the subjects are 'bounded by the River X' or 'by the sea'. Where that occurs consideration has to be given to the judicial interpretation of such references in order to determine where the particular boundary is deemed to fall. (See, for instance, Professor Halliday's *Conveyancing Law and Practice*[50], 2nd Edition, Volume II paragraph 18-11.)

Under registration of title the main difficulty with natural water boundaries derives from the fact that they may not remain static. The *medium filum*, for instance, is a fairly abstract notion as the width of a river is not constant. Similarly both the width of a river and sea boundaries can change with the seasons and be affected by other factors such as weather conditions and *alluvio* and *avulsion*. The practical consequence of the latter two events is that the actual course of a natural water boundary may at the time of registration be significantly different from the position revealed by the prior titles and may again change subsequent to the registration of the subjects.

Plotting natural water boundaries on the title plan poses a number of practical problems for the Keeper. Where the line of a natural water boundary is not straight, it can prove most difficult to accurately plot the precise line of the boundary. When attempting to plot natural water boundaries the Keeper is hampered by Ordnance Survey's policy of not updating water features as part of their ongoing revision programme. Consequently, the actual course of rivers and burns and position of foreshore *etc.* may differ from that shown on the most up to date ordnance maps. The scale of ordnance maps in rural areas can pose additional problems. At best they will be 1:2500, but in particularly sparsely populated areas they can be as great as 1:10000. As a result accurate plotting on the ordnance map can be almost impossible.

[50]Halliday, JM: *Conveyancing Law and Practice,* 2nd edition 1996-7, ed. IJS Talman, W Green, Edinburgh

Implications for the Land Register

6.101 In terms of section 6(1)(a) as amplified by rule 4 the property section of a title sheet must contain a description of the land based on the ordnance map. Unless section 12(3)(d) is applicable (where there is an inaccuracy in the boundaries which could not have been rectified by reference to the ordnance map) or there is an express exclusion of indemnity to the contrary, the Keeper guarantees the boundaries of registered subjects. In this respect, two problems arise where a boundary comprises a natural water feature. The first concerns identification of the boundary and the replication thereof on the title plan. The second problem is how to accommodate any subsequent moves in the boundary caused by *alluvio* or *avulsion*. Both problems were discussed at the May 1999 meeting of the Joint Consultative Committee of the Registers of Scotland and the Law Society of Scotland where it was agreed that the Keeper should retain the flexibility to be pragmatic and accordingly view each application on its own particular merits. The committee further agreed that the Keeper would apply the following broad guidelines:

Plotting the natural water boundary
1. Where the Keeper is in no doubt about the location of the natural water boundary that boundary would simply be red edged on the title plan in the same way as any other boundary would be. Given the potential problems outlined above it is likely this option will only apply in a limited number of instances.

2. The natural water boundary will be delineated by means of a red edge on the title plan and a qualifying note will be entered in the property section of the title sheet and/or on the title plan. The qualifying note will be to the effect that the natural water boundary shown on the title plan is only indicative of the position of the boundary feature, *i.e.* the medium filum of the river or the low water mark of ordinary spring tides *etc.* In some instances it may be appropriate to draw the red edge on the land abutting the natural 'water boundary and add a note to the property section of the title sheet indicating that, for example, 'the foreshore *ex adverso* the northern boundary is included within the title'.

3. The natural water boundary will not be red edged at all. Instead it will be arrowed and letter referenced and a note added indicating where the boundary lies. The note will be in terms similar to the following; 'the northern boundary comprises the *medium filum* of River X between the points arrowed and letter referenced A and B on the title plan'.

4. In situations where none of the foregoing three methods is appropriate the Keeper will exclude his indemnity as regards the position of the natural water boundary.

No hard and fast rules can be given as to which option will be pursued in any given circumstance. Factors which will have a bearing on the Keeper's decision will include:

- The state of the titles and in particular the description of the subjects conveyed.

- The length of the natural water boundary. The longer the boundary the more difficult it may prove to plot with any degree of accuracy on the ordnance map.

- Whether in any given circumstance the Keeper can actually identify, with reference to the ordnance map, the location of the natural water boundary. In areas of mountain and moorland where the scale of the ordnance map is 1:10000 small deviations in the course of a burn, or even a narrow river, may not appear as such on the ordnance map. In such circumstances the red edging on the title plan may not clearly reflect the intention of the deeds.

- Whether the course of the natural water feature has altered subsequent to the granting of the original foundation deed.

- Whether the natural water feature is one which is prone to change. Some rivers, particularly those which are tidal, and indeed certain stretches of particular rivers are, for example, noted for wide fluctuations in their natural course.

Alluvio and avulsion
Whilst the basic legal premise of *avulsion* is that the legal boundary is deemed not to have moved, debate exists as to what this actually means in practice. The Keeper will, therefore, view any suggestion that *avulsion* has occurred in light of the facts and circumstances surrounding any such claim. Where *alluvio* occurs the boundary is taken to have moved in accordance therewith. The nature of registration of title is such that it cannot cope easily with natural boundary changes. The result is that the original plotting of the subjects may, following the physical process of *alluvio*, no longer correspond with the actual position on the ground thereby potentially creating an inaccuracy in the Register. The Joint Consultative Committee concluded that the Keeper had two options for dealing with *alluvio*.

The first option would be to exclude indemnity at the time the subjects with a natural water boundary were being registered as regards any future changes in the position of the boundary caused by *alluvio*. This would bring the Keeper within the ambit of section 9 and enable him to rectify a title sheet where the course of a natural water boundary has altered over time. The Committee considered that such perpetual exclusions of indemnity were unsatisfactory and that option 2, as undernoted, was preferable. The Committee agreed the position should be monitored to establish if difficulties are encountered in practice as a consequence of pursuing option 2. If difficulties are found a change in the Keeper's policy may have to be considered.

The second option and the one the Keeper is currently following is to treat any question relating to *alluvio* subsequent to the original first registration as a matter of rectification. In doing so any application to rectify the extent of the subjects on the basis that *alluvio* has altered a boundary will be dealt with on its merits in the context of section 9. The Keeper will take account of factors such as possession, whether there is agreement from all interested parties and whether he is satisfied *alluvio* has actually occurred. As regards the latter this will be an evidential matter and, depending on the particular circumstances, it may be that the Keeper will require sight of a court declarator confirming that *alluvio* has occurred.

Salmon Fishings

6.102 The right to salmon fishings, being a separate tenement in land, falls within the definition of interest in land in section 28(1) of the 1979 Act. A transfer for value of the right to salmon fishings in an operational area will, therefore, require to be registered in the Land Register in order to establish a real right thereto. Considerable legal debate exists as to the ways in which a right to fish for salmon can properly be acquired and this uncertainty has led the Keeper to adopt a cautious approach when processing applications to register an interest in salmon fishings. His approach will, in turn, depend on the means by which it is claimed the right to salmon fishings has been constituted.

Express grant of salmon fishings by the Crown

6.103 Salmon fishings form part of the *regalia minora* and will normally originate in a conveyance by the Crown. The grant may exclusively refer to salmon fishings or it may be contained within a conveyance of land, the dispositive clause containing the phrase 'with salmon fishings' (*cum piscationibus salmonum* in older deeds). In the case of an express grant by the Crown of salmon fishings in appointed waters, the right vests in the grantee with no need of purification by prescription. Nor can it be lost through non-use under the long negative prescription. That said, it has been suggested by various legal commentators that the right could be supplanted by 20 years possession on a competing title. For that reason the Keeper will require to be satisfied that there is no risk to his indemnity from a competing title before he will issue a fully indemnified land certificate. The response given to question 3 of Part B of the application Form 1 (*'Is there any person in possession or occupation of the subjects or any part of them adversely to the interest of the applicant?'*) will obviously be important in this respect as will the level of warrandice contained in the Crown grant.

Grant by the Crown of a general title followed by prescriptive possession

6.104 In the absence of a specific Crown grant the right to salmon fishings can be acquired by prescription on a more general title granted by the Crown. For this to happen the title must be habile to found prescription for salmon fishings and must be augmented by possession for the prescriptive period. Where prescription is being pled against the Crown the requisite period is 20 years. It follows that not only will the Keeper have to be satisfied that any such general title is in fact habile to include salmon fishings, but he will also require to examine evidence that possession has been enjoyed for the prescriptive period.

The character of such evidence will depend on the particular circumstances surrounding each application, for just as the nature of possession can vary, so will the appropriate evidence. For example, the right to fish for salmon may be exercised personally, or through the grant of fishing leases or their equivalent, or by setting up a fishery. Thus, whilst in some instances documentary evidence such as fishing leases or licences or catch records may suffice, in others a court declarator may be required. If satisfactory evidence of possession cannot be produced the Keeper may, depending on the particular circumstances, be prepared to register the title to salmon fishings subject to an exclusion of indemnity for the prescriptive period.

Grant by a party other than the Crown followed by prescriptive possession

6.105 There is considerable debate as to whether a grant of salmon fishings by a party other than the Crown followed by prescriptive possession can ever be free from challenge by the Crown in circumstances where the Crown has yet to alienate such fishings by either express or implied grant. Until the matter has been judicially determined the Keeper will adopt a cautious approach and insist on evidence which demonstrates that the Crown has alienated the fishings in an earlier title or that the Crown will not seek to challenge the particular right of salmon fishings to which the application relates. As regards the latter, written confirmation to that effect from the Crown Estate Commissioners will suffice. In the absence of such evidence the Keeper may exclude indemnity.

In addition to evidence relating to the Crown's interest evidence of possession will also have to be submitted. The same considerations as detailed in paragraph 6.104 will apply.

Pro indiviso shares in salmon fishings

6.106 It is not uncommon for the owner of a right in salmon fishings to convey a *pro indiviso* share or shares in that right to some other party or parties. Such conveyances are, of course, wholly competent and the interest will be given effect to in the Land Register. However, some such conveyances contain clauses that restrict the right to fish for salmon to a set number of rods in a particular beat during a designated week(s). These conveyances provide that the disponee is barred from making any use of that part of the fishings at any other time in the year and of the remainder of the fishings at any time at all. The Keeper considers that such qualifications on occupation and exercise of the right are inconsistent with the unrestricted nature of a real right of common ownership. Consequently, the Keeper's policy, which was reached after consultation with the Joint Consultative Committee (Nov. 1999), is to reject any application for registration which is founded on such a conveyance. Solicitors who are concerned that any proposed scheme for disposing of shares in salmon fishings may not meet the Keepers requirements are invited to seek guidance from the Agency's Pre-Registration Enquiries Section.

Mapping considerations

6.107 In terms of section 4(2)(a) the Keeper must be able to identify with reference to the ordnance map the stretch of river or sea to which the right to fish for salmon relates. Practice has shown that it can be problematic for both the submitting solicitor and the Keeper to accurately relate the descriptions contained in some of the older Crown grants to the most up to date ordnance maps. Partly this stems from the absence of suitable deed plans and partly from descriptions which are less than complete. Nor are there likely to be any physical features on the actual river or sea of the kind normally found on land (hedges/walls/fences *etc.*) setting the parameters of a person's physical occupation and which in turn would be reflected on the ordnance map. In the event that the Keeper cannot determine exactly where the right to fish for salmon falls he will either reject the application or proceed with an exclusion of indemnity as regards the exact location. Further mapping considerations are discussed in the section on Natural Water Boundaries.

Mixed Estates

6.108 What is meant by a mixed estate is an estate which, through feuing, has come to include a mixture of property and superiority. The superiority interest will usually appear from the title deeds to be a title *ex facie* to the lands. Sometimes the property interest, or part of it, will be the subject of long leases. This is the sort of estate the transmission of which, for fear that some part be overlooked, has customarily been effected by a disposition describing the whole estate, under exception of any outright disposals, the rights of feuars and tenants being excepted only from warrandice.

When a disposition of a mixed estate induces first registration, the question arises as to what documents and other evidence the Keeper will require in addition to the normal forms and other documentation, such as a prescriptive progress ot title, deeds referred to for burdens *etc*. The natural starting point in the search for an answer is section 4 (2) (a), which provides that an application for registration shall not be accepted by the Keeper if it relates to land which is not sufficiently described to enable him to identify it by reference to the ordnance map. Because an application to register the title to a mixed estate is in effect an application to register more than one type of interest in land, the Keeper must be able to indentify the component interests seperately on the ordnance map. Attention is also drawn to question 13 on Form 1, which requires the disclosure of relevant deeds and documents not detailed in the Inventory (form 4). Feu writs and long leases are caught by this provision. In practice the Keeper will almost invariably requisition these deeds, so it is as well to detail them on Form 4 and submit them at the outset.

It can be seen that the applicant should be working towards supplying the deeds and documents necessary for identification of (1) superiority (2) property subject to long lease and (3) property not subject to long lease. A long lease which is also an overriding interest presents a complication in that there is no strict requirement to disclose its existence, the rationale being that the tenant's interest is unaffected by the omission of the lease from the proprietor's title. Neither is indemnity payable on such an omission (see section 12(3)(h)). It is suggested, however, that, for the sake of completeness, and to avoid any possible issue as to whether a particular lease is, or is not, an overriding interest, the applicant should ensure he is in a position to disclose the existence of all long leases out of the estate.

It is usual practice that a schedule of feus and/or long leases be annexed and signed as relative to the conveyance of a mixed estate. If this is not to be done, a separate schedule should be prepared for submission as part of the application for registration. A style of schedule is suggested in the Notes and Directions for Completion of Form 1, which for convenience are reproduced after Form 1 in the rules, although the Notes themselves are non-statutory. Any deed which affects the terms of a feuar's or tenant's title, *e.g.* a minute of waiver or minute of extension, must also be listed and produced. The relevant feus and leases and other deeds affecting the title will appear in a schedule forming part of the property section of the title sheet. Because the inclusion of feuduty in the schedule normally carries the Keeper's guarantee in respect of the same, the Keeper will require the applicant to certify that the feuduty was still exigible at the date of the application. It is, however, open to the applicant to ask the Keeper to omit the column of the schedule dealing with feuduty, in which case no investigation of the current position will be necessary.

As in other cases, consideration should be given to the situation on the ground as well as to the state of title, and in this connection attention is drawn to question 3 of Form 1 concerning adverse possession or occupation. In the case of a mixed estate, consideration should be given not only to the perimeters of the estate, but to adverse possession through encroachment by feuars and tenants under long leases within the estate. Where adverse possession by a feuar or tenant is uncovered, it is helpful if the applicant advises at the outset whether or not he is prepared to accept that the extent of the relevant feu or lease is as currently possessed.

Barony titles

6.109 Barony titles are dealt with at this point because, while a barony need not be a mixed estate, in practice subinfeudation by the Crown vassal has usually taken place, in which case what is said above applies. There are, however, additional considerations peculiar to baronies.

The description of the barony lands in the the Charters constituting and subsequently confirming the grant is almost invariably just a catalogue of names of various lands comprehended within the barony, with the result that it is often difficult, sometimes impossible, to establish either its past or present location and extent. While this difficulty is not unique to baronies, it may not be so readily resolved by consideration of possession as it could be in other cases. It is to the barony lands that the noble quality of a barony grant attaches, and the location and extent of the barony lands may be a matter of fact, requiring proof. It also appears that the noble quality of the grant may, without mention, be transmitted with the barony lands, wherever they may lie. The recent case of *Spencer-Thomas of Buquhollie v. Newell*[51] examines the nature of barony titles and provides a

[51] 1992 SLT 973

salutary insight into their potential complexities. It is therefore suggested that even prescriptive possession of particular land, upon a recorded conveyance of the lands and barony of X may not always result in an unchallengable title to the barony, for the lands may lie elsewhere. Similarly, the named barony might, for example, have disappeared on assimilation with another at some time in the past, or the lands now described as the barony may form part of the original, but have been severed at some intervening point in time. It may therefore be necessary to examine title back at least to the last charter by progress, and to establish that the lands currently held out as the barony have since that time always been possessed by reference to the chain of title to the barony.

There has in recent times been considerable interest in baronies as social or 'vanity' titles, which has in turn given rise to attempts to transfer them without transferring the barony lands, or the whole residue of them. The conveyance, typically, contrives to redefine the barony by reference to some, often insignificant, part of the barony lands, and to nominate that part as being, or including, the *principal messuage*. The competence and effect of this sort of approach is something of a grey area, there being no authority directly in point.

In view of the various uncertainties touched upon above, the Keeper can be expected to decline to be the arbiter of whether the identifiable land actually conveyed does, or does not, include or comprise the barony lands. Nor will he wish to assume any risk associated with that question. The Keeper feels, in any case, that there is no strict need for him to form a view as to whether the identifiable land sought to be registered is, or is not, the barony land. His statutory duty, as regards the description of a registered interest, which is set out at section 6(1)(a), can be fulfilled without consideration of that issue.

In practice the Keeper is likely to describe the land actually conveyed in a standardised manner, and without reference to the barony. He is not oblivious to the aspirations of purchasers, however, and will refer, in a note in the property section, to the terms of the description contained in the disposition. It will be made clear that the note is intended only to provide information about the terms of the disposition, and that it should not be inferred therefrom that the Keeper believes the land identified on the title plan to be or to represent the barony, or that he indemnifies the title in that respect. Title to the registered interest, as identified on the title plan, will usually be indemnified, if the Keeper is otherwise satisfied with the titles and other evidence produced.

School Sites Act 1841

6.110 Section 2 of the School Sites Act 1841[52] provides that land granted in terms thereof for use as a school or schoolhouse shall, when it ceases to be used for that purpose, revert back to the estate or land from which it originally derived. Problems can arise when the school or schoolhouse is no longer used as such and the local authority, or indeed some other party similarly not in right of the reversionary interest, attempts to convey the property. In light of the decisions in *Hamilton v. Grampian Regional Council*[53], the Keeper has adopted a cautious approach where there is any possibility that a right of reversion under section 2 exists. Accordingly, where the subject matter of an application for registration comprises an area of less than one acre which has at some time in the past been conveyed for use as a school or school house the Keeper will, except where the circumstances outlined in the following paragraph apply, exclude his indemnity in respect of any challenge to the title which may arise from the right of reversion. Until the matter has been judicially resolved, the Keeper will not presume that prescription, be it positive or negative, can remedy the situation whereby title does not stem from the party in right of the reversionary interest.

There are two circumstances in which an exclusion of indemnity can be avoided. The first is where the Scottish Ministers or the Court has ordered the sale under section 106 of the Education (Scotland) Act 1980[54]. The second is where the party in right of the reversion has granted a formal renunciation or waiver of the right.

Crofting

6.111 Crofting tenure occurs only in the Counties of Argyll, Inverness, Ross and Cromarty, Sutherland, Caithness, and Orkney and Shetland and is based on a one year lease. Consequently, the tenant crofter's interest is not a registrable interest in land. That said, the crofter's tenancy is specified by section 28(1) to be an overriding interest and so may be noted on the landlord's title sheet. It has to be remembered that section 12(3)(h) of the 1979 Act excludes any losses arising from an error in or omission to note an overriding interest. Accordingly the presence or absence of any note regarding crofting should not be seen as any guarantee that the subjects (or any part of them) are, or are not, a croft. The Crofters Commission in Inverness maintains a Register of Crofts which, although not conclusive, will provide a better indication of the crofting status of subjects than the Land Register.

[52] c.38
[53] 1995 GWD 8-443, 1996 GWD 5-227
[54] c.44

Under the Crofters (Scotland) Act 1993[55] crofters are given statutory rights to buy both their croft agricultural lands and also the dwellings pertaining thereto. Unless decrofted, these subjects are then regarded as being vacant crofts and as such remain subject to the controls contained in the 1993 Act and other crofting legislation. Thus where a crofter purchases his subjects the Keeper will, unless advised in the application for registration that the subjects have been decrofted, note on the crofter's title sheet that the subjects are a croft. If the subjects become decrofted the Keeper will remove the note if an application containing evidence of the decrofting is presented to him.

Standard securities

6.112 Under section 19(4) of the 1993 Act any subjects purchased under the right to buy provisions are automatically disburdened of any prior standard security granted by the former landlord without the need for any formal discharge or deed of disburdenment. In such cases the Keeper will require a written statement from the seller's solicitor confirming that the transaction was within sections 12 to 18 of the 1993 Act before the prior security will be omitted from the purchasing crofter's title sheet.

Section 19(3) of the 1993 Act provides that the Scottish Ministers and Highlands and Islands Enterprise may record standard securities over owner occupied crofts in relation to assistance given to the crofter whilst still a tenant and that such securities will rank ahead of any other security. It is further provided that a security in favour of the Scottish Ministers will rank ahead of a similar security in favour of Highlands and Islands Enterprise. Very often such securities may not be submitted for registration until some considerable time after the date of purchase of the croft. Accordingly, if another standard security is submitted in the interim the Keeper will add a qualifying note after its entry in the charges section noting that it will rank postponed to any security which may be granted to Scottish Ministers or Highlands and Islands Enterprise in terms of section 19(3). A similar note will be added after the entry for a standard security in favour of Highlands and Islands Enterprise noting the possibility of a later security in favour of the Scottish Ministers being registered with prior ranking.

Section 14(3) of the 1993 Act provides that the Land Court may stipulate for compensation to be payable to the landlord in the event of certain disposals by the former tenant, or a member of his family who has acquired title, within five years of the purchase under the right to buy provisions. This compensation may

[55]c.44

be secured by a standard security in favour of the landlord. If the five year period has clearly elapsed without any breach of the conditions secured by the security the Keeper will, either on specific application being made to him to do so or at the time of the next dealing, remove such a security from the title sheet without requiring a discharge to be produced. The Keeper will, of course, have to be satisfied that any standard security was indeed granted in terms of section 14(3).

Pre-emption rights

6.113 Section 17(3) of the 1993 Act disapplies any rights of pre-emption in relation to sales of crofts in pursuance of a Land Court Order. In the absence of any judicial authority on the point the Keeper will assume that the pre-emption right is not necessarily disapplied for any future sale and it will therefore be entered in the burdens section of the title sheet.

Common grazings

6.114 Where a crofter acquires croft land it is possible, though not usual, for some form of right in, or right of use of, common grazings to be granted. Because of the many varying situations that can arise with common grazings, the approach the Keeper will take will depend on the particular facts and circumstances surrounding the actual grant. As a consequence of the potential for diminution in the extent of the common grazings through apportionment it is unlikely the Keeper will delineate said extent on the title plan. Rather any right will be verbalised and a qualifying note will be added narrating the right is subject to the provisions on common grazings contained in sections 47 to 52 of the 1993 Act.

Chapter 7 - Rectification of the Register and Indemnity

Rectification

Rectification of inaccuracies: general

7.1 The title sheet prepared by the Keeper on first registration of an interest in land derives from a thorough examination and assessment of all relevant title deeds and documents submitted with the application. On completion the title sheet should reflect the rights and obligations of the registered proprietor as evidenced by the title deeds, including details of all outstanding standard securities and other relevant charges brought to the Keeper's attention. All subsequent applications affecting the title sheet will be dealt with in a similar fashion and the title sheet will be updated accordingly. The title sheet will, therefore, accurately reflect the extent and nature of the registered proprietor's title. It follows that when the title sheet is completed in such a manner, usually there will be no call for rectification of the register.

Inaccuracies in a title sheet do, however, occur for a variety of reasons. These include simple clerical errors, made by the Keeper's office in the compilation of title sheets, and erroneous information supplied to the Keeper in support of an application for registration. This latter category can give rise to decrees of reduction being pronounced by the court, the consequence of which may be that an inaccuracy is created in the register that requires consideration of the rectification provisions at section 9.

An obvious example of how an inaccuracy can occur is where the Keeper omits a particular burden from the title sheet because he deems it no longer enforceable. Such a decision may turn out to be wrong. Similarly, when the Keeper comes to delineate the extent of the subjects on the title plan there may be a discrepancy between the legal extent as depicted in the title deeds and the occupied extent as delineated on the ordnance map. The Keeper may decide the discrepancy is not material and so proceed to plot the subjects to the occupied extent. The registered proprietor or the neighbouring proprietor may disagree with that decision. Requests for the title sheet to be rectified may then follow.

Errors of a minor clerical nature: correction of title sheet

7.2 Title sheets do, from time to time, contain errors of a clerical nature. The most common example is that of a simple typographical error. Strictly speaking the correction of any inaccuracy in the title sheet can only be achieved by rectification of the register. Where the inaccuracy arises through a minor clerical error of the Keeper he will however normally be prepared to amend the inaccuracy without the need for a formal application for rectification of the register. If a typographical error is discovered, the certificate of title may either be returned for correction or it can be retained until the next application affecting the registered interest is submitted. The error should then be brought to the Keeper's attention. It is recommended that where the error is of a particularly minor nature, such as an incorrect spelling, the latter approach is appropriate. Conversely, where the nature of the error is such that it materially affects the interpretation of the certificate of title, such as a missed line in one of the burdens entries, it is recommended that the correction take place immediately. No application form is necessary when submitting a certificate of title for a minor correction. Should the Keeper agree with the request for correction, a fresh certificate of title will be issued.

Statutory authority for rectification

7.3 The statutory authority governing rectification is contained in section 9 and rule 20. Subsection (1) of section 9 confers on the Keeper a general power to rectify any inaccuracy in the register, either on his own initiative, or on being requested to do so. It also requires him to rectify an inaccuracy on being so ordered by the court or the Lands Tribunal for Scotland. Rectification may be by way of insertion, amendment or cancellation of anything in the register. Subsection (2) gives the court and the Lands Tribunal for Scotland power to make orders for the purposes of subsection (1). By subsection (3), however, if rectification of the register would prejudice a proprietor in possession, the Keeper`s power to rectify is limited, as is the power of the court or the Lands Tribunal for Scotland to order him to rectify. The circumstances in which, on the one hand, the Keeper may rectify an inaccuracy to the prejudice of a proprietor in possession and, on the other hand, the court or the Lands Tribunal for Scotland may order him to do so, are set out at, respectively, paragraphs (a) and (b) of subsection (3).

What constitutes an inaccuracy?

7.4 The word 'inaccuracy' is not defined in the Act, but it has come under judicial consideration. In the case of *Brookfield Developments Limited v. The Keeper of the Registers of Scotland* [1] it was held that the word 'inaccuracy' should be *'construed widely so as to include any incorrect or erroneous entry in or omission from the register'.* The inaccuracy identified by the Lands Tribunal in that case was that certain real burdens no longer subsisted at the time of first registration and should not have been entered in the title sheet. The concept of inaccuracy in the register is not, however, confined to error or omission at the hand of the Keeper, as may be evidenced from case law. In *Short`s Trustee v The Keeper of the Registers of Scotland* [2] it was held that the proper course for the petitioner, who had obtained a decree of reduction, was to apply to the Keeper for rectification of the register. It is clear from the decision that, reduction of the disposition created an inaccuracy in the register. In the case of *Kaur v Singh* and others (unreported on this particular point) the Lord Ordinary (Lord Hamilton) found the register to be inaccurate to the extent that an entry in it gave effect to a disposition on which the signature of one of the granters was found to have been forged.

An inaccuracy in the register may also arise upon the making of an order under section 8 of the Law Reform (Miscellaneous Provisions)(Scotland) Act 1985[3]. Where the register has given effect to terms of a document which are later judicially altered, the register will become inaccurate. By subsection 3(A) of section 9 of the 1979 Act the entry in the register is to have effect, as rectified, from the date when the entry was made. The court may, however, specify a later date to protect the interests of a person having the benefit of section 9 of the 1985 Act.

Who may apply for rectification?

7.5 The Act provides no guidance as to who may competently request the Keeper to rectify an inaccuracy in the register. The Keeper`s approach is that he will consider an application from anyone who can show title and interest to sue before the court or the Lands Tribunal for Scotland. If an application raises contentious issues, however, the court or the Lands Tribunal for Scotland may have to be approached for an order.

[1] 1989 S.L.T. (Lands Tr.) 105
[2] 1993 S.C.L.R. 242, affirmed 1994 S.C.L.R. 135
[3] c.73

When is rectification possible?

7.6 As indicated at paragraph 7.3, the Keeper`s power to rectify an inaccuracy in the register, and the power of the court or the Lands Tribunal for Scotland to order him to do so, is limited by subsection (3) of section 9. If rectification would prejudice a proprietor in possession, the Keeper may exercise his power to rectify the register only where:

- **The purpose of the rectification is to note an overriding interest or to correct any information in the register relating to an overriding interest.** A registered interest affected by an overriding interest continues to be affected by it whether the overriding interest is noted on the register or not (see sections 3(1)(a) and 28(1)). Rectification of the register, to note, or correct any information in the register relating to an overriding interest therefore merely reflects the existing legal position. The definition of an overriding interest is restricted in section 9(4) to exclude a lease which is not a long lease.

- **All persons whose interests in land are likely to be affected by the rectification have been informed by the Keeper of his intention to rectify and have consented in writing.** Where all interested parties, including the proprietor in possession and any prejudiced proprietor, consent in writing to rectification, there can be no bar to the Keeper in proceeding to rectify the register.

- **The inaccuracy has been caused wholly or substantially by the fraud or carelessness of the proprietor in possession.** The terms fraud and carelessness are not defined in the Act. It is thought that the known parameters of fraud as a civil wrong will apply. Determining what would constitute carelessness is more problematic. It is trite but true to say that what constitutes carelessness will depend on the circumstances of each specific case. The Keeper's view is that it is likely to include a material inaccuracy in the information furnished to the Keeper, or failure to disclose information of relevance to the outcome of the application. The case of *Dougbar v Keeper of the Registers of Scotland*[4] is instructive. The Lord Ordinary held that purchasing an interest in land where the purchaser knows there is an obvious error in the title sheet does not constitute carelessness. That case is presently on appeal to the Inner House of the Court of Session.

[4] 1999 SCLR 458

- **The rectification relates to a matter in respect of which indemnity has been excluded under section 12(2) of this Act.** Exclusion of indemnity by the Keeper preserves rectification as a remedy even to the prejudice of a proprietor in possession, should a relevant inaccuracy later be established. Exclusion of indemnity also allows the continued operation of positive prescription where that is relevant (see section 1, Prescription and Limitation (Scotland) Act 1973[5], as amended).

The court or the Lands Tribunal for Scotland may order the Keeper to rectify an inaccuracy in the register, to the prejudice of a proprietor in possession, only in the circumstances set out at paragraph (b) of subsection (3) of section 9. Those circumstances include that in which an order for rectification of the register is consequential on the making of an order for rectification of a defectively expressed document.

The interaction between sections 9 and 12 may be seen from the case of Taylor v Taylor and others (unreported at the time of publication). This case concerned a claim by Mrs Taylor that property held in her name, on a deed recorded in the Register of Sasines, had been transferred without her consent to Ms Houston. It was alleged that Mrs Taylors signature on the disposition to Ms Houston was a forgery. The transaction (which included the discharge of existing standard securities recorded in the Register of Sasines) had induced first registration in the Land Register. A land certificate showing Ms Houston as the registered proprietor was issued along with a charge certificate in respect of a standard security she had granted over the property in favour of the North of England Building Society.

Mrs Taylor raised an action in the Court of Session to (1) have the pretend disposition and standard security reduced (2) to have the register rectified to delete the entries relating to Ms Houston and the Building Society and (3) to have her name inserted in the proprietorship section. The Building Society and the Keeper defended the action; however, neither Mr Taylor nor Ms Houston submitted defences. The building Society had lodged a counterclaim in respect that should reduction and rectification be granted Mrs Taylor would have gained a gratuitous benefit at the expense of the Building Society. This was on the basis that should Mrs Taylor succeed in her action she would obtain an unencumbered title whereas the title she had prior to the pretend disposition had been burdened by pre-existing securities at least one of which she acknowledged.

[5]c.52

In terms of Section 12(1)(a) the Keeper, subject to the provisions of section 12(2) and (3), will indemnify a person who suffers loss as a result of a rectification of the register made under section 9. In this case if rectification of the register had been made under section 9, the Building Society would have had a claim on the Keeper's indemnity.

The case was heard before Lord Penrose in the Court of Session. The court found that Mrs Taylor's signature on the pretend disposition was a forgery. Accordingly the pretend disposition was reduced as was the standard security to the North of England Building Society. This created an inaccuracy in the Register. The Court then addressed the issue of proprietor in possession. Having established there was no proprietor in possession who could be prejudiced by rectification of the register he ordered the keeper to rectify the register on the terms noted above.

The authority of the Court was interponed to a Joint Minute between Mrs Taylor, the building society and the Keeper. This agreement, in consideration of the withdrawal of defenses, included *inter alia*:-

1. an undertaking that Mrs Taylor would grant a security over the property in favour of the Building Society's successors,
2. an undertaking by the Keeper to make a monetary payment to the Building Society in full and final settlement of the society's claim for indemnity under section 12(1)(a) as a result of the rectification of the register.and
3. an undertaking by the Building Society to the Keeper to make repayment, with interest at the judicial rate, if within two years of this minute an action is raised which results in a finding by a competent Court (That finding not successfully being appealed) that there was, in the period between the date of registration and the date of rectification, a "proprietor in possession" within the meaning of section 9(3), and such proprietorship in possession has been created as a result of the voluntary act of the Building Society.

The Building Society and the Keeper were found liable for their own expenses of the action and in the ratio of one third to the society and two thirds to the Keeper for Mrs Taylors expenses.

In cases where fraud is alleged the keeper will bring the matter to the attention of the Police should the parties not already have reported the matter.

Proprietor in possession

7.7 The term 'proprietor in possession' is not defined in the Act. Judicial comment on the matter has, in addition, been limited. Apart from the Taylor case where Lord Penrose arrived at a determination following submission by Counsel, the only other case where it has been addressed is that of *Kaur v Singh and others*[6]. In that case Lord Hamilton held that the holder of a standard security was not a proprietor in possession. His view was upheld on appeal to the Inner House where the Lord President further observed that merely exercising a right to sell the property by virtue of the power of sale provisions did not enhance the status of the creditor to that of proprietor. A creditor under a standard security could become a proprietor only where it had obtained a decree of foreclosure in terms of section 28 of the Conveyancing and Feudal Reform (Scotland) Act 1970[7]. The question of whether it was then 'in possession' would become relevant. Their Lordships took the view that the term 'proprietor in possession' contained two distinct elements. The relevant person had to be both 'a proprietor' and 'in possession'. The term proprietor, it was suggested, should be interpreted as applying *'only to someone who has a title as owner of the land in question'*. Commenting on possession the Inner House further observed that the term *'suggests possession of land or other heritable subjects rather than possession of a legal interest'*. Following that reasoning a landowner and the holder of a registered charge could not be considered as being in the same position.

Applying for rectification

7.8 Rule 20(1) stipulates that an application to the Keeper for rectification of the register should be made on Form 9. All relevant supporting deeds and documents should be submitted with the Form 9. For the fee payable in respect of such an application see the relevant fee order.

Decrees of reduction and the Land Register

7.9 In the case of *Short's Trustee v Keeper of the Registers of Scotland*[8], the House of Lords upheld the view that a decree of reduction of a disposition could not be registered in the Land Register under section 2(4) of the 1979 Act. Short's Trustee involved a bankrupt selling two flats, at under-value, to a third party within the two year period prior to his sequestration. The third party subsequently conveyed the flats to his wife for love, favour and affection. All the dispositions were subsequently

[6] 1997 S.C.L.R. 1075 (O.H.)
[7] c.35
[8] 1996 S.C. (H.L.)14

registered in the Land Register. The trustee successfully raised an action for reduction of the dispositions under section 34 of the Bankruptcy (Scotland) Act 1985[9]. The trustee then submitted applications to register the decree of reduction in the Land Register under section 2(4). The Keeper rejected the applications arguing that the decree of reduction of itself achieved nothing since title stemmed from the Register and not from prior dispositions, and so accordingly the correct procedure for giving effect to the decree was to apply for rectification of the Register. The trustee sought judicial review of the Keeper's decision. The trustee was unsuccessful. Appeals to the Inner House of the Court of Session and the House of Lords were also unsuccessful

The practical implications of *Short's Trustee* are as follows:

- Although the decision concerned a decree of reduction under section 34 of the Bankruptcy (Scotland) Act 1985 it appears not to depend on the ground of reduction or the authority therefore.

- A decree of reduction is not a dealing registrable under section 2(4).

- If the decree of reduction is to have any effect upon the registered title, that effect will be achieved only through rectification of the register under subsection (1) of section 9.

The decision in *Short's Trustee* highlights one of the primary distinctions between the Land Register and the Sasine Register. Whereas the former is a register of title the latter is simply a register of deeds. In the Sasine system a deed remains the document of title, whereas under Land Registration the register itself becomes, in effect, the document of title.

Indemnity

7.10 A major benefit of registration of title is the certainty that comes from a State guaranteed register of title to interests in land. Once an interest in land is registered in the Land Register, title to that interest flows from the register. The provisions at section 9 in Part I of the Act prohibit rectification of the register to the prejudice of a proprietor in possession except in limited circumstances. It follows that, regardless of the quality of the title prior to registration, the quality of the registered title depends on the quality of the indemnity given by the Keeper. If the Keeper registers the title with full indemnity, that title becomes all but indefeasible so long as possession is maintained.

[9] c.66

Subject to the provisions of section 9 then, the general effect of the Act is that, in a dispute, it is the registered proprietor who retains the property. The person who, but for the Act, would have been the true proprietor, is able to claim indemnity for the loss of the right. It is noted that Lord Hamilton in MRS Hamilton Ltd v Keeper of the Registers of Scotland (No.1)[10] suggested that claims for indemnity under section 12(1) were fully assignable A further effect is that the public can rely on the register in the knowledge that, if loss is suffered as a result of that reliance, the loss will attract indemnity.

The indemnity provisions in respect of registered interests in land are to be found in Part II of the Act at sections 12 and 13. Section 12(1) sets out those situations in which a claim for indemnity may arise; section 12(2) empowers the Keeper to exclude, on registration, any right to indemnity in respect of anything appearing in or omitted from the title sheet; and section 12(3) sets out the circumstances under which there is no entitlement to indemnity.

When indemnity may be payable

7.11 Section 12(1) provides that a person who suffers loss as a result of certain events shall be entitled to be indemnified by the Keeper in respect of that loss. The purpose of this section is to indemnify any person against loss suffered as a result of the register being rectified; the register not being rectified; the loss or destruction of any document while it is in the Keeper's custody; and any error or omission in any information from the register given formally by the Keeper. The Keeper's policy when dealing with the indemnity provisions is that loss must be demonstrable, real and actual, as opposed to hypothetical or speculative. Note also that the constraints set out at section 12(3) and the provisions of section 13(4) may affect the outcome of any claim.

12.(1)(a) Rectification of the register made under section 9 of this Act;
7.12 If the Keeper rectifies the register under section 9 to correct an inaccuracy and a party suffers loss as a consequence, under section 12(1)(a) the Keeper may have to make good that loss. For example, where two adjoining properties held under separate ownership are registered with an overlap causing the same area to be included in both titles with indemnity excluded in neither, and the Keeper subsequently corrects the anomaly by rectifying the register by removing the overlap from the title sheet of the proprietor who does not possess the land then that party would have a *prima facie* claim on the Keeper's indemnity under section 12(1)(a). By way of further illustration, suppose the Keeper receives an

---

[10]1999 SLT 829

application on Form 1 to register the title to one of a terrace of houses. These are served by a mutual access road. In error the Keeper includes part of the roadway within the registered title. The registered proprietor is issued with a land certificate and proceeds to build a wall along the boundary as disclosed by the title plan. This impedes the passage of the other proprietors who of course have an overriding interest in the form of an unfettered servitude right of passage. When the facts are explained, the registered proprietor consents to rectification; but, because loss is suffered as a direct result of the rectification, the Keeper reimburses directly incurred costs including the building and removal of the wall under his indemnity. Such a claim would typically also include the reimbursement of any associated expenses and would include reasonably incurred legal expenses.

12(1)(b) Refusal or omission of the Keeper to make such a rectification;
7.13 Where the register contains an inaccuracy, the Keeper's powers to rectify are circumscribed by the provisions of section 9(3)(a). However, where the Keeper refuses or omits to rectify the register, and loss results, section 12(1)(b) provides for indemnity. This may be seen from the case of *Kaur v Singh* where in terms of the declarator pronounced on 22nd February 1999, the pursuer's (Mrs Kaur's) signature was held to be forged, and therefore the disposition did not transfer the pursuer's interest in the flat to Mr Singh. Consequently the register was inaccurate insofar as it showed Mr Singh as proprietor of the interest that belonged to Mrs Kaur. Mrs Kaur was entitled to be indemnified in terms of section 12 (1)(b), because the Keeper was obliged to refuse to rectify the register against Mr Singh as he was a proprietor in possession and none of the circumstances at (i) to (iv) of subsection (3) of section 9 applied.

Another example of a claim litigated under this head is to be found in MRS Hamilton Ltd v the Keeper of the Registers of Scotland (No. 1). The inaccuracy in that case was that the extent of the registered interest of a tenant under a long lease considerably exceeded the square measurement contained in the lease itself. A speciality of the case was that it was only a number of years after the first registration of the tenant's interest that the pursuer acquired the estate from which the lease derived. The pursuer averred that both it and its immediate predecessor in title had acquired the estate in ignorance of the error (an averment the defender was not in a position to contradict) and that the consideration had in each case been unaffected. The court found that, where no previous owners had been compensated for the diminution of their rights because of the error in registration, the pursuers who had first become aware of the diminution and had been refused rectification could be regarded as having suffered a loss as a result of that refusal.

12(1)(c) Loss or destruction of any document while lodged with the Keeper.

7.14 Despite the enormous number of documents dealt with by the Registers, loss rarely occurs. Should this happen the Keeper will pay the reasonable costs incurred in reconstituting any lost deeds or documents. Alternatively the Keeper will pay for obtaining extracts if these are available, or the costs of a Court action to prove the tenor of a lost document if this becomes necessary.

12(1)(d) An error or omission in any land or charge certificate or in any information given by the Keeper in writing or in such other manner as may be prescribed by rules made under section 27 of the Act.

7.15 The event envisaged here is an error or omission in a land or charge certificate or in an office copy or report or other writing issued by the Keeper. The phrase *"such other manner as may be prescribed by rules"* foreshadows the possibility of the introduction of additional means of providing information such as electronic transmissions. If, for example, a pre-registration report supplied by the Keeper inadvertently fails to disclose an existing standard security affecting the subjects reported on, and a creditor lends money in reliance on that report and subsequently sustains loss through not being the prior chargeholder (in a situation, where the debtor defaults), the Keeper may be required to indemnify the disadvantaged creditor. Similarly, if a Form 10a report fails to disclose the fact that part of the subjects over which the report was requested are already registered without exclusion of indemnity, the Keeper may be liable in indemnity to a party suffering loss as a result of the reliance placed on the report.

The issue has arisen as to whether this head of claim includes the case where an error or omission in a title certificate is merely a perpetuation of an error or omission in the register itself. In the case of MRS Hamilton Ltd v Keeper of the Registers of Scotland (No.1) the court found that errors or omissions in a land or charge certificate as referred to under section12(1)(d) were not limited to mere errors of transcription between the title sheet and the certificate. The Lands Tribunal came to a similar conclusion in another case between the same parties, in which it found that "A Land Certificate which does not include a burden which should have appeared on it, can be said to contain an omission even if the explanation for the omission is that it was missed from the title sheet." The point was appealed from the Lands Tribunal to the Inner House, however, where the First Division took a different view[11]. The Lord President found that, on the plain language of the provision, section 12(1)(d) was designed to cover the situation where a certificate or office copy contained an inaccuracy when judged against the title sheet in the register. The loss to be indemnified was loss due to an error

[11] 2000 SLT 352

or omission in a certificate or office copy as opposed to loss due to an error or omission in the register. Another reason his Lordship did not favour the wider interpretation of 12(1)(d) was that it rendered 12(1)(b) and, arguably, 12(1)(a) redundant. A person affected by rectification of, or refusal to rectify, an inaccuracy in the register, as seen through a land certificate or office copy, could seek indemnity under 12(1)(d) without reference to 12(1)(a) or (b).

Qualifications and restrictions to indemnity

7.16 A person who has suffered loss as a consequence of one of the four events stipulated in section 12(1) will lose the entitlement to indemnity if the right has been qualified or restricted in terms of section 12(2) or (3).

(1) Keeper's power to exclude indemnity

12(2) Subject to section 14 of the Act, the Keeper may on registration in respect of an interest in land exclude, in whole or in part, any right to indemnity, under this section in respect of anything appearing in, or omitted from, the title sheet of that interest.

7.17 Under registration of title, the Keeper need not reject an application for registration simply because of a particular defect in the title. Instead, the Keeper may, under section 12(2), exclude indemnity as regards the whole or part of the title in respect of anything appearing in, or omitted from, the title sheet for the interest. This protects the Keeper from claims by persons suffering loss as a result of a defect in the title. The Keeper is also empowered expressly by section 9(3)(a)(iv) to rectify the register at a later date in respect of any matter which is subject to an exclusion of indemnity. The Keeper will exercise his authority to exclude indemnity cautiously. Not every title defect will necessarily lead to an exclusion of indemnity. Where the defect in title is minor and unlikely, in the Keeper's opinion, to induce a claim on the indemnity, effect may be given to the application without taking into account the defect. It is not possible to define the range of defects in title which the Keeper may be willing to overlook, as each application will be examined on its merits. In this connection, the Keeper's Pre-Registration Enquiries Section should be consulted for guidance on specific queries at the earliest opportunity.

Where the Keeper intends to exclude indemnity in whole or in part from a registered title, the applicant will be advised of this before the registration process is completed. The applicant will therefore have an opportunity to remedy the defect occasioning the exclusion of indemnity or to make the case that indemnity should not be excluded. If the defect cannot be cured (or the applicant wishes the application to proceed notwithstanding) and an exclusion of indemnity is unavoidable, the exclusion note may be inserted in whichever of the four sections of the title sheet the Keeper considers appropriate (as prescribed in rules 4 to 7). The relevant section is determined according to the nature of the defect for which the exclusion is to be made. For example, exclusions of indemnity relating to the validity of a heritable security or other charge will appear in the charges section, while exclusions relating to the lack of a valid prescriptive title will appear in the proprietorship section. A defect may warrant an exclusion in more than one section. For example, if the defect relates to the validity of the title, and there is a standard security over the interest registered, a note excluding indemnity may appear in both the B (proprietorship section) and the C (charges) sections of the title sheet.

An exclusion of indemnity note entered in the title sheet will generally take the following form:

'[As regards the part ... on the Title Plan] Indemnity is excluded in terms of section 12(2) of the Land Registration (Scotland) Act 1979 in respect that ...'

Removal of an exclusion of indemnity entered on the title sheet is discussed below.

(2) Statutory restrictions on indemnity

7.18 Section 12(1) places an onerous responsibility on the Keeper, so section 12(3) lists a number of particular situations where he is absolved from liability for the payment of indemnity. These are situations where it would be unreasonable to compel him to bear the burden of the loss, *viz.*:

12(3)   There shall be no entitlement to indemnity under this section in respect of loss where-

(a) the loss arises as a result of a title prevailing over that of the claimant in a case where

(i)   the prevailing title is one in respect of which the right to indemnity has been partially excluded under subsection (2) above, and

(ii) such exclusion has been cancelled but only on the prevailing title having been fortified by prescription;

Section 10 of the Act amends section 1 of the Prescription and Limitation (Scotland) Act 1973 to provide for the continuance of the operation of the positive prescription in relation to registered titles. The effect of this section is that positive prescription operates in relation to a registered interest in land but only in instances where the Keeper has excluded indemnity; this will have the effect of fortifying the title in relation to the matter in respect of which indemnity has been excluded.

The following example illustrates how this provision can operate. A applies to register title to subjects and receives a land certificate bearing no exclusion of indemnity. B then applies to register property, part of which overlaps with A's registered title. B is in possession of the overlap area. B's title is registered but indemnity is excluded in respect of the overlap. B possesses the property openly, peaceably and without judicial interruption for the ten year prescriptive period after which B can apply to the Keeper for removal of the exclusion of indemnity from his title sheet and for rectification of A's title sheet to remove the overlap. On production of satisfactory evidence of B's possession, the Keeper gives effect to B's application. The title sheet can be rectified against A because A is demonstrably not in possession of the overlap. Nor can A claim indemnity as B's prevailing title has been fortified by prescription which has run against A.

7.19 *(b) the loss arises in respect of a title which has been reduced, whether or not under subsection (4) of section 34, or subsection (5) of section 36, of the Bankruptcy (Scotland) Act 1985 (or either of those subsections as applied by sections 615A and 615B of the Companies Act 1985, respectively), as a gratuitous alienation or fraudulent preference, or has been reduced or varied by an order under section 6(2) of the Divorce (Scotland) Act 1976 or by an order made by virtue of section 29 of the Matrimonial and Family Proceedings Act 1984 (orders relating to settlements and other dealings) or has been set aside or varied by an order under section 18(2) (orders relating to avoidance transactions) of the Family Law (Scotland) Act 1985;*

A proprietor who acquires title by gratuitous alienation or fraudulent preference which would prejudice the creditor in bankruptcy proceedings is not deemed worthy of protection by the law. The same is true of a proprietor who acquires right by a deed which the court subsequently reduces by an order under section 6(2) of the Divorce (Scotland) Act 1976[12] on the grounds that it was made by one spouse to defeat an obligation to make financial provision for the other spouse and any children.

---

[12] c.39

The principle underlying section 12(3)(b) is that the applicant knew or should have known that the transaction in which he was involved was a gratuitous alienation, unfair preference, or potentially subject to reduction under the Divorce (Scotland) Act 1976. Such a material fact should, therefore, have been disclosed to the Keeper on the application form for registration in response to the question asking whether there are any facts or circumstances material to the title. Failure to disclose such information makes it possible for the Keeper to rectify the register against the interest of the proprietor in possession on the basis of section 9(3)(a)(iii) since the inaccuracy in the register has been caused wholly or substantially by the fraud or carelessness of the proprietor in possession. Assuming the Keeper can rectify the register under that provision, no indemnity will be payable for any loss arising as a result of the rectification.

7.20 *(c) the loss arises in consequence of the making of a further order under section 5(2) of the Presumption of Death (Scotland) Act 1977 (effect on property rights of recall or variation of decree of declarator of presumed death);*

Any interested party can apply under the 1977 Act[13] to have a person who has been missing for seven or more years declared dead. Any such declarator may be recalled or varied under section 4 of the 1977 Act. When this occurs the court can make a further order under section 5(2) of the 1977 Act in relation to any rights to or in property acquired as a result of the decree. If the person presumed dead reappeared and obtained an order recalling the original decree, the Keeper would not be able to rectify the register to re-invest that person as proprietor, as it is unlikely that any of the circumstances in section 9(3) would apply. The terms of section 12(3) would preclude the person originally presumed dead from claiming against the Keeper's indemnity in respect of the loss incurred by the Keeper's refusal to rectify the register.

7.21 *(d) the loss arises as a result of any inaccuracy in the delineation of any boundaries shown in a title sheet, being an inaccuracy which could not have been rectified by reference to the ordnance map, unless the Keeper has expressly assumed responsibility for the accuracy of that delineation;*

It is sometimes claimed that the ordnance map is a map of scientific accuracy, and within the limits of scaling this is so. The 1:1250 scale is generally available for urban and suburban property; the 1:2500 scale for agricultural and rural areas; and the 1:10,000 scale for mountain and moorland. The Keeper will use the largest scale available to him, but even on the 1:1250 scale, 1 millimetre on the map equals 1.25 metres on the ground. Thus a person suffering loss due to an inaccuracy in

[13] c.27

delineation by the Keeper of any boundary on the title plan will not qualify for indemnity if the Keeper could not have been aware of the inaccuracy because of the limitations imposed by the scale of the ordnance map. So, unless the Keeper has expressly assumed responsibility for the accuracy of the delineation of a boundary on the title plan, indemnity will not be payable. As a matter of practice, the Keeper rarely assumes responsibility for the accuracy of a boundary delineation.

7.22 *(e) the loss arises, in the case of land extending to 2 hectares or more the area of which falls to be entered in the title sheet of an interest in that land under section 6(1)(a) of this Act, as a result of the Keeper's failure to enter such area in the title sheet or, where he has so entered such area, as a result of any inaccuracy in the specification of that area in the title sheet;*

The purpose of the requirement to show the size of areas exceeding 2 hectares was to enable the public to identify the owners of large tracts of land and the extent of their holdings. However, the Land Register is concerned with quality of title. This is in no way affected if the Keeper misquotes or fails to quote the area of the subjects when it extends to 2 hectares or more. In any event, any calculation from a map is bound to be inaccurate since the map is flat and the land may not be. So, no indemnity is payable to anyone who suffers loss by relying on the measurement of the area as stated in the title sheet. Extent is, in any case, warranted by the accuracy of the plotting of the boundaries.

7.23 *(f) the loss arises in respect of an interest in mines and minerals and the title sheet of any interest in land which is or includes the surface land does not expressly disclose that the interest in mines and minerals is included in that interest in land;*

Whether or not mines and minerals under the surface of land are included within a title is very often obscure and can be difficult to establish. Prior to the first registration of a surface area, the minerals may have passed into separate ownership on a separate title as a separate tenement; or there may have been unrecorded mineral leases, no evidence of which was made available to the Keeper at the time of first registration. It is for this reason that the Keeper is under no statutory duty to guarantee the minerals position in any registered title. If the titles do contain specific information about minerals the Keeper will, if the evidence supports such an inclusion, enter the details in the property section of the title sheet. If there is no reference to minerals in a title sheet, despite proprietorship of land being assumed to be from the centre of the earth to the sky, it should not be assumed that the minerals are included within the title. There is, therefore, no liability for indemnity for loss in respect of an interest in mines and minerals where the title sheet does not expressly disclose that the interest in mines and minerals is included in the registered interest in land.

7.24 *(g) the loss arises from inability to enforce a real burden or condition entered in the register, unless the Keeper expressly assumes responsibility for the enforceability of that burden or condition;*

In terms of section 6(1)(e) the Keeper must enter in the title sheet any subsisting real burden or condition. If the Keeper is satisfied that any real burden or condition no longer subsists, it will be omitted. Prescription or obsolescence may apply, but the Keeper would not necessarily be aware this was the case. So, while the Keeper will guarantee that there are no burdens affecting the subjects other than overriding interests and those burdens contained in the title sheet, he is relieved of liability in respect of the continued subsistence of burdens or conditions entered in the title sheet except on the rare occasion when he expressly assumes responsibility for their enforceability.

7.25 *(h) the loss arises in respect of an error or omission in the noting of an overriding interest;*

In terms of section 6(4), the Keeper must note overriding interests if they are revealed in his examination of title and may note them if they otherwise come to his notice. There can never be, however, any certainty that all overriding interests affecting a registered interest have been noted. The Keeper is therefore not liable in indemnity for loss arising in respect of an error or omission in the noting of an overriding interest. Indemnity may, however, be payable where the Keeper has omitted to note, or made an error in noting, the discharge of or freedom from an overriding interest.

7.26 *(j) the loss is suffered by-*

(i) a beneficiary under a trust in respect of any transaction entered into by its trustees or in respect of any title granted by them the validity of which is unchallengeable by virtue of section 2 of the Trusts (Scotland) Act 1961 (validity of certain transactions by trustees), or as the case may be, section 17 of the Succession (Scotland) Act 1964 (protection of persons acquiring title), or

(ii) a person in respect of any interest transferred to him by trustees in purported implement of trust purposes;

Paragraph (j)(i) extends to the Keeper the protection afforded parties to transactions with trustees and executors by section 2 of the Trusts (Scotland) Act 1961[14] and section 17 of the Succession (Scotland) Act 1964[15]. Thus, while a beneficiary who suffers loss by the act of the trustee or beneficiary can have recourse against the trustee or executor, he cannot claim indemnity for the loss from the Keeper. Paragraph (j)(ii) provides that there shall be no entitlement to

[14] c.57
[15] c.41

indemnity for loss suffered by a person in respect of any interest transferred to him by trustees in purported implement of trust purposes. The Keeper is not required to examine the terms of any trust deed and must assume that the trustee is acting in accordance with the truster's instructions.

7.27 *(k) the loss arises as a result of an error or omission in an office copy as to the effect of any subsisting adverse entry in the Register of Inhibitions and Adjudications affecting any person in respect of any registered interest in land, and that person's entitlement to that interest is neither disclosed in the register nor otherwise known to the Keeper;*

When the Keeper registers a title, he is bound in terms of section 6(1)(c) to disclose on the title sheet any subsisting entry in the Register of Inhibitions and Adjudications adverse to the interest being registered. Thus, at the time of registration, the Keeper is able to establish from the deeds and documents presented with the application for registration the names and addresses of those parties who have a direct and obvious interest in the subjects. A search in the Register of Inhibitions and Adjudications will be made against those names and addresses. In addition, the applicant or his agents should have noted on the application form the names and designations of any other parties who have an interest in the subjects in order that these too can be searched against.

However, the situation is different when an office copy of a title sheet is ordered. Any member of the public can order an office copy and, unless it is otherwise made known to him, the Keeper's knowledge of the parties entitled to the interest in respect of which the office copy is ordered will be as disclosed on the register. Therefore, if the Keeper fails to reveal a subsisting adverse entry where information about an entitled party is outwith his knowledge, he is not liable in indemnity. For example, suppose at the time an office copy is issued, the registered proprietor is contractually bound under missives to dispone the subjects to another party. The existence of this other party would not be known to the Keeper and accordingly no search for a name and address match could be carried out.

7.28 *(l) the claimant is the proprietor of the dominant tenement in a servitude, except insofar as the claim may relate to the validity of the constitution of that servitude;*

Before disclosing the existence of a servitude right in a title sheet, the Keeper, on registration, must satisfy himself that the servitude has been validly constituted. No claim for indemnity will however arise if the servitude subsequently turns out to be unenforceable. A servitude may be lost by non-use or other supervening event and it would be impossible for the Keeper to investigate the reality of the position in every case to discover whether or not a servitude subsists.

Indemnity is payable only in respect of a claim relating to the validity of the constitution of a servitude. If the Keeper makes a mistake in that respect, the proprietor of the dominant tenement who suffers loss through the mistake may be entitled to indemnity.

7.29 *(m) the claimant is a superior, a creditor in a ground annual or a landlord under a long lease and the claim relates to any information-*

(i) contained in the feu writ, the contract of ground annual or the lease as the case may be, and

(ii) omitted from the title sheet of the interest of the superior, creditor or landlord,
(except insofar as the claim may relate to the constitution or amount of the feuduty, ground annual or rent and adequate information has been made available to the Keeper to enable him to make an entry in the register in respect of such constitution or amount or to the description of the land in respect of which the feuduty, ground annual or rent is payable);

The interests of a superior, a creditor in a ground annual and a landlord are all registrable in appropriate circumstances. While the Land Register strives to be as informative as possible, it would be impracticable when compiling, for example, a title sheet pertaining to a superiority to detail all the information relative to that superiority as narrated in the feu writs previously granted. By the same token a superior, a creditor in a ground annual or a landlord should have in their possession evidence of the conditions created by, respectively, the feu writs, contracts of ground annual or long leases. It is for these reasons that no indemnity is payable to a superior, a creditor in a ground annual or a landlord, where the claim relates to information in, respectively, a feu writ, a contract of ground annual or long lease, which has been omitted from the title sheet.

An exception to this arises where the Keeper has adequate information to enable him to make an entry in the title sheet in respect of the constitution or amount of the feuduty, ground annual or rent. Indemnity may be payable to anyone who suffers loss from any error in such an entry or from the Keeper's failure to make such entry. Likewise the Keeper may be liable in indemnity if the claim relates to the description of the land in respect of which the feuduty, ground annual or rent is payable.

In superiority *etc.* titles, the exact extent and location of feus *etc.* may not always be clear. There remains nevertheless an onus on the superior, creditor or landlord to supply enough information to enable the Keeper to identify the land by reference to the ordnance map. If the Keeper and the applicant are not sure about the extent of the land, they may agree that the doubtful area should be indicated on the title plan, but that indemnity be excluded as regards that area.

7.30 *(n) the claimant has by his fraudulent or careless act or omission caused the loss;*

It is inevitable that inaccuracies in the register will arise from time to time. These may result from an error on the part of the Keeper (discussed above) or because he has acted on information supplied by an applicant which subsequently proves to be erroneous. The Keeper will generally place reliance on information given in an application. This includes the answers to the questions on the application form. These answers are crucial to the Keeper's decision to confer or exclude indemnity. It is important too to ensure that the Keeper is informed timeously of any additions or changes to the information supplied which would be material to his deliberations in this regard. Accordingly, no indemnity is payable to a claimant who has caused the loss by his own fraudulent or careless act or omission. If the Keeper is induced to make an entry in the register on the basis of information supplied by an applicant which subsequently turns out to be false (due either to fraud or to a lack of proper care on the part of the applicant), the Keeper will resist any claim from that applicant for loss resulting from that error. (Attention is however drawn to the provisions of section 13(4) as they affect indemnity for loss payable to a fraudulent or careless claimant who is responsible only for a proportion of any loss).

For example, suppose that part of the subjects an applicant seeks to register are in fact possessed by another party, but the adverse possession is not disclosed to the Keeper on the application form. The Keeper then proceeds to register the subjects without excluding indemnity in respect of that part. Should the true owner of the part then obtain a declarator establishing his entitlement and seek to have the register rectified, the Keeper would, in terms of section 9(3)(a)(iii), be able to comply with the court order by removing the part in question from the relevant title sheet. The fraudulent or careless certification on the application form that no one was in adverse possession of any part of the subjects would preclude a claim on the Keeper's indemnity by the proprietor of the rectified title. Note however that the Keeper would remain liable to any third party for any loss suffered as a result of the error.

7.31 *(o) the claim relates to the amount due under a heritable security;*

While the Keeper will guarantee that a standard security which appears in the charges section of the title sheet, without exclusion of indemnity, has been validly constituted, he does not guarantee the amount due either at the time of registration or at any other given date. The Keeper is not in a position to know what sum is outstanding under a heritable security, although he will note in the charges section of the title sheet the amount borrowed as stated in the standard security (for example, £10,000 and further sums). If any assignee or other creditor is misled by such a statement, a claim for indemnity for loss will be disallowed in terms of section 12(3)(o).

7.32 *(p) the loss arises from a rectification of the register consequential on the making of an order under section 8 of the Law Reform (Miscellaneous Provisions)(Scotland) Act 1985.*

In the event of the court ordering rectification of a contract or deed under this section, no claim for indemnity is permitted against the Keeper for any loss that may arise as a result.

(3) Contributory negligence

7.33 In terms of section 13(4) the Keeper is under a duty to restrict the amount of indemnity payable to a successful claimant if it can be shown that the claimant has by his own fraudulent or careless act or omission, contributed to the loss. The amount of indemnity to which the claimant would otherwise have been entitled will be reduced proportionately by the extent to which the claimant himself has contributed to the loss.

Removal of exclusion of indemnity

7.34 Where a matter in respect of which indemnity has been excluded is cured by prescriptive possession, the exclusion will not be automatically removed from the title sheet at the end of the appropriate period. The exclusion note will remain on the title sheet, and in force, until the Keeper gives effect to an application for its removal. Such evidence as the Keeper deems sufficient to warrant the issue of a clear title must accompany the application.

The evidence the Keeper will require to examine will depend on the particular circumstances of each case. At the very least he will expect to have affidavit evidence to the effect that there has been continuous, open and peaceable possession for 10 years (or 20 years, depending on the nature of the right prescribed to) and that without judicial interruption. In some cases, it may suffice to submit affidavits from the party or parties exercising possession; in others, additional affidavits from neighbouring proprietors may be required. In yet other instances, the Keeper may not be content with affidavit evidence and may, for example, insist that the applicant obtains a court declarator to support the application.

Where a matter in respect of which indemnity is excluded cannot be cured by the passage of time, the exclusion of indemnity will remain on the title sheet until either (1) an application for the removal of the exclusion, supported by proof that the particular defect which gave rise to the exclusion has been cured, is given effect to by the Keeper, or (2) the matter giving rise to the exclusion is resolved by supervening events. For example, where indemnity has been excluded in respect that no evidence was supplied to the Keeper that a standard security granted by a limited company had been registered in the Charges Register within 21 days of its registration in the Land Register, the exclusion will remain on the title sheet until such time as either (1) an application, accompanied by evidence that the security was in fact registered in the Charges Register within the 21 days, is made to the Keeper, or (2) the standard security is discharged.

Submitting a claim on the Keeper's indemnity

7.35 A legitimate claimant must demonstrate loss and provide proof that it resulted from one or more of the events referred to in section 12(1) of the Act. The claimant should take all reasonable and appropriate steps to ensure that the loss is kept to a minimum.

There is no prescribed form for intimating a claim on the Keeper's indemnity. The claim should, however, be in writing and include detailed information about the nature and circumstances of the loss. It must be properly quantified and, where appropriate, vouchers such as receipts or invoices should be submitted in support of the claim.

Where the loss claimed is purely financial, for example, made up of legal fees, expenses or other outlays, it will usually be readily quantifiable. But where the loss is in respect of, say, the loss of a right in land, or of amenity, or of an incorporeal right, quantification may be more difficult. In all such cases, however, the loss must be converted into monetary terms and will normally require to be verified. No specific guidance can be given about the evidence the Keeper will need by way of verification. This will depend entirely on the particular circumstances of each case. Claims which appear speculative and claims which are poorly quantified will always be resisted by the Keeper.

On receiving a claim, the Keeper will undertake a full investigation of the facts and circumstances and the supportive evidence submitted. Additional information or such other evidence as the Keeper may consider necessary may be sought from the claimant. The merits of the claim will be assessed and the Keeper will advise whether or not the claim will be met and, if so, whether in whole or in part.

The Keeper will generally acknowledge a claim within 7 days of receipt. All claims are dealt with expeditiously. Where a matter is straightforward and additional information or evidence is not needed, acceptance or rejection of the claim will usually be advised timeously. However, where a matter is complex or particularly problematic, for example, where it involves two or more parties with differing points of view (say, in the case of a boundary dispute or a competition in title), it will inevitably take longer to conclude. It should be noted that the Keeper will normally decline to arbitrate in disputes about possession. Accordingly, where possession is an issue and the evidence of the parties conflicts, a judicial decision may be the only way forward.

Expenses

7.36 The legal expenses reasonably and properly incurred by a successful claimant in pursuit of a claim will generally be met by the Keeper. Expenses which in the Keeper's view were not proper to the claim or were incurred unnecessarily will be resisted. Section 13(1) requires the Keeper to reimburse any expenditure properly and reasonably incurred by a person who has pursued a *prima facie* well-founded claim against the Keeper under section 12, regardless of whether the claimant is successful or not. Should the claim reach the Lands Tribunal or the court, either of those bodies can make an order regulating expenses. The courts (Mrs Hamilton v Keeper of the Registers of Scotland (No2))[16] have upheld the view that where a claim on indemnity has not been finally determined the Keeper has discretion to decide on whether he is actually in a position to facilitate an application for expenses. The Inner House has suggested that such discretion is subject to appeal under section 25 or juducial review.

Subrogation and assignation

7.37 In terms of section 13(2), when the Keeper settles any claim to indemnity, all rights which would have been available to the claimant to recover the loss shall automatically be subrogated to the Keeper. In addition, section 13(3) authorises the Keeper to require, as a condition of payment of the claim, a formal assignation of the rights available to the claimant to recover the loss indemnified. The Keeper will be liable for the expenses of the assignation.

Right of appeal against rejection of a claim

7.38 If the Keeper rejects a claim on his indemnity, he will provide the claimant with the reason(s) for his decision. Should the claimant wish to appeal the Keeper's decision, the terms of section 25 will be relevant (paragraph 1.6 looks at this subject in detail).

---

[16] 1998 GWD 35-1813

CHAPTER 8 - Missives and Conveyancing Procedures

8.1 Both the Reid and Henry Committees recommended that registration of title should be introduced with as few substantive changes in conveyancing law as possible. The Act follows these recommendations and the principal changes in conveyancing law are outlined in chapter 1. The changes in conveyancing procedure are listed in paragraph 2.2 but procedure will vary depending on whether the transaction relates to an unregistered interest but induces first registration or relates to an interest already registered in the Land Register. In the following paragraphs conveyancing procedure on both first registration and in relation to a registered interest is discussed. In both cases the procedure has a simple house purchase/building society loan transaction in mind but much of what is discussed will also apply where the transaction is a grant of feu or a lease. It should be noted that where the grant of feu or long lease relates to either the whole or to part only of the registered interest the appropriate application form is a Form 3, as the granter is not divested of his whole interest.

8.2 This chapter examines a sale and purchase which takes place after an area has become operational, *i.e.* the subjects are sold and missives concluded after the date on which the area became operational. However, the commencement provisions relate not only to a transaction started after the commencement date but also to any transaction completed after the area in which the subjects lie has become operational. In other words a disposition (for value) delivered after an area has become operational must be registered in the Land Register if the purchaser is to obtain a real right in terms of section 3(1). The Keeper must, after the commencement date, reject any such disposition if it is presented for recording in the Sasine Register (section 8(4)). There will, however, be transactions where missives are concluded before an area has become operational but which are not due for settlement until after that date and again there will be transactions which should have been completed before an area has become operational but which for one reason or another are not settled before the commencement date. Transactions which fall within these categories are discussed in paragraphs 8.32 *et seq.*

Throughout this chapter, where reports are referred to, the reference is to reports provided by the Keeper, that is the statutory Form 10, 11, 12 and 13 reports and the non-statutory P16 and P17 reports. It should be remembered, however, that firms of Private Searchers also provide equivalent reports and the solicitor is at liberty to acquire his or her reports from whatever source he or she wishes.

In the near future the introduction of the Registers Direct service by the Keeper will mean that a solicitor acting in a Land Register transaction will not require to order reports from any intermediary. He or she will be able, if desired, to access the raw data from the Registers electronically. The service will provide on screen access to the Sasine Search Sheets, Land Register, Register of Inhibitions and Adjudications, Register of Deeds (Books of Council and Session) and Register of Judgements with the capacity to print off copies at no extra charge. This will enable the practitioner to examine the most up to date position in the relevant Register(s) for any particular type of transaction and make his or her own judgement on the state of the title and whether or not there are any matters of concern. The indemnity provisions in Section 12(1)(d) of the Act will apply to information so acquired and the Law Society's Master Policy will cover solicitors operating in this way. Providing all solicitors involved agree to proceed in this fashion there is no reason why they should not as long as the necessary adjustments to missives are made.

First registration - presale procedures

Do the registration provisions apply?

8.3 As will be seen in the following paragraphs the stipulations normally found in missives under the Sasine system dealing with the delivery or exhibition of a prescriptive progress of titles and clear searches are not appropriate to a transaction which will lead to first registration (or indeed to a transaction relating to a registered interest). A seller's solicitor must, therefore, before concluding missives, establish whether the registration provisions apply and, if so, whether the interest (*i.e.* the property) has or has not been registered already in the Land Register. As soon as an area becomes operational the registration provisions will apply although not all transactions will lead to registration.

In terms of section 11(2), where property lies partly within and partly outwith an operational area (*i.e.* a straddling plot), the subjects are to be treated as lying wholly within the operational area. The solicitor should, therefore, check the title deeds at this stage, even if the property seems to lie outwith an operational area if that property is on or near the boundary of such an area. In addition, the registration provisions may apply even where no part of the property in question lies in an operational area at all, *i.e.* where the Keeper accepts an application for voluntary registration under section 11(1).

Has the interest been registered?

8.4 Having established that the subjects lie in an operational area the next question is to establish whether the interest has been registered, as subsequent procedures differ where the transaction induces first registration or where the interest is already registered. If the seller's title is a land certificate clearly the interest is registered. It is however not necessarily safe to conclude if the seller produces a prescriptive progress of titles that the interest has not been registered in the Land Register, because the interest may have been registered voluntarily or part sold or the registration has not yet been completed.

Furthermore, the Keeper on registering adjoining subjects may have included in that registration part of the subjects contained in the seller's title. It is recommended, therefore, that a Form 10 report should always be instructed at this stage of a transaction in all cases where the seller's title is not a land certificate to make certain that the interest or part thereof has not been registered. The seller's solicitor will require to have his client's titles before him when completing the application for a Form 10 report.

Is the transaction registrable?

8.5 Where the seller's interest is registered in the Land Register all dealings with that interest are registrable. Where the seller's interest is still held on a Sasine title then those transactions listed in section 2(1)(a) will induce first registration.

Title and occupational boundaries

8.6 The difficulties which can arise where there are differences between the boundaries as contained in the seller's title and the occupational boundaries as disclosed on the ordnance map are discussed in paragraph 4.7. Serious problems could arise if the difference proved to be material and were not discovered until after missives had been concluded or came to light during the registration process. It is suggested, therefore, that at this stage of the transaction and certainly if the seller's title contains a bounding description the seller's solicitor should make certain that there are no material discrepancies between the title and the occupational boundaries. This can be done by a physical comparison on the ground. Alternatively it may be done by comparing the description in the title deeds or in the deed plan with the ordnance map. If the latter option is chosen the Keeper will confirm the position if application is made to him on Form P16. The information which the Keeper will require to deal with such an application is discussed in paragraph 4.9 and a fee will be charged for the Form P16 report. It should be stressed that as the Keeper will not at this stage have examined the seller's titles the Form P16 report does no more than confirm the boundary position as disclosed on the ordnance map. Such confirmation need not be sought if the transaction relates to flatted property unless any ground specifically pertaining to the flat in question requires to be identified from the ordnance map.

Presale examination of titles

8.7 It is particularly important that the seller's solicitor should examine the title deeds of a property which lies in an operational area at the pre-contract stage not only as regards the matters discussed in the preceding paragraphs but to enable the solicitor to ensure before concluding missives that there are no matters arising from the titles which might lead to registration in the Land Register being subject to exclusion of indemnity in whole or in part.

Recommended presale procedure

8.8 It is accordingly recommended that a seller's solicitor should at the earliest possible stage and certainly before missives are concluded:

- Examine the seller's title.

- Instruct a Form 10 report.

- Where appropriate instruct a Form P16 report.

Missives

8.9 In cases where the transaction will induce first registration (*i.e.* the subjects lie in an operational area, the interest has not been registered in the Land Register and the transaction is one specified in section 2(1)(a)), missives will be in normal form for a Sasine transaction but the clause dealing with the production of titles and Searches will require alteration and it is suggested that a clause in the following terms should be used:

> 'In exchange for the price the seller will deliver a duly executed disposition in favour of the purchaser and will exhibit or deliver a valid marketable title together with a Form 10 report brought down to a date as near as practicable to the date of settlement and showing no entries adverse to the seller's interest, the cost of said report being the responsibility of the seller. In addition, the seller will furnish to the purchaser such

documents and evidence including a plan as the Keeper may require to enable the Keeper to issue a land certificate in name of the purchaser as the registered proprietor of the whole subjects of offer and containing no exclusion of indemnity in terms of section 12(2) of the Land Registration (Scotland) Act 1979. Such documents shall include (unless the whole subjects of offer comprise only part of a tenement or flatted building and do not include an area of ground specifically included in the title to that part) a plan or bounding description sufficient to enable the whole subjects of offer to be identified on the ordnance map, and evidence (such as a Form P16 report) that the description of the whole subjects of offer as contained in the title deeds is habile to include the whole of the occupied extent. The land certificate to be issued to the purchaser will disclose no entry, deed or diligence prejudicial to the purchaser's interest other than such as are created by or against the purchaser, or have been disclosed to, and accepted by, the purchaser prior to the date of settlement. Notwithstanding any provision of the missives to the contrary, this clause shall remain in full force and effect until implemented and may be founded on.'

Some comments on the suggested clause may be helpful:

'A duly executed disposition'
This will be a disposition in normal Sasine form subject to the terms of section 16.

'Deliver or exhibit a valid marketable title'
The purchaser's solicitor will require to carry out a full examination of title as for a Sasine transaction. Unless the Keeper specifically (in the Form 10 report) indicates to the contrary, a prescriptive progress of titles must also be submitted to the Keeper to support the application for registration.

'A Form 10 report'
Where a transaction induces first registration it will not be appropriate to instruct or continue the search for incumbrances. Instead a Form 10 report will on application be issued by the Keeper and will cover the Sasine Register, the Land Register and the Personal Registers (but not the Register of Charges). A continuation of this report can be instructed shortly before settlement on Form 11. The Form 10 report (which takes the place of the Sasine search for incumbrances and interim report) will not be continued after settlement to disclose the disposition in favour of the purchaser, as is the search in the Sasine Register, because the land certificate, when issued, is in itself equivalent to a completed search, brought down to the date of registration of the title.

'Furnish such documents and evidence'
Basically, this will cover (1) those common titles which the seller would otherwise

retain or indeed may even have borrowed from other custodiers but which the purchaser will require to have delivered (on loan) at settlement to support the application for first registration, and (2) the information which the purchaser will require to complete the application form (Form 1).

'Without exclusion of indemnity'
This provision in the missives relates to specific exclusions of indemnity by the Keeper under section 12(2). It would not cover those matters in respect of which indemnity is excluded by section 12(3).

'The land certificate to be issued'
Under Sasine practice a purchaser is entitled to clear Searches unless the missives provide otherwise. Under registration of title, however, as stated above, a completed Search for Incumbrances will never be produced, the land certificate being equivalent to such a Search. It is suggested that it is prudent to stipulate precisely what the purchaser expects by way of a 'clear' land certificate and this clause attempts to do so.

Section 2 of the Contract (Scotland) Act 1997[1]
This section has encouraged the use of supersession clauses, which provide that the missives may not be founded on after a stipulated period, such as 2 years. The last part of this clause is to ensure that this clause survives such supersession. It is particularly important that the clause remains in effect in case the purchaser requires to obtain further information from the seller to support his application for registration.

It has already been suggested that a prudent seller's solicitor will obtain a presale Form 10 report and where appropriate confirm the boundaries, if necessary, by obtaining a Form P16 report. It is worth emphasising the wisdom of this course and stressing again the importance of examining the client's titles before missives are concluded.

There is no formal procedure open to the seller to 'test' his title by submitting it presale to the Keeper for confirmation as to what, if any, limitations of indemnity might be imposed. The seller could, of course, apply for voluntary registration but this could involve his client in unnecessary additional expense and such registration is at the Keeper's discretion. In some cases, however, this may be appropriate, for example at the commencement of a building development or where the title is known to be bad or doubtful. In other cases, such as complicated subdivisions or estate sales, the Keeper will welcome pre-registration discussions.

[1] c34

To assist the profession, the Keeper has established a Pre-Registration Enquiries Section which exists to give guidance to solicitors before applications for registration are submitted. Guidance can include views on defects in title, possible exclusions of indemnity, remedial conveyancing or additional evidence that may be required in any given case. The section can be contacted by writing to the Keeper marking the envelope for the attention of 'Pre-Registration Enquiries Section' or by phone at the Agency's Edinburgh number.

First registration - conveyancing procedures

Examination of title

8.10 Where a transaction induces first registration the examination of title involved is similar to that carried out in a transaction leading to a recording in the Register of Sasines in that a prescriptive progress of titles, including all burdens writs and links in title will require to be examined and the usual enquiries on title raised. A search for incumbrances in a form appropriate for the Sasine Register need not, however, be exhibited or examined. It should be remembered that as part of the process of registration the Keeper will re-examine all the title deeds and, therefore, the purchaser's solicitor's work will be subject to detailed scrutiny. In his examination however the Keeper may feel able to discount small conveyancing errors that may be found from time to time. For example, the Keeper will probably feel able to ignore an error in a recording date, or a blundered clause of deduction of title, providing in the latter case that the warrants (*i.e.* the links in title) for the deduction are in order. While, therefore, a transaction which leads to first registration will in general proceed to settlement in the same way as a normal Sasine transaction, the Act does introduce certain changes. These changes which are examined in greater detail in the following paragraphs are:

- A Form 10 (and Form 11) report replaces the search for incumbrances.

- A different form of letter of obligation is required.

- The Keeper must be able to identify the subjects with reference to the ordnance map.

- The Keeper will require additional information (Part B of Form 1) to complete registration.

- Section 16 (formal clauses) will apply to the form of disposition.

Form 10 and Form 11 reports

8.11 For a detailed statement on reports reference should be made to Chapter 3. A system of direct electronic access to the Registers is being introduced ('Registers Direct') and further information about this is available from the Keeper.

While the purchaser's solicitor will still require to ensure that the Sasine and Personal Registers are clear he will not, as in a Sasine transaction, have to examine a search for incumbrances or any prior searches. A Form 10 report supersedes this search entirely and also includes a report from the Land Register. Application for a Form 10 report should be made in duplicate. It should be applied for by the seller's solicitor as he is in the best position to give all the information required to identify the subjects to be searched against on the ordnance map. Great care must be taken to provide a description of the subjects that will enable the Keeper to identify them with reference to the ordnance map. As the Form 10 report is over the individual unit to be purchased/registered and contains all the entries relevant to that unit the practical problem of maintaining an up-to-date estate search for exhibition to each purchaser does not arise.

Once an area becomes operational a Form 10 report will disclose all entries relating to the interest in question in the Sasine, Personal and Land Registers up to the close of business at the Registers on the day before the report is issued provided that the correct forms are used and that they are completed correctly. The Sasine Register in a non-operational area will usually be some weeks out of date although the use of the computerised presentment book reduces some of the problems created by this. Under registration of title, however, the period not covered by the Form 10 (or Form 11) report is very short - for the purchaser's solicitor probably little more than the time taken to transmit it to him by post, fax, electronic mail etc from the Registers and/or the seller's solicitor. Where a Form 10 report is obtained prior to the conclusion of missives or some time prior to settlement a continuation of that report, a Form 11 report, should be applied for (in duplicate) as near as practicable to the date of settlement but a report should be instructed so that there is sufficient time after it is received to clear the relevant registers of an unexpected encumbrance or other adverse deeds which might appear. As the Form 10 report takes the place of the search it should be available for examination along with the title deeds. It is therefore recommended that the seller's solicitor should apply for a Form 10 report when he receives instructions for a sale and before missives are entered into and that a Form 11 report should be instructed as near as practicable to the date of settlement.

If a Form P16 is required it should be applied for at the same time as the Form 10 report.

Reports - recommended procedure

8.12 The following procedure is accordingly recommended:

• The seller should in all cases instruct a Form 10 report as soon as instructions are received to sell the property. In any event this report should be instructed before missives are concluded. Any existing search should not be submitted with the application for the report and need not be included with the titles sent to the purchaser's solicitor for examination.

• The Form 10 report should be exhibited to the purchaser's solicitors along with the title deeds. As the application for a Form 10 report (Form 10) and the report itself (Form 10A) comprise one document the purchaser's solicitor will be able to examine not only the report itself but also the instructions on which it has been prepared. It should be noted that the report in the Land Register is not for any specific period as the Land Register discloses the position of the title at any given moment and is not an historical record of entries since the Land Register was last searched.

• Along with the Form 10 report the seller's solicitor should submit a draft application for a Form 11 report for revisal by the purchaser's solicitor. This draft application takes the place of the Sasine transaction draft Memorandum for Continuation of Search. Where the purchaser is to grant a security over the property his solicitor should make certain at this stage that his client's name (and any others which may be appropriate) are added to the part of the Form 11 dealing with the Personal Register so that they are searched against in that Register and reported on. So far as the Sasine Register is concerned there is no need to instruct a continuation to disclose the disposition and standard security as would be done in a Sasine transaction. Nor need they be added to the instructions for the report on the Land Register as no final report (*i.e.* a continued search for incumbrances) will be prepared after completion of the transaction. The land certificate itself takes the place of any such final report.

• The continuation of the Form 10 report, *i.e.* the Form 11 report, should then be instructed by the seller's solicitor in accordance with the revised application. The application should also be adjusted with the lender's solicitor if separate solicitors are acting for the purchaser and the lender. The Form 11 report should be timed so that it is instructed as near as practicable to the date of settlement. If it is instructed from the Keeper the original Form 10 report need not be returned to the Keeper as he will have retained a copy of it but the number of the Form 10 report should be inserted in the appropriate space on the Form 11 application. A Form 11 report or its equivalent should always be ordered from the same source of supply as the Form 10 report or its equivalent.

- Immediately prior to settlement the Form 11 report should be exhibited to the purchaser's solicitor.

- Any adverse matters disclosed in either report should, of course, be dealt with before settlement as in a normal Sasine transaction.

It is not unusual for builder's missives for new houses to provide either that no reports will be made available or that, if they are, the cost will be borne by the purchaser. Irrespective of what is provided in the missives it has for long been recognised that the purchaser's solicitor should obtain the usual property, personal and charges searches or reports unless the purchaser, properly advised, has given specific written authority to his solicitor to dispense with such searches or reports. It is recommended that in every such case the seller's solicitor should provide a Form 10 report in respect of the individual property being sold even if the cost is recovered in terms of the missives from the purchaser. If further reports are required for the purchaser or the lender these can be obtained by the purchaser's solicitor.

It should be noted that the Form 10 and the Form 11 reports relate only to the Sasine, Personal and Land Registers and not to the Register of Charges or the Company File. If a Search in the Register of Charges and Company File is required this should be instructed from the Private Searchers.

Cost of reports

8.13 Fees for reports are set out in the current Fee Order. As reports will normally be instructed by the seller's solicitor their cost will be borne by the seller unless the relevant contract otherwise provides.

Letter of obligation - seller/purchaser - first registration

8.14 As a Sasine search will not be brought down on first registration the Sasine style of letter of obligation is not appropriate. There will however still be a gap, albeit very much reduced, between the date of the Form 10 or the Form 11 report and the date of the registration of the purchaser's interest (normally the date on which the application for registration (Form 1) is received by the Keeper). To cover this gap a letter of obligation by the seller's solicitor is required and a letter of obligation in the following style is recommended:

Dear Sirs

(Seller's name)
(Purchaser's name)
(Address of the subjects)

With reference to the settlement of the above transaction today we hereby (1) undertake to clear the records of any deed, decree or diligence (other than such as may be created by or against your client) which may be recorded in the Property or Personal Registers or to which effect may be given in the Land Register in the period from   * to
° inclusive (or to the earlier date of registration of your client's interest in the above subjects) and which would cause the Keeper to make an entry on or qualify his indemnity in the land certificate to be issued in respect of that interest and (2) confirm that to the best of our knowledge and belief as at this date the answers to the questions numbered 1 to 14 in the draft Form 1 adjusted with you (in so far as these answers relate to our client or to our client's interest in the above subjects) are still correct.

Yours faithfully

* *Insert date of certification of Form 11 report or, if only a Form 10 report has been instructed, the date of certification of that report.*

° *Insert date 14 days after settlement.*

As the seller's solicitor will wish to limit the duration of his obligation the foregoing style only covers the period from the date of the Form 10 (or the Form 11) report to the date of the receipt by the Keeper of the application for registration with a final cut-off date of fourteen days after the date of the letter of obligation (fourteen days being the recognised maximum period for a 'classic' letter of obligation). The purchaser's solicitor therefore has fourteen days to have the disposition completed and stamped and then submitted to the Keeper along with the application for registration (Form 1) and the appropriate deeds and documents conform to the inventory (Form 4). From the purchaser's point of view, it should be noted that an obligation which undertakes that the land certificate will contain no entries, *etc* 'provided that an application for registration is received by the Keeper within (   ) days' is not acceptable as if, for any reason, the application were received outwith that period, the obligation would not even cover adverse entries appearing between the date of the Form 11 or Form 10 report and the date of settlement.

The letter of obligation may cover other items which the seller has to produce but which are not available at settlement, for example, a feuduty redemption receipt. Under the Sasine system where an outstanding heritable security is being discharged an undertaking will be included to deliver the recorded discharge within an agreed period. Such an undertaking is no longer appropriate where the purchaser's interest is being registered as in the majority of cases the discharge will no longer be recorded in the Sasine Register at all. Even in these cases where recording is appropriate (*e.g.* where it also relates to other property not registered or not in an operational area) the purchaser's concern is not that the discharge has been recorded but that effect is given to the discharge in the Land Register when his interest is registered. There are occasions when a purchase has to be settled before a signed discharge is in the seller's solicitor's hands. It is not appropriate here to examine the difficulties and pitfalls which may exist in regard to settlement taking place on this basis and it is stressed that such settlements require the utmost care on the part of the purchaser's solicitor and must be approached with great circumspection. Where, however, settlement has to take place on this basis, an appropriate addition to the letter of obligation may be made undertaking delivery within a negotiated number of days of a duly executed discharge of the standard security (to be specified) in terms of the draft discharge approved, together also with a completed application for registration of the discharge duly signed (Form 2) and an inventory (Form 4) in duplicate to cover that application. It is again stressed that this practice is in no way recommended and is a matter for the judgement of the individual solicitor alone. This style is given for assistance only.

> '*We further undertake to deliver to you within (   ) days (1) a duly executed and completed discharge of the standard security granted by (   ) in favour of (   ) in terms of the draft discharge approved by you, (2) a completed application for registration of the said discharge duly signed together with a cheque in favour of the Registers of Scotland for the registration dues and (3) an Inventory (Form 4) completed in duplicate with reference to that application.*'

The following comments should be noted:

- If settlement is effected on the basis of later delivery of a discharge of a standard security, then the guidance given above is given on the basis that at settlement the purchaser's solicitor has already taken delivery of the standard security and any deeds of transmission or links in title. If the purchaser's solicitor has not, then the undertaking must be expanded to include these and they must be referred to in the Inventory - Item (3) set out in the style set out in the immediately preceding section.

- The purchaser on presenting his application for registration of his interest must include the discharge on the inventory which accompanies his application marking the entry 'to follow' (the standard security and any transmissions and links must also be noted). If the purchaser's solicitor fails to include the discharge in the inventory the Keeper will assume that the standard security is not to be discharged and will proceed to complete registration showing the standard security in the charges section of the title sheet as still outstanding.

- Even where the discharge is marked 'to follow' on the inventory, if it has not been submitted by the time the Keeper undertakes legal examination of the application he will complete registration showing the standard security in the charges section of the title sheet as still outstanding.

- As soon as the seller's solicitor receives the executed discharge from the lender he should complete the testing clause as necessary and then forward the discharge with completed supporting application Forms 2 and 4 along with a cheque to cover the registration dues to the purchaser's solicitor. On receipt, the purchaser's solicitor can mark the letter of obligation as implemented in this respect but should note that the letter of obligation is not fully implemented until a land certificate without exclusion of indemnity has been issued.

- The purchaser's solicitor should then send the discharge and supporting papers to the Keeper. The duplicate copy Form 4 in relation to the purchaser's application for registration will by this stage have been returned to the purchaser's solicitor and will give the title number. It would assist the Keeper if this title number were quoted on the application form for the discharge.

- If the Keeper does complete registration before the discharge is submitted, the purchaser's land certificate will have to be submitted with the discharge when application for registration of the discharge is eventually made.

- Even where the discharge falls to be recorded in the Sasine Register as well, for example, in the case of a partial discharge and deed of restriction, the purchaser's solicitor should still ensure, if settlement has taken place unavoidably before the discharge is to hand, that an undertaking is given on the lines suggested above, but the seller's solicitor should in this case remember to complete a warrant of registration on the deed and to attach a covering letter to the Keeper requesting that the deed be recorded in the Sasine Register as well.

Letter of obligation - Borrower/Lender where different solicitors act (purchase inducing first registration or purchase of registered interest with immediate grant of standard security)

8.15 The following style of letter of obligation to be granted by the borrower's solicitor is recommended:

Dear Sirs

(Borrower's name)
(Lender's name)
(Address of the subjects)

With reference to the settlement of the above transaction today we hereby undertake to deliver to you within   months of this date a land certificate issued by the Keeper of the Registers of Scotland in favour of our clients showing the interest of our client as registered proprietor of the above subjects which land certificate shall be unaffected by any deed, decree or diligence (other than such as may be created by or against your client) given effect to the Land Register in the period from   * to   ° inclusive (or to the earlier date of registration of your client's standard security over the above subjects) and further, will disclose the standard security granted in favour of your client (provided it is presented for registration in the Land Register within fourteen days of this date).

We further undertake (1) to exhibit to you along with the said land certificate all deeds, documents and other evidence which were submitted to the Keeper in support of our client's application for registration of his interest as registered proprietor of the above subjects and (2) confirm that, to the best of our knowledge and belief, as at this date the answers to the questions number 1 to 8 in the draft Form 2 adjusted with you (insofar as these relate to our client or to our client's interest in the above subjects) are still correct.

[We further undertake to exhibit to you within (   ) days of this date the duplicate Form 4 lodged with our client's application for the registration of his title to the above subjects with the Keeper's acknowledgement thereon].*

Yours faithfully

* *Insert date of certification of Form 10, 11, 12 or 13 report.*

° *Insert date 14 days after settlement*

+ *To be inserted where purchaser's solicitors lodge the purchaser's application with the Keeper or where there are two lenders one of whom will present that application.*

With regard to the foregoing style of letter of obligation it should be noted:

- This style is appropriate both where the interest to be secured is the subject of a first registration where the borrower is the applicant and where the interest to be secured is already registered and the borrower is acquiring that registered interest. It is not appropriate where the borrower is already the registered proprietor.

- An obligation to deliver the land certificate is necessary even although, at settlement, the lender's solicitor takes delivery of, and actually presents, the purchaser's application for registration, for the application must be signed by the purchaser or his solicitor on his behalf. On completion of registration the land certificate will be issued to the applicant *i.e.* the purchaser or his solicitor and not to the presenter of the application.

- As mentioned above, it is appropriate for the duration of the obligation under a letter of obligation to be limited. The words in the brackets at the end of the first paragraph of the foregoing style will protect the granter of the obligation against delay on the part of the creditor.

- On completion of registration, the lender's solicitor should check the terms of the land certificate issued as well as the terms of the charge certificate. To check the land certificate he will require to have all the title deeds and other evidence exhibited to him.

- Cases may arise where it is arranged that the purchaser's solicitor rather than the lender's will actually lodge the purchaser's application with the Keeper or, where there are two lenders one of whom will present that application. In such cases it may be appropriate, in order to confirm that the application has indeed been lodged, to add a further obligation as follows:

'We further undertake to exhibit to you within (   ) days of this date the duplicate Form 4 lodged with our client's application for the registration of his title to the above subjects with the Keeper's acknowledgement thereon.'

Identification of subjects

8.16 Registration of title is a map-based system. Properties are indexed by means of an index map and section 6(1)(a) provides that the title sheet of each registered interest will contain a description consisting of, or including, a description of that interest based on the ordnance map. In addition, section 4(2)(a) provides that the Keeper will reject any application for registration where the land to which it relates is not sufficiently described to enable him to identify the subjects by reference to the ordnance map. The purchaser's solicitor must ensure, therefore, as part of his examination of title, that the titles and deed plans produced will be sufficient to enable the Keeper to prepare the title and certificate plans. In cases where the Keeper's response to a P16 report narrates that the title boundaries coincide with the occupational boundaries as depicted on the ordnance map the purchaser's solicitor can assume that the Keeper can identify the property. However, the purchaser's solicitor must in this case not only examine the Form P16 report but examine the documents submitted to the Keeper in support of that enquiry. For example, the Keeper may have indicated that he can identify the property on the ordnance map with the boundaries disclosed in a deed plan submitted to him but the deed plan may only include part of the subjects covered by the missives. Where the property is a new one, the purchaser's solicitor must ensure that the deed plan contains sufficient information to enable the Keeper to locate the property accurately on the ordnance map - the physical boundaries will not at that stage be shown on the ordnance map. Where the deed plan is not sufficient, *i.e.* it is a 'floating' rectangle unrelated to physical features depicted on the ordnance map, a supplementary plan based on the ordnance map and supported by measurements will be required. Such a supplementary plan should be signed by the seller but need not be signed as relative to any deed forming part of the progress of titles.

Additional information required by the Keeper

8.17 In addition to a prescriptive progress of titles and to information required to enable him to identify the subjects, the Keeper will require additional information which cannot be obtained from the title deeds to enable him to complete registration. The standard information which he will require on first registration is contained in questions 1 to 14 in part B of the application for first registration, Form 1. Insofar as this information relates to the seller, the purchaser's solicitor should make certain, during the course of the transaction, that he obtains from the seller's solicitor sufficient information to complete the questionnaire in part B of the application form and a draft of the application form should be adjusted with the seller's solicitor during the course of the transaction. If there is a separate solicitor acting for a lender, then not only should a draft of the application form (Form 2) relating to the standard security be adjusted between the solicitors for the purchaser and the lender, but the draft Form 1 as adjusted between the solicitors for the seller and purchaser should be submitted to the lender's solicitor for approval. In addition, there may well be matters other than those covered by the questionnaire in Part B in respect of which the Keeper will require information or additional evidence. For example, where the seller originally held the property on a survivorship destination, the purchaser's solicitor should make certain that at settlement he is in a position to lodge with the Form 1 a death certificate of the former co-proprietor and evidence, *e.g.* by way of affidavit, confirming that the former co-proprietor had not evacuated the destination *quoad* his or her share.

The information which the purchaser's solicitor has obtained during the course of the transaction to enable him to complete Form 1 will have been obtained some time before the form is actually lodged with the Keeper. For this reason the purchaser's solicitor should seek from the seller's solicitor, at settlement, confirmation that the answers to the questions are still correct on the lines suggested in the second part of the style of Letter of Obligation given in paragraph 8.14. The purchaser's solicitor may not foresee all the additional information which the Keeper may request and it is important, therefore, that he should safeguard his client's right to seek further information from the seller. If the Keeper considers that the lapse of time between the date of signature of the application form and the date of its receipt by him is too great he may require a further certificate that the information was still correct at the date of his receipt of the application.

Style of disposition for first registration

8.18 The purchaser's solicitor will draft and then adjust a disposition to be granted to his client in the usual way. It should be noted that the further simplifications provided for in section 15 do not apply as that section only relates to an interest which has already been registered in the Land Register. Furthermore, although registration will be sought, section 4(2)(d) (reference to title number) will not apply as this also relates to a deed relating to a registered interest. The terms of section 15 will similarly not apply to any standard security granted by the purchaser and presented along with the application for registration of the purchaser's interest; nor will section 4(2)(d) apply to such a related standard security whether it is presented along with, or after, the application for registration induced by the disposition has been received, unless the standard security is dated after the date on which the Form 1 application is received by the Keeper. In this latter case the title number <u>must</u> be included. This does not mean that the standard security will require to be re-engrossed to include a reference description in terms of section 15(1). The provision in section 4(2)(d) will be sufficiently complied with if the title number is clearly marked on the deed, preferably on the top of the first page and certainly not on the backing. The title number can be obtained by reference to the duplicate Inventory (Form 4) which the Keeper will already have returned to the solicitor on receipt of the Form 1 application.

Section 16 abolished the requirement to include clauses of assignation of writs, assignation of rents, and the obligation of relief. The section does not, however, deal with warrandice. Furthermore, although some of the matters covered by the seller's warrandice may also be covered by the Keeper's indemnity, the purchaser's rights under the seller's warrandice remain unchanged. Where the purchaser has the benefit of the Keeper's indemnity, he has the choice of pursuing his claim against the Keeper under the indemnity provisions or against the seller under his warrandice. Indeed, where the Keeper settles a claim for indemnity, he is, in terms of section 13(2), subrogated to all rights which would have been available to the purchaser to recover the loss indemnified and may himself pursue the seller under his warrandice. Where the purchaser does not have the benefit of the Keeper's indemnity, that is where, in terms of section 12(3), there is no entitlement to indemnity or where indemnity has been excluded in terms of section 12(2), the purchaser's only remedy is against the seller under warrandice. For example, should the existence of a servitude right come to light, there would be no claim against the Keeper for, as the right is an overriding interest, the indemnity provisions do not apply (section 12(3)(h)). However, the emergence of such a right could found a claim on warrandice against the seller. A seller must, therefore, consider carefully whether the statutory form (sections 5 and 8 of the Titles to Land Consolidation (Scotland) Act 1868 and Schedule B to that Act) is appropriate. (See paragraph 6.12 to 6.16)

Parts previously sold

8.19 Special considerations arise where the interest to be registered consists of subjects out of which parts have previously been sold. In Sasine transactions it is common practice on the sale of the part remaining to describe that part by reference to the original description of the subjects under exception of the parts sold. In the normal case there is no objection to such a description in a deed in respect of which an application for first registration is made, provided that the subjects so described (*i.e.* the remaining part) can be identified by the Keeper by reference to the ordnance map. However, in cases where the description by reference to the title plan requires to be amplified by a more elaborate verbal description, for example tenement flats and flats resulting from conversions, the remainder should be particularly described, with the addition, where it is considered necessary, of a further description by reference to the original description under exception of parts sold. It is likely that parts previously sold will have been conveyed with rights over the remainder and under burden of rights in favour of the remainder. The Keeper may be in some difficulty in setting out such rights and burdens in the title sheet unless they are clearly stated in the disposition of the remainder. Bearing in mind that such rights and burdens may be lost forever if they are not set out in the title sheet, it is recommended that in such a disposition all rights and burdens affecting the subjects conveyed should be clearly stated and where appropriate be identified on a plan.

First registration - settlement

Same solicitor acting for both purchaser and lender

8.20 Settlement of the transaction will take place as for a Sasine transaction but the following differences should be noted. The purchaser's solicitor should take delivery of:

(a) The title deeds. This will include not only those writs which would fall to be delivered to the purchaser at settlement but also all common titles which under the Sasine system would not fall to be delivered but which under registration of title will be required to support the application for first registration.

(b) The Form 10 and Form 11 reports and also the Form P16 report (if any).

(c) Any additional plan which the seller is to provide to enable the subjects to be identified on the ordnance map.

(d) The letter of obligation in the form suggested in paragraph 8.14.

(e) The signed disposition in favour of the purchaser.

(f) If any existing heritable security is being discharged, the discharge (which does not require and should not include a warrant of registration, along with the relevant Forms 2 and 4 and a cheque for the registration dues.

Separate solicitors acting for purchaser and lender

8.21 If separate solicitors are acting for the purchaser and for any lender to the purchaser then the lender's solicitor should at settlement take delivery of:

(a) A completed and signed application for first registration, Form 1, which must be signed by the purchaser or by the purchaser's solicitor together with a cheque in respect of the registration dues of the disposition. The terms of the Form 1 should have been adjusted in draft among the seller's, the purchaser's and the lender's solicitors.

(b) An Inventory Form 4 completed by the purchaser's solicitor in duplicate.

(c) All the deeds and documents detailed in that Inventory being all the deeds and documents required to support the application for first registration.

(d) The items mentioned in (b), (c), (e) and (f) in the preceding paragraph.

(e) The signed standard security and a cheque for the registration dues. (No warrant of registration should be endorsed on the standard security).

(f) A letter of obligation in the terms set out in paragraph 8.15.

First registration application for registration

Purchase and loan transactions completed contemporaneously

Same solicitor acting for purchaser and lender
8.22 There should be submitted to the Keeper:

- A completed and signed application for first registration, Form 1, together with the deed inducing first registration; in this case the disposition in favour of the purchaser. No warrant of registration should be included.

- All the deeds and documents supporting the application for registration accompanied by an inventory Form 4 listing these deeds and documents.

The inventory should be completed in duplicate. One copy will be returned by the Keeper as an acknowledgement and will bear the title number allocated to the interest. The inventory should include deeds and documents which are not yet in the purchaser's solicitor's possession but which are to follow, for example the feuduty redemption receipt (see below); common deeds not meeting the criteria set out in paragraph 5.13 and any discharge of an outstanding heritable security. (NB while a separate application on Form 2 is required for registration of such a discharge, a fixed fee of (currently) £22 will be payable.)

- Any supplementary plan required to enable the Keeper to identify the subjects (this should be listed on the Inventory). The Form P16 report (if any) should be included with the Form 1 application but not any equivalent report from Private Searchers.

- Any additional evidence, for example, affidavits, death certificates or the like (these too should be listed on the Form 4).

- A completed and signed application for registration of a dealing, Form 2, together with the deed effecting that dealing; in this case the standard security. The standard security should not include a warrant of registration but it should be entered in the inventory. A reduced registration fee will be charged in respect of an application for registration of a standard security where that application is received along with the borrower's application for registration of his interest.

- Where there is additional evidence not available when the applications for registration are lodged, for example a feuduty redemption receipt or a certificate of registration of a charge from the Register of Charges such evidence should be accompanied by a further Inventory Form 4 in duplicate and clearly marked with the title number.

- The total amount of registration fees payable.

Separate solicitors acting for purchaser and lender
8.23 It is suggested that in this case the lender's solicitor will wish to ensure that the application for registration of the purchaser's (borrower's) interest is duly lodged. Accordingly, he will take delivery of all the items referred to in paragraph 8.21 and will lodge these with the Keeper along with an application for registration (Form 2) in respect of the standard security and an inventory (Form 4) listing the standard security only. In this case there are two additional points to note:

1. The purchaser or his solicitor must sign the Form 1. The lender's solicitor cannot do so. Similarly Form 2 must be signed by the lender or his solicitor.

2. The Keeper will return the duplicate inventory submitted with the Form 1 application to the purchaser's solicitor as an acknowledgement of receipt of the deeds and other documents submitted in support of the application for registration. The duplicate of the inventory accompanying the Form 2 application (the standard security) will be returned to the lender's solicitor. Both duplicate inventories will be marked with the title number allocated to the prospectively registered interest.

Where it is arranged that the purchaser's solicitor will submit the application for registration of his client's interest the lender's solicitor should lodge with the Form 2 and the standard security an inventory Form 4 in duplicate listing that standard security only. If the lender's solicitor wishes evidence that the Form 1 application and supporting evidence have been received by the Keeper he may either:

- attach a copy of the purchaser's inventory to the inventory Form 4 submitted with the lender's Form 2 application including on the latter Inventory (1) 'the deeds and documents listed on and submitted with the copy inventory attached' and (2) the standard security; or

- include, as is suggested at the end of paragraph 8.15, an undertaking to exhibit the keeper's acknowledgement, *i.e.* the purchaser's duplicate Form 4, within (   ) days in the letter of obligation.

The reduced registration fee for the standard security only applies if the two applications are received together.

Purchase and loan transactions not completed contemporaneously

8.24 In the majority of cases where a purchaser is financing the purchase by means of a secured loan the two transactions are completed together. There are, however, cases where settlement of the loan transaction is delayed but the purchase is duly settled by means of temporary bridging finance. It is suggested that these transactions should be dealt with as outlined in the following sections.

Same solicitor acting for purchaser and lender
Where the same solicitor is acting he should, on completion of the purchase, submit an application for registration of the purchaser's interest - Form 1. In due course, the standard security can be lodged with a Form 2 and an inventory Form 4

in duplicate, and the Keeper will complete registration in respect of both applications. The reduced registration fee for a standard security will not apply. The two applications must be received together for the reduced fee to apply. The standard security in this case should be framed in terms of section 15(1). The appropriate title number will be found on the duplicate inventory returned by the Keeper in acknowledgement of the Form 1 application. The standard security may, of course, be prepared as part of the purchase transaction, the security subjects being described according to Sasine practice. In this case the Keeper will still accept the standard security for registration provided the title number is clearly marked on it, preferably on the top of the first page. It is not sufficient to mark it on the backing as that is not part of the deed.

Separate solicitors acting for purchaser and lender
Where the loan transaction is going to be completed before the land certificate is issued the lender's solicitor proceeds by examination of the Sasine titles. If the title deeds are still required by the lender's solicitor when the purchaser is in a position to apply for registration of his interest, the purchaser's application can nevertheless proceed, the title deeds still in the lender's hands being marked on the inventory Form 4 'to follow'.

Discharge of outstanding heritable security

8.25 Reference has already been made to the discharge of an outstanding heritable security. Where this discharge relates entirely to the interest being acquired by the purchaser and accompanies the application for registration of the purchaser's interest and is listed on the inventory Form 4 then, although strictly speaking it should be recorded in the Sasine Register, the Keeper will on registering the purchaser's interest give effect to that discharge although it contains no warrant of registration nor is accompanied by an application for registration. The discharge will not be recorded in the Sasine Register at all. The foregoing applies equally to a deed of disburdenment, a discharge of an *ex facie* absolute security or a reconveyance by an *ex facie* absolute proprietor to the proprietor in reversion, provided that in each case the deed relates solely to the interest acquired by the purchaser.

Discharge not available at settlement

8.26 Where the discharge is not available at settlement, on being subsequently submitted to the Keeper it should be accompanied by an application for registration Form 2 signed by, or on behalf of, the seller together with an inventory Form 4 (in duplicate) listing the discharge. The letter of obligation granted at settlement should include an obligation to deliver to the purchaser's solicitor the executed and completed discharge, the completed and signed Form 2 and the inventory Form 4 in duplicate and a cheque in favour of the Registers of Scotland for the registration dues. The purchaser's solicitor should then present the application for registration. The discharge may be rejected by the Keeper if, in terms of section 4(2)(d), it requires to have the title number marked on it. A title number will at this stage have been allocated and the purchaser's solicitor will have a note of this from the duplicate Form 4 returned to the agent. Where a discharge has been marked 'to follow' on an inventory form 4 accompanying an application for registration, the Keeper will allow 60 days from the date of receipt of that application for the discharge to be submitted (as a separate application) before completing registration of the initial application. If the discharge is not submitted as an application within 60 days the initial application will be completed showing the outstanding standard security.

Discharge relating to additional subjects in Sasine Register

8.27 If the standard security is recorded in the Sasine Register, a partial discharge and deed of restriction, for example, will have to be recorded in the Sasine Register but effect will also have to be given to such a deed in the Land Register. In such a case the deed will have a warrant of registration endorsed on it. An application Form 2 will also be required, even if it accompanies an application for registration of the purchaser's interest. There should also be a Form CPB2 requesting the Keeper to record the deed.

First registration - procedure after registration

8.28 On completion of registration the Keeper will issue a land certificate in name of the purchaser to the purchaser's solicitor and where appropriate will issue a charge certificate to the lender's solicitor. The original standard security will be attached to the charge certificate. At the same time all deeds and other evidence exhibited to the Keeper in support of the application for registration will be returned to the applicant (*i.e.* the applicant's solicitor). Subsequent procedure will be as follows:

One solicitor acting for purchaser and lender

8.29 Where one solicitor is acting for both purchaser and lender he should, after registration:

- Check the land certificate. This will entail a detailed comparison of the land certificate with the title deeds to ensure that the entries in each section of the land certificate are correct; that the title plan, a copy of which will be attached to the land certificate, is in order; that the proprietorship section is in order and that, in appropriate cases, it contains a statement that there are no subsisting occupancy rights of spouses of former proprietors; and that any exclusions of indemnity are acceptable. Note that exclusions may be made to some or all of sections A, B, C or D of the land certificate.

- Check the charge certificate. In this connection it should be noted that the charge certificate will include an automatic exclusion of indemnity where the standard security has been granted by a Limited Company unless the Keeper has received a certificate of registration in the Register of Charges before the issue of the charge certificate.

- If appropriate, return the seller's letter of obligation, marked as implemented, and at the same time.

- Return to the seller any common titles that have merely been exhibited.

- Send the land certificate and charge certificate to the heritable creditor for safekeeping in accordance with the creditor's instructions.

- Dispose of the remaining title deeds (see paragraph 8.31).

Separate solicitors acting for purchaser and lender

8.30 Where there are separate solicitors acting, the purchaser's and lender's solicitors should after registration:

Purchaser's solicitor

- Check the land certificate.

- Send the land certificate to the lender's solicitor along with the title deeds and other documents which were submitted in support of the application for registration, at the same time indicating those titles which should be retained with the land certificate.

- In due course receive back from the lender's solicitor (a) the letter of obligation, marked as implemented, and (b) the remaining titles (*i.e.* those which are not to be retained with the land certificate).

- Return to the seller's solicitor any title deeds and other documents that have merely been exhibited by the seller's solicitor.

- Return the seller's solicitor's letter of obligation, marked as implemented.

- Check the charge certificate.

- Check the land certificate when received from the purchaser's solicitor.

- Send the land certificate, charge certificate and titles (if any) to the lender or otherwise deal with as instructed.

- Return the remaining titles to the purchaser's solicitor, together with the discharged letter of obligation.

Title deeds

8.31 Once an interest has been registered the title deeds cease to be of any importance except where the Keeper has registered the interest with an exclusion of indemnity either in whole or in part. Titles which have a bearing on that exclusion should be retained until that exclusion has been removed, for example by the operation of prescription. Even if unforeseen future circumstances should make it necessary to examine earlier deeds, for example to check the terms of the seller's grant of warrandice, this will still be possible either in the Sasine Register or, once the interest has been registered, by ordering office copies from the Land Register. The Keeper will retain on microfiche, as part of the Register, copies of all the deeds which have induced an entry on the title sheet. There is only one case where a Sasine Extract may not be sufficient, namely where the earlier deed contains a plan which has not been recorded either because the deed was recorded before plans were copied into the Register (*i.e.* before 1934) or because the plan was too large to photograph (in excess of 28 inches x 22 inches) and a duplicate plan was not recorded, or, although recorded, the colours will not show on an Extract. The solicitor may consider that such a plan should be retained, for example it may contain greater detail than can possibly be shown on the title plan. In such cases, of course, the Keeper may have decided to incorporate a copy of the earlier plan in the title sheet to supplement the title plan.

Subject to these preliminary remarks it is suggested that title deeds after registration should be dealt with as follows:

(a) Where the interest has been registered with qualified indemnity the title deeds so far as delivered to the purchaser should be retained intact insofar as these deeds relate to the matter in respect of which indemnity has been excluded. Where common writs that are not delivered have a bearing on the exclusion the purchaser's solicitor should retain a careful note of the custodian of these common writs and perhaps keep copies.

(b) Common titles which have merely been exhibited on loan to the purchaser to support the application for registration must be returned to the custodian.

(c) Common titles which have been delivered to the purchaser must be retained as, although the disposition in favour of the purchaser will not contain an assignation of writs clause and an obligation to make common writs forthcoming, there is now an implied statutory obligation to do so by virtue of section 16(1)(c). This obligation, however, ceases to operate in favour of any interest that has been registered in the Land Register unless that interest has been registered subject to an exclusion of indemnity (section 3(5)).

(d) With the exception of outstanding securities (see (e) below) title deeds which relate solely to the subjects will, after registration with full indemnity, and bearing in mind that a Sasine Extract or Office Copy can always be obtained, be of little significance (except perhaps as regards an unrecorded plan). In theory, such titles could be destroyed although this should not be done without specific instructions from the client.

(e) Where the purchaser has granted a standard security this will be entered in the title sheet and a charge certificate issued. However, the effect of such an entry in the title sheet merely guarantees that there is a valid security over the interest; the entry will not provide evidence of conditions relating to that security. It is important; therefore, that notwithstanding the issue of a charge certificate the original security writ must be retained until it has been discharged. In practice the Keeper will attach the principal security writ to the charge certificate. Less commonly the purchaser may take over the personal obligation in an existing heritable security recorded in the Sasine Register. The existence of this security will be noted in the charges section of the title sheet but a charge certificate will not be issued to the lender unless specifically applied for by him. In this case the principal security writ must be retained until ultimately discharged.

First registration - transactions commenced before but settled after the commencement date

8.32 A disposition for value delivered after an area becomes operational will induce first registration even if the deed is dated before the commencement date for that area. There will, therefore, be transactions entered into before an area has become operational but which are either not due to be settled until after the commencement date or, although due to be settled before that date are for one reason or another not so settled. The Keeper has undertaken to have the statutory instrument setting the commencement date for any given area promulgated at least 6 months before the commencement date and therefore it should be known at the missives stage of a transaction whether or not the subjects or any part of them will be in an operational area at entry/settlement.

Date of settlement after the commencement date

8.33 Where missives are being concluded for subjects in a non-operational area and the settlement date will definitely be after the commencement date the provisions of the missives with regard to the production of titles etc should be as recommended for a first registration transaction.

Because the entry date or the settlement date could be brought forward by agreement between the parties to a date before the relevant commencement date so that the transaction will fall to be settled as a Sasine transaction it is recommended that the missives contain alternative provisions covering not only those recommended for a first registration transaction but also the production of titles and clear searches as for a Sasine transaction. It is therefore recommended that missives contain the following alternative clauses:

'*In exchange for the price the seller will deliver a duly executed disposition in favour of the purchaser and will exhibit or deliver a valid marketable title together with either:*

(a) *clear Searches in the Sasine and Personal Registers (the Search in the Sasine Register being for a period of 40 years), if at the date of settlement the provision of sections 2(1) and 3(3) of the Land Registration (Scotland) Act 1979 do not apply to the transfer of the seller's interest; or*

(b) *if the provisions of the said sections do so apply, a Form 10 report brought down to a date as near as practicable to the date of settlement and showing no entries adverse to the seller's interest, the cost of said report being the responsibility of the seller. In addition, the seller will furnish to the purchaser such documents and evidence, including a plan, as the Keeper may require to enable the Keeper to issue a land certificate in name of the purchaser as the registered proprietor of the whole subjects of offer and containing no exclusion of indemnity in terms of section 12(2) of the said Land Registration (Scotland) Act 1979. Such documents shall include (unless the whole subjects of offer comprise only part of a tenement or flatted building and do not include an area of ground specifically included in that part) a plan or bounding description sufficient to enable the whole subjects to be identified on the ordnance map, and evidence (such as a Form P16 report) that the description of the whole subjects of offer as contained in the title deeds is habile to include the whole of the occupied extent. The land certificate to be issued to the purchaser will disclose no entry, deed or diligence prejudicial to the purchaser's interest other than such as are created by or against the purchaser, or have been disclosed to, and accepted by, the purchaser prior to the date of settlement.*

In either case the transaction should proceed as outlined in the earlier paragraphs of this chapter but it should be noted:

- The Keeper will issue a Form 10 report (and if necessary a Form 11 report) within three months before the commencement date for a new operational area.

- The Keeper will also issue a Form P16 report within three months before the commencement date for a new operational area. If, therefore, occupational boundaries have to be checked as part of the examination of title before that time, the parties will have to carry out their own comparison of the legal and occupational boundaries by reference to the ordnance map.

Dealing with a registered interest - presale procedures

Presale examination of title

8.34 Where the transaction relates to an interest which is already registered in the Land Register, the conveyancing procedures appropriate to that transaction will differ from those discussed in the previous paragraphs in relation to a sale/purchase which induces first registration in the Land Register.

A seller's solicitor should always examine his client's land certificate before concluding a bargain, not only to ensure that the seller has a title to the whole subjects of sale and that there are no material burdens which should be disclosed to a purchaser, but also to make certain that on registering the interest in the Land Register the Keeper has not excluded indemnity.

Where the transaction relates to an interest for which an application for registration in the Land Register has been made but the land certificate has not been issued, the conveyancing procedures appropriate to that transaction will differ from those discussed. Unless the Keeper is prepared to confirm that the land certificate is to be issued in terms of the application for first registration a purchaser's solicitor will need to carry out a complete examination of title as if the

the seller's solicitor must ensure that this is brought to the purchaser's notice before missives are concluded and the exclusion specifically referred to in the missives. This will normally be done by exhibiting the qualified land certificate before concluding a bargain, together with such title deeds as may be required to enable the purchaser's solicitor to evaluate the effect of the exclusion. The purchaser's solicitor should not accept any exclusion without first obtaining his client's authority to do so. The foregoing would not, of course, apply to exclusions of indemnity which related for example to securities granted by the seller and which fall to be discharged before settlement.

Dealing with a registered interest - conveyancing procedures

8.38 It is on a sale or other dealing with a registered interest that the full practical changes under registration of title come into play. These changes may be summarised as follows:

- Examination of title is much simpler.

- Just as Form 10 and Form 11 reports replace the Search for Incumbrances on first registration, these forms are in turn replaced by Form 12 and Form 13 reports where the subjects are already registered.

- Problems of identification should arise only where the dealing relates to part of the registered interest or where there were no physical boundaries when the interest was first registered.

- The Keeper will require additional information (Part B of Form 2/3) to enable him to complete registration.

- The form of disposition appropriate to a registered interest is much shortened.

Examination of title

8.39 In cases where there is no exclusion of indemnity, the only 'titles' which the purchaser's solicitor will require to examine are as follows:

- The land certificate.

- Any charge certificate.

- Draft discharges of any outstanding heritable securities.

- Any links in title connecting the proprietor as shown in the proprietorship section of the title sheet with the present seller or relating to an outstanding heritable security.

- Any deeds relating to dealings in the interest which have not been registered.

- A Form 12 (or Form 13) report.

- Any Form P17 report.

- Any documents relating to occupancy rights of spouses of the proprietor shown in the land certificate and any other person who subsequently had a right to the registered interest.

The principal differences in title examination where the subjects of purchase are a registered interest are:

- The purchaser's solicitor is not concerned with the sufficiency or validity of any deed which has resulted in an entry in the title sheet except where that deed relates to a matter in respect of which indemnity has been excluded. The purchaser's solicitor is, however, still concerned to check the sufficiency and validity of all deeds later in date than the date of last registration which affect the interest and have not been noted on the title sheet, for example links in title.

- Where a heritable security has been discharged and effect given to the discharge by registration there is no need to examine any discharged security writs. In fact any outstanding heritable securities will be disclosed in the charges section of the title sheet. When, however, they have been discharged, the Keeper will prepare a new charges section omitting any reference at all to the discharged security. Even in cases where the earlier Sasine titles have been preserved, there is no need to examine any security writs among those titles if these writs are not disclosed in the charges section of the land certificate. However, any outstanding standard securities, whether they are still in the Sasine Register or are in the Land Register, together with the relative draft discharges and links in title, will require to be examined in the usual way as for a Sasine transaction.

Where the title has been registered with an exclusion of indemnity (*i.e.* some aspect of the title is not warranted by the Keeper) then prior titles, insofar as they relate to that exclusion, require to be examined; and, where the statement in the land certificate relating to the subsistence of occupancy rights of spouses of former proprietors has been qualified, any documents relevant to that qualification require to be examined.

Form 12 and Form 13 reports

8.40 For a detailed statement on reports reference should be made to Chapter 3. A system of direct electronic access to the Registers is being introduced ('Registers Direct') and further information about this is available from the Keeper.

As the interest is registered, the purchaser's solicitor will only require to satisfy himself that the Land and the Personal Registers are clear. A Search in the Sasine Register is no longer appropriate as, in terms of section 8(4), the Keeper must reject any deed presented for recording in the Sasine Register which relates to an interest registered in the Land Register. The appropriate application form for the report is Form 12. Applications to the Keeper should be submitted in duplicate. The report is made against the subjects in (or remaining in) the title as at the date to which the land certificate was last updated (shown on the inside cover of the land certificate). Where the report is required over the whole of the registered interest, all that is required to enable the Keeper to identify the interest on the index map is the title number. The difficulties which could arise in identifying the subjects sufficiently to enable the Keeper to issue a Form 10 report should not arise.

As the Form 12 report (Forms 12A *etc*) will also cover the Personal Registers the parties to be searched against should include the registered proprietor and any other parties who have been interested in the subjects since the last update of the land certificate. Accurate details of the names and addresses of the parties to be searched against must be given on the application.

Where however the transaction relates to part only of the subjects registered, not only must the title number of the whole be given, but the part must be clearly identified to the Keeper either by a verbal description or by a plan which is included in or accompanies the deeds or documents which are submitted with the application for registration. In some cases the plan may be a suitably marked-up copy of the plan which forms part of the land certificate. The question of copyright and possible distortion in copying should be kept in mind. The most common example of a transaction relating to part only of a registered interest is of course the first disposal of a unit on a building development. In this case builders' solicitors should make use of the facility provided for submitting an estate plan for the Keeper's approval. If this is done, then reference to the plot number on that plan will be sufficient identification for the Keeper. In most transactions, it will be sufficient to instruct a Form 12 report during the course of the transaction so that it is available as near as practicable to the date of settlement. However where an earlier report is instructed, or where there is a delay in settlement, and a continuation of the Form 12 report is required, a continuation should be instructed on a Form 13.

Where there is no land certificate because first registration has not been completed, the Form 12 report in addition to covering the period from receipt of the application for first registration, will also provide a report from the Sasine Register and give the same information as would be contained in a Form 10 report brought down to the date of first registration. Similarly where a land certificate is not available because the registration of a previous dealing with the registered interest has not been completed, details of applications still in course of registration will be included in the Form 12 report but in these cases it will be stated specifically that registration has not yet been completed. No indemnity can be implied from the disclosure of an incomplete registration in a Form 12 report. The purchaser's solicitor will require to investigate the circumstances of any incomplete registrations and examine all the relevant titles submitted with the application for first registration and any subsequent dealings unless the Keeper is prepared to confirm that a land certificate is to be issued in terms of the application for registration.

There are five types of Form 12 report (Forms 12A, 12B, 12C, 12D and 12E). The type used by the Keeper will depend upon the stage which the registration of the title of the subjects (or any part thereof) has reached. Form 12A will be used if first registration of the subjects to be reported on has been completed. Details of the circumstances in which the other reports will be issued can be found in chapter 3.

Reports - recommended procedure

8.41 The following procedure is recommended:

- The seller's solicitor should prepare a draft application for a Form 12 report and submit this to the purchaser's solicitor for revisal when he sends the land certificate and other documents to the purchaser's solicitor for examination. (This draft application is equivalent to the Memorandum for Continuation of Search). There is, of course, no search to submit to the purchaser's solicitor, nor, where the seller's land certificate has been issued is there any need to exhibit any existing Form 10 report. Both have been superseded by the seller's land certificate. The Register of Inhibitions and Adjudications part of the form should include the names of the registered proprietors, together with all relevant addresses.

- In revising the application for a Form 12 report, the purchaser's solicitor should ensure that all additional parties against whom a search in the Personal Registers is required are added and designed accurately. All relevant addresses should be included.

- If there are separate solicitors acting for the purchaser and lender, then the lender's solicitor should also revise the draft application.

- A Form 12 report should be applied for in duplicate by the seller's solicitor as near as practicable to the date of settlement.

- Where a further report is required (because there has perhaps been some delay in settlement) the Form 12 report is continued by a Form 13 report. The draft application for the Form 13 report (*i.e.* the Form 13) should be prepared by the seller's solicitor and sent to the purchaser's solicitor for revisal along with the Form 12 report. The revised Form 13 should be submitted in duplicate. If the application is sent to the Keeper no copy of the Form 12 report needs to accompany it. If the application is sent to the Private Searchers a copy of the Form 12 report may have to accompany it.

The procedure to be followed where missives, such as builder's missives, make special provisions with regard to the availability of reports is similar to the procedure recommended for first registration *i.e.* it is recommended that the seller's solicitor should provide a Form 12 report irrespective of who is due to meet the cost; and unless specifically instructed otherwise the purchaser's solicitor should examine all the relevant reports.

The Form 12 and Form 13 reports only cover the Land Register and the Personal Registers. They do not cover the Register of Charges or the Company File and, if a search is required from them it should be instructed in the usual way.

Cost of reports

8.42 Fees for reports are set out in the current Fee Order. As reports will normally be instructed by the seller's solicitor their cost will be borne by the seller unless the relevant contract otherwise provides.

Letter of obligation seller/purchaser - registered interest

8.43 The style of letter of obligation recommended for a transaction which induces first registration is, subject to small adjustments, also appropriate to a transaction relating to a registered interest and the comments in paragraph 8.14 are equally applicable. The recommended style is:

Dear Sirs

(Seller's name)
(Purchaser's name)
(Address of the subjects)

With reference to the settlement of the above transaction today we hereby (1) undertake to clear the records of any deed, decree or diligence (other than such as may be created by or against your client) which may be recorded in the Personal Register or to which effect may be given in the Land Register in the period from   * to   ° inclusive (or to the earlier date of registration of your client's interest in the above subjects) and which would cause the Keeper to make an entry on, or qualify his indemnity in, the land certificate to be issued in respect of that interest, and (2) confirm that, to the best of our knowledge and belief, as at this date the answers to the questions numbered (1 to 8) (1 to 13) in the draft Form 2/3 adjusted with you (insofar as these answers relate to our client or to our client's interest in the above subjects) are still correct.

Yours faithfully

* *Insert date of certification of Form 12 report, or if a Form 13 report has been instructed, the date of certification of that report.*

° *Insert the date 14 days after settlement.*

As in a first registration transaction the seller's solicitor will wish to limit the duration of his obligation and so the foregoing style only covers the period from the date of the Form 12 (or the Form 13) report to the date of the receipt by the Keeper of the application for registration with a final cut-off date of fourteen days after the date of the letter of obligation (fourteen days being the recognised maximum period for a 'classic' letter of obligation). The purchaser's solicitor therefore has fourteen days to have the disposition completed and stamped and then submitted to the Keeper along with the application for registration (Form 2/3) and the appropriate deeds and documents conform to the inventory (Form 4).

Reference is made in the recommended style of letter to 'Form 2/3'. Both forms relate to registration of a dealing with a registered interest. The appropriate form depends on whether the Keeper, on registration of the dealing, will merely amend and re-issue an existing land certificate or open a new title sheet in respect of the interest. In the case of a purchase and loan transaction, the appropriate forms, where the purchase relates to the whole of the registered interest, are Form 2 (for the disposition) and another Form 2 (for the standard security). Where the purchase relates to part only of the registered interest, Form 3 must be used for the disposition and Form 2 for the standard security. If the transaction relates to a first sale of property in a building development in respect of which a layout plan has been approved, it is suggested that the purchaser's solicitor, and, indeed, the lender's solicitor, should, at settlement, confirm that the layout plan, on the basis of which the transaction has proceeded, has not been departed from. It is suggested that this confirmation might conveniently be included in the letter of obligation by adding:

> 'We further confirm that the estate layout plan approved by the Keeper on (   ) has not been departed from by our clients or approval in respect thereof been withdrawn by the Keeper.'

Letter of obligation (borrower/lender) where different solicitors act and the borrower is already the registered proprietor of interest to be secured

8.44 The form of letter of obligation discussed in paragraph 8.15 is appropriate in cases where the transaction relates to a registered interest and the lender is taking a charge over that interest. Where, however, the borrower is already registered in the Land Register as proprietor it is recommended that the letter of obligation should be in the following terms:

Dear Sirs

(Borrower's name)
(Lender's name)
(Address of the subjects)

With reference to the settlement of the above transaction today we hereby (1) undertake to clear the records of any deed, decree or diligence (other than such as may be created *by or against your client) which may be recorded in the Personal Registers or to which effect may be given in the Land Register in the period from   * to   ° inclusive (or to the earlier date of registration of your client's interest in the above subjects) which would cause the Keeper to make an entry on, or qualify his indemnity in, the title sheet relating to our client's interest in the above subjects and (2) confirm that to the best of our knowledge and belief, as at this date the answers in questions numbered 1 to 8 in the draft Form 2 adjusted with you (insofar as these answers relate to our client or to our client's interest in the above subjects) are still correct.*

Yours faithfully

*   *Insert date of certification of Form 12 report or, if a Form 13 report has been instructed, the date of certificate of that report.*

°   *Insert the date 14 days after settlement.*

The following comments on the style suggested in the preceding paragraph should be noted:

- In this case, *i.e.* where the borrower is the registered proprietor, there is no need to provide for delivery of the land certificate for the lender's solicitor will take delivery of this at settlement. It will then be submitted by or on behalf of the lender in support of the application for registration of the standard security and, on completion of that registration, will be returned by the Keeper to the lender's solicitor.

- The style is equally appropriate where the transaction is a second loan although in this case the second lender may be unable to produce the borrower's land certificate to support his application for registration because it is held by the first lender (rule 18). The second lender will be able to satisfy himself that the obligation has been implemented, *i.e.* the title sheet is 'clear' by obtaining an office copy when the registration is complete. The lender's solicitor should either recover the cost of an office copy from the borrower or take an obligation from the borrower (or his solicitor on his behalf) to deliver an office copy to him as soon as registration has been completed.

Identification of subjects

8.45 Where the dealing relates to the whole of a registered interest, no problems arise as to identification except in the case where the boundaries are still shown by dotted lines. In this case, there may be possible discrepancies between these dotted lines (the legal boundaries) and the actual physical boundaries. It is suggested that, where boundaries are so shown, they should be checked by the seller's solicitor at the pre-missives stage. The purchaser's solicitor should, if the matter has not been raised during completion of the missives, confirm the position with the seller's solicitors, and where the seller's solicitor has obtained a Form P17 report, examine the result of the report following on that enquiry. Where the dealing relates to part only of the registered interest, then identification should be dealt with as discussed in paragraph 4.20. It is not anticipated in these cases that problems will arise, but from the purchaser's solicitor's point of view he should make certain that a plan is provided by the seller, supported, where necessary, by measurements, and that the plan complies with the requirements set out in paragraph 4.20. A plan which is declared to be demonstrative only is not sufficient for the Keeper's purposes. Where the dealing relates to the first purchase of a property in a building development, the use of an approved estate layout plan should eliminate any problems of identification.

Additional information

8.46 Part B of both Forms 2 and 3 sets out the standard enquiries which the Keeper will require to be satisfied about before completing registration. There may be other matters which the Keeper will have to raise, but, normally satisfactory answers to the questions in Part B will enable the Keeper to complete registration of a dealing. The Form 2 or Form 3 should be prepared in draft by the purchaser's solicitor and adjusted with the seller's solicitor during the course of the transaction. Similarly, the style of letter of obligation should provide for confirmation at settlement that the answers previously adjusted are still correct.

Styles of disposition, feu charter, and standard security etc

8.47 Once an interest has been registered in the Land Register, not only does section 16 apply to any transfer of that interest but the terms of section 15, where applicable, also apply to deeds relating to that registered interest. Section 15 provides for a description by reference to the title number, dispenses with the need to repeat or refer to existing burdens and provides that a clause of deduction of title is no longer necessary. Neither the act nor the rules prescribe particular forms of deeds although section 27(1)(d) gives power to do so. Rule 25 and Schedule B of the Rules do, however, prescribe the form of reference description to be used in deeds relating to a registered interest. The styles which follow are not, therefore, statutory styles which must be used (apart from the reference description), but rather are illustrative of the much shortened forms appropriate to dealings with a registered interest.

Disposition of the whole of a registered interest
I A.B. (design), in consideration of (state price or other consideration) hereby dispone to C.D. (design) All and Whole the subjects (here insert postal address of subjects where appropriate) registered under title number(s) (   ); with entry on (date of entry); and I grant warrandice; (here insert stamp clause if appropriate).

Disposition of part of a registered interest
I A.B. (design), in consideration of (state price or other consideration) hereby dispone to C.D. (design) All and Whole (describe the part conveyed in sufficient detail, preferably by reference to a plan, to enable the Keeper to identify it on the ordnance map) being part of the subjects registered under title number(s) (   ) [All and Whole the subjects (First) registered under title number (   ) or All and Whole the subjects marked (   ) on the plan of title number (   )] [but always with and under the following reservations, burdens and conditions viz.:- (insert additional burdens or conditions where appropriate)] [but declaring that the following rights (burdens, conditions) set out in title number(s) (   ) are not to apply to the subjects hereby conveyed]; with entry on (date of entry); and I grant warrandice; (here insert stamp clause if appropriate).

In the foregoing styles the following points should be noted:

- **Granter**. It is common practice to describe the granter as 'heritable proprietor' or 'proprietor' in a disposition which falls to be recorded in the Sasine Register depending on whether the granter is infeft or not. This does not have the same practical significance in a disposition of a registered interest and there is no need in a disposition of a registered interest by an uninfeft (*i.e.* unregistered) proprietor for the deed to contain a clause of deduction of title (section 15(3)). All midcouples or links in title between the uninfeft granter and the person last infeft (*i.e.* in this case the registered proprietor as disclosed in the title sheet) must be produced to the Keeper in support of any application for registration of the dealing (the disposition). The provisions of section 15(3) apply equally to the grant of a standard security by an uninfeft proprietor. Furthermore, section 3(6) dispenses with the need for an uninfeft proprietor to expede a notice of title in order to complete his title to an interest already registered in the Land Register. In order to obtain infeftment in such a case, the uninfeft proprietor should submit the land certificate and all links in title to the Keeper in support of a Form 2 application.

- **Grantee**. The foregoing styles deal only with the case of an individual grantee. If the grantee is to hold the registered interest in any fiduciary capacity or under any special destination, the capacity or destination should be inserted as under normal Sasine practice.

- **Description**. Where the disposition relates to the whole of the registered interest, the subjects are sufficiently described by reference to the title number (section 15(1)). No further description is necessary although for the avoidance of doubt the postal address should be added. Where the disposition relates to part only of a registered interest, the description must be sufficient to enable the Keeper to identify the part affected on the ordnance map and therefore on the existing title plan. The guidelines set out in paragraph 4.20 apply to such a description which, in addition, should include a reference to the title number of the whole interest of which the subjects in question form part. In some cases the part in question may already be identified on the title plan and in such cases an expanded description is not necessary. Where the disposition relates to part of a building development in respect of which an estate layout plan has been approved, it should be remembered that mere reference to a plot number on that layout plan is not a sufficient description. A deed plan should still be attached to the disposition in favour of the purchaser and the description in the deed should refer to the title number of the builder's whole interest. Ideally, the deed plan should be a copy or excerpt from the approved layout plan and should be docqueted as such and give the date of the Keeper's approval.

- **Incidental rights and pertinents**:

Dealings with Whole
Where incidental rights are included in the title sheet of the registered interest there is no need on a subsequent dealing with the whole of that interest to repeat these rights. Reference to the title number is quite sufficient to carry them. Nor is there any need to include a general conveyance of parts and pertinents as the effect of section 3(1) is to vest in the registered proprietor on registration a real right in the interest and in and to any right or pertinent express or implied forming part of that interest.

Transfers of Part

Different considerations apply when the dealing is a transfer of part only of the registered interest. While in theory the same rule should apply there are dangers inherent in leaving the transfer of incidental rights and pertinents to implication in that a right or pertinent which was not intended to be transferred may be transferred inadvertently by an omission specifically to exclude it. It is not a practical proposition to expect the Keeper to form a judgement unaided regarding which of the rights and pertinents which run with the whole are also appropriate to the part transferred. Accordingly the Keeper will only include in the title sheet created for the part transferred such rights and pertinents as are specifically stated as being transferred in the deed inducing the transfer of part. In cases where the rights are narrated in a deed of conditions which is entered in the title sheet of the whole subjects a reference in the dispositive clause of the conveyance to the deed of conditions, such as 'together with the rights specified in the deed of conditions...', will suffice.

Equal care should be taken with dealings with parts of the whole which do not *per se* involve the creation of a new title sheet such as a standard security over a part of the registered interest. If, as may be the case, the heritable creditor exercises his power of sale it may be difficult to decide at that point in time which rights and pertinents are appropriate to the part in question. In consequence, in such a case, it is advisable to make the situation clear in the description in the security deed.

It is axiomatic that any rights being created in a dealing with a part of registered subjects must be narrated at length or by reference in the deed effecting that dealing.

- **Part previously sold**. Under normal Sasine practice where a property is being sold, it is common to describe the property by reference to the original description of the whole property under exception of the parts that have been sold off over the years. Where, however, the property is in the Land Register, on a subsequent sale of the property there is no need to exclude in the description the parts previously sold as, on the sale of each part, the Keeper will have removed that part sold from the title sheet of the property and by describing the property by reference to its title number the description will carry only the balance remaining in the title sheet at that time.

In the case of tenement flats or flats resulting from conversions where the title plan requires to be amplified by a more elaborate written description a deed conveying the remainder should particularly describe what remains in the title sheet. For example, the description in a disposition of the last flat in a tenement should be on the following lines 'the north house on the first floor of the tenement twenty-five Brunswick Street, Ayr, being the subjects registered under title number (   )' rather than simply 'the subjects in title number (   )'. Although the latter description complies with section 15(1), as the land certificate of what was originally the whole tenement will now relate to the remaining house only it does not clarify, in simple terms, what the title specifically now relates to.

- **Burdens**. In terms of section 15(2) it is no longer necessary to repeat or refer to any real burden, provision or other matter affecting the interest registered if the real burden etc has been entered in the title sheet of that interest. There are, however, two cases where such a reference is necessary but on a first sale only, namely (1) to import burdens contained in a deed of conditions executed prior to 4 April 1979 (the date on which section 17 came into force) or (2) to import burdens where the deed of conditions, although executed after that date, expressly excludes the operation of section 17. No reference is required on any subsequent transmission of that interest. Where new burdens are created, these must of course be set out at length and, where a burden affects part only of the interest being registered, that part must be sufficiently described to enable the Keeper to identify the part affected. Reference is made in (5) above to a conveyance of a registered interest from which parts have been previously sold. In many cases rights will have been granted over the subjects remaining in the title sheet in favour of the parts sold. The Keeper will, at the time of the sale of a part, have shown rights of access in favour of that part on the title sheet of the parent title. He will not, however, necessarily show all rights in favour of parts sold on the parent title sheet, for example the burden of maintenance of common parts, and it is unlikely that the parent title sheet already shows such a burden. In most cases such an apportionment must be expressly made in a conveyance of the remainder. The seller's solicitor should ensure that any burdens which are to be created over the remainder are expressly set out in the conveyance of the remainder if they are not already clearly set out in the title sheet. Upon registration of a conveyance containing these burdens they will be set out in the title sheet and thereafter a reference to the title number will be sufficient to import them.

- **Entry**. As short term leases are not covered by the normal grant of warrandice, if the missives provide for vacant possession, this clause should be amended accordingly.

- **Formal Clauses**. Care should be taken to ensure that the statutory import of these formal clauses truly reflects the bargain between the parties. Where the statutory import does not, individual clauses suitably qualified will have to be inserted. It should be noted that, where there is a special obligation of relief which has been noted in the title sheet, it is no longer necessary in a subsequent transfer of the interest to assign that right specifically or to narrate the series of writs by which the benefited proprietor became entitled to that right (section 15(4)).

- **Warrandice** It is still necessary to include a grant of warrandice and the seller's solicitor should consider carefully whether the statutory clause is appropriate without further qualification. For example, if the interest to which the transaction relates has been registered subject to an exclusion of indemnity in respect of part of the property, a conveyance of the property with a grant of absolute warrandice could result in a claim under warrandice against the seller should the proprietor be evicted from that part although the Keeper, having excluded indemnity, would be under no liability. In such circumstances the seller would be advised to limit his warrandice to fact and deed only in respect of that part.

Style of disposition - superiority
Under Sasine practice a disposition of a superiority takes the form of a conveyance of the lands with an exception of the feu rights from warrandice. In addition, the disposition will contain an assignation of feuduties, either generally or by reference to a Schedule of Feuduties. The superiority title is a title to the lands. However, once a superiority title is registered in the Land Register or on feus being granted out of any interest already registered, the superior's title will be expressly that of proprietor of the superiority interest only. The styles of disposition suggested above are therefore appropriate to a disposition of a superiority and the foregoing comments apply equally to such a disposition. However, the following further points should be noted:

- The land certificate will contain a schedule of feus and it is not therefore necessary to assign feuduties by reference to a schedule, provided the schedule reflects the current position. If, however, there have been intervening redemptions, the Keeper may not be aware of these and an up-to-date schedule should be included or alternatively, an up-to-date list attached to the application for registration.

- There is no need to except the feu rights from warrandice as the registered interest being transferred is that of the superiority only.

- The comments on mixed estates in chapter 6.

Feu charter and feu disposition

These deeds will normally contain feuing conditions and will create burdens over the *dominium utile* and these burdens in turn may be fenced with an irritancy clause. However, the foregoing styles of disposition amended so that the words of conveyance read 'in feu farm dispone', and a tenendas clause is inserted immediately after the date of entry will form the framework of a feu charter or feu disposition of a registered interest. The comments on the foregoing styles of disposition apply subject to the following additional points:

- **Granter**. Section 3(6) dispenses with the need for an uninfeft proprietor to expede a notice of title in order to complete his title, provided that sufficient links are produced to the Keeper. The section does not, however, alter the common law requirement for the granter of a feu (or a lease) to be infeft (*i.e.* a registered proprietor). Accordingly, while the descriptions 'heritable proprietor' or 'proprietor' have never been essential, it would still be appropriate in a feu deed to use the terms 'registered proprietor' or 'proprietor' to indicate whether the superior is infeft or not. On a grant of feu out of a registered interest by an uninfeft proprietor the feuar's application for registration (Form 3) should be preceded or accompanied by an application for registration (Form 2), completed on behalf of the uninfeft superior, and this latter application should be accompanied by sufficient links in title to link the superior with the last registered proprietor. If such an application is not made by the uninfeft superior, the Keeper will register the feuar's interest subject to an exclusion of indemnity in respect of the superior's lack of infeftment. Should the superior subsequently become infeft, accretion may operate in favour of the feuar.

- **Description**. The forms of description discussed with reference to a disposition of a registered interest are applicable to a feu deed. In particular, it should be noted that, where the feu relates to the whole of the superior's interest, no new description in the feu deed is necessary. Reference to the title number of the whole interest is all that is required.

- **Resolutive clause**. Under Sasine practice it is common to find that conditions in a feu deed are fenced not only with a conventional irritancy but with a resolutive clause requiring the conditions created in the feu deed to be recorded and thereafter repeated or referred to in all subsequent transmissions, under pain of nullity. Such a provision in the form appropriate to the Sasine system is no longer necessary in a feu of a registered interest as, by virtue of section 15(2), all conditions appearing in the title sheet will be imported into any deed relating to the interest without any reference being made to these conditions or to the deed creating them. A resolutive clause, therefore, will only be appropriate insofar as it requires the feuar to ensure that the conditions are entered on the title sheet. The Keeper is unlikely to omit any condition and thus to lay himself open to a claim by the superior. However, superiors may consider it appropriate, as a condition of granting a feu, to require the feuar to exhibit the land certificate for checking. Where it is considered appropriate to do so, a conventional irritancy should be included.

- **Assignation of writs**. Section 16(2) now implies an assignation of writs clause in each feu grant in the terms normally expressed. In fact, where the feu is granted out of a registered interest, the assignation of writs clause is of little significance except where the interest of the feuar has been registered subject to an exclusion of indemnity (section 1(5)).

- **Obligation of relief**. Section 16(3)(b) imports an obligation of relief from over feuduties in each feu grant. It is therefore no longer necessary to include such a clause except where the statutory meaning now implied is not appropriate to the contract between the parties.

Standard security

The form of standard security contained in schedule 2 of the Conveyancing and Feudal Reform (Scotland) Act 1970[2] is amended in two respects by the Act:

- Section 15(1) and rule 25 and schedule B of the Rules provide for the interest over which the security has been granted to be described by reference to the title number of that interest. Accordingly, the descriptions suggested in the two styles of disposition given above and notes (3) and (4) to these styles apply equally to a standard security.

- Under Sasine practice, where the transaction is a first split-off followed by a standard security to be recorded along with the purchaser's title, the security subjects are normally described by means of the statutory reference description amended to read - 'recorded of even date with the recording of these presents'. Section 29, which substitutes in the Conveyancing Statutes reference to the Land Register for references to the Register of Sasines, does not apply to this form of reference description which is no longer available for a registered interest. Nor, if the standard security is to be registered along with the purchaser's interest, can a section 15(1) reference to the title number be used as a title number will not yet have been allocated. The possible courses open are therefore:

[2] c.35

- Repeat the description contained in the disposition (or feu charter) in favour of the purchaser.

- If that description is dependent on a plan, prepare the plan in duplicate and use one for the description in the standard security.

Whichever course is followed, reference to the title number of the whole subjects from which the part purchased derives should be included.

- Section 15(3) dispenses with the need to deduce title in a standard security where the granter is the uninfeft proprietor of an interest registered in the Land Register but sufficient links in title must be produced to the Keeper along with the application for registration (Form 2).

Assignations, deeds of restriction and discharges of standard securities
The basic forms of these deeds are provided for in Schedule 4 of the Conveyancing and Feudal Reform (Scotland) Act 1970. Two matters should be kept in mind:

- Section 15(1) applies to the description in a deed of restriction and the interest disburdened should, therefore, be described as outlined above for a transfer of part of a registered interest. Neither assignations nor discharges contain a description of the subjects or interest secured and therefore section 15(1) is not relevant. However, in order to comply with the provisions of section 4(2)(d), such deeds must bear a reference to the title number of that interest. It is not necessary for that reference to appear *in gremio* of the deed. If it does not, then it should be clearly indicated on the top of the first page of the deed. In any event, it must appear on the deed proper and not, for example, on the backing. It is, however, suggested that the title number should appear in the body of the deed. The form of discharge of a standard security for a fixed amount by the original creditor would therefore be:

I, A.B. (design) in consideration of £X paid by C.D. (design) hereby discharge a Standard Security for £X by the said C.D. in my favour registered on (   ) over the subjects in title number(s) (   ) : (to be attested).

- While section 15(3) dispenses with the need to deduce title in the case of a disposition or standard security granted by an uninfeft proprietor of a registered interest, the section unfortunately has not dispensed with deductions of title in the case of these subsidiary writs. Strictly speaking, therefore, it is still necessary to deduce title in terms of note 1 to schedule 4 of the 1970 Act. However, as a practical matter, the Keeper will not reject an application for registration merely because the assignation, deed of restriction or discharge, as the case may be, does not contain a deduction of title provided sufficient links are produced to him in support of that application for registration.

Form of long lease
The effect of the act and rules on the form of a long lease and on assignations and other writs relating to such a lease are discussed in paragraph 5.57.

Dealing with a registered interest - settlement

One solicitor acting for both purchaser and lender

8.48 At settlement the purchaser's solicitor should take delivery of:

(a) The signed disposition in favour of his client.

(b) The signed and completed discharge of the seller's standard security (if any) together with the completed Form 2 and Form 4 in duplicate and a cheque in payment of the registration dues.

(c) The land certificate and the charge certificate relating to (b) above.

(d) Any links in title together with any evidence required in terms of the Matrimonial Homes (Family Protection) (Scotland) Act 1981[3].

(e) The seller's solicitor's letter of obligation.

(f) The Form 12 report (and the Form 13 report if any).

(g) Any Form P17 report.

(h) If the interest has been registered with limited indemnity, the pre registration titles relating to that exclusion in so far as these are in the seller's possession. A note of the present custodian of any other titles relating to the exclusion which are not delivered should also be obtained. (If the purchaser proposes to request the Keeper to cancel the exclusion of indemnity, then he should arrange for the seller to borrow these undelivered writs and make them available at settlement).

[3] c.59

(i) Any common titles held by the seller. By virtue of section 16, there is an implied obligation on the purchaser to make common titles available to parties having an interest in them. This obligation will cease in respect of any interest that has been registered in the Land Register, unless it has been registered subject to an exclusion of indemnity (section 3(5)).

(j) Where the original Sasine titles (relating exclusively to the interest) have not been destroyed the purchaser's solicitor should ensure that these too are delivered, if they have plans amending or showing the routes of pipes, cables etc. for which there are wayleaves or servitudes benefiting or burdening the property.

Separate solicitors acting for purchaser and lender

8.49 If separate solicitors are acting for the purchaser and for any lender to the purchaser, then the lender's solicitor should, at settlement, take delivery of:

(a) A completed and signed application for registration of the purchaser's interest (Form 2) together with a cheque for the registration dues. This Form must be signed by the purchaser or by the purchaser's solicitor. The terms of the Form should have been adjusted in draft by the solicitors for the seller, the purchaser and the lender.

(b) An inventory Form 4 completed by the purchaser's solicitor in duplicate.

(c) The land certificate and all the deeds and documents detailed in the Form 4, being all the deeds and documents required to support the application for registration of the purchaser's interest.

(d) The items mentioned in (f) - (j) in the preceding paragraph.

(e) The signed standard security and a cheque for the registration dues.

(f) A letter of obligation in terms suggested in paragraph 8.15.

Purchase of part only

8.50 If the purchase is of part only of the registered interest, then the application form will be a Form 3. Insofar as the existing land certificate plan or any plan attached to the disposition in favour of the purchaser is not sufficient to enable the Keeper to identify on the title plan the part affected by the dealing, a supplementary plan enabling the Keeper to do so should be delivered. The land certificate referred to as item (c) in the two preceding paragraphs will, in fact, be made available by the seller 'on loan' and, after amendment to give effect to the part sale, it will fall to be returned to the seller. The seller's land certificate does not, however, remain a 'common title'. The purchaser's 'title' will rest entirely on the land certificate issued to him and, on registration of the purchaser's interest, the seller's land certificate will thereafter be limited to the interest remaining with the seller. Nonetheless, there may be occasions when the purchaser might wish to borrow the seller's land certificate and the seller will remain under obligation to make it forthcoming by virtue of section 16 as read with section 3(5). If the purchase is part of a building development and the seller's land certificate has been deposited with the Keeper, a note of the deposit number should be obtained at settlement.

Dealing with a registered interest - application for registration

Purchase and loan transaction completed contemporaneously

Same solicitor acting for purchaser and lender
8.51 There should be submitted to the Keeper:

1. A completed and signed application for registration of the purchase (Form 2) together with the deed giving effect to that dealing *e.g.* the disposition. No warrant of registration should be endorsed on the disposition.

2. The land certificate and all deeds and other documents supporting the application for registration (for example links in title), accompanied by an inventory Form 4 listing the land certificate and the other deeds and documents. The Inventory should be completed in duplicate.

3. Any additional evidence, for example a death certificate with reference to a survivorship clause. This should also be listed in the Form 4.

4. Any existing charge certificate, together with the executed discharge. Strictly speaking an application for registration (Form 2) should be completed in respect of the discharge, but separate application is not insisted on, provided the discharge is noted on the Inventory. NB a fixed fee (currently £22) is payable.

5. A separate Form 2 applying for registration of the dealing effected by the standard security granted by the purchaser, together with the standard security. A

separate inventory Form 4 is not required, but the standard security must be included in the Inventory referred to in (ii) above.

6. Where the applications for registration of the purchaser's and lender's interests are submitted together, a reduced registration fee will be charged in respect of the standard security.

7. The total registration fees payable.

Separate solicitors acting for purchaser and lender
8.52 The lender's solicitor will wish to ensure that the applications for registration of the purchaser's (borrower's) interest is duly lodged. Accordingly, at settlement he should take delivery of all the items referred to in 1 - 4 in the preceding paragraph and lodge these with the Keeper, along with an application for registration in respect of the standard security (Form 2). In this case, there are two additional points to note:

- The application for registration of the purchaser's interest must be signed by the purchaser or by the purchaser's solicitor. The lender's solicitor cannot sign this application. Similarly, the application for registration of the standard security must be signed by the lender or by the lender's solicitor.

- Again the Keeper will return the duplicate copy of each inventory to the purchaser and lender or their respective solicitors, as the case may be, by way of acknowledgement. If the lender's solicitor wishes to have on his file evidence that the application for registration of the purchaser's interest has been received, he should attach a duplicate copy of the purchaser's inventory to his own. If the applications are lodged separately, the lender's solicitor may consider an addition to the borrower's solicitor's letter of obligation appropriate.

Purchase of part only of a registered interest
8.53 Where the purchase relates to part only of the registered interest, it should be noted that the appropriate application form for registration of the purchase is Form 3 and that any additional plan e.g. any plan in addition to that attached to the disposition, which may be needed to enable the Keeper to identify the part sold must be submitted with the application for registration. Any such plan should be listed on the inventory Form 4. If the purchase is part of a building development and the seller's land certificate has been deposited with the Keeper a note of the deposit number should be inserted in the Form 2.

Purchase and loan transactions not completed contemporaneously

8.54 Where settlement of the loan transaction has, for one reason or another, been delayed but the purchase has been settled in the meantime, the purchaser's solicitor should submit an application for registration of his client's interest and thus preserve his client's priority of registration. When, in due course, the standard security is submitted, it should be accompanied by an application Form 2 and an inventory Form 4 in duplicate. If application for registration of the purchaser's interest is delayed until the standard security is available the purchaser will not in the meantime obtain a real right. Where the two applications are lodged separately, a full registration fee will be charged for the standard security.

Outstanding heritable securities

Discharge available at settlement
8.55 As noted previously the Keeper will not require a separate application for registration to be submitted in respect of a discharge of an outstanding heritable security which relates solely to the registered interest, provided that the discharge is presented along with the application for registration of the purchase of that interest and is listed on the Form 4 accompanying that application, although, strictly speaking, a separate application should be lodged. The Keeper will, however, give effect to the discharge. The existing charge certificate must, of course, also be submitted. It is possible although the security subjects are registered in the Land Register and the standard security is noted on the title sheet, that the title to the standard security is still governed by a recording in the Sasine Register. Here again, however, the discharge should be submitted with the application for registration of the purchaser's interest and not presented for recording in the Sasine Register.

Where the discharge relates to both the seller's and purchaser's interest, for example a combined partial discharge and deed of restriction, a separate application for registration is required even if the deed accompanies the application for registration of the purchaser's interests. The Keeper will give effect to this deed as regards both interests. This he will do by noting the sum discharged on the seller's title sheet. He will not, however, amend either the charges section of the seller's title sheet or the seller's charge certificate to show the subjects disburdened. The subjects disburdened will be removed from the seller's title sheet by making the relevant alteration in the property section, including the plan, and thereafter the entries in the charges section and the charge certificate will relate only to the subjects remaining in the property section. No note at all will be made of the restriction in the purchaser's title sheet; effect will be given to that deed by making no reference in the charges section of the purchaser's title sheet to the standard security granted by the seller.

Discharge not accompanying application for registration
8.56 Where a discharge does not accompany an application for registration, the following points must be kept in mind:

- The discharge should be noted on the Form 4 accompanying the application for registration of the purchaser's interest but marked 'to follow'. Even where the discharge is marked 'to follow' on the inventory, if it has not been submitted by the time the Keeper undertakes legal examination of the application he will complete registration showing the standard security in the charges section of the land certificate.

- The discharge must be accompanied by an application for registration Form 2 completed by the solicitor for the seller/borrower, a Form 4 inventory in duplicate, the seller's charge certificate and any links in title insofar as the seller's charge certificate or links in title have not been included with the purchaser's original application for registration. Note that in cases where lenders have converted from building societies to banks, the links in title will usually have been lodged with the Keeper and further copies do not have to be submitted, provided they are listed on the Form 4. While the application for registration of the discharge should be completed and signed by the seller or his solicitor, it should be submitted by the purchaser's solicitor and delivery to the purchaser's solicitor of the executed discharge, the signed Form 2, and other supporting documents covered in the seller's letter of obligation.

Discharge relating to a number of properties
8.57 Where the discharge or deed of restriction (for example an omnibus deed of restriction) relates to a number of registered interests, then, even if it accompanies the application for registration of the purchaser's interest, a separate Form 2 must be lodged with it seeking registration in respect of each of the interests affected. All the title numbers of these interests must appear on the deed and be entered on the Form 2.

Dealing with a registered interest - procedure after registration

Purchase of whole registered interest

Same solicitor acting for purchaser and lender
8.58 The purchaser's solicitor should:

1. Check the land certificate. In this case all that is required is to see that it has been amended to give effect to the deeds submitted in support of the application for registration, and, where appropriate, to check that the proprietorship section contains a statement relative to occupancy rights of spouses of former proprietors.

2. Check the charge certificate. The standard security will be attached to the charge certificate and should be retained with it.

3. Return the seller's letter of obligation, marked as implemented.

4. If any titles have been borrowed from the seller's solicitors return these. For example, common writs may have been borrowed at settlement in connection with an exclusion of indemnity.

5. Send the land certificate and the charge certificate (with the principal security writ attached) to the lender for safe-keeping or otherwise as instructed. If there are any common titles held by the purchaser (*i.e.* titles which the purchaser is now under a statutory obligation to make forthcoming) these should be put up with the land certificate.

Separate solicitors acting for purchaser and lender
8.59 Where there are separate solicitors acting, the purchaser's and lender's solicitors should, after registration:

Purchaser's solicitor

1. Check the land certificate as in 1. above.

2. Send the land certificate to the lender's solicitor along with any other writs which were exhibited to the Keeper in support of the application for registration (at the same time indicating if any of these writs should be retained with the land certificate).

3. Receive back from the lender's solicitor (a) the implemented letter of obligation and (b) any deeds which are not to be retained with the land certificate.

4. Return any title deeds which have been borrowed from the seller for the purpose of supporting the application for registration, *e.g.* by reason of exclusion of indemnity.

5. Return seller's solicitor's letter of obligation.

Lender's solicitor

1. Check the charge certificate and make sure that the principal standard security is attached to it.

2. Check the land certificate when received from the purchaser's solicitor.

3. Send the land certificate, charge certificate and titles, if relevant, to the client or otherwise deal with them as instructed.

4. Return the remaining titles, and implemented letter of obligation to the purchaser's solicitors.

Purchase of part of the registered interest

Same solicitor acting for purchaser and lender
8.60 Where the transaction relates to part only, the purchaser's solicitor should, in addition to the steps outlined in paragraph 8.51, also return the seller's land certificate and the seller's creditor's charge certificate (if any).

Separate solicitors acting for purchaser and lender
8.61 In this case, in addition to the steps outlined in paragraph 8.52, the purchaser's solicitor should return the seller's land certificate and the seller's creditor's charge certificate (if any).

Seller's solicitor
8.62 Where part only of the seller's interest has been sold, the seller's solicitor should, on receiving the land certificate back from the purchaser's solicitor after registration of the purchaser's interest, check that the part sold has been correctly excluded from the seller's land certificate. He should also check that any charge

certificate has been suitably amended to reflect any partial repayments and that the charges section of the title sheet has been similarly amended. In cases where the seller's lender is also separately represented, he should, on receiving the seller's land certificate and charge certificate back from the seller's solicitor for safe-keeping, carry out a similar check.

Land Registration (Scotland) Act 1979[1]

An Act to provide a system of registration of interests in land in Scotland in place of the recording of deeds in the Register of Sasines; and for indemnification in respect of registered interests in land; to simplify certain deeds relating to land and to provide as to the effect of certain other such deeds; to enable tenants-at-will to acquire their landlords' interests in the tenancies; to provide for the fixing of fees payable to the Keeper of The Registers of Scotland; and for connected purposes.

[4th April 1979]

PART I

REGISTRATION OF INTERESTS IN LAND

The Land Register of Scotland

1.-(l)   There shall be a public register of interests in land in Scotland to be known as the "Land Register of Scotland" (in this Act referred to as "the register").

(2)   The register shall be under the management and control of the Keeper of the Registers of Scotland (in this Act referred to as "the Keeper") and shall have a seal.

(3)   In this Act "registered" means registered in the register in accordance with this Act and "registrable", "registration" and other cognate expressions shall be construed accordingly.

Registration

2.-(l)   Subject to subsection (2) below, an unregistered interest in land other than an overriding interest shall be registrable-

(a)   in any of the following circumstances occurring after the commencement of this Act-
 (i)   on a grant of the interest in land in feu, long lease or security by way of contract of ground annual, but only to the extent that the interest has become that of the feuar, lessee or debtor in the ground annual;
 (ii)   on a transfer of the interest for valuable consideration
 (iii)   on a transfer of the interest in consideration of marriage

[1] c33

(iv) on a transfer of the interest whereby it is absorbed into a registered interest in land;

(v) on any transfer of the interest where it is held under a long lease, udal tenure or a kindly tenancy;

(b) in any other circumstances in which an application is made for registration of the interest by the person or persons having that interest and the Keeper considers it expedient that the interest should be registered.

(2) Subsection (1) above does not apply to an unregistered interest which is a heritable security, liferent or incorporeal heritable right; and subsection (1) (a) (ii) above does not apply where the interest on transference is absorbed into another unregistered interest.

(3) The creation over a registered interest in land of any of the following interests in land-

(i) a heritable security;

(ii) a liferent;

(iii) an incorporeal heritable right, shall be registrable; and on registration of its creation such an interest shall become a registered interest in land.

(4) There shall also be registrable-

(a) any transfer of a registered interest in land including any transfer whereby it is absorbed into another registered interest in land;

(b) any absorption by a registered interest in land of another registered interest in land.

(c) any other transaction or event which (whether by itself or in conjunction with registration) is capable under any enactment or rule of law of affecting the title to a registered interest in land but which is not a transaction or event creating or affecting an over-riding interest.

(5) the Secretary of State may, by order made by statutory instrument, provide that interests in land of a kind or kinds specified in the order, being interests in land which are unregistered at the date of the making of the order other than overriding interests, shall be registered; and the provisions of this Act shall apply for the purposes of such registration with such modifications, which may include provision as to the expenses of such registration, as may be specified in the order.

(6) In this section, " enactment " includes sections 17, 18 and 19 of this Act.

Effect of registration

3.-(l) Registration shall have the effect of-
   (a) vesting in the person registered as entitled to the registered interest in land a real right in and to the interest and in and to any right, pertinent or servitude, express or implied, forming part of the interest, subject only to the effect of any matter entered in the title sheet of that interest under section 6 of this Act so far as adverse to the interest or that person's entitlement to it and to any overriding interest whether noted under that section or not;
   (b) making any registered right or obligation relating to the registered interest in land a real right or obligation;
   (c) affecting any registered real right or obligation relating to the registered interest in land,

insofar as the right or obligation is capable, under any enactment or rule of law of being vested as a real right of being made real or, as the case may be, of being affected as a real right.

In this subsection, "enactment" includes sections 17, 18 and 19 of this Act.

(2) Registration shall supersede the recording of a deed in the Register of Sasines but, subject to subsection (3) below, shall be without prejudice to any other means of creating or affecting real rights or obligations under any enactment or rule of law.

(3) A-
   (a) lessee under a long lease;
   (b) proprietor under udal tenure;
   (c) kindly tenant,

shall obtain a real right in and to his interest as such only by registration; and registration shall be the only means of making rights or obligations relating to the registered interest in land of such a person real rights or obligations or of affecting such real rights or obligations.

(4) The date-
   (a) at which a real right or obligation is created or as from which it is affected under this section;
   (b) of entry of a feuar of a registrable interest in land with his superior, shall be the date of registration.

(5)   Where an interest in land has been registered, any obligation to assign title deeds and searches relating to that interest in land or to deliver them or make them forthcoming or any related obligation shall be of no effect in relation to that interest or to) any other registered interest in land.

This subsection does not apply-
(a) to a land or charge certificate issued under section 5 of this Act;
(b) where the Keeper has, under section 12 (2) of this Act, excluded indemnity under Part II of this Act.

(6)   It shall not be necessary for an uninfeft proprietor of an interest in land which has been registered to expede a notice of title in order to complete his title to that interest if evidence of sufficient mid-couples or links between the uninfeft proprietor and the person last infeft are produced to the Keeper on any registration in respect of that interest and, accordingly, section 4 of the Conveyancing (Scotland) Act 1924 (completion of title by person uninfeft) shall be of no effect in relation to such an interest in land.

This subsection does not apply to the completion of title under section 74 or 76 of the Lands Clauses Consolidation (Scotland) Act 1845 (procedure on compulsory purchase of lands).

(7)   Nothing in this section affects any question as to the validity or effect of an overriding interest.

Applications for registration

4.-(1.) Subject to subsection (2) below, an application for registration shall be accepted by the Keeper if it is accompanied by such documents and other evidence as he may require.

(2)   An application for registration shall not be accepted by the Keeper if-
(a) it relates to land which is not sufficiently described to enable him to identify it by reference to the Ordnance Map;
(b) it relates to land which is a souvenir plot, that is a piece of land which, being of inconsiderable size or no practical utility, is unlikely to be wanted in isolation except for the sake of mere ownership or for sentimental reasons or commemorative purposes; or
(c) it is frivolous or vexatious;
(d) a deed which-

(i)   accompanies the application;

(ii) relates to a registered interest in land; and

(iii) is executed after that interest has been registered, does not bear a reference to the number of the title sheet of that interest;

(e) Payment of the fee payable in that respect under section 25 of the Land Registers (Scotland) Act has not been tendered.

(3)   On receipt of an application for registration, the Keeper shall forthwith note the date of such receipt, and that date shall be deemed for the purposes of this Act to be the date of registration either-

(a) where the application, after examination by the Keeper, is accepted by him, or

(b) where the application is not accepted by him on the grounds that it does not comply with subsection (1) or (2)(a) or (d) above but, without being rejected by the Keeper or withdrawn by the applicant, is subsequently accepted by the Keeper on his being satisfied that it does so comply, or has been made so to comply.

Completion of registration

5.-(1) The Keeper shall complete registration-

(a) in respect of an interest in land which is not a heritable security, liferent or incorporeal heritable right-

(i)   if the interest has not previously been registered, by making up a title sheet for it in the register in accordance with section 6 of this Act, or

(ii) if the interest has previously been registered, by making such amendment as is necessary to the title sheet of the interest;

(b) in respect of an interest in land which is a heritable security, liferent or incorporeal heritable right or in respect of the matters registrable under section 2(4) of this Act by making such amendment as is necessary to the title sheet of the interest in land to which the heritable security, liferent, incorporeal heritable right or matter, as the case may be, relates,

and in each case by making such consequential amendments in the register as are necessary.

(2)   Where the Keeper has completed registration under subsection (1)(a) above, he shall issue to the applicant a copy of the title sheet, authenticated by the seal of the register; and such copy shall be known as a land certificate.

(3) Where the Keeper has completed registration in respect of a heritable security, he shall issue to the applicant a certificate authenticated by the seal of the register; and such certificate shall be known as a charge certificate.

(4) A land certificate shall be accepted for all purposes as sufficient evidence of the contents of the title sheet of which the land certificate is a copy; and a charge certificate shall be accepted for all purposes as sufficient evidence of the facts stated in it.

(5) Every land certificate and charge certificate shall contain a statement as to indemnity by the Keeper under Part II of this Act.

The title sheet

6.-(1) Subject to subsection (3) below, the Keeper shall make up and maintain a title sheet of an interest in land in the register by entering therein-
   (a) a description of the land which shall consist of or include a description of it based on the Ordnance Map, and, where the interest is that of the proprietor of the *dominium utile* or the lessee under a long lease and the land appears to the Keeper to extend to 2 hectares or more, its area as calculated by the Keeper;
   (b) the name and designation of the person entitled to the interest in the land and the nature of that interest;
   (c) any subsisting entry in the Register of Inhibitions and Adjudications adverse to the interest;
   (d) any heritable security over the interest;
   (e) any enforceable real right pertaining to the interest or subsisting real burden or condition affecting the interest;
   (f) any exclusion of indemnity under section 12(2) of this Act in respect of the interest;
   (g) such other information as the Keeper thinks fit to enter in the register.

(2) The Keeper shall enter a real right or real burden or condition in the title sheet by entering its terms or a summary of its terms therein; and such a summary shall, unless it contains a reference to a further entry in the title sheet wherein the terms of the real right, burden or condition are set out in full be presumed to be a correct statement of the terms of the right, burden or condition.

(3)   The Keeper's duty under subsection (1) above shall not extend to entering in the title sheet any over-feuduty or over-rent exigible in respect of the interest in land, but he may so enter any such over-feuduty or over-rent.

(4)   Any overriding interest which appears to the Keeper to affect an interest in land-
        (a)   shall be noted by him in the title sheet of that interest if it has been disclosed in any document accompanying an application for registration in respect of that interest;
        (b)   may be so noted if-
              (i)   application is made to him to do so;
              (ii)   the overriding interest is disclosed in any application for registration; or
              (iii) the overriding interest otherwise comes to his notice.
                     In this subsection "overriding interest" does not include the interest of
              (i)   a lessee under a lease which is not a long lease and
              (ii)   a non-entitled spouse within the meaning of section 6 of the Matrimonial Homes (Family Protection) (Scotland) Act 1981.

(5)   The Keeper shall issue, to any person applying, a copy, authenticated as the Keeper thinks fit, of any title sheet, part thereof, or of any document referred to in a title sheet; and such copy, which shall be known as an office copy, shall be accepted for all purposes as sufficient evidence of the contents of the original.

Ranking

7.-(1) Without prejudice to any express provision as to ranking in any deed or any other provision as to ranking in, or having effect by virtue of, any enactment or rule of law, the following provisions of this section shall have effect to determine the ranking of titles to interests in land.

(2)   Titles to registered interests in land shall rank according to the date of registration of those interests.

(3)   A title to a registered interest and a title governed by a deed recorded in the Register of Sasines shall rank according to the respective dates of registration and recording.

(4)   Where the date of registration or recording of the titles to two or more interests in land is the same, the titles to those interests shall rank equally.

Continuing effectiveness of recording in Register of Sasines

8.-(1) Subject to subsection (3) below, the only means of creating or affecting a real right or a real obligation relating to anything to which sub-section (2) below applies shall be by recording a deed in the Register of Sasines.

(2)   This subsection applies to-

    (a) an interest in land which is to be transferred or otherwise affected by-

        (i)   an instrument which, having been recorded before the commencement of this Act in the Register of Sasines with an error or defect; or

        (ii) a deed which, having been recorded before the commencement of this Act in the Register of Sasines with an error or defect in the recording,

        has not, before such commencement, been re-presented, corrected as necessary, for the purposes of recording of new under section 143 of the Titles to Land Consolidation Scotland) Act 1868;

        In this paragraph, "instrument" has the same meaning as in section 3 of the said Act of 1868.

    (b)   A registered interest in land which has been absorbed, otherwise than by operation of prescription, into another interest in land the title to which is governed by a deed recorded in the Register of Sasines;

    (c)   anything which is not registrable under subsections (1) to (4) of section 2 of this Act and in respect of which, immediately before the commencement of this Act, a real right or obligation could be created or affected by recording a deed in the Register of Sasines.

(3)   Nothing in subsection (1) above shall prejudice any other means, other than by registration, of creating or affecting real rights or obligations under any enactment or rule of law.

(4)   Except as provided in this section, the Keeper shall reject any deed submitted for recording in the Register of Sasines.

Rectification of the register

9.-(1) Subject to subsection (3) below, the Keeper may, whether on being so requested or not, and shall, on being so ordered by the court or the Lands

Tribunal for Scotland, rectify any inaccuracy in the register by inserting, amending or cancelling anything therein.

(2)   Subject to subsection (3)(b) below, the powers of the court and of the Lands Tribunal for Scotland to deal with questions of heritable right or title shall include power to make orders for the purposes of subsection (1) above.

(3)   If rectification under subsection (1) above would prejudice a proprietor in possession-
(a)   the Keeper may exercise his power to rectify only where
(i)   the purpose of the rectification is to note an overriding interest or to correct any information in the register relating to an overriding interest;
(ii)   all persons whose interests in land are likely to be affected by the rectification have been informed by the Keeper of his intention to rectify and have consented in writing;
(iii) the inaccuracy has been caused wholly or substantially by the fraud or carelessness of the proprietor in possession; or
(iv)   the rectification relates to a matter in respect of which indemnity has been excluded under section 12(2) of this Act;
(b)   the court or the Lands Tribunal for Scotland may order the Keeper to rectify only where sub-paragraph (i), (iii) or (iv) of paragraph (a) above applies or the rectification is consequential on the making of an order under section 8 of the Law Reform (Miscellaneous Provisions) (Scotland) Act 1985.

(3A)   Where a rectification of an entry in the register is consequential on the making of an order under section 8 of the said Act of 1985, the entry shall have effect as rectified as from the date when the entry was made:

Provided that the court, for the purpose of protecting the interests of a person to whom section 9 of that Act applies, may order that the rectification shall have effect as from such later date as it may specify.

(4)   In this section-
(a)   "the court" means any court having jurisdiction in questions of heritable right or title;
(b)   "overriding interest" does not include the interest of (i) a lessee under a lease which is not a long lease and (ii) a non-entitled spouse within the meaning of section 6 of the Matrimonial Homes (Family Protection) (Scotland) Act 1981.

Positive prescription in respect of registered interests in land

10. Section 1 of the Prescription and Limitation (Scotland) 1975 shall have effect as if—
(a) after "followed" in paragraph (b) of subsection (1) there were inserted "(i)" and for the words from "then" to the end of that subsection there were inserted ", or
    (ii) registration of that interest in favour of that person in the Land Register of Scotland, subject to an exclusion of indemnity under section 12(2) of the Land Registration (Scotland) Act 1979,
then, as from the expiration of the said period, the validity of the title so far as relating to the said interest in the particular land shall be exempt from challenge.
(1A) Subsection (1) above shall not apply where—
    (a) possession was founded on the recording of a deed which is invalid *ex facie* or was forged; or
    (b) possession was founded on registration in respect of an interest in land in the Land Register of Scotland proceeding on a forged deed and the person appearing from the Register to be entitled to the interest was aware of the forgery at the time of registration in his favour";
at the end of subsection (2) there were added "or which is registrable in the Land Register of Scotland."

Transitional provisions for Part I

11.-(1) If an application for registration relates to land no part of which is in an operational area, the Keeper may nevertheless accept that application as if it related to land wholly within an operational area, and if the Keeper has so accepted such an application, the provisions of this Act relating to registration then in force shall apply in relation to that application.

(2) An application for registration which relates to land which is partly in an operational area shall be treated as if it related to land wholly in that area, and the provisions of this Act relating to registration in force shall in relation to that application.

(3) In this section an "operational area" means an area in respect of which the provisions of this Act relating to registration have come into operation.

PART II

INDEMNITY IN RESPECT OF REGISTERED INTERESTS IN LAND

Indemnity in respect of loss

12.-(l) Subject to the provisions of this section, a person who suffers loss as a result of -

    (a) a rectification of the register made under section 9 of this Act;

    (b) the refusal or omission of the Keeper to make such a rectification;

    (c) the loss or destruction of any document while lodged with the Keeper;

    (d) an error or omission in any land or charge certificate or in any information given by the Keeper in writing or in such other manner as may be prescribed by rules made under section 27 of this Act, shall be entitled to be indemnified by the Keeper in respect of that loss.

(2) Subject to section 14 of this Act, the Keeper may on registration in respect of an interest in land exclude, in whole or in part, any right to indemnity under this section in respect of anything appearing in, or omitted from, the title sheet of that interest.

(3) There shall be no entitlement to indemnity under this section in, respect of loss where-

    (a) the loss arises as a result of a title prevailing over that of the claimant in a case where-

        (i) the prevailing title is one in respect of which the right to indemnity has been partially excluded under subsection (2) above, and

        (ii) such exclusion has been cancelled but only on the prevailing title having been fortified by prescription;

    (b) the loss arises in respect of a title which has been reduced, whether or not under subsection (4) of section 34, or subsection (5) of section 36 of the Bankruptcy (Scotland) Act 1985 (or either of those subsections as applied by sections 615A and 615B of the Companies Act 1985, respectively) as a gratuitous alienation or fraudulent preference, or has been reduced or varied by an order under section 6(2) of the Divorce (Scotland) Act 1976 or by an order made by virtue of section 29 of the Matrimonial and Family Proceedings Act 1984 (orders relating to settlements and other dealings) or has been set aside or varied by an (order under section 18(2) (orders relating to avoidance transactions) of the Family Law (Scotland) Act 1985;

(c) the loss arises in consequence of the making of a further order under section 5(2) of the Presumption of Death (Scotland) Act 1977 (effect on property rights of recall or variation of decree of declarator of presumed death);

(d) the loss arises as a result of any inaccuracy in the delineation of any boundaries shown in a title sheet, being an inaccuracy which could not have been rectified by reference to the Ordnance Map, unless the Keeper has expressly assumed responsibility for the accuracy of that delineation;

(e) the loss arises, in the case of land extending to 2 hectares or more the area of which falls to be entered in the title sheet of an interest in that land under section 6(1)(a) of this Act, as a result of the Keeper's failure to enter such area in the title sheet or, where he has so entered such area, as a result of any inaccuracy in the specification of that area in the title sheet;

(f) the loss arises in respect of an interest in mines and minerals and the title sheet of any interest in land which is or includes the surface land does not expressly disclose that the interest in mines and minerals is included in that interest in land;

(g) the loss arises from inability to enforce a real burden or condition entered in the register, unless the keeper expressly assumes responsibility for the enforceability of that burden or condition;

(h) the loss arises in respect of an error or omission in the noting of an overriding interest;

(j) the loss is suffered by-
   (i) a beneficiary under a trust in respect of any transaction entered into by its trustees or in respect of any title granted by them the validity of which is unchallengeable by virtue of section 2 of the Trusts (Scotland) Act 1961 (validity of certain transactions by trustees), or as the case may be, section 17 of the Succession (Scotland) Act 1964 (protection of persons acquiring title), or
   (ii) a person in respect of any interest transferred to him by trustees in purported implement of trust purposes;

(k) the loss arises as a result of an error or omission in an office copy as to the effect of any subsisting adverse entry in the Register of Inhibitions and Adjudications affecting any person in respect of any registered interest in land, and that person's entitlement to that interest is neither disclosed in the register nor otherwise known to the Keeper;

(l) The claimant is the proprietor of the dominant tenement in a servitude, except insofar as the claim may relate to the validity of the constitution of that servitude;

(m) the claimant is a superior, a creditor in a ground annual or a landlord under a long lease and the claim relates to any information-
  (i) contained in the feu writ, the contract of ground annual or the lease, as the case may be, and
  (ii) omitted from the title sheet of the interest of the superior, creditor or landlord,
  (except insofar as the claim may relate to the constitution or amount of the feuduty, ground annual or rent and adequate information has been made available to the Keeper to enable him to make an entry in the register in respect of such constitution or amount or to the description of the land in respect of which the feuduty, ground annual or rent is payable);
(n) the claimant has by his fraudulent or careless act or omission caused the loss;
(o) the claim relates to the amount due under a heritable security;
(p) the loss arises from rectification of the register consequential on the making of an order under section 8 of the Law Reform (Miscellaneous Provisions) (Scotland) Act 1985.

(4) A refusal or omission by the Keeper to enter into a title sheet -
  (a) any over-feuduty or over-rent exigible in respect of a registrable interest;
  (b) any right alleged to be a real right on the ground that by virtue of section 6 of this Act he has no duty to do so since it is unenforceable, shall not by itself prevent a claim to indemnity under this section.

Provisions supplementary to section 12

13.-(1) Subject to any order by the Lands Tribunal for Scotland or the court for the payment of expenses in connection with any claim disposed of by the Lands Tribunal under section 25 of this Act or the court, the Keeper shall reimburse any expenditure reasonably and properly incurred by a person in pursuing a *prima facie* well-founded claim under section 12 of this Act, whether successful or not.

(2) On settlement of any claim to indemnity under the said section 12, the Keeper shall be subrogated to all rights which would have been available to the claimant to recover the loss indemnified.

(3) The Keeper may require a claimant, as a condition of payment of his claim, to grant, at the Keeper's expense, a formal assignation to the Keeper of the rights mentioned in subsection (2) above.

(4)   If a claimant to indemnity has by his fraudulent or careless act or omission contributed to the loss in respect of which he claims indemnity, the amount of the indemnity to which he would have been entitled had he not so contributed to his loss shall be reduced proportionately to the extent to which he has so contributed.

The foreshore

14.-(1) If-
    (a) it appears to the Keeper that-
        (i)   an interest in land which is registered or in respect of which an application for registration has been made consists, in whole or in part, of foreshore or a right in foreshore, or might so consist, and
        (ii) discounting any other deficiencies in his title in respect of that foreshore or right in foreshore, the person registered or, as the case may be, applying to be registered as entitled to the interest will not have an unchallengeable title in respect of the foreshore or the right in foreshore until prescription against the Crown has fortified his title in that respect, and
    (b) the Keeper wholly excludes or proposes wholly to exclude rights to indemnity in respect of that persons entitlement to that foreshore, and is requested by that person not to do so,
        the Keeper shall notify the Crown Estate Commissioners that he has been so requested.

(2)   If the Crown Estate Commissioners have-
    (a) within one month of receipt of the notification referred to in subsection (1) above, given to the Keeper written notice of their interest, and
    (b) within three months of that receipt informed the Keeper in writing that they are taking steps to challenge that title,
        the Keeper shall-
        (i)   during the prescriptive period, or
        (ii) until such time as it appears to the Keeper that the Commissioners are no longer taking steps to challenge that title or that their challenge has been unsuccessful,
          whichever is the shorter, continue wholly to exclude or, as the case may be, wholly exclude right to indemnity in respect of that person's entitlement to that foreshore or that right in foreshore.

(3)   This section, or anything done under it, shall be without prejudice to any other right or remedy available to any person in respect of foreshore or any right in foreshore.

PART III

SIMPLIFICATION AND EFFECT OF DEEDS

Simplification of deeds relating to registered interests

15.-(l) Land in respect of which an interest has been registered shall be sufficiently described in any deed relating to that interest if it is described by reference to the number of the title sheet of that interest, and accordingly, section 13 of and Schedule G to the Titles to Land Consolidation (Scotland) Act 1868, section 61 of the Conveyancing (Scotland) Act 1874, sections 8 and 24(2) of and Schedules D and J to the Conveyancing (Scotland) Act 1924 and Note 1 of Schedule 2 to the Conveyancing and Feudal Reform (Scotland) Act 1970 (sufficiency of description by reference) shall not apply to such a deed.

(2) It shall not be necessary in any deed relating to a registered interest in land to insert or refer to any real burden, condition, provision or other matter affecting that interest if that real burden, condition, provision, or other matter has been entered in the title sheet of that interest under section 6(l)(e) of this Act, and, accordingly, in such a case-

(a) sections 10 and 146 of and Schedule D to the Titles to Land Consolidation (Scotland) Act 1868, in section 32 of the Conveyancing (Scotland) Act 1874, the words from the beginning to "shall be sufficient" and in section 9 of the Conveyancing (Scotland) Act 1924, the proviso to subsection (1), subsections (3) and (4) and Schedule E to the said Act of 1924 (importation of burdens etc. by reference) shall not apply to such a deed; and

(b) such a deed shall import for all purposes a full insertion of the real burden, condition, provision or other matter.

(3) It shall not be necessary in any deed relating to a registered interest in land, being a deed referred to in section 3 of the Conveyancing (Scotland) Act 1924 or section 12 of the Conveyancing and Feudal Reform (Scotland) Act 1970 (dispositions *etc.* by persons uninfeft), to deduce title, if evidence of sufficient midcouples or links between the uninfeft proprietor and the person last infeft are produced to the Keeper on registration in respect of that interest in land and, accordingly, in such a case, section 5 of and Form 1 of Schedule A and Note 2 of Schedule K to the said Act of 1924 and Notes 2 and 3(b) of Schedule 2 to the Conveyancing and Feudal Reform (Scotland) Act 1970 (further provisions to deduction of title) as well as the said section 3 and the said section 12, shall not apply to such a deed, which shall be as valid as if it had contained a clause of deduction of title.

(4)   It shall not be necessary, in connection with any deed relating to a registered interest in land, to include an assignation of any obligation or right of relief or to narrate the series of writs by which the grantor of the deed became entitled to enforce that obligation or exercise that right if the obligation or right has been entered in the title sheet of that interest and, accordingly, in such a case-

(a)   section 50 of and Schedule M to the Conveyancing (Scotland) Act 1874 (form and effect of assigning right of relief or other right affecting land) shall not apply to such a deed; and

(b)   such a deed shall for all purposes import a valid and complete assignation of that obligation or right.

Omission of certain clauses in deeds

16.-(1) It shall not be necessary to insert in any deed executed after the commencement of this Act which conveys an interest in land a clause of assignation of writs and any such deed shall, unless specially qualified, import an assignation to the grantee of the title deeds and searches and all deeds not duly recorded, and shall-

(a)   impose on the grantor or any successor an obligation-

(i)   to deliver to the grantee all deeds and searches relating exclusively to the interest conveyed;

(ii)   to make forthcoming to the grantee and his successors at his or their expense on all necessary occasions any title deeds and searches which remain in the possession of the grantor or any successor and which relate partly to the interest conveyed; and

(b)   import an assignation to the grantee by the grantor of his right to require any person having custody thereof to exhibit or deliver any title deeds and searches remaining undelivered; and

(c)   impose on the grantee or any successor an obligation to make forthcoming on all necessary occasions to any party having an interest therein any deeds and searches which have been delivered to the grantee but which relate partly to interests other than the interest conveyed to the grantee.

(2)   It shall not be necessary to insert in any deed executed after the commencement of this Act which grants land in feu a clause of assignation of writs, and any such deed shall, unless specially qualified, import an assignation to the grantee of the title deeds and searches to the effect of maintaining and defending the right of the grantee in the feu; and the superior shall be held to be obliged for that purpose to make the title deeds and searches forthcoming to the grantee on all necessary occasions at the latter's expense.

(3)   It shall not be necessary to insert in any deed conveying an interest in land executed after the commencement of this Act a clause of assignation of rents or a clause of obligation of relief and any such deed so executed shall, unless specially qualified, import-

(a)   an assignation of the rents payable-

(i)   in the case of backhand rents, at the legal terms following the date of entry, and

(ii)   in the case of forehand rents, at the conventional terms following that date;

(b)   an obligation on the grantor to relieve the grantee of all feuduties, ground annuals, annuities and public, parochial and local burdens exigible in respect of the interest prior to the date of entry and, in the case of a grant of land in feu, of all feuduties payable by the grantor to his superiors from and after the date of entry.

Deeds of declaration of conditions

17.-(1) A land obligation specified in a deed executed after the commencement of this Act under section 32 of the Conveyancing (Scotland) Act 1874 (deeds of conditions etc.) shall-

(a)   on the recording of such deed in the Register of Sasines;

(b)   on the obligation being registered,

become a real obligation affecting the land to which it relates, unless it is expressly stated in such deed that the provisions of this section are not to apply to that obligation.

(2)   In this section "land obligation" has the meaning assigned to it by section 1(2) of the (Conveyancing and Feudal Reform (Scotland) Act 1970.

Variations and discharges of land obligations

18.-(1)The terms of any-

(a)   deed recorded in the Register of Sasines, whether before or after the commencement of this Act, whereby a land obligation is varied or discharged;

(b)   registered variation or discharge of a land obligation,

shall be binding on the singular successors of the person entitled to enforce the land obligation, and of the person on whom the land obligation was binding.

(2)   In this section "land obligation" has the meaning assigned to it by section 1(2) of the Conveyancing and Feudal Reform (Scotland) Act 1970.

Agreement as to common boundary

19.-(1) This section shall apply where the titles to adjoining lands disclose a discrepancy as to the common boundary and the proprietors of those lands have agreed to, and have executed a plan of, that boundary.

(2) Where one or both of the proprietors holds his interest or their interest in the land or lands by virtue of a deed or, as the case may be, deeds recorded in the Register of Sasines, the agreement and plan may be recorded in the Register of Sasines and on being so recorded shall be binding on the singular successors of that proprietor or, as the case may be, those proprietors and on all other persons having an interest in the land or, as the case may be, the lands.

(3) Where one or both of the interests in the lands is or are registered interests, the plan with a docquet thereon executed by both proprietors referring to the agreement shall be registrable as affecting that interest or those interests, and on its being so registered its effect shall be binding on the singular successors of the proprietor of that interest or, as the case may be, the proprietors of those interests and on all other persons having an interest in the land or, as the case may be, the lands.

PART IV

MISCELLANEOUS AND GENERAL

Tenants-at-will

20.-(1) A tenant-at-will shall be entitled, in accordance with this section, to acquire his landlord's interest as such in the land which is subject to the tenancy-at-will (hereinafter referred to as the "tenancy land").

(2) Subject to section 21(2) of this Act, a tenant-at-will who wishes to acquire his landlord's interest under this section shall serve notice on him in, or as nearly as may be in, the form set out in Schedule 1 to this Act.

(3) There shall be payable by the tenant-at-will to his landlord by way of compensation in respect of an acquisition of tenancy land such amount as may be agreed between them or, failing agreement, an amount equal to-
    (a) the value of the tenancy land, not including any buildings thereon, but assuming that planning permission for residential purposes has been granted in respect of it; or

(b) one twenty-fifth of the value of the tenancy land, including any buildings thereon,

whichever is the lesser, together with-

(i) subject to subsection (4) below, such further amount as may be required to discharge any heritable security over the tenancy land or, where the heritable security is granted over land including the tenancy land, such further amount (being such proportion of the sum secured over the land which includes the tenancy land as may reasonably be regarded as attributable to the tenancy land)as is required to restrict the heritable security so as to disburden the tenancy land; and

(ii) such further amount as may be required to redeem any feuduty, ground annual or other periodic payment falling to be redeemed under section 5 of the Land Tenure Reform (Scotland) Act 1974.

(4) In respect of any acquisition under this section, the amount mentioned in paragraph (i) of subsection (3) above shall not exceed ninety per cent. of the amount fixed by virtue of paragraph (a) or (b) of that subsection.

(5) The tenant-at-will shall reimburse the expenses reasonably and properly incurred by the landlord in conveying his interest in the tenancy land to the tenant-at-will, including the expenses of any discharge, restriction or redemption under subsection (3) above.

(6) The landlord shall, on there being tendered to him the compensation and expenses specified in this section, convey his interest in the tenancy land to his tenant-at-will on such terms and conditions (additional to those relating to compensation and expenses under subsections (3), (4) and (5) above) as may be agreed between them or, failing agreement, as may be a appropriate to the circumstances of the case and free of all heritable securities, and all such feuduties, ground annuals or other periodical payments as are mentioned in subsection (3)(ii) above.

(7) A heritable creditor whose security is over the tenancy land or land which includes the tenancy land, on there being tendered to him the amount mentioned in paragraph (i) of subsection (3) above (as read with subsection (4) above) and his reasonable expenses, shall discharge or, as the case may be, restrict the security so as to disburden the tenancy land.

(8) In this section and in sections 21 and 22 of this Act, "tenant-at-will" means a person-

(a) who, not being-
  (i) a tenant under a lease;
  (ii) a kindly tenant; or
  (iii) a tenant or occupier by virtue of any enactment,
    is by custom and usage the occupier (actual or constructive) of land on which there is a building or buildings erected or acquired for value by him or any predecessor of his;
(b) who is under an obligation to pay a ground rent to the owner of the land in respect of the said land but not in respect of the building or buildings on it, or would have been under such an obligation if the ground rent had not been redeemed; and
(c) whose right of occupancy of the land is without ish.

(9) In subsections (5) and (6) above, references to the conveying of the landlord's interest in tenancy land shall be construed in accordance with section 21(10) of this Act.

Provisions supplementary to section 20

21.-(1) Any question arising under section 20 of this Act as to-
  (a) whether a person is a tenant-at-will;
  (b) the extent or boundaries of any tenancy land;
  (c) the value of any tenancy land or as to what proportion of any sum secured over any land may reasonably be regarded as attributable to any tenancy land included in that land;
  (d) whether any expenses are reasonably and properly incurred;
  (e) what are appropriate terms and conditions,
    shall be determined, on the application of the tenant-at-will, a person claiming to be the tenant-at-will or the landlord, by the Lands Tribunal for Scotland.

(2) The Lands Tribunal for Scotland may, on the application of a tenant-at-will who wishes to acquire his landlord's interest in the tenancy land under section 20 of this Act, if they are satisfied that such landlord is unknown or cannot be found, make an order-
  (a) dispensing with notice under section 20(2) above;
  (b) fixing an amount by way of compensation in accordance with section 20(3) of this Act;
  (c) determining appropriate terms and conditions on which the landlord's interest in the tenancy land should be conveyed,
    for the purposes of the acquisition by the tenant-at-will of his landlord's said interest.

(3) If the landlord-

    (a) fails to convey his interest in accordance with section 20(6) of this Act, or

    (b) is unknown or cannot be found,

the tenant-at-will may apply to the sheriff for an order dispensing with the execution by the landlord of the conveyance in favour of the tenant-at-will and directing the sheriff clerk to execute the conveyance instead of the landlord, and on making such an order the sheriff may require the tenant-at-will to consign in court any sums payable by the tenant-at-will under section 20(3) and (5) of this Act or, as the case may be, any sums specified in an order under subsection (2) above.

(4) Where, in pursuance of an order made by the sheriff under this section, a conveyance is executed by the sheriff clerk on behalf of the landlord, such conveyance shall have the like force and effect as if it had been executed by such landlord.

(5) The sheriff may, on the application of any party, order the investment, payment or distribution of any sums consigned in court under subsection (3) above, and in so doing the sheriff shall have regard to the respective interests of any parties appearing to have a claim on such sums.

(6) Nothing in section 5 of the Sheriff Courts (Scotland) Act 1907 shall entitle any party to an application to the sheriff under this section to require it to be remitted to the Court of Session on the grounds that it relates to a question of heritable right or title.

(7) A landlord shall have power to execute a valid conveyance in pursuance of this section notwithstanding that he may be under any such disability as is mentioned in section 7 of the Lands Clauses Consolidation (Scotland) Act 1845.

(8) Where a person other than the landlord is infeft in the subjects to be conveyed, references in section 20 of this Act and in this section to the landlord shall be construed as references to the landlord and such other person for their respective rights.

(9) Any condition or provision to the effect that-

    (a) the superior of any feu shall be entitled to a right of pre-emption in the event of a sale thereof or any part thereof by the proprietor of the feu, or

    (b) any other person with an interest in land shall be entitled to a right of pre-emption in the event of a sale thereof or of any part thereof by the proprietor for the time being,

Interpretation, etc.

28.-(1) In this Act, except where the context otherwise requires-

> **"deed"** has the meaning assigned to it by section 3 of the Titles to Land Consolidation (Scotland) Act 1868, section 3 of the Conveyancing (Scotland) Act 1874 and section 2 of the Conveyancing (Scotland) Act 1924;

> **"feu"** includes blench holding and cognate expressions shall be construed accordingly;

> **"heritable security"** has the same meaning as in section 9(8) of the Conveyancing and Feudal Reform (Scotland) Act 1970;

> **"incorporeal heritable right"** does not include a right to salmon fishings; **"interest in land"** means any estate, interest, servitude or other heritable right in or over land, including a heritable security but excluding a lease which is not a long lease;

> **"the Keeper"** has the meaning assigned by section 1(2) of this Act;

> **"land"** includes buildings and other structures and land covered with water;

> **"long lease"** means a probative lease-
> (a)   exceeding 20 years; or
> (b)   which is subject to any provision whereby any person holding the interest of the grantor is under a future obligation, if so requested by the grantee, to renew the lease so that the total duration could (in terms of the lease, as renewed, and without any subsequent agreement, express or implied, between the persons holding the interests of the grantor and the grantee) extend for more than 20 years;

> **"overriding interest"** means, subject to sections 6(4) and 9(4) of this Act, in relation to any interest in land, the right or interest over it of-
> (a)   the lessee under a lease which is not a long lease;
> (b)   the lessee under a long lease who, prior to the commencement of this Act, has acquired a real right to the subjects of the lease by virtue of possession of them;
> (c)   a crofter or cottar within the meaning of section 3 or 28(4) respectively of the Crofters (Scotland) Act 1955, or a land-holder or statutory small tenant within the meaning of section 2(2) or 32(1) respectively of the Small Landholders (Scotland) Act 1911;

SCHEDULE 3

Section 29(3)

ENACTMENTS REFERRING TO THE REGISTER OF SASINES OR TO THE RECORDING OF A DEED IN THE REGISTER OF SASINES NOT AFFECTED BY SECTION 29(2)

1. *The Real Rights Act 1693*
   The whole Act.

2. *The Register of Sasines Act 1693*
   The whole Act.

3. *The Register of Sasines Act 1829*
   Section 1.

4. *The Infeftment Act 1845*
   Sections 1 to 4 and Schedule B insofar as relating to section 1.

5. *The Registration of Leases (Scotland) Act 1857*
   (a) In section 6, from the beginning of the section to "to the extent assigned" and Schedule D
   (b) Section 12
   (c) Section 15
   (d) Section 16

6. *The Land Registers (Scotland) Act 1868*
   (a) Sections 2 and 3
   (b) Sections 5 to 7
   (c) Section 9
   (d) Sections 12 to 14
   (e) In section 19, the proviso
   (f) Section 23

7. *The Titles to Land Consolidation (Scotland) Act 1868*
   (a) Sections 9 and 10 and Schedules C and D
   (b) Sections 12 and 13 and Schedules F and G insofar as relating to sections 12 and 13 respectively
   (c) Section 17
   (d) Section 19 and Schedule L

(e) Section 120

(f) Section 141

(g) Section 142

(h) Section 143

(i) Section 146

(j) Section D

(k) Section G

8. *The Conveyancing (Scotland) Act 1874*

(a) Section 8

(b) In section 32, from the beginning to "shall be sufficient" and Schedule H

(c) Section 61

(d) Schedule M

9. *The Writs Execution (Scotland) Act 1877*

Sections 5 and 6

10. *The Registration of Certain Writs (Scotland) Act 1891*

Section 1(2)

11. *The Conveyancing (Scotland) Act 1924*

(a) Section 3, form I of Schedule A and Note 2 to Schedule K

(b) Section 4 and, in Schedule B, forms I to 6 and Note 7, but not insofar as relating to the completion of title under section 74 or 76 of the Lands Clauses Consolidation (Scotland) Act 1845

(c) Section 8 and Schedule D

(d) Section 9(3) and (4)

(e) Section 10(1) to (5) and Schedule F

(f) In section 24(3) from "and such lease, before" to "Schedule B to this Act"

(g) Section 24(2) and (5) and Schedule J

(h) Section 47

(i) Sections 48 and 49(2)

12. *The Burgh Registers (Scotland) Act 1926*

(a) Section 1(1) (except the words from "and any writ" to "appropriate burgh register of sasines") and Schedule 1 insofar as relating to section 1(1) with that exception

(b) Section 1(2)

(c) Section 2 and Schedule 1 insofar as relating to section 2

(d) Section 5 and Schedule 1 insofar as relating to section 5

13.   *The Conveyancing Amendment (Scotland) Act 1938*
      Section 6(1) and (2)

14.   *The Public Registers and Records (Scotland) Act 1948*
      (a) Section 2
      (b) Section 4

15.   *The Public Registers and Records (Scotland) Act 1950*
      Section 1 (1)

16.   *The Conveyancing and Feudal Reform (Scotland) Act 1970*
      (a)   Section 12(1) and (2) and Notes 1, 2 and 3 to Schedule 2 insofar as
            relating to section 12(2)
      (b)   Section 28(3)

17.   *The Prescription and Limitation (Scotland) Act 1973*
      Section 1.

SCHEDULE 4

Section 29(4)

REPEALS

Chapter	Short Title	Extent of Repeal
1693 c 22	The Real Rights Act 1693.	The words "and priority"
1693 c 23	The Register of Sasines Act 1693	The words "and houre"
1868 c 64	The Land Registers (Scotland) Act 1868	In Section 6, the words "stamp", the words "by post", the words "and thereafter" and the words "transmitted by post" where secondly occurring
1868 c 101	The Titles to Land Consolidation (Scotland) Act 1868	In Section 142, the words "transmitted by post in terms of the Land Writs Regulation (Scotland) Act 1868

Land Registration (Scotland) Act 1979 (Commencement No.1) Order 1980

(S.I. 1980 No. 1412)

The Secretary of State, in exercise of the powers conferred on him by section 30(2) of the Land Registration (Scotland) Act 1979 and of all other powers enabling him in that behalf, hereby makes the following order:-

Citation and interpretation

1. This order may be cited as the Land Registration (Scotland) Act 1979 (Commencement No. 1) Order 1980.

2. In this order a reference to the Act is a reference to the Land Registration (Scotland) Act 1979.

Commencement

3. Subsections (1) and (2) of section 2 and subsection (3) of section 3 shall come into operation on 6th April 1981 in the area, for the purpose of registration of writs, of the County of Renfrew.

4. The other provisions of the Act, except those provisions which, under section 30 (2) of the Act, came into operation on the passing of the Act, shall also come into operation on 6th April 1981.

Land Registration (Scotland) Rules 1980 (as amended¹)

(S.I. 1980 No. 1413)

In exercise of the powers conferred on me by section 27 (1) of the Land Registration (Scotland) Act 1979 and of all other powers enabling me in that behalf, and after consultation with the Lord President of the Court of Session, I hereby make the following rules:

---

¹ As amended by SI 1998 No. 3100, SI 1982 No. 974, SI 1985 No.248

PART I

GENERAL

Citation and Commencement

1.   These rules may be cited as the Land Registration (Scotland) Rules 1980 and shall come into operation on 6th April 1981.

Interpretation

2.-(1) In these rules-

"**the Act**" means the Land Registration (Scotland) Act 1979.

"**certificate of title**" includes a land certificate and a charge certificate;

"**dealing**" means a transaction or event capable of affecting the title to a registered interest in land:

"**debt**" has the meaning assigned to it by section 9(8)(c) of the Conveyancing and Feudal Reform (Scotland) Act 1970; and

"**Registers Direct service**" means the service provided by the Keeper which allows remote direct access by computer for the purpose of searching and retrieving information in respect of the register.

(2)   In these rules any reference to a numbered rule or to a numbered form is a reference to, respectively, the rule bearing that number in these rules or the form bearing that number in Schedule A to these rules.

(3)   In a rule, any reference to a numbered paragraph is a reference to the paragraph in that rule bearing that number.

PART II

THE TITLE SHEET

Contents and Distinguishing Number of Title Sheet

3.-(1) A title sheet shall consist of the following sections: a Property Section, a Proprietorship Section, a Charges Section and a Burdens Section.

Application for Certificate of Title to be made to Correspond with Title Sheet

16.-(1) An application may be made to the Keeper for a certificate of title to be made to correspond with the relevant title sheet.

(2) Such an application shall be Form 8.

Amendment or Cancellation of Certificate of Title by Keeper

17.-(1) The Keeper shall have power to amend or cancel a certificate of title in order to make the certificate correspond with the relevant title sheet.

(2) Subject to rule 18, a certificate of title shall be produced to the Keeper for amendment or cancellation if the Keeper requests production.

(3) The Keeper shall not request production of a certificate of title in terms of the preceding paragraph where amendment of the certificate would inform the person entitled to the interest in land of the existence of a recorded deed or a registration upon which possession adverse to him may be founded in terms of section 1 of the Prescription and Limitation (Scotland) Act 1973.

(4) On being requested to do so, the Keeper shall make payment of such expenses occasioned by compliance with paragraph (2), as the Keeper considers to be reasonable.

Circumstances where Certificate of Title need not be Produced to Keeper

18.-(1) There shall be no obligation to produce the Certificate of title to the Keeper, in terms of rule 9 (3) or rule 17 (2), where the Keeper is satisfied of the existence of good cause for the failure to produce the certificate.

(2) For the purpose of the preceding paragraph, good cause will include-
(a) with reference to a land certificate or a charge certificate, the fact that the certificate has been lost or destroyed or is otherwise unobtainable; and
(b) with reference to a land certificate, the fact that the land certificate is held by a creditor.

Issue by Keeper of Substitute Certificate of Title

19. Where the Keeper is satisfied that a certificate of title has been lost or destroyed he shall issue a substitute certificate, marked " substitute " and shall note on the title sheet that a substitute certificate has been issued.

PART V

MISCELLANEOUS

Rectification of Register

20.-(1) An application to the Keeper, under section 9 (1) of the Act, for the rectification of the register shall be on Form 9.

(2)   Where it appears to the Keeper that proceedings in the court or the Lands Tribunal for Scotland may result in an order for rectification of the register under section 9(l) of the Act, the Keeper shall note the existence of such proceedings on the title sheet of the interest in land to which the proceedings relate.

Notifications by Keeper

21.-(1) The Keeper shall notify his decision on any matter affecting registration to any person whose interest appears from the register to be affected by that decision.

(2)   Notification shall not be made under the foregoing paragraph where notification would have the effect of informing the person entitled to the interest in land of the existence of a recorded deed or a registration upon which possession adverse to his interest may be founded in terms of section 1 of the Prescription and Limitation (Scotland) Act 1973.

(3)   A notification under paragraph (1) shall be made in such form as the Keeper shall think fit and shall be sufficiently made if sent by post to the person's last address shown on the register.

Affidavits to Accompany Applications for Registration

22.   Affidavits intended to accompany an application for registration may be made before a notary public.

Maps of Registered Interests and Index of Proprietors

23.   The Keeper shall make up and maintain-
    (a)   an index map, based on the Ordnance Map, of registered interests in land; and
    (b)   an index of the names of all persons currently entered in the proprietorship section of title sheets.

Application to Keeper for Report or Office Copy

24.-(1) Subject to paragraphs (2) and (3) below, an application to the Keeper for a report or office copy in terms of section 6(5) of the Act mentioned in column 1 of the following table shall be in the appropriate form as referred to in column 2 of the said table.

	Report or office copy applied for	*Form*
(1)	Report prior to Registration	10
(2)	Continuation of report prior to Registration	11
(3)	Report over registered subjects	12
(4)	Continuation of report over registered subjects	13
(5)	Report to ascertain whether or not subjects have been registered	14
(6)	Office copy (in terms of section 6(5) of the Act)	15

(2) An application for a report or office copy in terms of section 6(5) of the Act may be made by telephone provided the information which would have been included under an equivalent application under paragraph (1) above is supplied, together with such additional information as may be required by the Keeper.

(3) An application for a report or office copy in terms of section 6(5) of the Act may be made by facsimile or electronic mail provided the information which would have been included under an equivalent application under paragraph (1) above is supplied.

Application for Registers Direct service

24A.-(l) An application may be made to the Keeper for use of the Registers Direct service.

(2) On making an application, an applicant shall submit such information as will enable the Keeper to be satisfied that suitable arrangements have been made for payment of any fees incurred by the applicant.

(3) Any user of the Registers Direct service shall, on being required to do so by the Keeper submit such information as will enable the Keeper to be satisfied that the requirements of paragraph (2) above continue to be met.

Description of a Registered Interest in Land

25. Land in respect of which an interest has been registered shall be sufficiently described in any deed relating to that interest if it is described by reference to the number of the title sheet of that interest, in or as nearly as may be in, the manner prescribed by Schedule B to these rules.

SCHEDULE A

LIST OF FORMS TO BE USED IN CONNECTION WITH REGISTRATION

Form	Purpose	Reference to Act
1	Application for first registration	Section 4
2	Application for registration of a dealing (other than the transfer of part of a registered interest in land)	Section 4
3	Application for registration of a transfer of part of a registered interest in land	Section 4
4	Inventory of writs	Section 4
5	Application for noting of overriding interest or for entry of other information in terms of section 6(1)(g)	Section 6(4)
6	Land Certificate	Section 5(2)
7	Charge Certificate	Section 5(3)
8	Application for certificate of title to be made to correspond with title sheet	-
9	Application for rectification of the register	Section 9(1)
10	Application for report prior to registration	-
11	Application for continuation of report prior to registration	-
12	Application for report over registered subjects	-
13	Application for continuation of report over registered subjects	-
14	Application for report to ascertain whether or not subjects have been registered	-
15	Application for office copy	Section 6(5)

REGISTERS OF SCOTLAND
Executive Agency

APPLICATION FOR FIRST REGISTRATION

FORM 1

(Land Registration (Scotland) Rules 1980 Rule 9(1)(a))

Note: No covering letter is required.

VAT Reg No. GD 410 GB 888 8410 64

PART A

Please complete in BLACK TYPE

Typewriter Alignment Box. Type XXX in centre

1. **Presenting Agent. Name and Address**

FOR OFFICIAL USE

2. **FAS No.**

3. **Agent's Tel No.** *(include STD Code)*

4. **Agent's Reference**

5. **Name of Deed** in respect of which registration is required

6. **County** — Mark X in box if more than one county

7. **Subjects**

Street No.	Street Name	
Town		Postcode
Other		

8. **Name and Address of Applicant**

1. Surname	Forename(s)
Address	

2. Surname	Forename(s)
Address	

and/or company/firm or council, etc.	Mark X in box if more than 2 applicants
Address	

9. **Granter/Party Last Infeft**

1. Surname	Forename(s)
2. Surname	Forename(s)
and/ or company/ firm or council, etc.	Mark X in box if more than 2 granters

10. **Consideration**	Value
Fee A	Date of Entry

11. If a Form 10 Report has been issued in connection with this Application, please quote Report No. _____

12. I/we apply for registration in respect of Deed(s) No. _____ in the Inventory of Writs (Form 4). I/We certify that the information supplied in this application is correct to the best of my/our knowledge and belief.

Signature _____

Date _____

Meadowbank House, 153 London Road, Edinburgh EH8 7AU

www.ros.gov.uk

PART B

Delete **YES** or **NO** as appropriate

N.B. If more space is required for any section of this form, a separate sheet, or separate sheets, may be added.

1. Do the deeds submitted in support of this application include a plan illustrating the extent of the subjects
    to be registered? **YES/NO**
    If **YES**, please specify the deed and its Form 4 Inventory number:

    If **NO**, have you submitted a deed containing a full bounding description with measurements? **YES/NO**

    If **YES**, please specify the deed and its Form 4 Inventory number:

    N.B. If the answer to both the above questions is **NO** then, unless the property is part of a tenement or
    flatted building you must submit a plan of the subjects properly drawn to a stated scale and showing
    sufficient surrounding features to enable it to be located on the Ordnance Map. The plan should bear a
    docquet, signed by the person signing the Application Form, to the effect that it is a plan of the subjects
    sought to be registered under the attached application.

2. Is a Form P16 Report issued by the Keeper confirming that the boundaries of the subjects coincide with
    the Ordnance Map being submitted in support of this Application? **YES/NO**

    If **NO**, does the legal extent depicted in the plans or descriptions in the deeds submitted in support of the
    Application cohere with the occupational extent? **YES/NO**

    If **NO**, please advise:-

    (a) the approximate age and nature of the occupational boundaries, or

    (b) whether, if the extent of the subjects as defined in the deeds is larger than the occupational extent, the
         applicant is prepared to accept the occupational extent as viewed, or **YES/NO**

    (c) whether, if the extent of the subjects as defined in the deeds is smaller than the occupational extent, any
         remedial action has been taken. **YES/NO**

3. Is there any person in possession or occupation of the subjects or any part of them adversely to the interest
    of the applicant? **YES/NO**
    If **YES**, please give details:

4. If the subjects were acquired by the applicant under any statutory provision, does the statutory provision
    restrict the applicant's power of disposal of the subjects? **YES/NO**
    If **YES**, please indicate the statute:

5.(a) Are there any charges affecting the subjects or any part of them, except as stated in the Schedule of
      Heritable Securities etc. on page 4 of this application? **YES/NO**
      If **YES**, please give details:

  (b) Apart from overriding interests are there an burdens affecting the subjects or any part of them, as stated in
      the Schedule of Burdens on page 4 of this application? **YES/NO**
      If **YES**, please give details:

(c)   Are there any overriding interests affecting the subjects or any part of them which you wish noted on the Title Sheet?

      If **YES**, please give details:

YES/NO

(d)   Are there any recurrent monetary payments (e.g. feuduty, leasehold casualties) exigible from the subjects or any part of them?

      If **YES**, please give details:

YES/NO

6.   Where any party to the deed inducing registration is a Company registered under the Companies Acts

      Has a receiver or liquidator been appointed?

      If **YES**, please give details:

YES/NO

      If **NO**, has any resolution been passed or court order made for the winding up of the Company or petition presented for its liquidation?

      If **YES**, please give details:

YES/NO

7.   Where any party to the deed inducing registration is a Company registered under the Companies Acts can you confirm

(a)   that it is not a charity as defined in section 112 of the Companies Act 1989 and

YES/NO

(b)   that the transaction to which the deed gives effect is not one to which section 322A of the Companies Act 1985 (as inserted by section-109 of the Companies Act 1989) applies?

YES/NO

      Where the answer to either branch of the question is NO, please give details:

8.   Where any party to the deed inducing registration is a corporate body other than a Company registered under the Companies Acts

(a)   Is it acting *intra vires*?

      If **NO**, please give details:

YES/NO

(b)   Has any arrangement been put in hand for the dissolution of any such corporate body?

      If **YES**, please give details:

YES/NO

9.   Are *all* the necessary consents, renunciations or affidavits in terms of section 6 of the Matrimonial Homes (Family Protection)(Scotland) Act 1981 being submitted in connection with this application?

YES/NO

      N.B. if sufficient evidence to satisfy the Keeper that there are no subsisting occupancy rights in the subjects of this application is not submitted with the application then the statement by the Keeper in terms of rule 5(j) of the Land Registration (Scotland) Rules 1980 will not be inserted in the Title Sheet or will be qualified as appropriate without further enquiry by the Keeper.

10. Where the deed inducing registration is in implement of the exercise of a power of sale under a heritable security

Have the statutory procedures necessary for the proper exercise of such power been complied with? **YES/NO**

11. Where the deed inducing registration is a General Vesting Declaration or a Notice of Title pursuant on a Compulsory Purchase Order

Have the necessary statutory procedures been complied with? **YES/NO**

12. Is any party to the deed inducing registration subject to any legal incapacity or disability? **YES/NO**
If **YES**, please give details:

13. Are the deeds and documents detailed in the Inventory (Form 4) all the deeds and documents relevant to the title? **YES/NO**
If **NO**, please give details:

14. Are there any facts and circumstances material to the right or title of the applicant which have not already been disclosed in this application or its accompanying documents? **YES/NO**
If **YES**, please give details:

SCHEDULE OF HERITABLE SECURITIES ETC.
N.B. New Charges granted by the applicant should not be included

SCHEDULE OF BURDENS

NOTES AND DIRECTIONS FOR COMPLETION OF FORM I (PINK)-APPLICATION FOR FIRST REGISTRATION[2]

The Form 1 is to be used in the case of an application for first registration of an interest in land. Any application for voluntary first registration made in terms of either section 2(1)(b) or 11(l) of the Act should be accompanied by a letter explaining the circumstances signed by the applicant or his solicitor.

The information contained in Part A of the Form 1 will be machine scanned in the Land Register; all boxes in Part A should therefore be completed in typescript.

Please type in the white response areas only. Do not staple or pin other documents to the Form. Care should be taken to ensure that the Form 1 is not torn, crumpled or excessively folded.
*

Part A-The Notes 1 to 9 referred to on Form 1

Note 1 Presenting Agent
> The name and address of the presenting agent should be inserted in the space provided.

Note 2 FAS No
> Insert Digits only

Note 3 County
> (i)   Insert the full name of the county within which the subjects to be registered are principally situated. Place an X in the box provided if the subjects fall within more than one county.
> (ii) Deeds which are also to be recorded in the Sasine Register will require the appropriate application form for each register.

Note 4 Subjects
> (i)   Insert the full postal address of the subjects (including the postcode) if possible, using the boxes provided.
> e.g. for "The Cedars", 22 Merryfield Avenue, Leven, KY12 IDV

[2]The notes do not form part of the S.I.

insert

Street No	22	Street Name	Merryfield Avenue
Town	Leven	Post code	KY12 IDV
Other	The Cedars		

(ii) Additional information assisting the identification of the subjects (*e.g.* the location of a house within a tenement, or a plot number on a builder's estate) should be inserted in the box marked "other".

(iii) Where the property does not have a postal address, as full a description of the subjects as is necessary for identification should be inserted in the "other" box.

(iv) In cases where the subjects comprise or include superiorities or landlord's interests in registered leases, a schedule of feus or leases must accompany the application if an up-to-date list is not included in the title. Where possible, identification should be made on a plan.

Any schedule may be in the following form:-

Writ	Feuar (or Tenant)	Date of Recording	Subjects	Feuduty (or rent)
Feu Contract	Adam Young and another	4 September 1898 G.R.S (Renfrew)	129 Old Road Renfrew	£5
(Lease	Ian Gow	1 May 1928 G.R.S. (Renfrew)	1 Hay Road Renfrew	£10)

Note 5 Applicant
(i) Insert the full names and addresses of the applicants in box 8 as appropriate.
(ii) Place an X in the box provided if there are more than two applicants. If there are more than two applicants, the additional parties should be clearly identified and designed on a separate sheet lodged with the application. N.B. The names and (where appropriate) the addresses of all applicants must be given.

(iii) Where the applicant is acting in a fiduciary or other capacity, the information required is the name and address of the party for whom he is acting and the capacity in which he is acting, e.g. where the applicant is George Campbell, Trustee of Robert Gordon Campbell late of 27 Princes Avenue, Girvan the insertion should be:

Surname	Forename
CAMPBELL	ROBERT GORDON, TR. OF

Address

27 PRINCES AVENUE, GIRVAN

This applies where the relationship results from a deed of trust, testamentary deed or court appointment etc. Where the applicants are the trustees for a club etc. the name and address of the club are what is required and should be inserted in the space for "company/firm or council"

(iv) Where the applicants are the trustees of a firm the names and addresses of the trustees should be inserted as if they were individuals and the name and address of the firm inserted in the appropriate space as well. If there are more than two trustees the names and addresses of the additional ones must be given on a separate sheet lodged with the application.

Note 6 Granter/party last infeft
   (i) Insert the full names of the party last infeft or the granter, whichever is appropriate, in box 9.
   (ii) Place an X in the box provided if there are more than two parties selling or last infeft. It is not necessary to list the extra names separately as long as they can be ascertained from the supporting documents.
   (iii) The names of *ex officio* trustees or executors should not be inserted in the party last infeft's response boxes.
   (iv) The names of trustees and partners for firms should be inserted in full as well as the name of the firm. If there are two or more trustees, the details of the trustees should be provided outwith the form, but the

details of the party for whom they act should when-ever possible, be included on the form itself.

Note 7 Consideration

Insert the consideration in figures. If there is a non-monetary consideration, abbreviate to fit, e.g. love favour and affection could be inserted as LF&A. If the latter is the case, please ensure that the value is inserted in the next box.

Note 8 Value

Where the consideration is either less than the true value of the subjects or not expressed in monetary terms, then the full value should be inserted (in figures).

Note 9 Fees

Please insert the amount due for this registration (in figures).

Explanatory notes relevant to Part B

Adverse possession. Rights of possession under a lease granted by any person entitled to grant the same are not to be regarded as adverse to the interest of the applicant.

The schedule of heritable securities. Must list all existing heritable securities which may be specified by reference to the inventory (Form 4) Intromissions (*i.e.* partial discharges and assignations) need not be listed in the schedule but should be included in the inventory.

The schedule of burdens. May be completed by reference to the inventory (Form 4). It must specify at length or by specific reference to the writs containing them all burdens affecting the subjects and any variation thereof.

Overriding interests. Where an overriding interest, as defined in section 28(1) of the Act, is constituted otherwise than by writ, particulars of its mode of constitution must be given. In terms of section 6(4) of the Act, the provisions for noting an overriding interest do not apply to the interest of a lessee under a lease which is not a long lease.

Deeds and documents are:-
    (i)   a sufficient progress of titles including the deed inducing registration and unrecorded links in title,

(ii) all prior writs containing rights or burdens affecting the subjects,

(iii) any document evidencing the extinction of an obligation to make a recurrent monetary payment, such as feuduty, leasehold casualty etc.

(iv) any existing heritable securities and deeds relating thereto,

(v) where appropriate, consents to leases and sub-leases and assignations of recorded or registered leases,

(vi) Form P16, if obtained,

(vii) any other relevant documents.

An applicant should be prepared to submit common titles (*i.e.* title deeds or burdens writs relating to a substantial development) to the Keeper if requested to do so. Such titles should not however be submitted in the first instance, although all those relevant to the application must be listed on Form 4.

REGISTERS OF SCOTLAND
Executive Agency

APPLICATION FOR REGISTRATION OF A DEALING

FORM 2

(Land Registration (Scotland) Rules 1980 Rule 9(1)(b))

Note: No covering letter is required.

VAT Reg No. GD 410 GB 888 8410 64

PART A

Please complete in BLACK TYPE

Typewriter Alignment Box. Type XXX in centre

FOR OFFICIAL USE

1. **Presenting Agent. Name and Address**

2. **FAS No.**		3. **Agent's Tel No.** *(include STD Code)*

4. **Agent's Reference**	

5. **Name of Deed** in respect of which registration is required	

6. **County**		Mark X in box if more than one county	

7. **Title No**(s) of registered interest(s) affected by this application		Mark X in box if more than 3 title numbers	

8. **Subjects**

Street No.		Street Name	
Town			Postcode	
Other				

9. **Name and Address of Applicant**

1. Surname		Forename(s)	
Address			
2. Surname		Forename(s)	
Address			
and/or company/firm or council, etc.		Mark X in box if more than 2 applicants	
Address			

10. **Consideration** - or amount of loan		**Value** - or amount of loan	
Fee A/B/C		**Date of Entry**	

11. I/we apply for registration in respect of Deed(s) No. _____ in the Inventory of Writs (Form 4). I/We certify that the information supplied in this application is correct to the best of my/our knowledge and belief.

Signature _____ Date _____

Meadowbank House, 153 London Road, Edinburgh EH8 7AU
www.ros.gov.uk

REGISTERS OF SCOTLAND
Executive Agency

APPLICATION FOR REGISTRATION OF A DEALING

FORM 2

PART B

Delete **YES** or **NO** as appropriate

N.B. If more space is required for any section of this form, a separate sheet, or separate sheets, may be added.

---

1. Where the dealing in respect of which registration is sought transfers the interest specified in the Property Section of the Title Sheet

(a) Is there any person in possession or occupation of the subjects or any part of them adversely to the interest of the applicant?
    If **YES**, please give details:

    YES/NO

(b) If the subjects were acquired by the applicant under any statutory provision, does the statutory provision restrict the applicant's power of disposal of the subjects?
    If **YES**, please indicate the statute:

    YES/NO

(c) Apart from overriding interests are there any burdens affecting the subjects or any part of them, except as already disclosed in the Land Certificate and in the documents produced with this application?
    If **YES**, please give details:

    YES/NO

(d) Are there any overriding interests affecting the subjects or any part of them which you wish noted on the Title Sheet?
    If **YES**, please give details:

    YES/NO

(e) Are there any recurrent monetary payments (e.g. feuduty, leasehold casualties) exigible from the subjects or any part of them?
    If **YES**, please give details:

    YES/NO

---

2. Where any party to the dealing is a Company registered under the Companies Acts
    Has a receiver or liquidator been appointed?
    If **YES**, please give details:

    YES/NO

    If **NO**, has any resolution been passed or court order made for the winding up of the Company or petition presented for its liquidation?
    If **YES**, please give details:

    YES/NO

---

3. Where any party to the dealing is a Company registered under the Companies Acts can you confirm

(a) that it is not a charity as defined in section 112 of the Companies Act 1989 and

    YES/NO

(b) that the transaction to which the deed gives effect is not one to which section 322A of the Companies Act 1985 (as inserted by section 109 of the Companies Act 1989) applies?

    YES/NO

    Where the answer to either branch of the question is **NO**, please give details:

---

4. Where any party to the dealing is a corporate body other than a Company registered under the Companies Acts

(a) Is it acting *intra vires*? YES/NO
If **NO**, please give details:

(b) Has any arrangement been put in hand for the dissolution of any such corporate body? YES/NO
If **YES**, please give details:

5. Are *all* the necessary consents, renunciations or affidavits in terms of section 6 of the Matrimonial Homes
(Family Protection)(Scotland) Act 1981 being submitted in connection with this application? YES/NO

N.B. If sufficient evidence to satisfy the Keeper that there are no subsisting occupancy rights in the subjects
of this application is not submitted with the application then the statement by the Keeper in terms of rule
5(j) of the Land Registration (Scotland) Rules 1980 will not be inserted in the Title Sheet or will be
qualified as appropriate without further enquiry by the Keeper.

6. Where the dealing is in implement of the exercise of a power of sale under a heritable security

Have the statutory procedures necessary for the proper exercise of such power been complied with? YES/NO

7. Where the dealing is a General Vesting Declaration or a Notice of Title pursuant on a Compulsory Purchase Order

Have the necessary statutory procedures been complied with? YES/NO

8. In all cases

(a) Is any party to the dealing subject to any legal incapacity or disability not already disclosed on the Land Certificate? YES/NO
If **YES**, please give details:

(b) Are the deeds and documents detailed in the Inventory (Form 4) all the deeds and documents relevant to
the application? YES/NO
If **NO**, please give details:

(c) Are there any facts and circumstances material to the right or title of the applicant which have not already
been disclosed in this application or its accompanying documents? YES/NO
If **YES**, please give details:

NOTES AND DIRECTIONS FOR COMPLETION OF FORM 2 (BLUE)- APPLICATION FOR A DEALING WITH REGISTERED INTEREST(S) (EXCLUDING DISPOSITION, FEU OR LONG LEASE OF PART OF THE PROPERTY OR A FEU OR LONG LEASE OF THE WHOLE OF THE PROPERTY)[3]

The Form 2 is to be used in the case of an application for registration of a transaction or event which deals with or affects a registered interest or interests in land. The following are examples of such transactions:-

(a) disposition of the whole interest in one registered title;
(b) standard security over the whole of the interest(s) in one or more registered titles;
(c) standard security over part of the interest in one registered title;
(d) discharge of a registered standard security;
(e) deed of conditions affecting all or part of the interest in a registered title;
(f) renunciation of a registered lease.

The above list is demonstrative only. It should be noted that the only type of transaction affecting a registered interest for which a Form 2 is not suitable is a disposition of part of property forming a registered interest in land, or a feu or lease of the whole or part of that property.

The information contained in Part A of the Form 2 will be machine scanned in the Land Register; all boxes in Part A should therefore be completed in typescript.

Please type in the white response areas only. Do not staple or pin other documents to the Form 2. Care should be taken to ensure that the Form 2 is not torn, crumpled or excessively folded.

Part A-The Notes I to 10 referred to on Form 2

Note 1 Presenting agent
 The name and address of the presenting agent should be inserted in the space provided.

Note 2 FAS No
 Input Digits only

---

[3] The notes do not form part of the S.I.

Note 3 Name of deed

Insert the full name of the deed if possible. Where space does not permit of this, an abbreviated version of the deed name may be used. (*E.g.* "Notice of Payment of Improvement Grant" could be shortened to "Improvement Grant".)

Note 4 County

(i)   Insert the full name of the county within which the subjects to be registered are principally situated. Place an X in the box provided if the subjects fall within more than one county.

(ii) Deeds which are also to be recorded in the Sasine Register will require the appropriate application form for each register.

Note 5 Title number

All the appropriate Title Numbers must be listed. If there are more than three, then insert an X in the box provided and list the additional Title Numbers on a separate sheet.

Note 6 Subjects

(i)   Insert the full postal address of the subjects (including the postcode) if possible, using the boxes provided.
      e.g. for "The Cedars", 22 Merryfield Avenue, Leven KY12 1DV

insert

Street No	22	Street Name	Merryfield Avenue
Town	Leven	Post code	KY12 IDV
Other	The Cedars		

(ii)   Additional information assisting the identification of the subjects (*e.g.* the location of a house within a tenement, or a plot number on a builder's estate) should be inserted in the box marked "other".

(iii) Where the property does not have a postal address, as full a description of the subjects as is necessary for identification should be inserted in the "other" box.

(iv)   In cases where the subjects comprise or include superiorities or landlord's interests in registered leases, a schedule of feus or leases must accompany the application if an up-to-date list is not included in the title. Where possible, identification should be made on a plan.

Any schedule may be in the following form:

Writ	Feuar (or Tenant)	Date of Recording	Subjects	Feuduty (or rent)
Feu Contract	Adam Young and another	4 September 1898 G.R.S (Renfrew)	129 Old Road Renfrew	£5
(Lease	Ian Gow	1 May 1928 G.R.S. (Renfrew)	1 Hay Road Renfrew	£10)

Note 7 Applicant

    (i)   Insert the full names and addresses of the applicants in box 8 as appropriate.

   (ii)   Place an X in the box provided. If there are more than two applicants, If there are more than two applicants, the additional parties should be clearly identified and designed on a separate sheet lodged with the application; N.B. The names and (where appropriate) the addresses of all applicants must be given.

  (iii) Where the applicant is acting in a fiduciary or other capacity, the information required is the name and address of the party for whom he is acting and the capacity in which he is acting, *e.g.* where the applicant is George Campbell, Trustee of Robert Gordon, Campbell late of 27 Princes Avenue, Girvan the insertion should be:

Surname   Forename

CAMPBELL	ROBERT GORDON, TR. OF

Address

27 PRINCES AVENUE, GIRVAN

This applies where the relationships results from a deed of trust, testamentary deed or court appointment etc. Where the applicants are the trustees for a club etc. the name and address of the club are what is required and should be inserted in the space for "company/firm or council etc."

(iv) Where the applicants are the trustees of a firm the names and addresses of the trustees should be inserted as if they were individuals and the name and address of the firm inserted in the appropriate space as well. If there are more than two trustees the names and addresses of the additional ones must be given on a separate sheet lodged with the application.

Note 8 Consideration/amount of loan

Insert the consideration or the amount of the loan in figures. If there is a non-monetary consideration, abbreviate to fit, *e.g.* love favour and affection could be inserted as LF&A. If the latter is the case or if the amount of the loan is not shown in the writ, please ensure that the value or the amount of loan is inserted in the next box.

Note 9 Value

Where the consideration is either less than the true value of the consideration or not expressed in monetary terms, then the full value should be inserted, in figures. If the amount of the loan is not shown in the writ, then ensure it is set out here.

Note 10 Fees

Please insert the amount due for this registration in figures, placing an X over the two letters which do not apply, *e.g.* if the deed for which registration is sought is a standard security, then the B table of fees applies, therefore the A and the C should be crossed out.

Explanatory notes relevant to Part B

Adverse possession. Rights of possession under a lease granted by any person entitled to grant the same are not to be regarded as adverse to the interest of the applicant.

Overriding interests. Where an overriding interest, as defined in section 28(l) of the Act, is constituted otherwise than by writ, particulars of its mode of constitution must be given. In terms of section 6(4) of the Act, the provisions for noting an overriding interest do not apply to the interest of a lessee under a lease which is not a long lease.

Deeds and documents are:-
(i)   the Land Certificate,
(ii) any relevant Charge Certificate,

(iii) all writs which affect the registration, including all writs containing burdens not already specified in the Land Certificate or varying or discharging burdens since the certificate was last issued,

(iv) where appropriate, consents to leases and sub-leases and assignations of recorded or registered leases,

(v) Form P17, if obtained,

(vi) all unregistered links in title.

All the above documents should be submitted along with the application.

APPLICATION FOR REGISTRATION OF A TRANSFER OF PART

FORM 3

(Land Registration (Scotland) Rules 1980 Rule 9(1)(c))

Note: No covering letter is required.

VAT Reg No. GD 410 GB 888 8410 64

PART A

Please complete in BLACK TYPE

Typewriter Alignment Box. Type XXX in centre

1. **Presenting Agent. Name and Address**

FOR OFFICIAL USE

2. **FAS No.**	

3. **Agent's Tel No.** *(include STD Code)*	

4. **Agent's Reference**	

5. **Name of Deed** in respect of which registration is required	

6. **County**		Mark X in box if more than one county	

7. **Title No**(s) of registered interest(s) affected by this application		Mark X in box if more than 3 title numbers	

8. **Subjects**

Street No.	Plot No.		Street Name	
Town			Postcode	
Other				

9. **Name and Address of Applicant**

1. Surname		Forename(s)	
Address			
2. Surname		Forename(s)	
Address			
and/or company/firm or council, etc.		Mark X in box if more than 2 applicants	
Address			

10. **Consideration**		**Value**	
Fee A		**Date of Entry**	

11. I/we apply for registration in respect of Deed(s) No. _____ in the Inventory of Writs (Form 4). I/We certify that the information supplied in this application is correct to the best of my/our knowledge and belief.

Signature _____   Date _____

Meadowbank House, 153 London Road, Edinburgh EH8 7AU
www.ros.gov.uk

REGISTERS OF SCOTLAND
Executive Agency

APPLICATION FOR REGISTRATION OF A TRANSFER OF PART

FORM 3

PART B

Delete **YES** or **NO** as appropriate

N.B. If more space is required for any section of this form, a separate sheet, or separate sheets, may be added.

---

1. Is there any person in possession or occupation of the subjects or any part of them adversely to the interest of the applicant?
   If **YES**, please give details: **YES/NO**

---

2. If the subjects were acquired by the applicant under statutory provision, does the statutory provision restrict the applicant's power of disposal of the subjects?
   If **YES**, please indicate the statute: **YES/NO**

3.(a) Apart from overriding interests are there any burdens affecting the subjects or any part of them, except as already disclosed in the Land Certificate and in the documents produced with this application?
   If **YES**, please give details: **YES/NO**

   (b) Are there any overriding interests affecting the subjects or any part of them which you wish noted on the Title Sheet?
   If **YES**, please give details: **YES/NO**

   (c) Are there any recurrent monetary payments (e.g. feuduty, leasehold casualties) exigible from the subjects or any part of them?
   If **YES**, please give details: **YES/NO**

---

4. Where any party to the dealing is a Company registered under the Companies Acts
   Has a receiver or liquidator been appointed?
   If **YES**, please give details: **YES/NO**

   If **NO**, has any resolution been passed or court order made for the winding up of the Company or petition presented for its liquidation?
   If **YES**, please give details: **YES/NO**

---

5. Where any party to the dealing is a Company registered under the Companies Acts can you confirm

   (a) that it is not a charity as defined in section 112 of the Companies Act 1989 and   **YES/NO**

   (b) that the transaction to which the deed gives effect is not one to which section 322A of the Companies Act 1985 (as inserted by section 109 of the Companies Act 1989)applies?   **YES/NO**

   Where the answer to either branch of the question is **NO**, please give details:

---

6. Where any party to the dealing is a corporate body other than a Company registered under the Companies Acts

(a) Is it acting *intra vires*? **YES/NO**
    If **NO**, please give details:

(b) Has any arrangement been put in hand for the dissolution of any such corporate body? **YES/NO**
    If **YES**, please give details:

7. Are *all* the necessary consents, renunciations or affidavits in terms of section 6 of the Matrimonial Homes (Family Protection)(Scotland) Act 1981 being submitted in connection with this application? **YES/NO**

    N.B. If sufficient evidence to satisfy the Keeper that there are no subsisting occupancy rights in the subjects of this application is not submitted with the application than the statement by the Keeper in terms of rule 5(j) of the Land Registration (Scotland) Rules 1980 will not be inserted in the Title Sheet or will be qualified as appropriate without further enquiry by the Keeper.

8. Where the dealing is in implement of the exercise of a power of sale under a heritable security

    Have the statutory procedures necessary for the proper exercise of such power been complied with? **YES/NO**

9. Where the dealing is a General Vesting Declaration or a Notice of Title pursuant on a Compulsory Purchase Order
    Have the necessary statutory procedures been complied with? **YES/NO**

10. Is any party to the dealing subject to any legal incapacity or disability not already disclosed on the Land Certificate? **YES/NO**
    If **YES**, please give details:

11. Are the boundaries of the subjects defined o the ground by fencing or other type of enclosure? **YES/NO**

12. Are the deeds and documents detailed in the Inventory (Form 4) all the deeds and documents relevant to the application? **YES/NO**
    If **NO**, please give details:

13. Are there any facts and circumstances material to the right or title of the applicant which have not already been disclosed in this application or its accompanying documents? **YES/NO**
    If **YES**, please give details:

NOTES AND DIRECTIONS FOR COMPLETION OF FORM 3 (YELLOW)- APPLICATION FOR REGISTRATION OF A TRANSFER OF PART OF REGISTERED SUBJECTS[1]

The Form 3 is to be used in the case of an application for registration of a transfer of part of property comprised in one or more registered titles. The following are examples of such transactions:-

(a) disposition of part of the property;
(b) feu of part of the property;
(c) long lease of part of the property;
(d) feu of the whole of the property;
(e) long lease of whole of the property.

The information contained in the Form 3 should reflect the information in the writ to which effect is to be given.

The information contained in Part A of the Form 3 will be machine scanned in the Land Register; all boxes in Part A should therefore be completed in typescript.

Please type in the white response areas only. Do not staple or pin other documents to the Form 3. Care should be taken to ensure that the Form 3 is not torn, crumpled or excessively folded.

Part A-The Notes 1 to 9 referred to on Form 3

Note 1 Presenting agent
　　The name and address of the presenting agent should be inserted in the space provided.

Note 2 FAS No.
　　Insert Digits Only

Note 3 County
　(i)　Insert the full name of the county within which the subjects to be registered are principally situated. Place an X in the box provided if the subjects fall within more than one county.
　(ii)　Deeds which are also to be recorded in the Sasine Register will require the appropriate application form for each register.

---

[1] The notes do not form part of the S.I.

Note 4 Title number

All the appropriate Title Numbers must be listed. If there are more than three, then insert an X in the box provided and list the additional Title Numbers on a separate sheet.

Note 5 Subjects

(i) Insert the full postal address of the subjects (including the postcode) if possible, using the boxes provided.
   In addition insert the plot number, if available.
   e. g. for Upper villa flat, plot 22A, 1 1 North Road, St Andrews, KY22 7UP

insert

Street No	11	Street Name	North Road
Town	St Andrews	Post code	KY22 7UP
Other	Upper villa flat Plot 22A		

(ii) Additional information assisting the identification of the subjects (*e.g.* the location of a house within a tenement, or a plot number on a builder's estate) should be inserted in the box marked "other".

(iii) Where the property does not have a postal address, as full a description of the subjects as is necessary for identification should be inserted in the "other" box.

(iv) In cases where the subjects comprise or include superiorities or landlord's interests in registered leases, a schedule of feus or leases must accompany the application if an up-to-date list is not included in the title. Where possible, identification should be made on a plan.

Any schedule may be in the following form:-

Writ	Feuar (or Tenant)	Date of Recording	Subjects	Feuduty (or rent)
Feu Contract	Adam Young and another	4 September 1898 G.R.S (Renfrew)	129 Old Road Renfrew	£5
(Lease	Ian Gow	1 May 1928 G.R.S. (Renfrew)	1 Hay Road Renfrew	£10)

    (i) Insert the full names and addresses of the applicants in box 8 as appropriate.

   (ii) Place an X in the box provided if there are more than two applicants. If there are more than two applicants, the additional parties should be clearly identified and designed on a separate sheet lodged with the application. N.B. The names and (where appropriate) the addresses of all applicants must be given

  (iii) Where the applicant is acting in a fiduciary or other capacity, the information required is the name and address of the party for whom he is acting and the capacity in which he is acting, e.g. where the applicant is George Campbell, Trustee of Robert Gordon Campbell late of 27 Princes Avenue, Girvan the insertion should be:

Surname	Forename
CAMPBELL	ROBERT GORDON, TR. OF

Address

27 PRINCES AVENUE, GIRVAN

This applies where the relationship results from a deed of trust, testamentary deed or court appointment etc. Where the applicants are the trustees for a club etc. the name and address of the club are what is required and should be inserted in the space for "company/firm or council etc."

  (iv) Where the applicants are the trustees of a firm the names and addresses of the trustees should be inserted as if they were individuals and the name and address of the firm inserted in the appropriate space as well. If there are more than two trustees the names and addresses of the additional ones must be given on a separate sheet lodged with the application.

Note 7 Consideration

Insert the consideration in figures. If there is a non-monetary consideration, abbreviate to fit, *e.g.* love favour and affection could be inserted as LF&A. If the latter is the case, please ensure that the value is inserted in the next box.

Note 8 Value

Where the consideration is either less than the true value of the consideration or not expressed in monetary terms, then the full value should be inserted (in figures).

Note 9 Fees

Please insert the amount due for this registration (in figures).

Explanatory notes relevant to Part B

Adverse possession. Rights of possession under a lease granted by any person entitled to grant the same are not to be regarded as adverse to the interest of the applicant.

Overriding interests. Where an overriding interest, as defined in section 28(1) of the Act, is constituted otherwise than by writ, particulars of its mode of constitution must be given. In terms of section 6(4) of the Act, the provisions for noting an overriding interest do not apply to the interest of a lessee under a lease which is not a long lease.

Deeds and documents are:-
   (i)   the Land Certificate,
   (ii) any relevant Charge Certificate,
   (iii) all writs which affect the registration, including all writs containing burdens not already specified in the Land Certificate or varying or discharging burdens since the certificate was last issued,
   (iv) where appropriate, consents to leases and sub-leases and assignations of recorded or registered leases,
   (v) Form P17, if obtained,
   (vi) all unregistered links in title.

All the above documents should be submitted along with the application.

REGISTERS OF SCOTLAND
Executive Agency

INVENTORY OF WRITS RELEVANT TO APPLICATION FOR REGISTRATION

FORM 4

(Land Registration (Scotland) Rules 1980 Rule 9(2))

Name and Address

Please complete in DUPLICATE and in BLACK TYPE

Typewriter Alignment Box. Type XXX in centre

Title number(s) (to be completed for a dealing with registered interest in land)

Subjects

Registration County

Applicant's Reference

Please complete Inventory overleaf as in this specimen (see example below)

Particulars of Writs

Item No.	Please mark "S" against writs submitted	Writ	Grantee	Date of Recording
		Land Certificate*		
		Charge Certificate*		
1	-	Feu Charter	Upright Builders Ltd	2 May 1938

*Delete if inapplicable

Meadowbank House, 153 London Road, Edinburgh EH8 7AU
www.ros.gov.uk

REGISTERS OF SCOTLAND
Executive Agency

INVENTORY

Particulars of Writs continuation

Item No.	Please mark "S" against writs submitted	Writ	Grantee	Date of Recording

FOR OFFICIAL USE ONLY

Application Number	Date of receipt	Title Number

The writs marked "S" on this inventory were received on the Date of Receipt stamped on this page.

NOTES AND DIRECTIONS FOR COMPLETION OF FORM 4 (WHITE)- INVENTORY OF WRITS RELEVANT TO APPLICATION FOR REGISTRATION[5]

Please read the following instructions carefully before completing the Form 4.
The Form 4 must be completed in black type.
Please type in the white response areas only.

The Notes 1-4 referred to on Form 4

1. Each application for registration must be accompanied by a Form 4 listing all deeds and documents relevant to the application whether or not such are submitted with the case. In cases where effect is to be given to, for example a disposition and two standard securities affecting the same interest, the application forms for which are all completed by one solicitor, it is sufficient for him to submit one Form 4 listing all the deeds and documents for the three applications. Where more than one solicitor or application is involved, each should complete a Form 4 for his own deeds. The Form 4 should be completed in duplicate. One copy will be returned by the Keeper as his acknowledgement of receipt.

2. Insert the name and address of the party or the solicitor who is submitting the writs.

3. A short description only of the subjects is required, *e.g.* a postal address.

4. (a) In the case of an application for first registration (Form 1), the relevant deeds and documents to be listed on the Form 4 are:
    (i) a sufficient progress of titles included the deed inducing registration and unrecorded links in title,
    (ii) all prior writs containing rights and burdens affecting the subjects,
    (iii) any document evidencing the extinction of an obligation to make a recurrent monetary payment, such as feuduty, leasehold casualty etc.
    (iv) any existing heritable securities and deeds relating thereto.
    (v) where appropriate, consents to leases and sub-leases and assignations of recorded or registered leases,
    (vi) Form P16, if obtained,
    (vii) any other relevant documents

---

[5] The notes do not form part of the S.I.

All the above documents should be submitted along with the application, but if any are not available when the application is lodged, they should be listed on the inventory but not marked "S".

(b) In the case of an application on Form 2 or 3, the relevant deeds and documents to be listed on the Form 4 are:

(i)   the Land Certificate,

(ii)   any relevant Charge Certificate,

(iii) all writs which affect the registration, including all writs containing burdens not already specified in the Land Certificate or varying or discharging burdens since the certificate was last issued,

(iv)   where appropriate, consents to leases and sub-leases and assignations of recorded or registered leases.

(v)   Form P17, if obtained,

(vi)   all unregistered links in title.

All the above documents should be submitted along with the application, but if any are not available when the application is lodged, they should be listed on the inventory but not marked "S".

(c) The details of the deeds should be entered as per the specimen on the front page of the Form 4. The deed name can be abbreviated to fit the space. The briefest of details necessary to identify the grantee can be inserted, *e.g.* Mary Irene Wallis or Cameron can be shortened to MIW Cameron. Where there are two or more grantees, the first once can be inserted and the rest covered by "and spouse" or "and another" or "and others". The recording date (or the date of registration in the Books of Council and Session) can be inserted as "18 Jan. 1961".

FORM 5

REGISTERS OF SCOTLAND EXECUTIVE AGENCY
(Land Registration (Scotland) Rules 1980 Rule 13)

APPLICATION FOR NOTING OR ENTERING ON THE REGISTER

Note:No covering letter is required.

Please complete in BLACK TYPE

Typewriter Alignment Box
Type XXX in centre

TO
Keeper of the Registers of Scotland

Meadowbank House
153 London Road
EDINBURGH EH8 7AU

Telephone: 01 31 659 61 11

FOR OFFICIAL USE
DATE OF RECEIPT

APPLICATION NUMBER

Title No(s)

Mark X in box if more
than 3 Title Numbers 1

Short description
of Subjects

*I/We apply to have the information set out below noted or entered on the Title Sheet(s) of the above Title(s) viz.

*I/We apply to have the information set out below deleted from the Title Sheet(s) of the above Title(s) viz.

The appropriate fee is enclosed   please place a cross here.

To support this application, I/We*enclose the documents listed on the Inventory (Form 4).

Signature of Applicant or
Applicant's Solicitor

Full Name of Applicant

Address of Applicant

Name of Solicitor

Address of Solicitor

Reference   Telephone No.

Date of Application   FAS No.

1. Please list additional Title Numbers on a separate sheet.
*Delete whichever is inapplicable

Printed in Scotland for HMSO by (13161)
Dd 8409700 C50 3/95

(Land Registration (Scotland) Rules 1980, Rule 14)

LAND REGISTER OF SCOTLAND

LAND CERTIFICATE

TITLE NUMBER

SUBJECTS

This Land Certificate, issued pursuant to section 5(2) of the Land Registration (Scotland) Act 1979, is a copy of the Title Sheet relating to the above subjects.

STATEMENT OF INDEMNITY

Subject to any specific qualifications entered in the Title Sheet of which this Land Certificate is a copy, a person who suffers loss as a result of the events specified in section 12(1) of the above Act shall be entitled to be indemnified in respect of that loss by the Keeper of the Registers of Scotland in terms of that Act.

ATTENTION IS DRAWN TO THE NOTICE AND GENERAL INFORMATION OVERLEAF.

Printed for TSO Scotland Dd 8457077 C700 3/97 25364

FORM 6 427

NOTICE

This Land Certificate was made to agree with the Title Sheet of which it is a copy on the most recent date entered below.

This Land Certificate may be made to agree with the Title Sheet at any time on payment of the appropriate fee. Application should be made on Form 8.

GENERAL INFORMATION

1.   **OVERRIDING INTERESTS**. A registered interest in land is in terms of section 3(l) of the Land Registration (Scotland) Act 1979 subject to overriding interests defined in section 28 of that Act (hereinafter referred to as 'the 1979 Act') as amended by the Matrimonial Homes (Family Protection) (Scotland) Act 1981, the Telecommunication Act 1984, the Electricity Act 1989 and the Coal Industry Act 1994 as:

     in relation to any interest in land, the right or interest over it of

     (a)   the lessee under a lease which is not a long lease;

     (b)   the lessee under a long lease who, prior to the commencement of the 1979 Act, has acquired a real right to the subjects of the lease by virtue of possession of them;

Continued on inside back cover.

428	**FORM 6**

(c)   a crofter or cottar within the meaning of section 3 or 28(4) respectively of the Crofters (Scotland) Act 1955, or a landholder or statutory small tenant within the meaning of section 2(2) or 32(l) respectively of the Small Landholders (Scotland) Act 1911;

(d)   the proprietor of the dominant tenement in a servitude;

(e)   the Crown or any Government or other public department, or any public or local authority, under any enactment or rule of law, other than an enactment or rule of law authorising or requiring the recording of a deed in the Register of Sasines or registration in order to complete the right of interest;

(ee)   the operator having a right conferred in accordance with paragraph 2, 3 or 5 of schedule 2 to the Telecommunications Act 1984(agreements for execution of works, obstruction of access, etc.);

(ef)   a licence holder within the meaning of Part I of the Electricity Act 1989 having such a wayleave as is mentioned in paragraph 6 of Schedule 4 to that Act (wayleaves for electric lines), whether granted under that paragraph or by agreement between the parties;

(eg)   a licence holder within the meaning of Part I of the Electricity Act 1989 who is authorised by virtue of paragraph I of Schedule 5 to that Act to abstract, divert and use water for a generating station wholly or mainly driven by water;

(eh)   insofar as it is an interest vesting by virtue of section 7(3) of the Coal Industry Act 1994, the Coal Authority;

(f)   the holder of a floating charge whether or not the charge has attached to the interest;

(g)   a member of the public in respect of any public right of way or in respect of any right held inalienably by the Crown in trust for the public;

(gg)   the non-entitled spouse within the meaning of section 6 of the Matrimonial Homes (Family Protection) (Scotland) Act 1981;

(h)   any person, being a right which has been made real, other wise than by the recording of a deed in the Register of Sasines or by registration; or

(i)   any other person under any rule of law relating to common interest or joint or common property, not being a right or interest constituting a real right, burden or condition entered in the title sheet of the interest in land under section 6(l)(e) of the 1979 Act or having effect by virtue of a deed recorded in the Register of Sasines,

but does not include any subsisting burden or condition enforceable against the interest in land and entered in its title sheet under section 6(l) of the 1979 Act.

2.   THE USE OF ARROWS ON TITLE PLANS

(a)   Where a deed states the line of a boundary in relation to a physical object, e.g. the centre line, that line is indicated on the Title Plan, either by means of a black arrow or verbally.

(b)   An arrow across the object indicates that the boundary is stated to be the centre line.

(c)   An arrow pointing to the object indicates that the boundary is stated to be the face of the object to which the arrow points.

(d)   The physical object presently shown on the Plan may not be the one referred to in the deed. Indemnity is therefore excluded in respect of information as to the line of the boundary.

3.   Lineal measurements shown in figures on title plans are subject to the qualification "or thereby". Indemnity is excluded in respect of such measurements.

4.   SUBMISSION OF LAND CERTIFICATE WITH SUBSEQUENT APPLICATIONS FOR REGISTRATION

In terms of Rule 9(3), this Land Certificate should be submitted to the Keeper of the Registers of Scotland with any application for registration.

5.   CAUTION. No unauthorised alteration to this Land Certificate should be made.

Printed by The Stationery Office, C300, 10/98, J63463 (188719)

FORM 6 | 429

(Land Registration (Scotland) Rules 1980, Rule 15)

LAND REGISTER OF SCOTLAND

CHARGE
CERTIFICATE

TITLE NUMBER

SUBJECTS

The within-mentioned Charge has been registered against the subjects in the above Title

STATEMENT OF INDEMNITY

Subject to any specific qualifications entered in the Title Sheet of which this Charge Certificate relates a person who suffers loss as a result of the events specified in section 12(1) of the Land Registration (Scotland) Act 1979 shall be entitled to be indemnified in respect of that loss by the Keeper of the Registers of Scotland in terms of that Act.

NOTICE

1. This Certificate must be presented to the Keeper on every transaction affecting the interest of the within-mentioned Registered Creditor.

2. The relative Title Sheet contains a specification of the reservations and burdens affecting the subjects in the above title. An Office Copy of the Title Sheet may be obtained on application to the Keeper.

3. No authorised alterations to this Charge Certificate should be made.

Printed in the UK for The Stationery Office C300 8/98 J55650 CCN 025364

430 | **FORM 7**

NOTICE

This Charge Certificate was made to agree with the Title Sheet of which it relates on the most recent date entered below.

This Charge Certificate may be made to agree with the Title Sheet at any time on payment of the appropriate fee. Application should be made on Form 8.

LAND REGISTER OF SCOTLAND

CHARGE CERTIFICATE

TITLE NO:

SUBJECTS:

Registered Proprietor of subjects:

THIS IS TO CERTIFY that

Is the Registered Creditor in the heritable security attached
registered on
to the extent of

NOTE
There are no heritable securities ranking prior to or *pari passu* with the above mentioned heritable
security appearing on the Register affecting the subjects (except as stated in the schedule annexed).

REGISTERS OF SCOTLAND EXECUTIVE AGENCY **FORM 8**
(Land Registration (Scotland) Rules 1980 Rule 16 (2))

APPLICATION FOR LAND OR CHARGE CERTIFICATE TO BE MADE TO CORRESPOND WITH THE TITLE SHEET
Note:No covering letter is required.
Please complete in BLACK TYPE

TO
    Keeper of the Registers of Scotland

    Meadowbank House
    153 London Road
    EDINBURGH EH8 7AU

    Telephone: 01 31 659 61 11

FOR OFFICIAL USE
DATE OF RECEIPT

APPLICATION NUMBER

Title Number

Short description
of Subjects

i/We apply for the accompanying Land Certificate/ Charge Certificate to be made to correspond with the Title Sheet

To assist the Keeper to disclose in the Land Certificate any relevant entries from the Register of Inhibitions and Adjudications, the full name and designation of any party who has acquired an interest in the subjects in the title since the Land Certificate was last made to correspond with the Title Sheet should be inserted.

1. Surname(s)   Forename(s)

   Address(es)

2. Surname(s)   Forename(s)

   Address(es)

3. Surname(s)   Forename(s)

   Address(es)

The appropriate fee is enclosed   Please place a cross here

Signature of applicant or
Applicant's Solicitor

Full name of applicant

Address of Applicant

Reference   Telephone No.

Date of Application   FAS No.

*Delete whichever is inapplicable

FORM 8 433

FORM 9

REGISTERS OF SCOTLAND EXECUTIVE AGENCY
(Land Registration (Scotland) Rules 1980 Rule 20)

APPLICATION FOR RECTIFICATION OF THE REGISTER
Note:No covering letter is required.
Please complete in BLACK TYPE

Typewriter Alignment Box
Type XXX in centre

TO
Keeper of the Registers of Scotland

Meadowbank House
153 London Road
EDINBURGH EH8 7AU

Telephone: 01 31 659 6111

FOR OFFICIAL USE
DATE OF RECEIPT

APPLICATION NUMBER

Title No

Short description
of subjects

*I/We apply for rectification of the Title Sheet for the above Title No. as follows:

To support this application, I/We*enclose the documents listed on the Inventory (Form 4).

The appropriate fee is enclosed ☐ please place a cross here.

Signature of Applicant or
Applicant's Solicitor

Full Name of Applicant

Address of Applicant

Name of Solicitor

Address of Solicitor

Reference

Telephone No.

Date of Application

FAS No.

*Delete whichever is inapplicable

Printed in Scotland for HMSO by (13161)
Dd 8409719 C200 9/95

REGISTERS OF SCOTLAND
Executive Agency

· p r o p e r t y **REPORTS** s e r v i c e ·

FORM 10

(Land Registration (Scotland) Rules 1980 Rule 24(1))

APPLICATION FOR A REPORT PRIOR TO REGISTRATION OF THE SUBJECTS DESCRIBED BELOW

Note: No covering letter is required and an existing Search should not be submitted.
VAT Reg No. GD 410 GB 888 8410 64

Please complete in DUPLICATE and in BLACK TYPE   Typewriter Alignment Box. Type XXX in centre

From		FOR OFFICIAL USE
		Report Number
		Date of Receipt
		Search Sheet Nos.
		Fee

County		**FAS No.**	

Applicant's Reference		**FAX No.**	

Telephone No.		**FAX response required (X here)**	

POSTAL ADDRESS OF SUBJECTS

Street No.	**House Name**		**Street Name**	

Town		**Postcode**	

OTHER:

Description of Subjects	

The above subjects being	**edged red on the accompanying plan,** [2]
	being (part of) [1] **the subjects described in** [3]

I/We apply for a report

(1) on the subjects described above, for which an application for registration in the Land Register is to be made, from

(a) the **REGISTER OF SASINES** and

(b) the **LAND REGISTER** stating whether or not registration of the said subjects has been effected [4]

1. Delete if inapplicable
2. A plan need not be attached if a verbal description will sufficiently identify the subjects
3. Describe by reference to a writ recorded in the Register of Sasines
4. If the subjects have been registered, the Keeper will supply an Office Copy of the Title Sheet only on specific request.

Faxed applications should not be followed up by a written request and may not be accepted if a plan is included.

DIARY SERVICE:

Please state date and time you require report

Date _____ Time _____

NOTE: If you do not state we will assume a 48 hour turnaround

Meadowbank House, 153 London Road, Edinburgh EH8 7AU
www.ros.gov.uk DX 555338 EDINBURGH 15 reports@ros.gov.uk
Tel: 0845 6070162 Fax: 0131 479 3651/3683/3667

---

and (2) from the Registers of Inhibitions and Adjudications for 5 years prior to the date of Certificate against in the Register of Inhibitions and Adjudications, viz.

Typewriter Alignment Box. Type XXX in centre

1. Surname(s)		**Forename(s)**	

Address(es)

2. Surname(s)		**Forename(s)**	

Address(es)

3. Surname(s)		**Forename(s)**	

Address(es)

4. Surname(s)		**Forename(s)**	

Address(es)

5. Company/ Firm/ Corporate body

Address(es)

6. Company/ Firm/ Corporate body

Address(es)

NOTE: Insert full names and addresses of the persons on whom a Report is required.

Signature: _____   **Date:** _____

REGISTERS OF SCOTLAND
Executive Agency

· property **REPORTS** service ·

FORM 11

(Land Registration (Scotland) Rules 1980 Rule 24(2))

APPLICATION FOR CONTINUATION OF REPORT PRIOR TO THE REGISTRATION OF THE SUBJECTS DESCRIBED BELOW

Note: No covering letter is required and an existing Search should not be submitted.

VAT Reg No. GD 410 GB 888 8410 64

Please complete in DUPLICATE and in BLACK TYPE

Typewriter Alignment Box. Type XXX in centre

From		**FOR OFFICIAL USE**
		Report Number
		Date of Receipt
		Fee

County		**Previous Report No.**	
Search Sheet No. [1]		**FAS No.**	
Applicant's Reference		**FAX No.**	
Telephone No.		**FAX response required (X here)**	

POSTAL ADDRESS OF SUBJECTS

Street No.	**House Name**		**Street Name**	
Town			**Postcode**	

OTHER:

Description of Subjects	

I/We apply for the Report to _____ [2] **against the above subjects to be brought down to date.**

1. Number obtainable from previous Report.
2. Date obtainable from previous Report.

Faxed applications should not be followed up by a written request and may not be accepted if a plan is included.

DIARY SERVICE:

Please state date and time you require report

Date _____ Time _____

NOTE: If you do not state we will assume a 48 hour turnaround

Meadowbank House, 153 London Road, Edinburgh EH8 7AU
www.ros.gov.uk DX 555338 EDINBURGH 15 reports@ros.gov.uk
Tel: 0845 6070162 Fax: 0131 479 3651/3683/3667

The following parties (in addition to those noted on the previous report) should be searched against in the Register of Inhibitions and Adjudications, viz.

Typewriter Alignment Box. Type XXX in centre

1. Surname(s)		Forename(s)	

Address(es)

2. Surname(s)		Forename(s)	

Address(es)

3. Surname(s)		Forename(s)	

Address(es)

4. Surname(s)		Forename(s)	

Address(es)

5. Company/ Firm/ Corporate body

Address(es)

6. Company/ Firm/ Corporate body

Address(es)

NOTE: Insert full names and addresses of the persons on whom a Report is required.

Signature: .... Date: ....

REGISTERS OF SCOTLAND
Executive Agency

· property **REPORTS** service ·

FORM 12

(Land Registration (Scotland) Rules 1980 Rule 24(3))

APPLICATION FOR A REPORT OVER REGISTERED SUBJECTS

Note: No covering letter is required.
VAT Reg No. GD 410   GB 888 8410 64

Please complete in DUPLICATE and in BLACK TYPE

Typewriter Alignment Box. Type XXX in centre

From

FOR OFFICIAL USE
Title Number
Date of Receipt
Report Number
Fee

Applicant's Reference

FAX No.

Telephone No.

FAX response required (X here)

FAS No.

Title number(s)

Title number(s)

Title number(s)

Mark X in box if more than 3 Title Numbers [1]

I/We apply for a report (1) from the Land Register against:

Short Description of Subjects [2]	

Please cross appropriate box

(a) ☐ being the whole subjects in the above Title

(b) ☐ being part of the subjects in the above Title and edged red on the attached plan [3]

(c) ☐ being part of the subjects in the above Title and comprising the plot numbered _____ on the estate plan approved by the Keeper

From the date to which the Land Certificate was last brought down to the date of the Certificate.

1. Please list additional Title Numbers on a separate sheet.
2. If (a) applies, take the description from the title page of the Land Certificate; if (b) or (c) applies, the description must be sufficient to allow the subjects to be identified.
3. A plan need not be attached if a verbal description will sufficiently identify the subjects.

Faxed applications should not be followed up by a written request and may not be accepted if a plan is included.

DIARY SERVICE:
Please state date and time you require report
Date _____ Time _____
NOTE: If you do not state we will assume a 48 hour turnaround

Meadowbank House, 153 London Road, Edinburgh EH8 7AU
www.ros.gov.uk DX 555338 EDINBURGH 15 reports@ros.gov.uk
Tel: 0845 6070162 Fax: 0131 479 3651/3683/3667

FORM 12 | 439

and (2) from the Registers of Inhibitions and Adjudications for 5 years prior to the date of Certificate against

Typewriter Alignment Box. Type XXX in centre

1. Surname(s)		Forename(s)	
Address(es)			

2. Surname(s)		Forename(s)	
Address(es)			

3. Surname(s)		Forename(s)	
Address(es)			

4. Surname(s)		Forename(s)	
Address(es)			

5. Company/ Firm/ Corporate body	
Address(es)	

6. Company/ Firm/ Corporate body	
Address(es)	

NOTE: Insert full names and addresses of the persons on whom a Report is required.

Signature: —————————————————   Date: —————————————————

REGISTERS OF SCOTLAND
Executive Agency

· property **REPORTS** service ·

FORM 13

(Land Registration (Scotland) Rules 1980 Rule 24(4))

APPLICATION FOR CONTINUATION OF REPORT OVER REGISTERED SUBJECTS

Note: No covering letter is required.
VAT Reg No. GD 410   GB 888 8410 64

Please complete in DUPLICATE and in BLACK TYPE

Typewriter Alignment Box. Type XXX in centre

From	FOR OFFICIAL USE
	Title Number
	Date of Receipt
	Report Number
	Fee

Previous Report No. [1]	FAS No.

Applicant's Reference	FAX No.

Telephone No.	FAX response required (X here)

1. Title number	2. Title number

3. Title number	Mark X in box if more than 3 Title Numbers [2]

Description of Subjects	

I/We apply for the Report from the Land Register to _____ [3] against the above subjects to be brought down to date.

1. *Number obtainable from previous Report.*
2. *Please list additional Title Numbers on a separate sheet.*
3. *Date obtainable from previous Report.*

Faxed applications should not be followed up by a written request and may not be accepted if a plan is included.

DIARY SERVICE:
Please state date and time you require report
Date _____ Time _____
NOTE: If you do not state we will assume a 48 hour turnaround

Meadowbank House, 153 London Road, Edinburgh EH8 7AU
www.ros.gov.uk   DX 555338 EDINBURGH 15   reports@ros.gov.uk
Tel: 0845 6070162 Fax: 0131 479 3651/3683/3667

FORM 13 | 441

The following parties (in addition to those noted on the previous report) should be searched against in the Register of Inhibitions and Adjudications, viz.

Typewriter Alignment Box. Type XXX in centre

1. Surname(s)	Forename(s)

Address(es)

2. Surname(s)	Forename(s)

Address(es)

3. Surname(s)	Forename(s)

Address(es)

4. Surname(s)	Forename(s)

Address(es)

5. Company/ Firm/ Corporate body

Address(es)

6. Company/ Firm/ Corporate body

Address(es)

NOTE: Insert full names and addresses of the persons on whom a Report is required.

Signature: _____ Date: _____

REGISTERS OF SCOTLAND
Executive Agency

· property REPORTS service ·

FORM 14

(Land Registration (Scotland) Rules 1980 Rule 24(5))

APPLICATION FOR A REPORT TO ASCERTAIN WHETHER OR NOT SUBJECTS HAVE BEEN REGISTERED

Note: No covering letter is required.

VAT Reg No. GD 410 GB 888 8410 64

Please complete in DUPLICATE and in BLACK TYPE

Typewriter Alignment Box. Type XXX in centre

From

FOR OFFICIAL USE
Report Number
Date of Receipt
Fee

County

FAS No.

Applicant's Reference

FAX No.

Telephone No.

FAX response required (X here)

Postal Address of Subjects

Street No.	House Name

Street Name

Town

Postcode

Other:

Description of Subjects

The above subjects being   **edged red on the accompanying plan,** [3]

being (part of [1]**) the subjects described in** [2]

I/We apply for a report from

(I) the Land Register stating whether or not registration of the said subjects has been effected

1. Delete if inapplicable
2. Describe by reference to a writ recorded in the Register of Sasines
3. A Plan need not be attached if a verbal description will sufficiently identify the subjects

Faxed applications should not be followed up by a written request and may not be accepted if a plan is included.

DIARY SERVICE:

Please state date and time you require report

Date —————— Time ——————

NOTE: If you do not state we will assume a 48 hour turnaround

Meadowbank House, 153 London Road, Edinburgh EH8 7AU
www.ros.gov.uk DX 555338 EDINBURGH 15 reports@ros.gov.uk
Tel: 0845 6070162 Fax: 0131 479 3651/3683/3667

and (2) from the Registers of Inhibitions and Adjudications for 5 years prior to the date of Certificate against

Typewriter Alignment Box. Type XXX in centre

1. Surname(s)   **Forename(s)**

Address(es)

2. Surname(s)   **Forename(s)**

Address(es)

3. Surname(s)   **Forename(s)**

Address(es)

4. Surname(s)   **Forename(s)**

Address(es)

5. Company/ Firm/ Corporate body

Address(es)

6. Company/ Firm/ Corporate body

Address(es)

NOTE: Insert full names and addresses of the persons on whom a Report is required.

Signature: _____   **Date:** _____

REGISTERS OF SCOTLAND
Executive Agency

FORM 15

(Land Registration (Scotland) Rules 1980 Rule 24(0))

APPLICATION FOR AN OFFICE COPY

Note: No covering letter is required.
VAT Reg No. GD 410 GB 888 8410 64

Please complete in DUPLICATE and in BLACK TYPE   Typewriter Alignment Box. Type XXX in centre

From

| **FOR OFFICIAL USE** |
| **Application Number** |
| **Date of Receipt** |
| **Fee** |

Applicant's Reference   **Telephone No.**

FAS No.   **Title No.**

Short description of subjects

I/We apply for
(1) An Office Copy of
Cross appropriate box(es)

☐ **Full Title Sheet with Plan**   ☐ **Proprietorship Section only**

☐ **Full Title Sheet excluding Plan**   ☐ **Charges Section only**

☐ **Title Plan only**   ☐ **Burdens Section only**

☐ **Property Section only**   ☐ **The undernoted documents**

Meadowbank House, 153 London Road, Edinburgh EH8 7AU
www.ros.gov.uk DX 555338 EDINBURGH 15 reports@ros.gov.uk
Tel: 0845 6070162 Fax: 0131 479 3651/3683/3667

and (2) A search in the Register of Inhibitions and Adjudications for 5 years prior to the date of the Office Copy against any party who has acquired an interest in the subjects since the last date on which the Land Certificate was made to correspond with the Register,

Typewriter Alignment Box. Type XXX in centre ☐ ☐

1. Surname(s)		Forename(s)	
Address(es)			

2. Surname(s)		Forename(s)	
Address(es)			

3. Surname(s)		Forename(s)	
Address(es)			

4. Surname(s)		Forename(s)	
Address(es)			

5. Company/ Firm/ Corporate body	
Address(es)	

6. Company/ Firm/ Corporate body	
Address(es)	

NOTE: Insert full names and addresses of the persons on whom a Report is required.

Signature: _____   Date: _____

SCHEDULE B

DESCRIPTION OF REGISTERED INTERESTS IN LAND

In any conveyance of, or other dealing with, or reference to, an interest in land which has been registered in the Land Register of Scotland the interest should be described as: "the subjects registered under Title Number(s) [*here insert the appropriate number(s)*]"

NOTES

    (a) If part only of the registered interest in land is being conveyed or otherwise dealt with for the first time, such part should either be described adequately adding "being part of the subjects registered under Title Number(s) [*here insert the appropriate number(s)*]"or thus: "All and whole the subjects registered under Title Number(s) [*here insert the appropriate number(s)*]with the exception of [*describe the part excepted*]."

    (b) If several subjects are registered under the one Title Number and it is desired to specify one or more of them, these may be distinguished thus: "All and whole the subjects (first) registered under Title Number [*here insert the appropriate number*]" or "the subjects (Second) and (Third) registered under Title Number [*here insert the appropriate number*]."

Index

C

CERTIFICATE OF REGISTRATION OF CHARGE
Confirmation of date of registration, **5.48**
Exclusion of indemnity, **5.49**
Major ownership schemes, **5.50**
CERTIFICATE OF TITLE (SEE ALSO LAND CERTIFICATE AND CHARGE CERTIFICATE)
Definition of, **5.79**
CHARGE CERTIFICATE
Combined charge certificates, **5.85**
Consists of, **5.84**
Error/omission in, **7.15**
COAL (SEE COAL AUTHORITY)
COAL AUTHORITY
Minerals, **6.90, 6.91, 6.97**
Overriding interest, **5.68**
COMMENCEMENT PROVISIONS, 1.7
Deeds unrecorded at commencement date, **2.6**
Timetable, **1.8**
Transactions not completed by commencement date, missives, **8.2** *et seq.*
COMMON BOUNDARIES
Agreement as to, **6.64**
Confirmation of position, **4.30**
Discrepancies, **1.5**
COMMON LINKS INDEX, 5.31
COMMON PROPERTY
Warrandice and, **6.15.11**
COMMON TITLES
Guidelines for submission of, **5.13**
COMPANY TRANSACTIONS
Certificate of registration of charge, **5.48**
Certificate of registration of charge; exclusion of indemnity, **5.49**
Certificate of registration of charge; major ownership schemes, **5.50**
Change of company name, **5.39**
Completion of application form, **5.46**

Conveyance by company in liquidation, **5.38**
Conveyance by company in receivership, **5.36**
Floating charge, overriding interest, **5.68**
Matrimonial homes evidence, **6.36**
Sharp v Thomson: Keeper's response, **5.37**
Standard securities, **5.47**
COMPULSORY ACQUISITION
Application for registration following a, **5.61**
CONSOLIDATION (SEE ABSORPTION)
CONTRIBUTORY NEGLIGENCE
Impact on indemnity, **7.33**
CONVEYANCING PROCEDURES (SEE ALSO MISSIVES)
Changes in, **2.2**
Comparing legal and occupied extent, **4.7, 8.6**
Dealing with a registered interest, application for registration, **8.51-57**
    Outstanding heritable security, discharge available at settlement, **8.55**
      discharge not available at settlement, **8.56**
      discharge relating to a number of properties, **8.57**
    Purchase and loan transactions completed contemporaneously, **8.51**
    Purchase and loan transactions not completed contemporaneously, **8.54**
Dealing with a registered interest, conveyancing procedures, **8.38-8.47**
    Burdens, **8.47**
    Completion of application form, **8.46**
    Examination of title, **8.39**
    Form 12 and 13 reports, **8.40, 8.41, 8.42**
    Identification of subjects, **8.45**
    Incidental rights and burdens, **8.47**

Keeper's requirements, **4.16**
DESIGNATION
Inhibitions, 'present whereabouts unknown', **6.18**
DESTINATIONS
General destinations, **6.17**
Special destinations, **6.17**
DEVELOPMENT LAND
Benefit of report when subjects bounded by development land in non operational area, **3.15**
Voluntary registration, **2.9, 2.10**
DIGITAL MAP, 4.3, 4.4, 4.25
Discrepancies, **4.25**
DISCHARGE (SEE ALSO STANDARD SECURITIES AND *EX FACIE* ABSOLUTE DISPOSITION)
Available at settlement, **8.14, 8.55**
Marked 'to follow', **8.14**
Outstanding at first registration, **5.24, 5.29, 5.30, 8.14, 8.25**
Outstanding at first registration, registration of creditor's interest, **5.29**
Not available at settlement, **8.26, 8.56**
Relating to additional subjects,
    in Land Register, **8.57**
    in Sasine register, **8.27**
Style, registered subjects, **8.47**

E

ENTITLED SPOUSE (SEE MATRIMONIAL HOMES (FAMILY PROTECTION) (SCOTLAND) ACT 1981)
ESTATE LAYOUT PLANS
Application for approval, **4.40**
Benefit of approved layout plan, **4.38**
Circumstances in which application may be made, **4.39**
Departure from approved plan, **4.41**
Deposit of Land Certificate, **4.43**

Reference to approved plans, **4.42**
Submitting plan to the Keeper, **4.37**
EVEN DATE REFERENCE
In standard security, **6.70**
In standard security over registered subjects, **8.47**
***EX FACIE* ABSOLUTE DISPOSITIONS**
Discharge or reconveyance of, **6.49**
Transfer of an e*x facie* absolute proprietor's interest, **6.49**
Transfer of reversionary proprietors interest, **6.49**
EXAMINATION OF TITLE
Dealing with a registered interest, **8.39**
First Registration, **2.2**
EXCLUSION OF INDEMNITY (SEE ALSO INDEMNITY)
Inhibitions, **6.18**
Foreshore, applicant's right to challenge, **6.84**
Keeper's power to exclude indemnity, **7.17**
Limitations of, re servitude, **6.57**
Limited company standard security, **5.49**
Minerals, **6.93**
Prescription, **6.2, 6.3**
Removal of exclusion of indemnity, **7.34**
Standard security, inadequate description, **6.69**
Style of exclusion note, **7.17**
EXECUTORS
Executry conveyancing, links in title, **5.32, 5.33**
Matrimonial homes evidence, **6.39, 6.40**
EXTENT OF SUBJECTS
Application form 1, completion of questions 1-3, Part B, **4.16**
Boundaries, position and length, **4.27**
Comparing legal title with ordnance map, **4.5, 4.7**
Discrepancies between legal and

minerals, **6.94**
Disclosure in title sheet, **6.88, 7.22**
Exclusion of indemnity as regards minerals, **6.93**
General rule, land carries minerals under surface, **6.89**
Identification of, **4.14.6**
Inclusion of, in title sheet, **6.92**
Indemnity, **7.22**
Minerals which do not pass with the surface land, **6.90**
Reservation of minerals, **6.91, 6.96**
Warrandice, **6.15.3**
MISSIVES (ALSO SEE CONVEYANCING PROCEDURES)
Comparing legal and occupied extent, **4.7, 8.6**
Dealing with a registered interest, application for registration, **8.51-57**
    Outstanding heritable security, discharge available at settlement, **8.55**
    discharge not available at settlement, **8.56**
    discharge relating to a number of properties, **8.57**
    Purchase and loan transactions completed contemporaneously, **8.51**
    Purchase and loan transactions not completed contemporaneously, **8.54**
Dealing with a registered interest, conveyancing procedures, **8.38-8.47**
    Burdens, **8.47**
    Completion of application form, **8.46**
    Examination of title, **8.39**
    Form 12 and 13 reports, **8.40, 8.41, 8.42**
    Identification of subjects, **8.45**
    Incidental rights and burdens, **8.47**
    Letter of obligation, **8.43, 8.44**
    Parts previously sold, **8.47**
    Standard security, description, **8.47**
    Style of conveyance, **8.47**

Superiority, description of, **8.47**
Dealing with a registered interest, missives, **8.37**
Dealing with a registered interest, pre-sale procedures, **8.34-8.36**
    Occupational boundaries, **8.36**
    Examination of title, **8.34**
    Report, **8.35**
Dealing with registered interest, procedure after registration,
    purchase of whole registered interest, **8.58, 8.59**
    purchase of part of registered interest, **8.60-62**
Dealing with a registered interest, settlement, **8.48-50**
First registration, application for registration, **8.22-8.27**
    Discharge of outstanding heritable security, **8.25**
    Discharge not available, **8.26**
    Discharge relating to additional subjects in Sasine register, **8.27**
    Purchase and loan transactions completed contemporaneously, **8.22, 8.23**
    Purchase and loan transactions not completed contemporaneously, **8.24**
First registration, conveyancing procedures, **8.10-8.19**
    Additional information required by the Keeper, **8.17**
    Examination of title, **8.10**
    Form 10 and 11 reports, **8.11**
    Form 10 and 11 reports, cost, **8.13**
    Form 10 and 11 reports, recommended procedure, **8.12**
    Form p16 report, **8.11**
    Identification of subjects, **8.16**
    Letter of obligation, **8.14, 8.15**
    Outstanding standard security, **8.14**

Conveyance by *ex officio* trustees, **5.35**
Matrimonial homes evidence, **6.39, 6.40**

U

UDAL TENURE
Acquiring a real right, **1.5, 6.86**
UNFAIR PREFERENCE, 5.46, 7.19
UNINFEFT PROPRIETOR
Deduction of title, **2.12**
Feu grant by, **6.80**
Minute of waiver by, **6.80**

V

VALUABLE CONSIDERATION
Examples of, **2.5**
Interpretation of, **2.5**
Keeper's understanding of, **2.5**
VOLUNTARY REGISTRATION
Criteria Keeper will apply in deciding
whether or not to accept, **2.9, 2.10**
Development land, **2.9, 2.10**
Fees, **2.8**
In operational area, **2.8, 2.9**
In non operational area, **2.8**
Keeper's discretion, **2.8**
Pro indiviso shares, **2.9**
Report request, **3.3, 3.15**
Request for voluntary registration, **2.8**

W

WARRANDICE
Common interest, **6.15.9**
Common property, **6.15.11**
Warrandice continued
Continuing importance of, **6.12**
Heritable security, **6.15.8**
Incorporeal rights, **6.15.10**
Minerals, **6.15.3**
Operation of warrandice in Sasine
and Land Registers, **6.15**
Prior recorded title to dominium utile

only of part of subjects, **6.15.2**
Prior recorded title to part of the
subjects, **6.15.1**
Property subject to recorded lease, **6.15.4**
Property subject to unrecorded lease,
6.15.5
Qualifications to, **6.13**
Real burdens, **6.15.7**
Servitude, **6.15.6**
Subrogation, **6.14**
Transfer of registered interest in
whole or in part, **6.16**
WARRANT OF REGISTRATION, 2.2
WATER BOUNDARIES
Alluvio and avulsion, **6.101**
Plotting on title plan, **6.101**
Problems with, **6.100**